EVIDENCE-BASED PRACTICE IN SCHOOL MENTAL HEALTH

A Primer for School Social Workers, Psychologists, and Counselors

James C. Raines

OXFORD WORKSHOP SERIES

OXFORD
UNIVERSITY PRESS

2008

OXFORD
UNIVERSITY PRESS

Oxford University Press, Inc., publishes works that further
Oxford University's objective of excellence
in research, scholarship, and education.

Oxford New York
Auckland Cape Town Dar es Salaam Hong Kong Karachi
Kuala Lumpur Madrid Melbourne Mexico City Nairobi
New Delhi Shanghai Taipei Toronto

With offices in
Argentina Austria Brazil Chile Czech Republic France Greece
Guatemala Hungary Italy Japan Poland Portugal Singapore
South Korea Switzerland Thailand Turkey Ukraine Vietnam

Published by Oxford University Press, Inc.
198 Madison Avenue, New York, New York 10016

www.oup.com

Oxford is a registered trademark of Oxford University Press

Library of Congress Cataloging-in-Publication Data
Raines, James Curtis.
Evidence-based practice in school mental health / James C. Raines.
p. cm.—(Oxford workshop series)
Includes bibliographical references and index.
ISBN 978-0-19-536626-6
1. School children—Mental health services. 2. School social work—United States.
3. Evidence-based social work—United States. 4. Evidence-based
psychiatry—United States. 5. Students with disabilities—Services for—United States.
I. School Social Work Association of America. II. Title. III. Series.
[DNLM: 1. School Health Services. 2. Adolescent. 3. Child. 4. Evidence-Based Medicine.
5. Mental Disorders—therapy. 6. Mental Health Services. WA 352 R155e 2008]
LB3430.R35 2008
371.7'130973   dc22   2008001223

1 3 5 7 9 8 6 4 2

Printed in the United States of America
on acid-free paper

Contents

Preface

Evidence-based practice has become a common expression in the helping professions over the last decade. Beginning with medicine and moving to fields such as psychology and social work, the number of books on evidence-based practice has grown significantly. What makes this book different? This book is aimed at preservice and in-service school-based mental health service providers, such as school counselors, school psychologists, and school social workers. It is not a research book. It is a book about research-infused practice. What does this mean? It means that this book aims to give school service providers a pragmatic approach to informing every major practice decision with the appropriate research so that students receive the best possible services. The book addresses how to use research to make reliable and valid assessments, how to use research to choose the best intervention, and how to use research to evaluate student progress.

Estimates of child and adolescent mental health problems range from 10% to 20% (Roberts, Attkinson, & Rosenblatt, 1998). The best estimate is that at least 10% of youths suffer from serious behavioral or emotional problems (National Advisory Mental Health Council, 2001). If there are 70 million school-age children in the United States (Kazdin, 2003), then at least 7 million need help. Unfortunately, up to 70% of these children never receive any mental health services. Of those who do get help, schools are the primary providers (Burns et al., 1995; Rones & Hoagwood, 2000).

Child and adolescent psychotherapy has not always had a history of being effective. Levitt (1957) came to the conclusion that children who received treatment were no better off than those who did not. By the year 2000, however, approximately 1,500 outcome studies have been completed on youth treatment (Durlak, Wells, Cotton, & Johnson, 1995; Kazdin, 2000). The later studies have overcome earlier methodological weaknesses and demonstrated significantly stronger results (Weisz, 2004).

This book, however, is not about evidence-based practices, which may be defined as techniques or treatments that have empirical support. This book is about evidence-based practice or the process of continually infusing practice with the current best research (Drake, Hovmand, Jonson-Reid, & Zayas, 2007; Evidence-Based Medicine Working Group, 1992). Why choose a process approach? Paul (2004) describes the problem when he reviews multiple books about empirically supported treatments:

> Even books published in the last year, are 3 to 4 years behind the times. By virtue of the lag between writing and publication, even the most recently released book will have citations that are a few years old. Journals and conventions remain the best vehicle to stay on top of the learning curve (p. 39).

Staying on top of the curve is what professional practice is all about. Each new client brings a unique amalgam of strengths and problems, developmental issues, cultural diversity, and value preferences. There are no clinicians who can sit back and comfortably assume that they have no more to learn. The world is changing much too fast to believe that we can stop growing along with it.

What's up ahead in this book? In Chapter 1—Introduction—I provide five compelling reasons for evidence-based practice. They include ethical, legal, clinical, educational, and economic justifications. I also describe the philosophy of science that undergirds this book. In Chapter 2—Evidence-Based Practice: Definition and Process—I define evidence-based practice and dispel some myths. I also describe the five basic steps of evidence-based practice. These include determining answerable questions, investigating the evidence, appraising the evidence, adapting and applying the evidence, and evaluating the results. In the next six chapters, I describe each step in much more detail, providing user-friendly tips along the way as well as illustrations about how this process works in an applied setting. In Chapter 9—Ethics for Evidence-Based Practice—I address some of the important concerns about evaluating results with children. Such issues include informed consent, client self-determination, and parental access and control. In Chapter 10—Systemic Change—I address what has changed to facilitate evidence-based practice and what still needs to change to make it work smoothly and seamlessly within our schools.

Finally, each chapter offers a brief preview of what's ahead for the reader, a summary of what has been covered in the chapter, suggestions for further reading, and Internet resources. I hope that you will approach this material with an open mind and an open heart. Overall, I hope that the book is both intellectually stimulating and useful in your daily practice.

EVIDENCE-BASED PRACTICE IN SCHOOL MENTAL HEALTH

I

Introduction

Preview

Thirty years ago, in a classic article that examined comparative outcomes from several types of therapy, Luborsky, Singer, and Luborsky (1975) concluded that the Dodo bird from *Alice in Wonderland* was right after all: "Everyone has won and all must have prizes." It was a generous verdict akin to the more recent Lake Wobegon conclusion that "all the children are above average." Alas, the days have changed substantially since the Dodo bird or Lake Wobegon, and it is improbable that today's educational administrators and school board members would be nearly so magnanimous (Winter, 2006).

This chapter will introduce both the reasons and the philosophy of science behind evidence-based practice (EBP). The "Reasons to Practice EBP" section includes ethical, legal, clinical, educational, and economic reasons. The subsection on ethical reasons examines the code of ethics for each of the three major student service provider groups: school social workers, school psychologists, and school counselors. Despite their differences in training and perspective, all three groups concur about the necessity for EBP. The subsection on legal reasons is split into two parts: case law and federal legislation. Case law looks at three U.S. Supreme Court cases that have clarified the question, "What is scientific evidence?" Federal legislation looks at the two most important laws governing both general and special education. The No Child Left Behind Act is the latest reauthorization of the Elementary and Secondary Education Act (1965) and has demanded accountability from every school based on student results. The Individuals with Disabilities Education Improvement Act of 2004 is the latest reauthorization of the Education of All Handicapped Children's Act (1975) and has aimed to align the accountability mandates of general education with those of special education. Both use the same definition of scientifically based research provided here. The subsection on clinical reasons is divided into "Standards of Care," "Avoiding Harm," and "Optimal Treatment." "Standards of Care" represent the expectations of an ordinary school service provider based on similar circumstances in similar locales, while "Avoiding Harm" addresses the iatrogenic or treatment-related damage that can occur. I provide three true cases of children who have been killed by inept service providers. "Optimal Treatment" looks at seven ways by which EBP can be used to provide the best care for students in our schools. The subsection "Educational Reasons" examines the effect on learning when mental health practitioners eliminate some of the barriers to learning for children with social or emotional difficulties. The subsection "Economic Reasons" argues that EBP can help schools and society save time, money, and resources while still providing excellent student support services.

The section "Philosophy of Science" briefly addresses three major schools of thought: positivism, constructivism, and critical realism. It identifies the strengths and weaknesses of the first two and argues that the third perspective combines the best of both to provide the most cogent philosophical foundation for EBP.

Reasons to Practice EBP

There are five major reasons for practicing EBP. These include ethical, legal, clinical, educational, and economic reasons.

Ethical Reasons

First and foremost, there is an *ethical* requirement to provide the highest quality of services to our clients (Franklin, 2001). The National Association of Social Workers' (NASW, 1999) *Code of Ethics*, for example, states that "social workers should critically examine and keep current with emerging knowledge relevant to social work and fully use evaluation and research evidence in their professional practice" (section 5.02 (d)). The National Association of School Psychologists' (NASP, 2000a) *Principles for Professional Ethics* concurs: "School psychologists use assessment techniques, counseling and therapy procedures, consultation techniques and other direct and indirect service methods that the profession considers to be responsible, research-based practice" (section IV.C.4.). The American School Counselor Association's (ASCA, 2004) *Code of Ethics* also confirms that the professional school counselor "strives through personal initiative to maintain professional competence including technological literacy and to keep abreast of professional information" (section E.1.C.). The American Counseling Association's (ACA, 2005) *Code of Ethics* further states that "counselors have a responsibility to the public to engage in counseling practices that are based on rigorous research methodologies" (section C). Thus, all the major professional associations agree that its practitioners must stay current with and utilize the professional literature when providing service to their clients.

Legal Reasons

Second, there is a *legal* mandate to practice EBP. This mandate rests on both case law and federal legislation.

Case Law

Case law requires experts to use scientific support for their conclusions. In *Daubert v. Merrell Dow Pharmaceuticals* (1993), two children and their parents alleged that the children's birth defects had been caused by the mother's ingestion of the antinausea drug, bendectin, while she was pregnant. The initial District Court found that the drug did not cause human birth defects. The parents appealed against the verdict and produced eight experts who claimed on the basis of their unpublished studies that bendectin could have caused birth defects. Both the District Court and the Court of Appeals determined that the parents' experts did not meet the 1923 standard (*Frye v. United States*) according to which experts could use only techniques "generally accepted" in their chosen field. In 1975, however, Congress passed the Federal Rules of Evidence (1975), which introduced the standards of *relevance* and *reliability*—the evidence had to be relevant to the issue at hand and experts had to be qualified on the basis of reliable foundation of scientific, technical, or other specialized knowledge. The two pertinent federal rules of evidence are as follows.

Rule 401. Definition of "*Relevant* Evidence"

"*Relevant* evidence" means evidence having any tendency to make the existence of any fact that is of consequence to the determination of the action more probable or less probable than it would be without the evidence.

Rule 702. Testimony by Experts

If scientific, technical, or other specialized knowledge will assist the trier of fact to understand the evidence or to determine a fact in issue, a witness qualified as an expert by knowledge, skill, experience, training, or education, may testify thereto in the form of an opinion or otherwise, if (1) the testimony is based upon sufficient facts or data, (2) the testimony is the product of *reliable* principles and methods, and (3) the witness has applied the principles and methods *reliably* to the facts of the case (italics added).

The U.S. Supreme Court in a rare unanimous verdict ruled that the Federal Rules of Evidence took precedence over the *Frye* standard and that Rule 702 required that expert testimony had to be based on "scientific" knowledge. Trial judges must make a preliminary judgment about whether the proffered testimony was *reliable*. Evidence should be considered reliable only if it is based on "sound science" and meets one of four criteria: (1) whether the theory or technique can be (or has been) tested, (2) whether the theory or technique has been subject to peer-review and publication, (3) whether or not the theory or technique has a known error rate and standards controlling its operation, or (4) whether the underlying science has attracted widespread acceptance by the scientific community.

The *Daubert* finding was reinforced in two succeeding cases. In *General Electric Co. v. Joiner* (1997), a lung cancer patient sued his employer for his exposure to polychlorinated biphenyls. The U.S. Supreme Court decided that the *Daubert* case required judges to fulfill a "gatekeeper" role to screen expert testimony to ensure it was both relevant and reliable. The Federal Rules of Evidence did not require a court to admit expert opinion solely on the *ipse dixit* (say so) of the supposed expert.

In *Kumho Tire Co. v. Carmichael* (1999), the survivor of a deadly car crash sued the manufacturer of the tire that blew out; he produced a tire-failure expert who intended to testify that a defect had caused the accident. The U.S. Supreme Court decided that judges could not be expected to make distinctions between "scientific" and "technical or specialized" knowledge. The court elaborated that the *Daubert* criteria were not meant to be an exhaustive list, but an illustrative one that gave judges broad discretion to screen all expert testimony.

Psychologists have been the first to understand the implications of federal case law on the practice (Youngstrom & Busch, 2000). Mental health practitioners have to become wary of pseudoscience (Lilienfeld, Lynn, & Lohr, 2003). Assessment techniques based on projective testing (e.g., Rorschach ink blot tests) and controversial diagnoses (e.g., dissociative identity disorder) have become suspect under these standards (Grove & Barden, 1999). Likewise, unsupported experimental treatments for children with attention-deficit/hyperactivity disorder and autism should warrant extreme caution (Reamer, 2006a; Romanczyk, Arnstein, Soorya, & Gillis, 2003; Waschbusch & Hill, 2003). Just because desperate parents will try almost anything for the benefit of their children does not mean that school service providers should join them in their quixotic quests.

Legal experts have also noticed an important difference between judges and scientists: "Judges cannot suspend judgment until research studies have addressed their sources of doubt" (Rothstein, 2005, p. S4). School-based clinicians are more like judges than social scientists—they cannot suspend judgment and wait until research catches up with their needs. Mental health practitioners must be able to make an immediate judgment about the evidence they have at their disposal. When the current state of the evidence does not apply to the client in front of them, clinicians must use their best judgment on the basis of what they know. Greenhalgh (2006) describes the quandary of coping with ever-changing scientific evidence thus: "It is not so much about what you have read in the past, but about how you go about applying your knowledge appropriately and consistently in new clinical situations" (p. 9).

Federal Legislation

There are also two important laws passed in the last 5 years that require school-based professionals to use EBP. The No Child Left Behind Act of 2001 (P.L. 107-110) mentions more than 100 times that educational service personnel must use "scientifically based research" to support their interventions (Olson & Viadero, 2002). The most recent reauthorization of the Individuals with Disabilities Act (P.L. 108-446) mentions more than 80 times that school-based professionals must use "scientific, research-based" interventions. What is the legal definition of scientifically based research? Both sets of federal regulations include the same definition, as given in the following (U.S. Department of Education, 2006):

Scientifically based research

a) Means research that involves the application of rigorous, systematic, and objective procedures to obtain reliable and valid knowledge relevant to education activities and programs; and
b) Includes research that
  1. Employs systematic, empirical methods that draw on observation or experiment;
  2. Involves rigorous data analyses that are adequate to test the stated hypotheses and justify the general conclusions drawn;

3. Relies on measurements or observational methods that provide reliable and valid data across evaluators and observers, across multiple measurements and observations, and across studies by the same or different investigators;
4. Is evaluated using experimental or quasi-experimental designs in which individuals, entities, programs, or activities are assigned to different conditions and with appropriate controls to evaluate the effects of the condition of interest, with a preference for random assignment experiments, or other designs to the extent that those designs contain within-condition or across-condition controls;
5. Ensures that experimental studies are presented in sufficient detail and clarity to allow for replication or, at a minimum, offer the opportunity to build systematically on their findings; and
6. Has been accepted by a peer-reviewed journal or approved by a panel of independent experts through a comparably rigorous, objective, and scientific review. (§ 300.35)

When one considers the continuum of evidence (see Figure 1.1), one cannot help but notice that the U.S. Department of Education has clearly chosen a standard in which randomized controlled trials and quasi-experimental designs are the only type of research that can be considered for their systematic reviews. Randomized controlled trials are experimental designs in which participants are randomly assigned to either a no-treatment control group or a treatment group. Measures are taken at the beginning to establish a baseline and to ensure that both groups are relatively equal. Treatment is carefully administered so that threats to internal validity are minimal. Finally, the same measures are taken at the end to determine if the treatment group has changed significantly more than the control group. Quasi-experimental designs are similar, but they do not use a control group. This

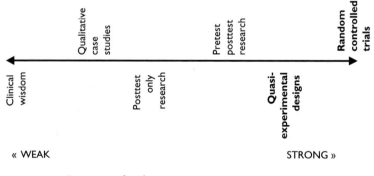

FIGURE 1.1. Continuum of evidence.

Evidence-Based Practice in School Mental Health

is often done due to ethical concerns that denying treatment to some clients (e.g., rape survivors) would be unconscionable (O'Leary & Borkovec, 1978). Thus comparison groups (e.g., individual vs. group treatments) are used instead of a control versus treatment group (Hoag & Burlingame, 1997).

There are four other forms of evidence that clinicians regularly use that do not meet the current standards. The first type of evidence is pretest-posttest designs where measures are used before and after treatment, but clients are not put in different groups, or even if they are assigned to different treatment conditions it is not done randomly. The second type is post-test-only designs where treatment is given and a measure is given at the end to see if they report improvement (e.g., client satisfaction surveys). The third type is qualitative case studies, where clients are described in rich detail at the beginning, middle, and end of treatment so that the reader can judge the amount of change that has taken place. Freud's famous case studies are an excellent example of this type. The final type of evidence is clinical wisdom, where experts provide their opinions of what constitutes best practice for a certain group of clients.

Clinical Reasons

There are three clinical reasons for doing EBP. These include treating clients using a standard of care, avoiding iatrogenic or treatment-caused harm, and providing optimal treatment.

Standards of Care

The standard of care is what ordinary, reasonable, and prudent professionals with similar training would do under similar circumstances (Reamer, 2006b). Practitioners who do not meet the standard of care for clients make themselves liable for malpractice. Gambrill (2006a) identifies four essential elements in professional liability. First, there has to be a fiduciary relationship—one that involves a commitment of trust between the helper and client. Second, the practitioner's treatment must be below the accepted standard for the profession. Third, the client must have sustained some kind of injury (emotional, physical, psychological, or social). Fourth, the practitioner's substandard treatment must be the proximate cause of the client's injury. Where does a professional find these standards of care? Each of the school-based helping professional associations publish and update these standards regularly.

The *NASW Standards for School Social Work* (National Association of Social Workers, 2002) addresses the importance of research-infused practice in two standards. First, "School social workers shall use research to inform practice and understand social policies related to schools" (Standard 17). Second, "School social workers shall be able to evaluate their practice and disseminate the findings to consumers, the local education agency, the community, and the profession" (Standard 23).

The National Association of School Psychologists (2000b) also has two standards that explicitly require practitioners to keep abreast of current research:

> School psychologists must (a) utilize current professional literature on various aspects of education and child development, (b) translate research into practice through the problem-solving process, and (c) use research design and statistic skills to conduct investigations to develop and facilitate effective services. (*Practice Guideline 1*)

> School psychologists (in collaboration with others) develop challenging but achievable cognitive and academic goals for all students, provide information about ways in which students can achieve these goals, and monitor student progress towards these goals. (*Practice Guideline 3*)

The American School Counselor Association (2001) addresses the importance of accountability in practice. The association's national model for school counseling programs states, "School counselors and administrators are increasingly challenged to demonstrate the effectiveness of the school counseling program in measurable terms. To evaluate the program and to hold it accountable, school counseling programs must collect and use data that link the program to student achievement" (p. 3).

Thus, each of the three major school-based helping professions state unequivocally that EBP is one of the standards of good practice. Providing interventions that are not evidence-based puts clients at risk of personal injury and professionals at risk of charges of malpractice.

Although the standard of care was originally thought to mean what was customarily done, the claim or excuse that a practitioner was merely following standard operating procedures has not stood the test of time. Why? The reason is that both health care and mental health care are constantly evolving (Scheflin, 2000). Let us use a school-based example.

In 1977, 2 years after the Education for All Handicapped Children Act (P.L. 94-142) was passed, federal regulations devised a standard way to evaluate whether a child has a learning disability. This involved finding a "severe discrepancy" between the child's intellectual potential and their academic achievement (Raines, 2003b). The discrepancy was usually determined by whether the child's discrepancy was one to two standard deviations (Mercer, Jordan, Allsopp, & Mercer, 1996). This standard of care resulted in what the President's Commission on Excellence in Special Education called a "wait-to-fail" model, wherein children were often not identified as being eligible for assistance until the 3rd or 4th grade, losing precious years of early intervention (Shaywitz et al., 1999; U.S. Department of Education, 2002a). In 2004, Congress decided that this standard method was insufficient and passed the Individuals with Disabilities Education Improvement Act (P.L. 108-446), which allowed states to evaluate how a child responds to scientific research-based intervention. This response to intervention approach does not have a long or wide track record for identifying children with learning disabilities (Bender, Ulmer, Baskette, & Shores, 2007; Kavale, Holdnack, & Mostert, 2006). It has been recommended since the turn of the century (Fletcher et al., 2001; Marston, 2001) and has primarily focused on response to reading interventions (Lyon et al., 2001). Thus, the adoption of response to intervention reflects what the philosopher of science Thomas Kuhn called faith in a new paradigm:

> The man who embraces a new paradigm at an early stage must often do so in defiance of the evidence provided by problem-solving. He must, that is, have faith that the new paradigm will succeed with the many large problems that confront it, *knowing only that the older paradigm has failed* with a few. A decision of that kind can only be made on faith.
>
> Kuhn, 1970, p. 158, italics added

So what is the current "standard of care" for evaluation of children who are suspected to have learning disabilities? The answer must be that we do not know—the standard is evolving and this kind of uncertainty is what requires school-based professionals to stay current with the most recent research.

Avoiding Harm

What is the worst that can happen? Consider real life examples in Boxes 1.1, 1.2, or 1.3. Although these cases represent the extreme, children and youth have died from a variety of mental health treatments, including antidepressant medications (Green, 2001; Nelson, 2004; Potter, Padich, Rudorfer, & Krishnan, 2006) or unsupervised seclusion and restraint procedures (Busch & Shore, 2000; Masters & Bellonci, 2001). The youth also suffer personal injury when school systems rigidly employ zero tolerance and automatic suspensions or expulsions for petty crimes (Meyer, Reppucci, & Owen, 2006; Sprott, Jenkins, & Doob, 2005); segregate violent, antisocial youth into self-contained special education programs (Arnold & Hughes, 1999; Dishion, McCord, & Poulin, 1999; Dodge, 1999); or refer children to physicians who are too quick to medicate without consideration of the potential side effects on learning or other behavior (Breggin, 2003; Handler & DuPaul, 1999; Kanner & Dunn, 2004). Further, child and adolescent mental health practitioners are regularly at risk for negligence—failing to protect children when making decisions about whether to report child abuse or neglect (Pollack & Marsh, 2004; Small, Lyons, & Guy, 2002); how to intervene with suicidal adolescents (Capuzzi, 2002; Judge & Billick, 2004); and what to do about autoerotic asphyxia (Urkin & Merrick, 2006). Some psychologists have even been sued for failing to accurately diagnose a child with dyslexia (Wheat, 1999).

I invite you to read (and share) the three true stories of treatment-related deaths detailed in Boxes 1.1, 1.2, and 1.3. Each one serves as a reminder of the power of adults to cause harm even when they are well-intentioned.

Optimal Treatment

There is a bewildering number of treatment techniques used to help children and adolescents. A conservative estimate places this number at over 550 different interventions (Kazdin, 2003). How can mental health practitioners choose between them? Weisz (2004) cites seven reasons why school-based clinicians ought to welcome EBP. First, meta-analytic findings show that the average effect sizes for empirically supported treatments for children and adolescents are medium to large. In other words, they don't just help a little; they make a substantial difference (Christopherson & Mortweet, 2001). Second, the treatment effects have demonstrated durability. In follow-up studies, the results maintained their effectiveness 5 to 6 months after intervention had ended. Third, the results were quite specific. Youth treated with empirically supported interventions showed more progress in the target problems than they did with their untargeted problems. Fourth, the results were wide-ranging in two ways. There are empirically supported treatments for a wide variety of problems—attention-deficit disorders, anxiety, conduct disorders, depression, and eating disorders, and so forth. There are also interventions available for a wide range of ages from preschool to late adolescence. Fifth, there are an increasing number of models for treatment delivery. The traditional weekly individual therapy model still predominates, but creative approaches that include environmental approaches, group therapy, parent guidance, and even summer camps are being found successful. As practitioners aim to be both efficient and effective, the long-term individual therapy model will have to give way to group and short-term approaches. Sixth, researchers are finding new ways to evaluate results. They are increasingly using multiple informants

BOX 1.1 Death by Therapy: Candace Newmaker

In April 2000, a 10-year-old girl named Candace Newmaker underwent treatment for reactive attachment disorder at the request of her adoptive mother. Candace's story begins with her removal from her birth parents by child welfare workers in North Carolina. Her natural mother, Angie Elmore, was a rural teenage mother with a violent husband who attempted to evade investigations into child neglect by moving to a different county. Eventually, social services tracked them down and placed all three of their children in foster care. Candace was placed in five different foster homes before being adopted at age six by registered nurse, Jeanne Newmaker.

According to her adoptive mother, Candace was always difficult—hitting other children and starting a fire at home. Her adoptive mother sought help from child psychiatrists who never bothered to seek input from Candace's teachers or neighbors. The doctors diagnosed her with reactive attachment disorder and gave Ms. Newmaker a referral for attachment therapy. Unable to find an attachment therapist in North Carolina, she was told about a prominent leader in the field, Connell Jane Watkins (a.k.a. C. J. Cooil), who operated out of her home in Evergreen, Colorado.

Working with licensed marriage and family therapist Julie Ponder, C. J. Watkins determined that what Candace needed was a rebirthing ritual to help her relive the emotional distress

(continued)

of the birth process, accept her infantile helplessness, and learn to trust her adoptive mother. Watkins routinely videotaped her sessions so that prospective clients and trainees could learn from her successes. Candace was told to curl herself into a fetal position while Ponder and Watkins wrapped her with a flannel "womb," tied the ends together, piled a dozen pillows on top, and then laid on top of Candace's 75 lb body with two other assistants for a combined weight of over 670 lbs. Candace succeeded in ripping a hole in the flannel womb, but the therapists retied the sheet and urged her to try harder. She screamed that she couldn't breathe and felt sick. She vomited and urinated on herself. When Candace warned the therapists that she felt she was going to suffocate, one of them replied, "Go ahead, die right now." Her adoptive mother pleaded with Candace, "Don't you want to be reborn?" and Candace whispered, "No." The therapists sat on top of her silent body for another 20 minutes before pulling her out. She was blue and limp. Paramedics were called, but it was too late. Candace's pupils were fixed and dilated. She was pronounced dead April 18, 2000 from cerebral edema.

Prosecutors used a videotape of the incident the two therapists made as evidence against them. The two therapists were convicted of reckless child abuse resulting in death and sentenced to 16 years in Colorado State Prison (Advocates for Children in Therapy, 2006; Mercer, Sarner, & Rosa, 2003).

Questions for Discussion

1. What evidence was there that Candace had a "reactive attachment disorder"?
2. What forms of therapy exist for such a problem?
3. What were the warning signs that C. J. Watkins was not properly qualified?
4. What should have told the therapists to stop the intervention?
5. Was the punishment fair?

BOX 1.2 Death by Restraint: Angie Arndt

Angie was a foster child taken in by Dan and Donna Pavlik. They enrolled her in the Marriage & Family Health Services "Mikan" program, where she made progress for 8 weeks. Then an agency social worker recommended day treatment in order for her to get caught up in school. She was admitted to Northwest Guidance & Counseling's Day Treatment clinic in Rice Lake, Wisconsin, in the Spring of 2006. At the time, she was seven years old and weighed 56 lbs. Soon afterward, her parents noticed a negative change in her behavior and made an appointment with the Director for June.

On May 24, Angie arrived late in the morning. While having lunch she was reprimanded for blowing bubbles in her milk and laughing. When she laughed again, she was taken to a "time-out" room where she was told to sit on a hard chair. She crossed her legs and rested her head in her lap. Since this was not exactly what she had been told to do, she was taken to a "cool down" room, consisting of another chair, a mat on a cement floor, and blank walls. She cried and protested that she didn't want to go there.

In the cool down room, she curled up on the chair and fell asleep. Staff woke her up and told her to sit head up, feet down, and be quiet. She dozed off again. Staff woke her up again. She became agitated and staff restrained her in the chair. She was warned that if she struggled, it would be considered "unsafe" behavior and she would be put in a face-down floor restraint. She started to cry and staff told her to control her emotions. She fell out of the chair and pleaded not to be restrained. Staff put her in a face-down floor restraint with one holding her ankles while another one, weighing 250 lbs., pressed his weight against her shoulders for 98 minutes. (The customary rule is 1 minute per year of age.)

Angie screamed for help, lost bladder and bowel control, vomited, and passed out. When she was finally released, she was not moving. Staff rolled her body over and noticed her face was blue. CPR was started but it was too late. The Medical Examiner concluded her death was caused by positional asphyxia as a result of the restraint

(continued)

and ruled it a homicide. Northwest Counseling & Guidance Clinic was charged with a felony and fined $100,000. The staff person pleaded no contest to a misdemeanor and received 60 days in jail and a $10,000 fine (Coalition Against Institutionalized Child Abuse, 2006; Harter, 2007).

Questions for Discussion
1. Should day treatment facilities have an "open door" policy for parents who would like to observe?
2. What kind of behavior should be labeled "unsafe" and require restraint?
3. How should seven-year-old children be disciplined?
4. Who was most at fault—the agency or the staff member?
5. Was the punishment fair?

BOX 1.3 Death by Medication: Rebecca Riley

Rebecca was diagnosed with attention-deficit hyperactivity disorder and bipolar disorder (ADHD) at 28 months by a psychiatrist who based her assessment of the family's medical history, parental descriptions of her behavior, and brief office visits. Other adults, such as preschool teachers, were never consulted. She was prescribed both clonidine (for the ADHD) and Depakote (for the bipolar disorder). Both medications are approved by the FDA for adults only, though doctors have been known to prescribe them for children as well. School teachers, the school nurse, the child's therapist, and social workers with the Massachusetts Department of Social Services all raised concerns about the side effects of the medications to no avail. The psychiatrist and the medical center where she worked assured the other professionals that the prescriptions

(continued)

were appropriate even though Depakote carries the following two black box warnings:

Hepatotoxicity: hepatic failure resulting in fatalities has occurred in patients receiving valproic acid and its derivatives. Experience has indicated that children under the age of two years are at considerably increased risk of developing fatal hepatotoxicity.

Pancreatitis: cases of life-threatening pancreatitis have been reported in both children and adults receiving valproate. Some of the cases have been described as hemorrhagic with a rapid progression from initial symptoms to death.

While Rebecca's parents have been charged with overdosing their child, the psychiatrist ignored many red flags. Rebecca's mother reported that she had independently increased the child's bedtime dose without prior authorization. Pharmacists at the local Walgreens called the psychiatrist twice to complain that the mother was seeking refills that were not due yet. On one occasion the mother claimed to have lost some pills and on another claimed she ruined them by getting them wet. The psychiatrist began prescribing 10-day refills instead of 30-day supplies, but the pharmacists reported that two of these 10-day refills were prescribed on consecutive days. Altogether, the mother managed to obtain 200 more pills than she should have been given for 1 year. On December 13, 2006, Rebecca died from an overdose and her siblings were removed by the Department of Social Services. Rebecca was four years old at the time of her death. Her parents were arrested for murder. They claim that they were only following doctor's orders. The medical examiner ruled that Rebecca died from a lethal combination of clonidine, Depakote, a cough suppressant, and an antihistamine. The amount of clonidine alone was enough for a fatal dose (Alliance for Human Research Protection, 2007; Lavoie, 2007).

Discussion Questions

1. At what age should children be diagnosed with ADHD or bipolar disorder?

(continued)

2. What evidence existed that she actually had these problems?
3. Were there other therapies the doctor did not consider for these problems?
4. What should the other professionals have done to prevent this tragedy?
5. Who do you think is most at fault?

and direct observation rather than merely relying on youth self-report or parental-report measures. Finally, empirically supported treatments are becoming more widely available and user-friendly. Treatment manuals have increased their flexibility and creativity for children. Some use modules that can be used for short-term, pinpointed problems. Others use decision-trees so that clinical judgment remains intact (Spirito & Kazak, 2006).

Educational Reasons

Schools are under enormous pressure to do more than just educate America's country's school children. As the President's New Freedom Commission on Mental Health (2003) observed:

> Schools are in a key position to identify mental health problems early and to provide a link to appropriate services. Every day more than 52 million students attend over 114,000 schools in the U.S. When combined with the six million adults working at those schools, almost one-fifth of the population passes through the Nation's schools on any given weekday. Clearly, strong school mental health programs can attend to the health and behavioral concerns of students, reduce unnecessary pain and suffering, and help ensure academic achievement. (p. 59)

There are now three national centers devoted to understanding the role of mental health services in schools. These include the Center for School Mental Health Analysis and Action at the University of Maryland, the Center for Mental Health in Schools at University of California at Los Angeles, and the newest, the National Center for School Counseling Outcome Research at the University of Massachusetts-Amherst. The first offers a national conference each fall and has just started its own scholarly journal, *Advances in School Mental Health Promotion*. The second offers technical assistance and toolkits and publishes a free newsletter, *Addressing Barriers to Learning*. Both are partly funded by the Office of Adolescent Health within the Department of Health and Human Services. The third conducts research in school counseling, publishes quarterly research briefs, and offers a summer leadership institute on using data to help children succeed. Over time, these three university centers should enable more rigorous research to be conducted in schools and disseminated online.

The first systematic review of the effect of mental health interventions on school-related results was conducted by Hoagwood et al. (2007). They examined 2,000 studies between 1990 and 2006 and found 64 that met rigorous methodological standards for quality. Only 24, however, examined both mental health and academic outcomes. Of these 24 studies, 15 (62.5%) showed a positive impact on both. This is not surprising given that academic competencies and social-emotional competencies have a reciprocal relationship (Welsh, Parke, Widaman, & O'Neill, 2001). Several types of educational outcomes were positively affected by mental health interventions. First, school behavioral measures indicated increases in school attendance and school bonding as well as decreases in disciplinary referrals, grade retention, school nurse visits, and tardiness (Jennings, Pearson, & Harris, 2000). Second, academic measures showed improved grades and math and reading scores. Finally, parental school involvement improved temporarily during and shortly after treatment. Clearly, researchers have just begun to examine the relationship between mental health intervention and school performance, but the initial results are promising—nearly two thirds of the studies examining the relationship found progress on both fronts, but this was not an easy task. As Hoagwood et al. (2007) concluded, "The majority of the interventions that were effective in both domains were time-intensive as well as complex, with multiple targets (e.g., students, parents, and teachers) and across multiple contexts (school and home)" (p. 89).

Economic Reasons

Finally, there are *economic* reasons for EBP. In a recent national survey, Raines (2006b) found that the greatest looming threat to the provision of school-based and related services was state and national budget cuts. When local educational agencies face reduced expenses, pupil personnel services are often the first to be affected because they are often considered supplemental to the academic enterprise. As school districts employ fewer practitioners (often due to attrition), the remaining ones have to cover more needs with less time. It behooves them to practice in the most effective and efficient manner. Economic reasons include more than just money. It also includes time, effort, and human resources.

For now, however, let's just address the issue of money. Consider, for example, the problem of teenage pregnancy. Medical costs associated with prenatal care for adolescent mothers are higher than those for older mothers because of pregnancy-induced hypertension, anemia, sexually transmitted diseases, and cephalopelvic disproportion (Brown & Eisenberg, 1995). The medical cost of neonatal care for their infants is also higher because of low birth weight, which increases the chances of respiratory disease, developmental disorders, and mental retardation (Maynard, 1996). Add to these costs the fact that less than one third of these mothers earn a high school diploma, probably end up on welfare, and are more likely to abuse or neglect their children, and that their children are less likely to complete high school education and more likely to repeat the cycle of teenage pregnancy themselves. These facts make the aggregate cost over $40 billion per year (Flinn & Hauser, 1998). Currently, the Bush administration is committed to spending millions of dollars using abstinence-only education although this approach has not been found effective (Hauser, 2004; Kirby, 2002; Klein, 2005). Use of a more scientific and holistic approach would save taxpayers millions of dollars every year (Franklin, Grant, Corcoran, O'Dell, & Bultman, 1997; Moncloa et al., 2003; Santelli, Ott, Lyon, Rogers, & Summers, 2006).

This concern for economical interventions does not mean that interventions should be solely based on cost minimization. Greenhalgh (2006) is correct when she observes that "clinical decision-making *purely* on the grounds of cost is usually both senseless and cruel" (p. 7, emphasis as in the original). Teenage pregnancy is a complex social problem and therefore will probably require complex solutions of the type that Hoagwood (2007) reviewed. Nonetheless, we should be cautious about expensive programs, such as Baby-Think-It-Over infant simulators that are no more effective than other inexpensive programs (Barnett, 2006). Economic evaluations of child and adolescent interventions are still in the early stages of development (Romeo, Byford, & Knapp, 2005).

Philosophies of Science

Although most mental health practitioners do not study the social sciences to learn about philosophy, they do have philosophical assumptions that undergird their approach to research. There are three different philosophical approaches to EBP. These include positivism, constructivism, and critical realism.

Positivism

Positivism is the oldest and most established philosophy of science. As Unrau, Grinnell, and Williams (2008) explain, positivists are scientists who believe in one objective reality, try to be objective by putting aside their own values, test hypotheses through deductive logic and experimental research, rely on standardized measuring instruments, and strive for highly generalizable findings. The U.S. Department of Education adopted this philosophy of science when they first defined scientifically based research.

Constructivism

At the opposite end of the philosophical spectrum is the constructivist or interpretivist viewpoint. Constructivists believe in multiple subjective realities, recognize and readily admit their own biases and values, seek to understand social phenomena through inductive logic and qualitative data, rely on the researcher as the primary measuring instrument, and strive for contextually generalizable findings. Most qualitative researchers are constructivists and take issue with the U.S. Department of Education's narrow view of research (Lincoln & Cannella, 2004).

Critical Realism

A third perspective emerged during the 1980s—critical, fallibilistic, or transcendental realism (Manicas & Secord, 1983). It agrees with the positivists on the issue of ontology that there is a socially shared or objective reality, but it also agrees with the constructivists on the issue of epistemology that no one has an "immaculate perception" of reality. Philosopher Roy Bhaskar (1989) explains,

> Transcendental realism explicitly asserts the non-identity of the objects of the transitive and intransitive dimensions, of thought and being. And it relegates the notion of correspondence between them to the status of metaphor for the aim of *adequating practice*. It entails acceptance of (i) the principle of *epistemic relativity*, which states that all beliefs are socially produced, so that all knowledge is transient, and neither truth-values nor criteria of rationality exist outside historical time. But it entails the rejection of (ii) the doctrine of *judgmental relativism*, which maintains

that all beliefs are equally valid, in the sense that there can be no rational grounds for preferring one to another. (pp. 23–24, emphasis as in the original)

In other words, fallible realists believe that the common mistake of both positivists and constructivists is that they equate their ontology with their epistemology. Ontology is the branch of philosophy that asks "What is real?" Epistemology, however, asks "How do we know?" Fallibilistic realism assumes that there is one objective reality (like the positivists) but admits that human beings are time-bound and culture-bound to such a degree that we can have only subjective knowledge (like the constructivists). The advantages of such a position are twofold. First, it rejects the postmodern position that every belief or source of evidence is equally valid with no way to determine which one is correct. Second, it allows us to move forward with the purpose of establishing an adequate, not absolutely proven, basis for practice. This is especially important because EBP is an evolving method for determining what works in clinical practice (Gambrill, 2007). The next chapter will define the process of EBP in greater detail and differentiate it from similar terms.

Summary

This chapter addressed five major reasons for EBP and three philosophies of science that might serve to undergird it. The five reasons included ethical, legal, clinical, educational, and economic reasons. The ethical reasons found that in every major code of ethics for school service providers, there was a mandate for staying current with the research literature, applying the literature to one's practice, and evaluating the results. The legal reasons included both case law and federal legislation. Case law looked at three U.S. Supreme Court rulings that define the legal standard for scientific evidence. Such evidence had to meet four criteria: (1) whether the theory or technique can be (or has been) tested; (2) whether the theory or technique has been subject to peer-review and publication; (3) whether or not the theory or technique has a known error rate and standards controlling its operation; or (4) whether the underlying science has attracted widespread acceptance by the scientific community. Federal legislation looked at both the No Child Left Behind Act and the Individuals with Disabilities Improvement Act. Both use the same definition of scientifically based research, leaving very little "wiggle room" for school-based practitioners who would rather use clinical wisdom or personal experience as the basis for their interventions. Clinical reasons included standards of care, avoiding harm, and optimal practice. Under standards of care, all three professional groups espoused a similar principle for student services—all practitioners must evaluate their practice by measuring their results. Avoiding harm means not causing damage by the use or misuse of therapeutic interventions that have been demonstrated to be dangerous. Optimal treatments are best for seven reasons: (1) they make a substantial difference, (2) they are durable, (3) they are problem-specific, (4) they are wide-ranging, (5) they have diverse modes of delivery, (6) they have new ways to evaluate results, and (7) they are user-friendly. Educational outcomes that can be improved include school behavior, academic performance, and parental school engagement. Economic reasons include greater efficiency in use of time, money, and resources.

The major philosophies of science include positivism, constructivism, and critical realism. The latter is the only one to truly distinguish between the philosophical concepts of ontology and epistemology. It combines the best of both positivism and constructivism. From positivism, it takes the belief in a mind-independent reality. From constructivism, it takes the belief in multiple ways of knowing, which values both quantitative and qualitative research. Critical realism is preferable for the evolutionary process of EBP.

Suggested Reading

1. Dishion, T., McCord, J., & Poulin, F. (1999). When interventions harm: Peer groups and problem behavior. *American Psychologist, 54*, 755–764.

2. Handler, M. W., & DuPaul, G. J. (1999). Pharmacological issues and iatrogenic effects on learning. In R. T. Brown (Ed.), *Cognitive aspects of chronic illness in children* (pp. 355–385). New York: Guilford.

3. Romanczyk, R. G., Arnstein, L., Soorya, L. V., & Gillis, J. (2003). The myriad of controversial treatments for autism: A critical evaluation of efficacy. In S. O. Lilienfeld, S. J. Lynn, & J. M. Lohr (Eds.), *Science and pseudoscience in clinical psychology* (pp. 363–395). New York: Guilford.

4. Waschbusch, D. A., & Hill, G. P. (2003). Empirically supported, promising, and unsupported treatments for children with Attention-Deficit/ Hyperactivity Disorder. In S. O. Lilienfeld, S. J. Lynn, & J. M. Lohr (Eds.), *Science and pseudoscience in clinical psychology* (pp. 333–362). New York: Guilford.

Internet Resources

Advocacy Groups

Advocates for Children in Therapy
http://www.childrenintherapy.org

Alliance for Human Research Protection
http://www.ahrp.org

Coalition Against Institutionalized Child Abuse
http://caica.org

Professional Associations

American Counseling Association
http://www.counseling.org/index.asp

American Psychological Association—Division of School Psychology
http://www.indiana.edu/~div16/index.html

American School Counselor Association
http://www.schoolcounselor.org

National Association of School Psychologists
http://www.nasponline.org

National Association of Social Workers
http://www.socialworkers.org

School Social Work Association of America
http://www.sswaa.org

University Research Centers

Center for Mental Health in Schools—UCLA
http://smhp.psych.ucla.edu/

Center for School Mental Health Analysis and Action—University of Maryland
http://csmh.umaryland.edu/

National Center for School Counseling Outcome Research
http://www.umass.edu/schoolcounseling/

2

Evidence-Based Practice: Definition and Process

Preview

The last chapter identified five reasons for evidence-based practice and provided a philosophy of science that undergirds it. In this chapter, the parallel processes of practice and research will be integrated using the evidence-based practice model. I will define what is meant by the phrase, evidence-based practice (EBP). I will differentiate it from similar terms, such as empirically supported treatments and outcome-based practice. The definition of EBP that I suggest focuses on a practical process that aims first and foremost to benefit clients. Next, I will carefully describe the five major steps in evidence-based practice. These steps include the following: asking answerable questions, investigating the evidence, appraising the evidence, adapting and applying the evidence, and evaluating the results. Finally, I will dispel two widespread caricatures of EBP, identify a middle ground between them, and offer some caveats about the EBP process.

Parallel Practices or Integrated Practices?

Some authors (Monette, Sullivan, & DeJong, 2002) have observed that there are parallels between research and practice. Usually, the parallel looks something like the following.

PRACTICE STEPS	RESEARCH STEPS
Assessment of the problem	Statement of the problem
Intervention planning	Research planning
Intervention implementation	Data collection
Evaluation of effectiveness	Data analysis
Documentation of results	Dissemination of results

The EBP approach aims for an integration of the steps, as shown:

1. Assessment of the problem using reliable and valid measures
2. Intervention planning using relevant, strong, and consistent research
3. Intervention implementation that adapts and applies the research in ways that account for client characteristics and complexity, clinician experience and expertise, and contextual constraints
4. Evaluation of effectiveness using the same reliable and valid measures from Step 1
5. Documentation of results, including dissemination to constituent groups (e.g., building principals, superintendents, and/or school-board members)

Definition of EBP

In the Preface, I stated that this is a book about research-infused practice. Practice is defined here as the process of helping people adapt to the demands of their environment, or modifying the environment to meet the needs of the people who inhabit it, or both. Although this person-in-environment perspective has been central to social work (Germain, 1979; Pardeck, 1996; Saari, 1986; Winters & Easton, 1983), it is also being increasingly used by counselors (Conyne & Cook, 2004) and psychologists (Dishion & Stormshak, 2007; Garbarino, 2001; Munger, 2000). This model is based on research that demonstrates that there is a strong reciprocal relationship between children's emotional-behavioral health and the instructional environment. This mutual influence between child and context can be seen in several types of research. First, interventions that are integrated into the curriculum achieve more positive results and last longer than interventions

Evidence-Based Practice in School Mental Health

offered adjunctively away from class (Hoagwood et al., 2007). Second, social-emotional learning has been linked to school success (Welsh, Parke, Widaman, & O'Neill, 2001; Zins, Bloodworth, Weissberg, & Walberg, 2004). Third, positive school and classroom climates have been shown to prevent behavioral problems and school violence (Adams, 2000; Gettinger & Kohler, 2006; Welsh, 2000). Thus, practice must encompass the larger process of enabling a better "fit" between students and their instructional milieu. For this reason, I do not use the word practice to denote a specific counseling technique, treatment, or intervention. The originators of EBP defined it as the "conscious, explicit, and judicious use of current best evidence in making decisions about the care of individual patients" (Sackett, Rosenberg, Gray, Haynes, & Richardson, 1996, p. 71). It involves a process of integrating the "best research evidence with clinical expertise and patient values" (Sackett, Strauss, Richardson, Rosenberg, & Haynes, 2000, p. 1).

Most school-based practitioners will be familiar with the comical children's character, Amelia Bedelia, whose consistent misunderstanding of common phrases (like "steal second base") leads to a series of misadventures (Parrish, 1992). Similarly, it is important to distinguish EBP from two other often-used phrases—empirically supported treatments and outcome evaluation.

Empirically Supported Treatments

It is important not to confuse EBP with empirically supported treatments (ESTs) (Westen, Novotny, & Thompson-Brenner, 2005). A treatment is defined as the application of remedies to help a person recover from an illness or injury. Treatment assumes a medical model and presumes that the problem lies with the person, not the environment (Fonagy, Target, Cottrell, Phillips, & Kurtz, 2002). There are ESTs for a wide variety of psychosocial problems, but they are not the primary focus of this book. The reason that ESTs do not qualify as EBP is that they cover only the first two steps of integrating research and practice and leave out the final three steps (Rubin & Parrish, 2007; Walker, Briggs, Koroloff, & Friesen, 2007). Furthermore, it is more important to show clinicians how to find the latest ESTs than to give them a list of ESTs that will be outdated by the time they read about them.

Outcome Evaluation

It is also important not to confuse EBP with outcome evaluation (Constable & Massat, in press). Outcome evaluation is concerned with carefully measuring the results of one's interventions (Bloom, Fischer, & Orme, 2006). Outcome evaluation is a critical component of EBP, but it is not synonymous with EBP. The reason that outcome evaluation does not qualify as EBP is that it does not require that practitioners ever use the professional literature. It simply jumps to the fourth step in the integrated process and leaves out the first three steps.

In short, the problem with both of the positions discussed here is that there is a philosophical error called a "category mistake" (Meiland, 1999). Both the "EST = EBP" and the "Outcome Evaluation = EBP" folks mistake a part of the process for the whole. Like the famous Indian story of the blind men and the elephant, they are partially correct, but cannot see the larger picture. EBP takes both into account.

Evidence-Based Practitioners

What is the definition of an evidence-based practitioner? Gibbs (2003) defines it as follows:

> Placing the client's benefits first, evidence-based practitioners adopt a *process* of lifelong learning that involves continually posing specific questions of direct *practical* importance to clients, searching objectively and efficiently for the current best evidence relative to each question, and taking appropriate action guided by evidence. (p. 6, italics added)

Two parts of this definition are worth noting. First, an evidence-based practitioner assumes that there are no facts, theories, or research that practitioners can learn in graduate school and then depend upon for the rest of their professional careers. Good clinical practice requires that all professional helpers become self-regulated "lifelong learners" (Howard, McMillen, & Pollio, 2003; Masui & DeCorte, 2005; Murphy, 2005; Slawson & Shaughnessy, 2005). Second, evidence-based practitioners seek satisfactory or "good-enough" evidence about current practice questions. There is seldom unequivocal evidence so that clinicians can know that they are making exactly the right choices. At the very least, practitioners should be able to identify which interventions, such as Scared Straight programs, are harmful to children (Beutler, 2000; Petrosino, Turpin-Petrosino, & Buehler, 2003; Verhulst, 2002).

Process of EBP

According to the originators of EBP, there are five basic stages in the process (Ollendick & Davis, 2004; Sackett et al., 2000). Let's review each one in

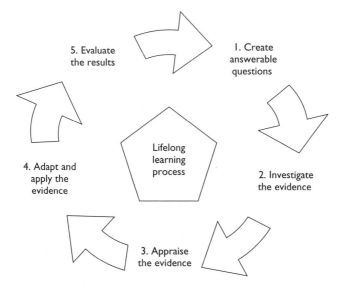

5. Evaluate
the results

1. Create
answerable
questions

Lifelong
learning
process

4. Adapt and
apply the
evidence

2. Investigate
the evidence

3. Appraise
the evidence

FIGURE 2.1. Process of evidence-based practice.

order (see Figure 2.1), and see how it fits into the integrated research-practice approach discussed.

Answerable Questions

First, practitioners must convert their need for information into answerable questions. This will be explicated in more detail in Chapter 3. An important caveat, however, is that not all questions are answerable by science. For example, science cannot help us determine if it is "right" for a pregnant 15-year old to have an abortion. That kind of question can be answered only on ethical or moral grounds. Professional associations offer codes of ethics to guide clinicians' decision making about these questions. Although science may be able to help clinicians determine the negative and positive sequelae of decisions already made, it cannot offer ethical guidance. This stage is similar to the assessment step mentioned earlier—it requires practitioners to identify the crux of the problem by formulating intelligent questions that need to be answered before treatment planning begins.

Investigation of the Evidence

Second, practitioners must be able to efficiently and effectively investigate the best evidence. Although these terms are often used in tandem, they do not mean the same. They are really separate dimensions that can be used orthogonally to create a typology of investigations, as shown in the following table.

Efficient and ineffective	Efficient and effective
Inefficient and ineffective	Inefficient and effective

Efficiency means being able to do something with a minimum of time and effort; it requires acquiring specific skills in using electronic databases. Some computer savvy investigators are efficient, but not effective. They can locate research quickly, but it is often irrelevant, weak, or inconsistent. Using Google is a great example of this approach. Even using Advanced Search to narrow down the number of irrelevant hits still leads to thousands of citations with no way of weeding out the necessary from the unnecessary. This is due to the fact that there is so much information available that Perelman (1992) compared it to trying to drink from a fire hose! Worse, if they do manage to find academic articles, they are only available for an exorbitant fee (e.g., $35/article).

Effectiveness, however, requires that users actually find the evidence that they are looking for. Typically, this requires that they learn to triangulate their search. Scholars across several fields suggest that there is no substitute for searching journals by hand (Lindo, 2006; Raines, 2006a; Seethaler & Fuchs, 2005; Stone & Gambrill, 2007). This is due to two facts. First, abstracting services often do not publish studies until 6 months after they appear. Second, abstracting services occasionally lose or misplace abstracts that are sent in by journals, resulting in gaps in coverage. If school-based practitioners wanted to stay current with the latest research in special education as well as their chosen discipline of counseling, psychology, or social work, they would have to review at least a dozen journals regularly (see Box 2.1). This would involve hand searching these 12 journals on a quarterly basis. They would go to a university library, locate the journals in the library stacks, and spend hours carefully sifting through hundreds of abstracts of the articles, hoping to find a few that are relevant. Along the way, many may become distracted by other interesting articles that have little to do with the original topic. I sometimes refer to this as academic attention deficit disorder. They eventually find what they want after an exhaustive (and exhausting) search, but they do not allow the computer databases to filter the information for them.

The best investigators are both effective and efficient. To become proficient at both requires access to what Alexander and Tate (2005) call the private Web.

BOX 2.1 Core Professional Journals for School-Based Practitioners

Special Education

Behavioral Disorders

Education & Treatment of Children

Exceptional Children

Journal of Applied Behavior Analysis

Journal of Behavioral Education

Journal of Emotional and Behavioral Disorders

Journal of Evidence Based Practices in Schools

Journal of Experimental Education

Journal of Special Education

Preventing School Failure

RASE: Remedial and Special Education

Counseling

Career Development Quarterly

Guidance and Counseling

Journal of Counseling & Development

Journal of Multicultural Counseling & Development

Measurement and Evaluation in Counseling and Development

Personnel and Guidance Journal

Professional School Counseling

Psychology

Contemporary Educational Psychology

Educational Psychologist

Educational Psychology

Journal of Applied School Psychology

(continued)

Journal of Psychoeducational Assessment

Journal of School Psychology

Psychology in the Schools

School Psychology International

School Psychology Quarterly

School Psychology Review

Social Work

Child and Adolescent Social Work Journal

Children and Schools

Children and Youth Services Review

Families in Society

Research on Social Work Practice

School Social Work Journal

Social Work Research

Unlike the public Web accessible through Google and other search engines, information on the private web is fee-based and edited for content. Efficient and effective investigators know how to search multiple databases and allow the computer to sift through mountains of data in a matter of minutes. This stage is similar to the treatment planning step—it requires practitioners to go beyond mere brainstorming and investigate which interventions are most likely to help the client. This is exactly what I intend to describe in Chapter 4.

Critical Appraisal

Third, practitioners should critically appraise the evidence for its validity and applicability to the practice problem that motivated the initial investigation. This is one of the ways in which EBP differs from the usual treatment—it requires critical thinking to determine what is the "best evidence." Let's discuss two common problems faced by those who lack either efficiency or effectiveness in their search strategies. First, the efficient but ineffective practitioners have learned to use Google to easily locate sources, but how can they evaluate these sources? Unfortunately, this kind of search tends to lead to biased or authority-based evidence. The experts at information management at most schools and universities are the librarians. They are not only skilled at finding information, but also in evaluating the trustworthiness of information they find. They were among the first professionals to realize that people needed help in appraising the information they found on the Internet. In order to take advantage of their expertise, readers may refer to Box 2.2 and try the experiment described there. On the other hand, effective but inefficient practitioners get bogged down in the immensity of scientific data available on the scholarly databases. After a while, they often yield to the temptation of only reviewing the abstracts rather than reading whole articles. This is fine for an overview of the research that exists on a topic, but it is insufficient for clinical decision making.

Appraising the abstracts is as simple as asking whether a trusted database accurately summarizes the authors' position. For example, while browsing for iatrogenic practices in the reputed PsycINFO database, I found this curious statement about stimulant medication for children with attention deficit/hyperactivity disorder: "Longer term studies are few in number but have produced conclusive evidence that careful therapeutic use of these medications is harmful" (accession number 1999-13939-007). Since this contradicted what other research indicated, I looked up the original article and read this statement again in the published abstract: "Longer term studies are few in number but have produced *no* conclusive evidence that careful therapeutic use of these medications is harmful" (Greenhill, Halperin, & Abikoff, 1999, p. 503, emphasis added). What a difference one two-letter word makes! Both kinds of practitioners need to keep their heads on and think critically about the "facts" that they uncover (Gambrill, 2006a). I will address ways to appraise scientifically based research in Chapter 5.

Adaptation and Application

Fourth, practitioners should apply and adapt the results to their own clients. This step requires both cultural sensitivity and clinical practice wisdom. Seldom will a research study's participants be similar to the actual clients we are trying to help so we must custom-tailor the intervention to fit the students in our school. This will involve a step that many browsers of research work are likely to skip: reading the method section of the research. Good method sections have a paragraph on the population, sampling plan, and response rate. All three are vitally important for different reasons. First,

BOX 2.2 Using the Web to Evaluate the Web

Begin by going to Google's Advanced Search page at http://www.google.com/advanced_search. In the **Find Results** section, go to the second blank (with the exact phrase) and type: *evaluating Web-based*. Then go to the third blank (with at least one of the words) and type two words: *library librarian*. Across from **Language**, tell Google to return pages written in the language with which you are most comfortable (e.g., English). Across from **Date**, tell Google to return Web pages updated in the "*past year.*" Finally, across from **Domain**, tell Google to only return results from the site or domain *.edu*. Now press the **Google Search** button or hit return. You will receive a few hundred results that will link you to trustworthy librarians who will give some pointers on how to evaluate Web-based information. Read at least five of these and ask these questions:

1. On which points did they concur?
2. On which points did they conflict?
3. On which points did they complement each other?

Based on what you've learned, answer these three questions:

1. What ideas have the most support?
2. What ideas were completely new to you?
3. What ideas would you share with others?

Now use the principles you have learned to evaluate the five web sites that you just read. Did they measure up to their own standards? Were there ways they could be improved? If they didn't measure up, were there other web sites that were better? Prioritize the top three and add them to your favorites or bookmark them for future reference. Share them with your school librarian and/or information technology specialist.

the population should be similar to the children or adolescents that attend our school. Applying the results of a study of white middle-class suburban kids to minority low-income urban children will inevitably cause problems. Second, the study should have used a representative or probability sample that makes the results generalizable to the population of interest. Third, the response rate should be high enough (generally 50% or better) that we can be confident that respondents did not bias the sampling plan. This step has been a part of EBP in medicine since the beginning. Sackett et al. (1996) explain the need for adaptation and application as follows:

> Good doctors use both individual clinical expertise and the best available external evidence, and neither alone is enough. Without clinical expertise, practice risks becoming tyrannized by evidence, for even excellent external evidence may be inapplicable to or inappropriate for an individual patient. Without best current evidence, practice risks becoming rapidly out of date, to the detriment of patients. (p. 72)

This stage is similar to the intervention implementation step—practitioners must put what they have learned into action to initiate the change process. Other ways to adapt and apply results will be explored in Chapter 6.

Outcome Evaluation

Finally, since adapting interventions automatically changes them, we must begin to track and evaluate progress. It is this step that completes the circle and turns EBP into practice-based evidence (Barkham & Mellor-Clark, 2003; Evans, Connell, Barkham, Marshall, & Mellor-Clark, 2003). One of the major weaknesses of research by related services personnel has been the failure to link mental health interventions with improved academic outcomes. In a systematic review of 2,000 studies, Hoagwood et al. (2007) found only 24 that examined this relationship. Educational outcomes included attendance, disciplinary actions, grades, special education placement, and standardized test scores. The good news is that 15 (62.5%) of these studies found positive outcomes for both mental health and academic success. Hoagwood et al. (2007) concluded that

> Mental health cannot afford to continue to exist in isolation; it needs to be reframed, mainstreamed, and folded into the broader mission of schools. To this end, attention to indigenous

resources, supports, and opportunities in schools that may provide entry points for delivery of mental health services in support of the school's mission are needed. (p. 89)

Outcome evaluation can be accomplished using either case-level or group-level designs. Case-level designs enable practitioners to track the progress of individual students over time. Group-level designs enable professionals to track and compare groups of students over time. Group-level designs will be discussed in Chapter 7, and case-level designs will be discussed in Chapter 8. This stage is similar to the final two steps in the integrated research-practice model—it requires practitioners to carefully evaluate their own effectiveness and share the results with vested constituencies, including clients, parents, and school administrators.

Caricatures of EBP

As I have spoken to school-based mental health professionals around the country, I find that there are two primary misunderstandings of EBP. These misunderstandings cause many practitioners to view EBP with either skepticism or trepidation. Frankly, if either of these misperceptions were indeed accurate, I would not be writing this book!

Emperor's New Clothes

The first major caricature of EBP is that it is simply authority-based practice in disguise. We call this the Emperor's New Clothes approach (Gambrill, 2003). According to this viewpoint, EBP has been around for decades (e.g., Jayaratne & Levy, 1979; Marks, 1974; Mullen & Dumpson, 1972). The "evidence" includes not only randomized controlled trials, but also "opinions of respected authorities, based on clinical experiences, descriptive studies, or reports of expert consensus ... anecdotal case reports, unsystematic clinical observation, descriptive reports, [and] case studies" (Roberts & Yeager, 2004, p. 6). In other words, it is "business-as-usual" in the world of psychotherapy. Many clinicians like this caricature because it requires very little change from what they have always done—read books by authorities in the field, attend entertaining workshops from senior professionals, and produce anecdotal reports of their own effectiveness by providing thank-you notes and client testimonials. What is wrong with this? It simply does not meet the legal and ethical requirements as discussed in the introduction.

Consider, for example, Corcoran and Vandiver's (2004) recommendation, "A useful Web site for guidelines on a number of psychiatric conditions is www. psychguides.com" (p. 17). Upon further investigation, we found that there were at least three major flaws in the development of these new guidelines. First, consider the following excerpts from the Web site's discussion of its methods.

Creating the Surveys

We first create a skeleton algorithm based on the existing research literature and published guidelines to identify key decision points in the everyday treatment of patients with the disorder in question. We then highlight important clinical questions that had not yet been adequately addressed or definitely answered. Then we develop written questionnaires concerning medication and psychosocial treatments.

Expert Consensus Guideline Series, 2006, p. 1

At first glance, this sounds fairly scientific, but upon closer examination we realized that there were three major flaws. First, they were developing the "skeleton algorithm" (whatever that means) from *both* research literature and published guidelines. This means that these "new" (and improved) guidelines are based on old guidelines!

Second, we read this excerpt about how their instrument was constructed.

The Rating Scale

The survey questionnaires use a 9-point scale slightly modified from a format developed by the RAND Corporation for ascertaining expert consensus. We present the rating scale to the experts with the following instructions:

Extremely inappropriate	1 2 3 4 5 6 7 8 9	Extremely appropriate

Expert Consensus Guideline Series, 2006, p. 1

At first glance this sounds fairly scientific again, but there is *no* mention of their sampling method. How were these "experts" identified? How many were included in their sample? What percentage responded? Did they receive any remuneration? An e-mail query to the webmaster went unanswered. Without knowing the answers to these important questions, we cannot draw any conclusions whatsoever about the reliability or validity of the results. There is simply too much that is unknown to rely on these guidelines for clinical decision making.

A third problem is fortunately acknowledged by the Web site—that it is funded by major pharmaceutical companies. The list of sponsors is a veritable "Who's Who" of corporate producers of psychotropic medications:

Abbott Laboratories

Alza Pharmaceuticals

AstraZeneca Pharmaceuticals

Bristol-Myers Squibb

Celgene Corporation

Eli Lilly and Company

Forest Pharmaceuticals, Inc.

GlaxoSmith-Kline

Janssen Pharmaceutica, Inc.

Medeva Pharmaceuticals

Novartis Pharmeceuticals Corporation

Ortho-McNeil Pharmaceutical

Pfizer, Inc.

Shire Richwood

Solvay Pharmaceuticals

In short, these "expert consensus guidelines" are just a pseudoscientific approach to practice without answers to some very important questions. Greenhalgh (2006, p. 6) calls this type of evidence GOBSAT guidelines ("Good Old Boys Sat Around a Table"). Blindly following them won't hold up in a court of law and places practitioners who do so at risk for malpractice. Perhaps most importantly to school service personnel, the new Individuals with Disabilities Education Act regulations clearly differentiate between "best practices" and "scientifically based research." According to the new federal rules (U.S. Department of Education, 2006),

> The statute and regulations do not refer to "recommended practices," which is a term of art that, generally, refers to practices that the field has referred to as "best practices," and which may or may not be based on evidence from scientifically based research. (p. 89)

As we have seen from the "expert consensus guidelines" above, some "best practices" are highly suspect. School-based practitioners should read them very cautiously.

Cookbook Practice

The second major caricature of EBP is that it is a rigidly controlled treatment. I call this approach the clinical cookbook approach (Howard et al., 2003; Shlonsky & Gibbs, 2006). It presumes that if practitioners will follow each carefully measured step with clients, then the results will turn out as well as one of Martha Stewart's recipes. If the previous approach waters EBP down to the lowest possible denominator, this approach views it as a rigid application of research to clinical practice. It presumes that EBP requires the use of treatment manuals and ignores the unique personal characteristics of both the client and the therapist.

There are also three major problems to the clinical cookbook approach: client characteristics and complexity, clinician experience and expertise, and contextual constraints (Addis, Wade, & Hatgis, 1999). Let's examine each of these in detail.

First, rarely do students get referred for just one problem. Each problem has the potential to create other concomitant issues as well. Take the most common problem that schools face: learning disabilities (U.S. Department of Education, 2002b). Most students with learning disabilities have self-esteem problems and/or social skills deficits (Raines, 2006a). Treating one problem in isolation from the others is likely to be an exercise in futility. What is needed is a set of interventions that addresses all the concerns that teachers and parents have. Treating just a part of a person is insufficient.

Second, clinicians are seldom interchangeable. We each bring our own unique set of knowledge, experience, and skill to the exchange (Elkin, 1999). No one likes to color by numbers and practitioners are not automatons. Cognitive behavioral therapy may be an EST for depression, but poorly executed cognitive behavioral therapy is unlikely to be helpful to anyone (Sholomskas et al., 2005). There is really no point in learning what works if we are not willing to take the time to learn how it works through supervision or consultation (Addis, 2002; Secemsky & Ahlman, 2003).

Third, contextual concerns about the realities of school-based interventions limit what can reasonably be accomplished. Most schools do not meet the No Child Left Behind Act's recommendation of one school counselor per 250 students; one school social worker per 800 students; and one school psychologist per 1,000 students (Title V). Many school-based professionals, in fact, will be shocked that such recommendations exist in federal law! Low pay, high turnover, too many clients, too little supervision, and low morale negatively affect the quality of services that are provided (Dishion & Stormshak, 2007). Many school-based practitioners are often forced to choose short-term individual or group interventions simply due to the constraints of time and resources (Lomonaco, Scheidlinger, & Aronson, 2000).

Remember that Sackett et al. (1996, p. 71) defined EBP as "the conscientious, explicit, and judicious use of the current best evidence in making decisions about the care of individual patients." In essence, this model of the "best evidence" is the convergence of four factors (see Figure 2.2).

Middle Ground

EBP occupies a middle ground between the extremes of authority-based practice and cookbook practice. It does not allow either the clinician or the researcher to be a tyrant. It respects practitioners for their clinical judgment with their clients, but it does not elevate clinical wisdom to a position that is higher than scientifically based research. Careful evaluation of practice serves as an important counterbalance against potential self-deception. A personal anecdote will illustrate the difference. While working in a community-in-schools program in New York, I provided mental health services to students with emotional disturbances in an intermediate school (grades 6–8). The staff learned that 100% of students dropped out of high school

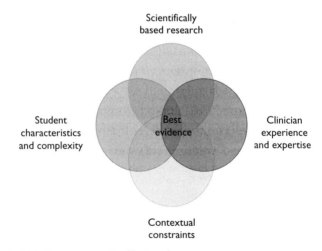

FIGURE 2.2. Four components of best evidence.

in their first year and decided that we had to do something. A colleague and I developed a "graduation group" for the eighth graders, whereby we met each Friday afternoon and took them to visit the high schools that they might attend, meet some key people at the schools, and discuss how high school was going to be different from intermediate school. After 10 weeks, we asked both students and teachers how they felt about the group and got rave reviews. A year later, however, we followed up on our graduates and learned that 100% of them had dropped out of high school! Clearly, simple customer satisfaction with the program was insufficient to measure its effectiveness.

EBP also respects the importance of using an empirically supported intervention in the way researchers intended it to work, but this does not imply that such interventions should be employed in a wooden manner. For example, clinicians will want to adjust how they communicate key concepts to their clients, using both vocabulary and metaphors that clients will understand. Insufficient attention to generic factors, such as client strengths and the therapeutic relationship (Murphy, 1999), will doom any empirically supported intervention. This may explain why Carr (2000) stated that "up to one-third of all cases do not respond to the best available psychological treatments" (p. 313).

Foolproof Process?

EBP is not a foolproof process. It is an established method in medicine that is mandated by educational laws, but is a promising rather than proven approach in schools (Powers, 2005). There are, therefore, some common pitfalls that need to be avoided along the way. First, some practitioners will have a difficult time identifying the exact question that needs to be answered. A child who may be referred for one problem may not have that problem at all but a different one entirely. Another child may be referred for only one problem and turn out to have two or three. Kauffman (2005) demonstrates, for example, that the symptom of inattention can be caused by multiple underlying problems, including anxiety disorders, thought disorders, mood disorders, and conduct disorders—it doesn't automatically mean that we should equate it with attention deficit/hyperactivity disorder. A misleading reason for referral will necessarily slow the process down, but it will not render it ineffective, just more time-consuming. Good questioning, like good clinical interviewing, takes practice and I will discuss this in detail in Chapter 3. Second, the investigation of the evidence can be frustrating at first and some practitioners may conclude that it is more trouble than it is worth. I can only urge new investigators to stay the course and have faith that technology will eventually catch up with our needs. I will discuss this in more detail in Chapter 4. Third, sometimes there are no studies that will stand up to rigorous appraisal. A practitioner recently contacted me about empirically supported interventions to help an adolescent girl with cerebral palsy to relax more at school. While I was able to locate a book describing detailed exercises for the student to do with a caregiver for exactly this purpose, it contained no evidence regarding its effectiveness. In cases such as this, we must supply the intervention and build the evidence from the ground up. This is one reason that I will address both group-level and case-level designs in Chapters 7 and 8. Fourth, the primary danger of adaptation is that clinicians can "gut" an intervention of its core components rendering it both unrecognizable and worthless. Adaptation requires a delicate balance between fidelity to an intervention's primary principles and faithfulness to meeting our clients' needs. Finally, outcome evaluation can be thwarted most easily by using an inappropriate instrument by which to measure results. Sometimes this occurs because practitioners use whatever rating scale they have on hand rather than purchase one that is more pertinent to the problem. Gradually identifying and obtaining the best measures takes time, money, and effort. The goal of the rest of this book is to make EBP as practical as possible for school-based practitioners.

Summary

EBP aims to integrate research and practice so that they are not parallel processes, but intimately integrated at every step. EBP is not to be confused with ESTs or outcome evaluation. Both confuse the part for the whole. Evidence-based practitioners use a practical process that places client's benefits as the highest priority. This process has five major stages: asking answerable questions, investigating the evidence efficiently and effectively, appraising the evidence, applying and adapting the evidence, and evaluating the results. There are two major caricatures of EBP, which distort its definition. One of these is so flexible, it accepts virtually anything as evidence. The other is so rigid, it does not allow for any flexibility. I have argued for a middle path—one with high scientific standards as well as clinical sensitivity. I also addressed a common pitfall for each stage in the process. I will address all five of these stages in greater detail over the next five chapters of the book.

Suggested Reading

1. Gambrill, E. (2003). Evidence-based practice: Sea change or the emperor's new clothes? *Journal of Social Work Education, 39*, 3–23.

2. Shlonsky, A., & Gibbs, L. (2004). Will the real evidence-based practice please stand up? Teaching the process of evidence-based practice to the helping professions. *Brief Treatment and Crisis Intervention, 4* (2), 137–153.

3. Westen, D., Novotny, C. M., & Thompson-Brenner, H. (2005). EBP ≠ EST: Reply to Crits-Christoph et al. (2005) and Weisz et al. (2005). *Psychological Bulletin, 131* (3), 427–433.

Internet Resources

Library Critiques of Web-Based Information

Association of College and Research Libraries
http://www.ala.org/ala/acrl/acrlpubs/crlnews/backissues1998/julyaugust6/
teachingundergrads.htm

Library of Congress
http://www.loc.gov/rr/business/beonline/selectbib.html

Hope Tillman—Librarian, Babson College
http://www.hopetillman.com/findqual.html

University of California–Los Angeles (UCLA's librarian, Esther Grassian)
http://www.library.ucla.edu/libraries/college/help/critical/index.htm

3

■ ■ ■

Creating Answerable Questions

Preview

The last chapter clarified the five-step process of evidence-based practice. This chapter will orient the reader to the first step of asking answerable questions. There are five types of answerable questions in evidence-based practice. These questions include assessment, description, risk, prevention, and intervention questions. The chapter will also include the legal guidance found in the Individuals with Disabilities Education Improvement Act (IDEA) for each type of inquiry. Each question will also include some school-related examples so that readers can envision how they might benefit from the answers. A case example focusing on the childhood and adolescence of the Virginia Tech shooter Seung-Hui Cho is highlighted in the section on risk. An important caveat on unanswerable questions is included in the same category.

Introduction

Len Gibbs (2003) has recommended that questions must have three fundamental qualities. They must be client-oriented, practical, and evidence-search questions. By being client-oriented, questions have to address the problem for which the student has been referred. By being practical, questions must address pragmatic issues that practitioners face on a daily basis. By being evidence-search, questions must facilitate the electronic search strategies, which are the subject of the next chapter. Gibbs has also identified five basic types of practice-related inquiries, including assessment, description, risk, prevention, and intervention questions (see Figure 3.1). There is no reason to ask all five types of questions in every case. Which question to ask will

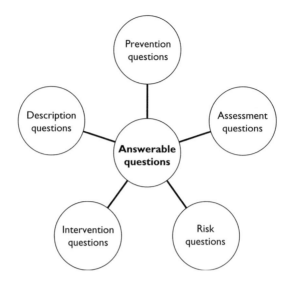

FIGURE 3.1. Five types of answerable questions.

depend on two primary factors—the practitioner's current knowledge and the clinical conundrum that he or she wishes to resolve (Fineout-Overholt & Johnston, 2005). The descriptions below are meant to help clinicians identify the precise question that they hope to answer from current research.

Assessment Questions

As mentioned at the end of Chapter 2, assessment is the first step in the provision of student services. The No Child Left Behind Act (P.L. 107-110, Title V) recommends the following ratios for student service personnel: 1 school counselor per 250 students; 1 school social worker per 800 students; and 1 school psychologist per 1,000 students. Clinicians who work in community mental health centers are often shocked by these ratios. It is more common for them to have caseloads of 30 to 40 clients. They frequently spend the first month doing an in-depth assessment of each client and then bring it to a case conference for intervention planning. There are two realities that differentiate school-based practitioners from their community-based peers. First, school-based clinicians do not have the luxury of assessing students over multiple sessions—they must get the job done effectively and efficiently. Second, school-based practitioners are legally required to identify a child's strengths as well as weaknesses. This requirement is actually mentioned thrice in the IDEA.

First, in developing the Individualized Family Service Plan for infants and toddlers, schools must provide

(1) A multidisciplinary assessment of the unique *strengths* and needs of the infant or toddler and the identification of services appropriate to meet such needs;
(2) A family-directed assessment of the *resources*, priorities, and concerns of the family and the identification of the supports and services necessary to enhance the family's capacity to meet the developmental needs of the infant or toddler; and
(3) A written individualized family service plan developed by a multidisciplinary team, including the parents, as required by subsection (e), including a description of the appropriate transition services for the infant or toddler.

Section 636 (a), emphasis added

Second, while formulating the student's individualized education program, IDEA requires that

The IEP Team, subject to subparagraph (C), shall consider

(i) The *strengths* of the child;
(ii) The concerns of the parents for enhancing the education of their child;
(iii) The results of the initial evaluation or most recent evaluation of the child; and
(iv) The academic, developmental, and functional needs of the child.

Section 614 (d)(3)(A), emphasis added

Finally, the definition of transition services requires that schools develop a coordinated set of activities that

(A) Is designed to be within a results-oriented process, that is focused on improving the academic and functional *achievement* of the child with a disability to facilitate the child's movement from school to post-school activities, including post-secondary education, vocational education, integrated employment (including supported employment), continuing and adult education, adult services, independent living, or community participation;
(B) Is based on the individual child's needs, taking into account the child's *strengths*, preferences, and interests; and
(C) Includes instruction, related services, community experiences, the development of employment and other post-school adult living objectives, and, when appropriate, acquisition of *daily living skills* and functional vocational evaluation.

Section 602 (34), emphasis added

In brief, the message seems clear—school-based professionals should take a strengths-based approach to students throughout their entire time at school from pre-K to graduation. This has some important implications for assessments—any standardized instrument used should report on both strengths and weaknesses. Those tools that are driven only by a search for psychopathology have no place in school-based practice. Unfortunately, this applies to many commonly used instruments developed in psychiatric or mental health settings.

School-based assessments typically have one of three purposes: screening, diagnosis, and intervention planning (Kazdin, 2005; Kelley, 2003). Each of these is improved by the use of standardized instruments that have proven to be reliable and valid measures of student behavior. Why should practitioners use standardized instruments? There are two major reasons. First, several studies have concluded that clinician-only-based assessments of children and youth are biased and haphazard (Jensen & Weisz, 2002; Lewczyk, Garland, Hurlburt, Gearity, & Hough, 2003). Incorporating standardized instruments into clinical assessment protocols improves objectivity and determines a baseline by which to measure future change (Doss, 2005). Second, IDEA requires that schools

(A) Use a variety of assessment tools and strategies to gather relevant functional, developmental, and academic information, including information provided by the parent,
(B) Not use any single measure or assessment as the sole criterion for determining whether a child is a child with a disability or determining an appropriate educational program for the child, and
(C) Use *technically sound instruments* that may assess the relative contribution of cognitive and behavioral factors, in addition to physical or developmental factors.

Section 614 (b)(2), emphasis added

Screening

Screening is a process of quickly determining which children are at risk and deserve more attention (Doll & Haack, 2005). Many schools continue to rely on teachers to make appropriate referrals for mental health interventions, but research has demonstrated that, even with training, many simply will not make needed referrals for services (Moor et al., 2007). According to IDEA, screening is not part of the child evaluation process and therefore does not require parental consent. The relevant section reads,

The screening of a student by a teacher *or specialist* to determine appropriate instructional strategies for curriculum implementation shall not be considered to be an evaluation for eligibility for special education and related services.

Section 614 (a)(1)(E), emphasis added

Screening questions are phrased, "What is the best measure to determine which children should receive closer scrutiny for [psychosocial problem]?" Screening instruments should be broad, brief, and easy to score. Examples include the Children's Global Assessment Scale or the Strengths & Difficulties Questionnaire.

The Children's Global Assessment Scale is the child and adolescent equivalent of the Global Assessment of Functioning scale that is used in Axis V of the multiaxial assessment in the *Diagnostic and Statistical Manual of Mental Disorders, 4th ed.* It is meant to be filled out by a clinician who is familiar with the child's complete situation and involves assigning a single number from 1 to 100 to describe the child's overall functioning within the past month (Shaffer et al., 1983). A newer nonclinician version is also available (Bird et al., 1996). A cutoff score of below 70 differentiates children who need further evaluation. It has been evaluated in over 69 studies and is probably the most widely used scale for children in the United States (Schorre & Vandvik, 2004). It has also been translated into Spanish (Ezpeleta, Granero, & de la Osa, 1999).

The Strengths and Difficulties Questionnaire is a broad measure of 25 questions that can be answered by the child's primary caregiver (or teacher) or by self-report (age 11 and above). It measures five broad areas (emotional symptoms, hyperactivity-inattention, prosocial behavior, peer problems, and conduct problems) of the child's functioning over the past 6 months (Goodman, 2001).

The Strengths and Difficulties Questionnaire was developed in England and has been translated into more than 60 languages across the globe (Vostanis, 2006; Woerner et al., 2004). An American evaluation of the Strengths & Difficulties Questionnaire has suggested that it measures three broad areas (internalizing, externalizing, and positive) of student functioning (Dickey & Blumberg, 2004).

An excellent example of a complete screening process is the Columbia TeenScreen Program that employs a multistage procedure. First, parental consent and teen assent is obtained. Second, students fill out a brief (14-item), self-report questionnaire, called the Columbia Health Screen. Third, those students whose scores place them in the risk category are interviewed by a mental health professional. (Those whose scores do not place them at risk are merely debriefed by a mental health professional.) Finally, those students whose interviews confirm that they are at risk are then seen by a clinician who does an individualized treatment plan in collaboration with the teen and his or her parents. The program also recommends that there is a case manager who works with the family around intervention compliance issues (Kalafat, 2005).

Diagnosis

When reauthorizing IDEA, Congress explicitly stated that it was concerned about the misdiagnosis of minority students: "Greater efforts are needed to prevent the intensification of problems connected with *mislabeling* and high dropout rates among minority children with disabilities" (section 601(c)(12)(a), emphasis added). So IDEA encouraged the Secretary of Education to help school-based personnel to begin

> Implementing effective teaching strategies, classroom-based techniques, and interventions to ensure appropriate identification of students who may be eligible for special education services, and to prevent the *misidentification, inappropriate overidentification, or underidentification* of children as having a disability, especially minority and limited English proficient children.
>
> Section 662(b)(2)(A)(iii), emphasis added

Diagnosis questions usually get worded as "What is the best method to determine which [psychosocial problem] a student has?" These scales should be comprehensive, culturally sensitive, normed, include multiple informants, and help practitioners do differential diagnosis. Examples include the Achenbach System of Empirically Based Assessment, formerly known as the Child Behavior Checklist, and the Behavior Assessment System for Children (2nd ed.) (BASC-2).

The Achenbach System of Empirically Based Assessment is a multidimensional, multimethod, and multiple-informant assessment system designed for children 1.5 to 18 years of age. For school-aged children, it includes a Child Behavior Checklist (for parents), Teacher's Report Form, Youth Self-Report Form (ages 11–18), a Semi-Structured Clinical Interview for Children & Adolescents, and a Direct Observation Form. The manual contains information on reliability and validity as well as multicultural norms (Achenbach & Rescorla, 2007) and relevance to diagnoses based on *Diagnostic and Statistical Manual of Mental Disorders*, 4th ed. (Achenbach & Rescorla, 2001). A quick reference guide for school-based practitioners is also available (Achenbach, 2007). Both the Child Behavior Checklist and Youth Self-Report are available in Spanish.

The BASC-2 is also a multidimensional, multimethod, and multiple-informant assessment system designed for children 2 to 21 years of age. It is composed of five main measures including the Teacher Rating scale, the Parent Rating scale, the Self-Report of Personality (ages 8–11 and 12–21), the Structured Developmental History, and the Student Observation System. It has good reliability and validity as well as general and clinical norms (Tan, 2007; Weis & Smenner, 2007). The BASC-2 manual gives clinicians instructions for administration, scoring, validation, norming, and interpretation (Kamphaus, VanDeventer, Brueggemann, & Barry, 2007). The BASC-2's Parent Rating scale, Self-Report of Personality, and Structured Developmental History are also available in Spanish (McCloskey, Hess, & D'Amato, 2003; Pearson Education, 2007).

Intervention Monitoring

IDEA requires schools to ensure that "assessment tools and strategies that provide relevant information that *directly assists* persons in determining the educational needs of the child are provided" (section 614 (b)(3)(C), emphasis added). Intervention-planning questions are often framed as "What is the best measure to monitor the progress of a student with [psychosocial problem]?" These scales should be specific, brief, and sensitive to small changes (Mash & Hunsley, 2005). In the academic arena, these instruments are often called "curriculum-based measurements." In the functional arena, these instruments are sometimes called "rapid assessment instruments" (Springer, Abell, & Hudson, 2002a, 2002b). Fischer and Corcoran (2007) have compiled an entire volume of rapid assessment measures that every school district should own, including nearly 60 for children and adolescents. Some of the more helpful ones for school-related issues include Child and Adolescent Social and Adaptive Functioning scale, Children's Thoughts Questionnaire, Eyberg Child Behavior Inventory, Hare Self-Esteem scale, Homework Problem Checklist, Index of Peer Relations, the Mood and Feeling Questionnaire, and the Urban Hassles scale.

Two measures stand out for their attention to both environmental issues, measurement of strengths, and help with intervention planning. The Elementary School Success Profile and the School Success Profile (for middle and high school students) assess 15 dimensions of the student's social environment and 7 dimensions of the student's individual adaptation. Students fill out online surveys and school administrators are provided with both individual and grouped data by which to plan either individual or group interventions (Bowen, Richman, & Bowen, 1997). Developers have also recently developed the School Success Profile—Learning Organization, a 36-item scale that evaluates the entire school environment along 12 dimensions (Bowen, Ware, Rose, & Powers, 2007). Finally, the authors have provided links to empirically supported interventions based on the results at www.schoolsuccessonline.com (check under the "community" link).

Description Questions

In order to meet the needs of students, it helps to know the constellation of symptoms that a student with a specific disorder will possess. Turning to a new example of emotional-behavioral disorders, we may benefit from knowing the answers to two related questions: taxonomy and clinical description. Clinical description asks, "What are the characteristics of the disorder?"

The descriptive literature provides information on several aspects of a disorder. There are five common characteristics: symptoms, comorbid diagnoses, associated adaptive impairments, contextual factors, and demographic differences (Mash & Hunsley, 2005). Let's use the example of attention-deficit/hyperactivity disorder. Symptoms may include inattention, hyperactivity, and impulsiveness. Common comorbid diagnoses include oppositional defiant disorder, conduct disorder, learning disabilities, and memory impairments (Martinussen, Hayden, Hogg-Johnson, & Tannock, 2005). Associated adaptive impairments include academic problems, clumsiness, and poor social skills. Contextual factors include lead-based paint and chaotic family functioning. Demographic differences may be found for gender, race, or age (Gaub & Carlson, 1997; Pelham, Fabiano, & Massetti, 2005). Without knowing what to look for, clinicians are unlikely to completely meet the child's needs.

For school-based practitioners, one of the most important aspects of each disorder is its effect on school performance. This is because in educational policy there are three categories of students with disabilities. In the largest group are all students who have a disability—they are covered by section 504 of the Rehabilitation Act of 1973 (P.L. 93-112). Under this law, a handicap must "substantially limit a major life activity." Such students may have either a permanent (e.g., orthopedic) or temporary (e.g., drug addiction) handicap and schools are required to accommodate their needs. A subset of this large group is those students whose disability also affects their academic performance. Such students might be mildly visually or hearing impaired. Schools often assess their needs, but determine they do not require further services. A further subset is those students whose disabilities are of sufficient duration or intensity that they require ongoing services. Only these students are covered by the IDEA.

We might expect the externalizing disorders to lead to disruptions both within the classroom and outside of it. Students who disturb the peace of the instructional setting are more likely to experience such consequences as being asked to report to the principal's office, getting suspended from school, and even becoming expelled and/or dropping out. School practitioners also need to consider what co-occurring problems might also be present. For example, an estimated 30% to 50% of students with attention-deficit/hyperactivity disorder also have a learning disability (Silver, 2004). They are also likely to exhibit coexisting conduct disorders and/or oppositional defiant disorders (August, Braswell, & Thuras, 1998). Knowing which "comorbid" disorders are likely to be present helps both the child and the school cope with them and reduce the chance of negative outcomes.

With internalizing disorders, however, it may be more difficult to delineate the negative consequences on school performance. Anxious students may have trouble attending school or arriving on time due to worries about school performance or social acceptance. They also might have a difficult time paying attention in class due to unmanageable worries. They may have somatic concerns and complain of headaches or stomachaches. They might not turn homework in on time due to constantly trying to perfect their work. Teachers may consider them daydreamers with their heads in a cloud (Sink & Igelman, 2004). Depressed students may be irritable or cry with little provocation. They might find it hard to work up the energy to give an assignment their best effort or reach out to peers for help with academic problems. Teachers may consider them lazy, dull, or slow learners. Such students are often hypersensitive to perceived criticism (Jones, 2004).

Risk Questions

After the 1999 Columbine and 2007 Virginia Tech shootings, no one can pretend that schools are safe places to work and learn. It is vital that school-based mental health professionals be able to perform threat assessments of potentially violent students. The Virginia Tech incident is discussed in detail in Box 3.1. Multiple-victim school shootings are not the only risks that practitioners must be able determine. Other common scenarios include suicide, self-mutilation, drug and alcohol overdoses, and reckless driving accidents. Risk questions are framed as "Which students with [psychosocial problem] are most likely to commit [severe behavior]? Examples would be, "Which students with depression are most likely to commit suicide?" or "Which students with an alcohol problem are most likely to get alcohol poisoning?"

BOX 3.1 The Virginia Tech Tragedy

Virginia Tech shooter Seung-Hui Cho was born January 18, 1984 into an intact family with an older sister. The family was poor and lived in a small basement apartment in Korea. Relatives describe him as a "cold" child who did not like to be hugged and would punch his sister in a rage. He seldom talked and a doctor diagnosed him as autistic, but he was never treated (Baxter, 2007; Churcher, 2007).

At age nine, his family immigrated to the United States, where they opened a dry cleaning shop in suburban Virginia, 25 miles from Washington, DC. He would join what Korean Americans refer to as the 1.5 generation—neither first generation because they immigrated as children nor second generation because they immigrated late enough that they would never lose their Korean accent. Like many immigrant families, the generation gap was probably exacerbated by the cultural divide. His older sister maintained that they "have always been a close, peaceful and loving family" (Lee, 2007). Both of his parents worked long hours and had little time for socializing with the tight-knit Korean American community. Arriving during the middle of 3rd grade, Seung-Hui was placed in an English-as-Second-Language program.

Before attending middle school, his parents followed up on a recommendation that he receive therapy from the elementary school. They took him to the Multicultural Center for Human Services, where a psychiatrist diagnosed him with a social anxiety disorder and he was assigned to an art therapist. He attended Stone Middle School, where classmates recalled that he wouldn't respond to teachers' attempts to engage him. His fellow students would tease him by offering him dollar bills just to hear him talk. Shortly after the Columbine massacre, Seung-Hui wrote an English paper that was filled with hateful writings. The school contacted his sister, Sun, and she accompanied her brother to his next therapy appointment. The psychiatric intern met with the parents who worried that after his sister left for college, Seung-Hui would not communicate with anyone. He was then diagnosed with selective mutism and major depression and received antidepressant medication for one year (Virginia Tech Review Panel, 2007).

(continued)

After attending the overcrowded Centreville High School for one year, he transferred to the new and affluent Westfield High School, where a teacher once threatened him with a failing grade for class participation if he refused to read aloud. When he finally did read in a strange deep voice, the whole class laughed and ridiculed, "Go back to China!" (CBS/AP, 2007). In gym class, his own teammates would throw balls at his face during a dodge ball and slam his locker shut as they walked by. His only extracurricular activity was the science club when he was a sophomore (Krishnamurthy, 2007). Eventually Westfield High School evaluated him and determined that he qualified for an Individualized Education Program under the emotionally disturbed and speech & language categories. He continued to receive counseling through the Multicultural Center for Human Services throughout his junior year and received good grades. His treatment stopped when he complained about going, and his parents recognized that at almost 18, he could make his own decisions. During his senior year, he was accepted by Virginia Tech and decided to attend, against the advice of his counselors and parents who felt the university was too large for him to get the individual support he needed (Virginia Tech Review Panel, 2007).

At Virginia Tech, his suitemates took him to a frat party where he was served vodka and beer, but he never loosened up. He rode a red bicycle to his classes and shot hoops by himself. Seung-Hui first caught officials' attention in the Fall of 2005, 18 months before his rampage. He refused to sign his name on a poetry class roll, writing a question mark instead. He took pictures of his female classmates with his cell phone and they started avoiding class because of him. The professor threatened to quit teaching if he wasn't forced to drop the class due to his menacing behavior (Seper, 2007). The department head decided to tutor him privately rather than let him attend class, but she was unnerved enough to arrange a private code with her assistant. If she mentioned the name of a dead professor, the assistant was to immediately call security (Kleinfield, 2007). She also notified student affairs, the university counseling center, and the campus police. During that same semester, two co-eds complained about Seung's stalking behavior, but they ultimately declined to press charges.

(continued)

In December of 2005, after the second rejection, Seung told one of his suitemates that he "might as well kill himself" (Thomas, 2007). His suitemate was so alarmed he alerted the campus police. The police called a community mental health agency, whose social worker evaluated him and advised that Seung was "mentally ill and in need of hospitalization and presents an imminent danger to self or others as a result of mental illness as to be substantially unfit to care for self, and is incapable of volunteering or unwilling to volunteer for treatment" (Goldstein, 2007, p. 1) A magistrate signed a temporary order of commitment and had Seung transported to a private mental hospital for further evaluation (Goldstein, 2007). There the psychologist concluded that Seung was

> Oriented × 4 [person, place, time, and situation]. Affect is flat and mood is depressed. He denies suicidal ideation. He does not acknowledge symptoms of a thought disorder. His insight and judgment are normal
>
> Goldstein, 2007, p. 4

There is no record that the hospital ever contacted any of Seung's parents, suitemates, professors, or campus police to substantiate their findings. As a result of the mental examination, the judge ruled that Seung "presents an imminent danger to himself as a result of mental illness," but did not conclude that he "presents an imminent danger to others as a result of mental illness." He ruled that "the alternatives to involuntary hospitalization and treatment were investigated and deemed suitable" and ordered Seung to attend outpatient care and "to follow all recommended treatments" (Goldstein, p. 6). There is no evidence, however, that Seung ever attended treatment or that anyone ever followed-up on the referral (Schulte & Jenkins, 2007).

During the Fall of 2006, in a playwriting class, yet another professor was concerned about the violent and profane language in his plays. An excerpt of a 13-year-old stepson's part reads:

> John (in his room, he smiles and throws darts on the target that is the face of Richard). I hate him. Must kill Dick. Must kill Dick. Dick must die. Kill Dick...

(continued)

In both plays available on the Internet, the male protagonist dies a failure. Altogether eight of his professors expressed fears about his mental state; one of them was among the five teachers killed by Seung. On at least two occasions, they tried to have the university administrators intervene to no avail (Santora & Hauser, 2007). During February and March of 2007, Seung bought two handguns, successfully circumventing a Virginia law that required self-disclosure regarding his court-ordered mental health treatment. He bought ammunition off the Internet. He rented a cargo van where he planned and videotaped his preparation for the attack. On April 16, he killed 32 people before killing himself in the worst campus shooting spree in history.

Questions for Discussion
I strongly recommend reading the FBI report mentioned in the text (O'Toole, 1999, pp. 2–3). It recommends a four-pronged assessment approach that includes personality factors, family dynamics, school dynamics, and social dynamics.

1. What personality traits or behavior seemed to offer clues that Seung-Hui was at risk?
2. What family dynamics might have increased his stress or served as barriers to help?
3. What events at Virginia Tech and previous schools might have contributed to his problems?
4. What social dynamics in his community and broader society might have contributed?
5. What did the mental health community do right and do wrong?
6. How does your school staff communicate concerns about students at risk?
7. What barriers to communication exist in your school?

family, including the frequency, intensity, and method of delivering services" (section 636 (d)(4), emphasis added). For school-age children, IDEA also encourages the U.S. Department of Education to assist schools in "implementing effective strategies for addressing inappropriate behavior of students with disabilities in schools, including strategies to *prevent* children with emotional and behavioral problems from developing emotional disturbances that require the provision of special education and related services" (section 663 (b)(1), emphasis added). Most importantly, schools should intervene before a student is at risk for causing harm to self or others. Experienced practitioners know that the beginning of the school year is an ideal time to do prevention programs. The first 10 weeks before report cards come out is usually the slowest time of their year so they have the time and the opportunity to do some whole-school or whole-classroom intervention. Prevention questions are usually worded as "What is the best way to prevent [social problem]?" "Social problems" can refer to any widespread psychosocial problem faced by the local school. These might include bullying, drug abuse, teen pregnancy, or a host of other ills.

As discussed in the introduction, the Bush administration's approach to teen pregnancy has been one that required an abstinence-only message, similar to Nancy Reagan's famous "Just say no" approach to drug prevention. These kinds of prevention programs are driven more by ideology than by scientifically based research. Despite the establishment of a national registry to promote the adoption of evidence-based prevention programs by the Substance Abuse and Mental Health Services Administration in 1996, Rohrbach, Ringwalt, Ennett, and Vincus (2005) found that less than half of school districts used an evidence-based substance abuse prevention curriculum. Many districts are still using the Drug Abuse Resistance Education program despite multiple studies that show it to be ineffective (Ennett, Tobler, Ringwalt, & Flewelling, 1994; Lynam et al., 1999; West & O'Neal, 2004). Moreover, many districts also use sanctions-based policies where students are suspended or expelled from schools for drug use (Martin, Levin, & Saunders, 1999). Although there is some evidence that the Drug Abuse Resistance Education program is losing support in communities (Weiss, Murphy-Graham, & Birkeland, 2005), its popularity among parents, local advisory groups, and key decision makers keeps it alive (Birkeland, Murphy-Graham, & Weiss, 2005; Donnermeyer, 2000; Ringwalt, Ennett, Vincus, Rohrbach, & Simons-Rudolf, 2004). School-based mental health professionals are in an ideal position to correct some of the misperceptions of ineffective programs and to advocate for empirically supported programs.

Evidence-Based Practice in School Mental Health

Intervention Questions

This question is the one that school-based professionals most want to know. The U.S. Department of Education has adopted a medical model to determine what works in schools, just as physicians have tried to determine what works in medicine (Morris, 2004). IDEA requires that the Individualized Education Program contain

> A statement of the special education and related services and supplementary aids and services, *based on peer-reviewed research* to the extent practicable, to be provided to the child, or on behalf of the child.
>
> Section 614 (d)(1)(a)(i)(IV), emphasis added

In short, they seek answers to the inquiry, "What works for whom?" These questions are usually framed as "What are the empirically supported interventions for [psychosocial problem]? While this is a simple question, there is not a simple answer. Researchers have created a distinction between efficacy and effectiveness.

Efficacy

Efficacy is defined as the potency of a particular intervention when assessed under highly controlled conditions (Bower, 2003). Efficacy research aims to discover whether a specific intervention has a measurable effect as well as determine its safety, feasibility, side effects, and optimal dose (Barkham & Mellor-Clark, 2003). It is usually done under university laboratory conditions—called a randomized controlled trial. Participants are carefully recruited and screened that there is a homogeneous group sharing just one diagnosis. Participants are then randomly assigned to a control group or intervention group. Much attention is given to "treatment fidelity" so treatment manuals or protocols are employed to make sure that every participant gets the same intervention (e.g., cognitive-behavioral therapy) in the same dose (1x/week). Multiple measures are completed at the beginning, middle, end, and follow-up period (usually 3–6 months later) to make sure the intervention was both helpful and had enduring power. All this is done to ward off every possible threat to internal validity so that the researchers know that the intervention was the sole cause of change (Grinnell, Unrau, & Williams, 2008).

School-based practitioners know that in the real world, this level of control is completely unrealistic. Students often have multiple problems and

what works for whom. An important distinction was made between efficacy and effectiveness and how they can complement each other to provide a solid base for empirically supported interventions.

Suggested Reading

1. Barkham, M., & Mellor-Clark, J. (2003). Bridging evidence-based practice and practice-based evidence: Developing rigorous and relevant knowledge for the psychological therapies. *Clinical Psychology & Psychotherapy, 10* (6), 319–327.

2. Kelley, M. L. (2003). Assessment of children's behavior in the school setting. In M. L. Kelley, G. H. Noell, & D. Reitman (Eds.), *Practitioner's guide to empirically based measures of school behavior* (pp. 7–22). New York: Kluwer Academic.

3. Mash, E. J., & Hunsley, J. (2005). Evidence-based assessment of child and adolescent disorders: Issues and challenges. *Journal of Clinical Child and Adolescent Psychology, 34* (3), 362–379. Special issue on evidence-based assessment.

4. O'Toole, M. E. (1999). *The school shooter: A threat assessment perspective.* Quantico, VA: US Department of Justice/Federal Bureau of Investigation. Retrieved May 19, 2002 from http://www.fbi.gov/publications/school/school2.pdf

5. Ringwalt, C., Ennett, S. T., Vincus, A. A., Rohrbach, L. A., & Simons-Rudolf, A. (2004). Who's calling the shots? Decision-makers and the adoption of effective school-based substance use prevention curricula. *Journal of Drug Education, 34* (1), 19–31.

Internet Resources

Achenbach System of Empirically Based Assessment
http://www.aseba.org/

Behavior Assessment System for Children
http://ags.pearsonassessments.com/Group.asp?nGroupInfoID=a30000

Children's Global Assessment Scale
http://www.southalabama.edu/nursing/psynp/cgas.pdf

Columbia University TeenScreen Program
http://www.teenscreen.org/

Mood and Feeling Questionnaire
http://devepi.mc.duke.edu/MFQ.html

School Success Profile
http://www.schoolsuccessprofile.org/

Strengths and Difficulties Questionnaire
http://www.sdqinfo.com/

Primary and Secondary Research

In Chapter 2, a distinction was made between efficient and effective searches. Younger practitioners are highly efficient at using Google and other search engines to find something on virtually any subject. In 2000, there were an estimated seven million web sites and the number is still growing (Oder, 2000). While these searches are easy, the results are seldom research based. Older practitioners may have the patience to do very effective hand searches on relevant journals, such as the *School Social Work Journal* or *Psychology in the Schools*, but it takes an inordinate amount of time. Ideally, there would be summaries of the existing research on the topic of interest that practitioners could find easily and read quickly. This leads to an important distinction within the research evidence.

There are two major kinds of research studies. These include primary research studies such as the ones described in the Introduction (see Figure 1.1) and secondary studies. Primary research refers to those studies where the researcher collected the data, analyzed the results, and did the interpretation. Secondary research refers to those studies that utilize the data collected by others or the results produced by others and then combine them into a summary.

Secondary Research

Secondary research broadly falls under the rubric of "literature reviews." Greenhalgh (2006) describes two widely different approaches to literature reviews—journalistic reviews and systematic reviews. All of us, at some point in our education, have probably done a journalistic review. It involved three simple steps. We identified a hypothesis, then diligently searched for evidence to support the hypothesis, and then concluded that we proved our hypothesis was correct. As we grew older and wiser, we hopefully realized how biased this method was. Systematic reviews are quite different. Researchers identify an issue, diligently search for evidence on all sides of the issue, and then conclude which side has the most evidentiary support.

Reasons for Secondary Research

Mulrow (1995) identified eight rationales for systematic reviews, but let's identify the three reasons most pertinent for practitioners. First, there is an enormous amount of published literature on almost any topic. PsycINFO, for example, contains over 350,000 references to school-related research, over 750,000 references to intervention, and about 500,000 references to children and adolescents. While some of these will overlap, reading even 1% would be overwhelming; so systematic reviews enable practitioners to digest large quantities of data in an efficient manner. Second, systematic reviews allow practitioners to avoid the mistake of "missing the forest for the trees." Reading a systematic review first will enable clinicians to put subsequent evidence in its proper context. Third, related services professionals can get an idea of what issues enjoy clear consensus while others are still mired in controversy. For example, there is so much consensus about the efficacy of stimulant medication for the vast majority of children with attention deficit/ hyperactivity disorder (Banaschewski et al., 2006; Brown et al., 2005) that a cost-benefit analysis has even been done to determine which stimulant medication is most economical (Marchetti et al., 2001). On the other hand, the use of diets that reduce or eliminate artificial food colors for the same children remains controversial (Schab & Trinh, 2004). Finally, there is a subtype of systematic review called meta-analysis that attempts to provide a quantitative summary of the results. The implications of these systematic reviews for the purpose of searching will now be addressed.

Guidelines for Going Beyond Secondary Research

In an ideal world, Steps 2 and 3 of the process of evidence-based practice (see Chapter 2) process could be combined, so that practitioners could do one-stop shopping on their way to improving client outcomes. Sackett, Strauss, Richardson, Rosenberg, and Haynes (2000) posit using three criteria to determine when to go beyond secondary research. First, ask if the problem is central to one's regular practice (e.g., students with disruptive behavior). If the issue is a central and recurring one, then, clinicians should access both secondary and primary research. Second, ask if the problem is peripheral to one's regular practice (e.g., students with reading problems). If the issue is peripheral, then secondary research might be sufficient. Third, ask if the problem is of marginal importance and unlikely to be encountered again (e.g., children with Marfan's syndrome); if it is, one can seek consultation from an expert who can provide the evidence upon which the problem depends.

There are, of course, a couple of caveats to these guidelines. First, sometimes what initially appears to be a relatively rare occurrence turns out to be more common than originally thought. Just a few years ago, for example, autism was thought to only occur once in every 500 youths. Now we believe it occurs once in every 150 youths (Centers for Disease Control

BOX 4.1 The What Works Clearinghouse (http://ies.ed.gov/ncee/wwc/)

The What Works Clearinghouse (WWC) was created shortly after the passage of the No Child Left Behind Act, which mandated educational personnel to use scientifically based research. Its purpose was to provide "educators, policymakers, researchers, and the public with a central and trusted source of scientific evidence of what works in education" (U.S. Department of Education, 2007). Initially, the WWC only provided evidence about academic topics such as reading and math. More recently, it has also provided scientific research on psychosocial issues, such as dropout prevention and character education.

Features

Unlike the databases discussed in text, the WWC does not just collect scientific information; it screens it for quality before identifying the intervention. It provides two kinds of reports: topic reports and intervention reports. *Topic reports* cover general issues like reading, math, character education, and dropout prevention. *Intervention reports* appraise a specific program for effectiveness. Each intervention receives three ratings: intervention rating, improvement index, and extent of evidence. The *intervention rating* provides the direction (positive or negative), size, and statistical significance of the intervention's effect. This rating scheme has six points: positive effects; potentially positive effects, mixed effects, no discernable effects, potentially negative effects, and negative effects. The *improvement index* is a translation of the effect size of the intervention so that users can know what to expect if an average student received the intervention. This rating scheme is expressed as a percentile from 0 to 100. The *extent of evidence* tells educators how much evidence was used to determine the intervention rating. This is a simple two-level rating system of small or moderate-large. Small evidence usually means that there was only one study, done in only one school, or done with less than 350 students. Moderate-large evidence means that there was more than one study conducted in more than one school with over 350

(continued)

students. All of this quality control is supported by an expanding set of technical working papers that define their terms and how they arrive at their conclusions. This will be discussed in greater detail in Chapter 5: Appraising the Evidence.

Search

Dropout prevention examines programs for students in middle school through high school to help them stay in or complete school. As of this review, the WWC had reviewed eight different programs across three criteria. These criteria included the following: staying in school, progressing in school, and completing school. On the initial screen, only one program received the highest intervention rating for positive effects: the Check and Connect Program. The program relies on a two-pronged strategy. The "check" part involves continual monitoring of the students' attendance, suspensions, grades, and credits by a case worker. The "connect" part involves giving basic attention (at least twice a month) and intensive intervention (i.e., problem-solving, academic support, and community services) to the individual student as well as collateral contact with parents. The WWC's rating for effectiveness gave the Check and Connect program a positive effects rating for helping pupils stay in school, a potentially positive effects rating for helping students progress in school, and a no discernible effects rating for helping adolescents complete school. The WWC's improvement index gave the program +25 percentile points for helping pupils stay in school, +30 percentile points for helping students progress in school, and only +1 percentile point for helping adolescent complete school (U.S. Department of Education, 2006). It was not easy to identify an extent of evidence rating. Since there was only one study that met all of the WWC evidence standards (Sinclair, Christenson, Evelo, & Hurley, 1998) and one other study that met the standards with reservations (Sinclair, Christenson, & Thurlow, 2005) with a combined total of less than 350 students in the sample, one could conclude that the extent of evidence was small.

(continued)

Weaknesses

There are three primary weaknesses in this web site. First, the WWC appears to primarily focus on program evaluation, not studies involving individual intervention. School-based practitioners will find the site primarily useful for large prevention programs rather than small group or individual interventions. Second, the information on intervention specifics is rather vague and reduces replicability (e.g., What does "problem-solving" look like?). This forces investigators to look up the original research in Education Abstracts or ERIC for a clearer description. Third, even though an "extent of evidence" rating was promised, it had to be inferred from a description of the underlying research.

BOX 4.2 The Campbell Collaboration (http://www.campbellcollaboration.org/)

The Campbell Collaboration (C2) is an international nonprofit network of social scientists that aims to "produce, maintain and disseminate systematic reviews of research evidence on the effectiveness of social interventions." It currently contains two sets of systematic reviews: the C2 Register of Interventions and Policy Evaluations (C2-RIPE) and the C2 Social, Psychological, Education, and Criminological Trials Registry (C2-SPECTR). It is a partner of the American Institutes for Research, which provide financial, human resources, and in-kind support for the Campbell Collaboration as well as conference support for the annual Campbell Colloquium. Within the C2, there is an Education Coordinating Group, which "aims to help people make well-informed decisions about the effects of interventions in the social, behavioral, and educational arenas."

Features

Begin by selecting the Education tab at the top of the home page and then choose Reviews, Protocols, and Related Papers on the left menu. As of now, there are 5 completed reviews and 14 reviews in

(continued)

progress. Choose any of the completed reviews and you will find three documents. The Title Registration Form serves as a type of abstract for the review. It provides the reviewer's name, affiliation, study participants, and intended outcomes. The Review Protocol includes background literature and methodological information about how the review was conducted. It provides the eligibility criteria, search strategy, and how the studies were evaluated, how the data was extracted, and how the data was analyzed. The Review provides the complete report, including the background literature, the methodology, the results, conclusions, and how often the review will be updated.

Search
Given the limited number of completed reviews, there is no need for searching at this juncture. Hopefully, in time, this will eventually be necessary as more reviews move out of the in-progress column. Unlike the WWC, each completed review lists every study included in the review so that searchers do not have to go to a database to find the reference (only to find the article).

Weaknesses
The Campbell Collaboration (like the WWC) does not provide specifics on the interventions it reviews, nor does it state which variant of the intervention works best.

BOX 4.3 SAMHSA's Registry of Evidence-Based Programs and Practices (http://www.nrepp.samhsa.gov/index.htm)

This national registry is a service of the U.S. Department of Health and Human Services' Substance Abuse and Mental Health Services Administration (SAMHSA). It began in 1997 to identify model programs for substance abuse prevention. In 2004, SAMHSA expanded the registry to include empirically supported

(continued)

interventions in mental health and substance abuse prevention and treatment. In 2005, they redesigned and strengthened their rating system. SAMHSA currently has 200 interventions under review and expects to add 5 to 10 new interventions each month.

Features

In March 2007, they launched the current registry with three new features. First, they provided more description of the interventions. Second, they provided separate ratings for individual outcomes rather than an aggregate rating for all outcomes. Finally, they provided a new rating for dissemination readiness—a measure of the intervention's availability, quality of training, and training materials. The Registry provides two kinds of ratings: quality of research and readiness of dissemination. *Quality of research* summarizes the amount and scientific quality of the evidence, that it was the intervention that produced the positive effects. Each outcome (e.g., alcohol use or behavioral problems in school) is rated separately. *Readiness for dissemination* summarizes the amount and quality of the resources available to help practitioners employ the intervention. Both are measured on a scale from 0.0 to 4.0.

The registry has evaluated over 50 different interventions, divided into five types: mental health promotion, mental health treatment, substance abuse prevention, substance abuse treatment, and co-occurring disorders. The search can be done by using a search term and/or the search menu. Under the menu, users can combine one of the five types of interventions above with an area of interest (e.g., alcohol, seclusion and restraint, or suicide prevention), a study design (experimental, quasi-experimental, or preexperimental), implementation history (international, replicated, or NIH funded), age range, race/ethnicity, gender, setting (e.g., school), and whether the intervention is public, proprietary, or a mix of both.

Search

I searched for the term "alcohol" and checked the menu items: substance abuse treatment, experimental, adolescence, and school. The registry returned one intervention—a description of

(*continued*)

multisystemic therapy for juvenile offenders. The initial screen provided a list of potential outcomes (e.g., arrest rates, alcohol or drug use, or peer aggression), a paragraph description of multisystemic therapy, and a set of keywords presumably used by the search engine. Clicking on the program name gives users a complete screen with seven features. First, it provides a lengthy description, including populations, settings, replications, costs, adaptations, and adverse effects. Second, it provides outcome details, including key findings, studies, type of study design, and the quality of the research. Third, it provides a summary of the outcome ratings (with strengths and weaknesses) and readiness for dissemination (with strengths and weaknesses). Fourth, it gives study demographics, including age, gender, and race/ethnicity. Fifth, it provides a list of the studies and materials reviewed, including dissemination materials, published by the developers. Sixth, it provides a list of replication studies (by researchers other than the developers). Finally, it provides contact information for the developers.

Weaknesses

This registry has two weaknesses. First, SAMHSA explicitly denies that it has a definition of what constitutes "evidence," arguing that users will probably have their own definitions in mind. The only clear statement is that it does not include "tradition, convention, belief, or anecdotal evidence." This leaves users, however, in the position of having to infer the hierarchy of evidence that undergirds the agency's criteria. Apparently, the agency identifies three levels of evidence as satisfactory—randomized controlled trials, quasi-experimental designs, and pretest/posttest designs. The second weakness is a result of the history of the registry—it currently focuses primarily on prevention rather than intervention. While there was only 1 intervention for treating alcohol problems in youth, there were 11 identified for preventing those problems.

following: "Always look first for that which disconfirms your beliefs; then look for that which supports them. Look with equal diligence for both. Doing so will make the difference between scientific honesty and artfully supported propaganda" (p. 89).

The Incredible Invisible Web

French mathematician Pierre-Simon Laplace was one of the first astronomers to propose that black holes existed in the universe. Consisting of collapsed stars, they are so dense that not even light can escape their gravitational pull. At the turn of the 21st century, a parallel phenomenon was observed when information specialists began to realize that search engines could find no more than 20% to 30% of available Web pages even with megacrawlers (Descry, 2004; Devine & Egger-Sider, 2004; O'Leary, 2000). They named these inaccessible Web pages or Internet black holes the "invisible Web" (O'Leary, 2000; Price & Sherman, 2001). For example, it wasn't until 2002 that search engines could find portable document files. The size of the invisible Web is enormous—400 to 550 times larger than the easily accessible web (Descry, 2004). It is also the fastest growing portion of the Internet. The irony is that 80% to 90% of the invisible Web is public information, but about half resides in topic-specific databases, such as ERIC, the Library of Congress, and PubMed, which search engines cannot penetrate because of the way they are programmed (Devine & Egger-Sider, 2004; Oder, 2000). Specifically, most Web crawlers spend only a specified amount of time at each Web site, meaning that the largest (or deepest) sites are the least visible. The other 10% to 20% of the invisible Web is private or proprietary, meaning that it is password protected or only available for a fee (Wouters, Reddy, & Aguillo, 2006).

Four-Part Search

Remember that the model of "best evidence" involved the intersection of four overlapping circles: scientifically based research, client characteristics and complexity, contextual constraints, and clinical expertise and experience (see Figure 2.2). If we presume that practitioners already know their own expertise and experience without having to look it up, then we are left with three major areas to search in addition to the type of question (see Figure 4.2). For each sample search below, we will subdivide the search into four important practical parts: (1) locate the best scientifically based research, (2) locate research that is children and adolescents oriented, (3) locate research that is school related, and (4) locate research addressing

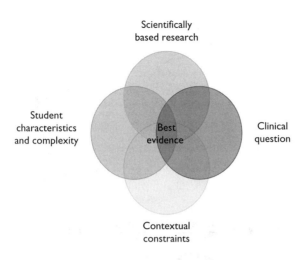

Scientifically
based research

Student
characteristics
and complexity

Best
evidence

Clinical
question

Contextual
constraints

FIGURE 4.2. Four components of a search strategy.

the specific clinical question. To accomplish this kind of complex searching, we will have to utilize Boolean logic.

Boolean Logic

George Boole was a 19th-century British mathematician who invented an algebraic system of logic that is the foundation for all modern search engines. Understanding Boolean logic is essential for knowing how to combine terms to obtain the results that are desired in any computerized search. Boolean operators will be illustrated through a series of Venn diagrams. Boolean syntax allows investigators to combine operators to locate materials as accurately as possible.

Boolean Operators

In its simplest form, Boolean logic differentiates between three terms, AND, OR, and NOT. The term AND combines only those members of two sets that belong to both sets (see Figure 4.3). For example, we typically use AND to combine dissimilar terms, such as children and depression. This eliminates the vast amount of literature on children as well as the vast amount of literature on depression and gives only those results that match both terms. The term OR combines the members of two sets that belong to either set (see Figure 4.4). For example, we typically use OR to combine similar terms, such as adolescents or teenagers. This helps us to avoid inadvertently excluding any studies that may use one term, but not the other. The term

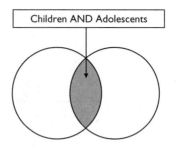

FIGURE 4.3. The Boolean operator AND.

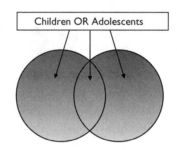

FIGURE 4.4. The Boolean operator OR.

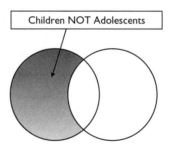

FIGURE 4.5. The Boolean operator NOT.

NOT subtracts the members of one set that may also belong to another set (see Figure 4.5). For example, we typically use NOT to exclude terms that may serve as a false lead or distraction, such as excluding colleges or universities from the general term "schools." Throughout this chapter, these terms will be capitalized when used as Boolean operators.

Boolean Syntax

Combining Boolean operators allows search engines to search efficiently for exactly the information required. This is accomplished through the use of parentheses. The search for relations within the parentheses always occurs first, then the search commences for results outside the parentheses. It is not uncommon to combine OR first and then use AND. For example, we may want the computer to find results for the algorithm (children OR adolescents OR teenagers) AND depression AND (schools NOT (colleges OR universities)). Given this scenario, the computer would first solve the problem in the double parenthesis: (colleges OR universities). Then the computer would solve the two problems in the single parentheses: (children OR adolescents OR teenagers) as well as (schools NOT (colleges OR universities)). Finally, the computer would solve the problems outside the two parentheses.

Our goal is to utilize the Boolean operators to allow us to do a detailed search in less than 1 hour. Ideally, following the instructions of the sample searches in the next section should enable investigators to narrow down the number of research studies to less than 100 abstracts (Sandieson, 2006). Assuming that it takes about 30 seconds to read an abstract, this will accomplish our goal.

Public Databases

Most Americans now use e-mail and eBay on a regular basis. They are comfortable using search engines, such as Google and perhaps a few others. There are some specialized Web sites with which every school-based professional should be familiar. This section will introduce two of the most important: ERIC and PubMed.

Education Resource Information Center

ERIC bills itself as the world's largest digital library of education literature. It contains over 1.2 million records and adds about 5,000 records each month. It is also currently working on the digitization of an additional 340,000 records (from 1966 to 1992) that were formerly available only on microfiche.

Features

One of the useful features of ERIC is the thesaurus that allows users to learn how it categorizes materials, updated in June 2007. For example, if you click on "counseling," it will expand into nearly 70 subcategories ranging from academic advising to teacher guidance. One of these subcategories is "school counseling," which is defined as "Assistance given to students by the school or college in order to help them understand and cope with adjustment problems—includes the administration and interpretation of tests" (ERIC, 1980). Clearly, understanding how ERIC uses these terms aids in knowing what terms to use in the keyword search process. It allows users to enter up to three terms connected by any of the Boolean operators. (Note that users can add another row if desired.) At the bottom of the page, there is a small bar for Search Help. This page explains how to use Advanced Search most efficiently. One of the quirks of ERIC is that the operator AND takes precedence over the other Boolean operators even if it does not appear first. For example, a search for effectiveness OR outcomes AND therapy OR guidance will actually return the results for the algorithm (outcomes AND therapy) OR effectiveness OR guidance. This counterintuitive approach requires inserting parentheses into the search bars. To obtain the correct results, you would have to enter the following in the first line: (effectiveness OR outcomes), then select AND type: (counseling OR guidance) in the second line. As explained in the section on Boolean logic, the parentheses will then take precedence over the AND operator. ERIC allows users to limit searches by full-text availability, publication date, and nearly 40 publication types. The most recommended is to change the publication date to the last 10 years. Finally, the truncation character * for ERIC is the same one for PsycINFO and Social Work Abstracts (SWAB).

Sample Search

Let's assume you are interested in the needs of special education students who must begin the transition from school to work. This description question could be phrased as "What are the needs of special education students who transition from school to work?" As we will do for the private databases, we will search for evidence that is scientifically based, child and adolescent oriented, school related, and question focused, but we will have to do this differently than before.

Secondary Research Overview. Let's begin by getting an overview of the previous research by looking for the best secondary research. Go to the Advanced Search page and put the limits for publication date and publication type mentioned earlier in place. Now enter the following two terms in the first row: "systematic review" OR "meta analysis", being sure to include both the double quotation marks and the parentheses. Then enter transition* in the second row. In the third row, type "special education," being sure to use the quotation marks. Leave the Boolean operator between the two lines at AND to OR and press the Search key. Done correctly, you should receive about 10 results. At the top of the results page, users can read the Boolean algorithm that ERIC used to do the search so one can see if it was done correctly or not. Users may save the search by creating their own (free) My ERIC account.

Primary Research Specifics. Now let's look for the best original or primary research. Return to the Advanced Search page. Click on the "Add Another Row" button twice and wait a moment for the two rows to be added. In the first row, type the broadest of the scientifically based indicators (SBIs) from Box 4.4 as follows: research*. In the second row, type three of four youth-oriented terms as follows: adolescen* OR teen* OR youth*. (This is presuming we are not interested in transitions from preschool to elementary school.) In the third row, type the School-Related term: "special education" only. In the fourth row, type the Question-Focused purpose term: need*. In the fifth row, type the Question-Focused problem term: transition*. Correctly combined together, the search should net less than 40 results. Click on the first result to see how ERIC provides more detailed information. The abstract will indicate the complete title of the work, ERIC's identifier number, the source, the publication type, whether it has been peer-reviewed, descriptors of the content, a complete summary, and full-text availability options. For those who want an explanation of these terms, ERIC offers a "Help reading these results" button on the top left side. There is also a list of Related Items that includes similar studies or other suggested search terms from ERIC's thesaurus. Finally, at the top right of each result, there is an Add button, which copies the results on to the user's clipboard for future reference.

Weaknesses

There are three major problems with the ERIC databases as of this review. The first weakness is that ERIC does not have a way to change the display setting so investigators who just want to browse can read the whole abstract from the initial screen. ERIC provides just over two lines of text and then users must click on the Show Full Abstract button to see the complete abstract. Another weakness is that few of the abstracts are available in full-text. The others would have to be found in a library or ordered from a

BOX 4.4 Scientifically Based Indicators (SBIs) by Type of Question

ASSESSMENT SBI	DESCRIPTION SBI	RISK SBI	PREVENTION SBI	INTERVENTION SBI
Psychometric	Random	False negative	Clinical trial	Clinical trial
Reliability	Representative	False positive	Comparison	Comparison group
Sensitivity	Research		Control group	Control group
Specificity	Survey		Effectiveness	Effectiveness
Validity			Efficacy	Efficacy
			Evaluation	Evaluation
			Quasi-experimental	Multiple baseline
			Random	Quasi-experimental
				Random

journal. This weakness is partially offset by one handy feature—the "Find in a library" button, added in March 2007. This takes the user out of ERIC to the World Catalog (World Cat) and looks up the work by its ISBN (for books) or ISSN (for journals). Users simply type in their personal zip code and the closest libraries with the material are listed. This is one reason to not limit searches to "full-text only." The results can be copied onto "My clipboard" and then printed, e-mailed, exported to another program, or saved in "My ERIC" for future use. The last option is best for two reasons. Each user can store a maximum of 10 folders with each folder holding up to 50 records. The other benefit is that users can upload these results at the library after they arrive and obtain more information than would normally be printed or exported. The final weakness is that the peer-reviewed category was just added in 2005 for materials published in 2004 and onwards; so there is no way to know if older works meet this basic requirement for scientifically based research mentioned in the Introduction. It would be helpful if ERIC would gradually apply this important qualifier to works going back at least 10 years. This would actually be a better use of government funding than adding microfiche sources back to 1966.

PubMed

PubMed is part of the National Center for Biotechnology Information that includes the U.S. National Library of Medicine's resources for physicians and other health care personnel. PubMed primarily consists of Medline, the national database that contains over 15 million references to journal articles on biomedicine. Medline goes back to 1950 and indexes 5,000 journals in 37 languages. Since 2005, over 600,000 references are added annually (U.S. National Library of Medicine, 2006).

Features

Since school-based personnel deal with similar issues as pediatricians and child psychiatrists, PubMed is a very appropriate tool. Like ERIC, one of the handy features of PubMed is that users may also access the Medical Subject Headings (MeSH), an online thesaurus. Also like ERIC, PubMed allows users to set up their own "My NCBI Account" on the first page. Doing so allows investigators to save searches and set up personal limits or filters for future searches. Since PubMed is so large, setting up limits ahead of time makes good sense. The most useful include the following: links to full-text, dates (published in the last 10 years), humans (vs. animals), language-English, subsets-Medline, type of article (clinical trial, meta-analysis, practice guideline, randomized controlled trial, and review), and ages (all children: 0–18 years). When you press the "Go" key at the bottom of the page, PubMed actually runs these limits as a search and returns over 100,000 results. Be sure to save this search to My NCBI Account since you are likely to use this Limits search again.

Sample Search

Let's assume that we interested in the differential diagnosis and clinical description of children with attention deficit/hyperactivity disorder. Users must enter their search term into the MeSH thesaurus to ensure that they are using a term that Medline recognizes. Change the default: Search: PubMed to Search: MeSH to check each term before you continue. If we type attention deficit hyperactivity disorder (without quotation marks) into the search bar for MeSH, then the medical thesaurus will inform us that the primary term within the database is Attention Deficit Disorder with Hyperactivity. It also provides a definition, subheadings, other entry terms, and where the term fits in Medline's taxonomy of subjects. Note that three of the subheadings are especially relevant to our purpose: classification, complications, and diagnosis.

Now return to Search: PubMed and type in attention deficit disorder with hyperactivity. With limits in place, this will return over 1,200 results. Go back to the top and type: classification. Do the same for complications and diagnosis separately. Now go the History tab to see all the searches. This is where searches can be combined with Boolean operators. In the Search PubMed for line, type: #2 OR #3 OR #4 to get combined results for classification, complications, or diagnosis. Then return to the History tab and search for #5 AND #1. With search limits in place, this will lead to over 800 results, still too many to browse through in 1 hour.

We have to remember that our contextual constraints include working in elementary and secondary schools, so using the MeSH thesaurus, enter schools. MeSH considers schools to be any educational institution, including universities as well as dental, medical, and nursing schools. These will probably prove more of a distraction. It does, however, provide separate categories for primary schools, secondary schools, and "education, special." Return to Search: PubMed and use each of the terms (without quotation marks). Go the History tab and combine them with the Boolean operator OR. This will also lead to over 800 results. Return to the History tab and type: #6 AND #10. This will lead to about two dozen results, easily meeting our goal for browsing. Those who want to browse the abstracts can change the Display to "Abstract" to see the full abstract. At the far right, there are two useful buttons. The first is a "Related Articles" link to other studies on the same topic in PubMed. The second is a "Links" button that will take you to external links where you may be able to obtain the full-text. This includes the publisher of the journal (fee-based full-text), libraries, or related Medline resources. The latter are especially useful for reliable, user-friendly literature to give to parents, students, or teachers. Practitioners can check off the abstracts they find most interesting, then go to the bottom of the page and click on "Send to" for a menu that allows them to save them as text, save them as a file, send them to a printer, copy them to a clipboard, e-mail them, or order them from "LoanSome Doc" for a fee. This latter option may be especially helpful for those who work in rural areas far from a university library. PubMed allows registered users to keep up to 500 items on the clipboard for future reference; this is especially helpful for those who want to access these records after they go to a university library.

Weaknesses

By now, investigators have also learned some weaknesses of PubMed. First, the terms are clearly made for physicians, not for lay people. Terms have to be searched in MeSH before they are used in PubMed in order to guarantee accurate results. It would be more helpful if terms automatically mapped to Subject Headings. Second, while many articles are available in full-text, most are only available for a fee. Even the list of university libraries is small since they are only voluntarily associated with PubMed and they are the ones responsible for keeping the list current. It would be better if PubMed linked to World Cat like ERIC so that users could simply plug in their zip code to find the closest library.

Gaining Access to Private Databases

In general, all clinicians should have regular access to proprietary scholarly databases. The two cheapest ways to gain access are not ideal at this juncture. First, publicly supported state universities provide "courtesy cards" to state citizens. Members of the community simply have to bring in a valid driver's license or state ID card to obtain this privilege. Second, both public and private universities offer free library cards to their alumni. This is done, of course, in the hope that alumni will bequeath some of their assets to their alma mater, but it is a service that is usually free to graduates of the institution. The reason that neither of these is ideal is because while the courtesy card or alumni card allow users to use the databases at the library, most universities still do not give the cardholder a user ID and password to use university databases from the convenience of their home or office.

There are three other sure-fire ways to gain access, but these require more effort. The first is to collaborate with a university faculty member. Researcher-practitioner partnerships have proven to be effective models for helping scientists increase the relevancy of their studies as well as helping clinicians gain objectivity for their results (Kalodner, Alfred, & Hoyt, 1997; Lopez, Torres, & Norwood, 1998; Weisz, Chu, & Polo, 2004). Another possibility is for seasoned professionals to offer to be a field instructor or adjunct faculty member. Even teaching for one semester is likely to grant the adjunct access for a full year. Third, practitioners can subscribe directly to the databases by going to the sponsor or owner of the search engine on the Web. For example, PsycINFO can be accessed for a fee through www.apa.org, and SWAB can be accessed through www.ovid.com.

Private Databases

There are two databases in the private web that should be familiar to all school-based practitioners. These include PsycINFO and SWAB.

PsycINFO

PsycINFO is the oldest and largest of the nonmedical databases, going back to 1806 and encompassing over 2.5 million abstracts of scholarly works. These include peer-reviewed articles, editorially reviewed book chapters, book reviews, and dissertations in the social sciences.

Features

PsycINFO opens with the keyword Search page and this is an excellent place to begin. The keyword search allows the user to enter a single word or phrase. Note that in the parenthesis, there is the hint (use "*" or "$" for truncation). These truncation characters allow searchers to use just a word root and find all of its variations. For example, if you type adolescen*, you will get results for both adolescence and adolescents. If you type child$, you will get results for child, childhood, childish, childlike, and children. PsycINFO also allows the user to "map term to Subject Heading." This lets searchers know what category the database uses to group similar articles together under one heading. Users can also click on limits that can narrow down the search—these should be employed judiciously. The ones that are most useful include abstracts, human, and English language. Publication year can be used to limit the search to the last 10 years (Berliner, 2002), but since the results are usually provided in reverse chronological order (most recent first), there is little reason to employ this feature. Finally, PsycINFO allows users to save searches, a feature that is especially useful for our purposes. It also saves an enormous amount of time for those who want to do similar searches in the future.

Sample Search

Let us explore the issue of autism since it is the fastest growing diagnostic category that schools now use, with an estimated 1-in-150 prevalence rate (Centers for Disease Control and Prevention, 2007). We will use an intervention question framed as "What are the most effective interventions for children with autism in schools?" The best research will be scientifically based, children and adolescents oriented, school related, and question focused.

Scientifically Based Research. We will begin by searching for the best evidence available in two stages. First, to get on overview of the subject, we will look for the secondary research called systematic reviews or meta-analyses. Second, we will look for recent primary research called randomized controlled trials and quasi-experimental designs. To obtain the best secondary research, we will use two different terms. First, type the phrase "systematic review" into the Keyword search box and leave the box "Map term to Subject Heading" checked. You will notice that there is a subject heading for Literature Reviews, but remembering Greenhalgh's (2006) warning about journalistic reviews, do *not* check it! Scroll down and check the box next to systematic reviews and press the Continue button at the top of the page. Then repeat this process with the term, "meta-analysis." This time there is a subject heading for Meta Analysis, so check it and the term meta-analysis since the American Psychological Association's (2001) *Publication Manual* suggests this is the proper spelling (p. 92). Note that PsycINFO automatically assumes you will combine these with the Boolean operator OR, so leave this default as it is. Under the Keyword Search section at the top of the page, click the Search History button to reveal the two searches. Select Searches #1 and #2, and combine them with OR. (If you make a mistake, simply select the search you wish to delete and click on "Remove Selected.") When correctly combined with OR, you should obtain over 9,000 results. Save this search by pressing the Save Search History button. You will have to create a personal account and password before you can save it. Save it using the name "systematic reviews." Be sure to change the default from "temporary" to "permanent" before pressing the Save button.

This step will save an enormous amount of time in future searches. Back at the key work search page, clear this search by selecting all three searches and pressing the "Remove selected" button.

When you have finished entering all of the Intervention SBIs (from Box 4.4), some of them will have disappeared from view, so press the down arrow above "Expand" on the far right. Correctly combined with OR, you should obtain over 289,000 results. Press the "Save Search History" button and save it using the name "SBIs." Again be sure to change the default from temporary to permanent before pressing the Save button. Clear this search by selecting all of the searches and pressing the "Remove selected" button.

Child- and Adolescent-Oriented Research. Our second task is to look for any studies related to children or adolescents. This time search for the following key words: adolescents, children, teenagers, and youth *without* mapping to the Subject Headings. Combine all of the searches with OR. Completed correctly, this should give you over 355,000 results. Save this search history using the name "Children," change the default to permanent, and press Save. Clear this search by selecting all of the searches and pressing the "Remove Selected" button.

School-Related Research. Third, let's look for any studies related to a school-based setting. Search for the key words, education, schools, students, and teachers. Combine them with OR as usual. Done correctly, you should receive nearly 500,000 results. Save them permanently under the name "school-based." Delete this search as before.

Question-Focused Research. While we have already addressed the issue of question-specific SBIs, we must identify the two primary parts of our question—our purpose (i.e., intervention) and our problem (i.e., autism). Note that we did not begin with a preconceived idea for effective interventions (see Box 4.5). To find our *purpose*, use all of the possible synonyms for intervention, including counseling, intervention, and psychotherapy (see Box 4.6). As we did earlier, we search for each of these four terms while mapping them to the Subject Headings. Then combine all of the results with the Boolean operator OR. Done correctly, you should obtain over 400,000 results. Now save them permanently under the name "intervention."

To find our *problem*, search for the word "autism" and map it to the Subject Heading and note that it is in bold print; click on the word autism. Press the Continue button at the top of the page. Done correctly, you should receive over 11,000 results. You can save this search under the name "autism" if you wish, but do not go back and delete it!

BOX 4.5 Searching for Empirically Supported Treatments: The Cart Before the Horse Problem

Some professionals have asked why they cannot simply look up their favorite techniques to help children or adolescents. It is possible to search for specific techniques and utilize such phrases as "evidence-based" or "empirically supported." Unfortunately, EBP has become a byword for almost any kind of evidence ranging from clinical wisdom to randomized controlled trials. This is the reason that we deliberately excluded partially correct as well as entirely wrong definitions of evidence-based practice in Chapter 2. As an example of this phenomenon, look up the following article: Hall, T. M., Kaduson H. G., & Schaefer, C. E. (2002). Fifteen effective play therapy techniques. *Professional Psychology, 33* (6), 515–522.

This article was found by several of my graduate students while searching for empirically supported treatments for children and adolescents. Unfortunately, they put the proverbial cart before the horse. They knew that play therapy was a common intervention for children, so they substituted the technique for the specific problem, such as anxiety, depression, or impulsivity. What is wrong with this approach?

There are two problems with focusing on a treatment technique rather than a specific problem. First and foremost, it is usually an indication that the investigator is doing a journalistic review. They are already familiar with play therapy and they find it an enjoyable way to build rapport with a wide variety of children. They are primarily looking for confirmation that they can continue to do what they are already doing. After they receive confirmation, they tend to discontinue searching lest they discover any contradictory research. The second problem is that there are famous authors, journals, and even entire organizations (e.g., the Association for Play Therapy) that will only provide a one-sided view of play therapy. No one expects Charles E. Schaefer to write a critical article on play therapy. No one anticipates that the *International Journal of Play Therapy* will publish an article that states that play therapy works with one problem, but is ineffective with another. The article cited

(continued)

above states that the authors have found 15 effective play therapy techniques, but if one searches the article for even one research study demonstrating the efficacy or effectiveness of any of the techniques, then they will be sorely disappointed. Evidently, what the authors mean as "effective" is that the techniques are endorsed by their clinical wisdom, not by scientifically based research. At this point, some play therapy proponents will get angry and argue that the Association for Play Therapy's Web site (http://www.a4pt. org/) includes a "Research and Practices" page, including one study that purports to give a "summary of meta-analytic findings." The authors of this meta-analysis, however, provide this caveat about their results:

> A word of caution is offered when reviewing the following summaries. Some studies may have noted a significant change on a particular variable, but did not find any differences on another variable. In this case, the authors reported only the statistics that were significant. For example, in a study that found significant decreases in social maladjustment after play therapy treatment but no statistical differences in anxiety, the authors may have reported only the significance of the social maladjustment. We used this method due to space limitations and a focus on the effectiveness of play therapy treatments.
>
> Ray & Bratton, 1999, p. 3

The authors seem to admit in the last line that they were only interested in taking a strengths-based approach to the play therapy research. A strength-based approach is fine for clients (as long as it doesn't result in Pollyannaism—see Saleebey, 1996, 2002). It results in what Greenhalgh (2006) calls a journalistic review because it lacks the essential characteristic of scientific objectivity. Those who are truly interested in discovering what technique works best will not search for their preferred method. They will use intervention questions to search for the problem and all of the empirically supported treatments.

(continued)

Questions for Discussion

1. Do you have a familiar or favorite technique that you use regularly with clients?
2. What would you do if scientific evidence demonstrated there were better techniques?
3. What other journals can you identify with a specific technique or therapy?
4. What associations sponsor these journals?
5. Where might you find an opposing point of view?

Putting It All Together. In order to get both a broad view and a narrow view of the research, it is a good idea to do this in two parts. Let's call these the Forest and Trees.

To get an overview of the forest of autism research, we will combine the autism search with the already combined systematic review or meta-analysis search. Press the "View Saved" in the Search History section of the page. At the Saved Searches page, select the box directly above the term Systematic Reviews and press Run. At the next pop-up page, click on the Main Search Pay button. Combine the autism search and the search labeled (2 or 3) using AND. Done correctly, this should give you about 30 results. Scroll down to see the results. Then press the Customize Display button at the top of this section. Under Display Fields, select Citation + Abstract. Under Page Size, change the default from 10 citations per page to 50 and press Continue. This allows for faster scrolling and quicker browsing. You can save this search under the name "Autism-Forest." Select searches 2 to 5 (all except Autism) and remove them as usual.

To see the trees of the most recent primary research, we will combine Autism AND all of the remaining combination search results. Press the View Saved button again and select the saved searches, Children, Intervention, SBIs, and School-Based. Back at the Main Search Page, select Autism and all of the searches with the word "or" and combine selections with AND. Done correctly, this should give you about 100 results. You won't have to customize the display again because the program will remember your preferences. You can save this search under the name "Autism-Trees."

BOX 4.6 Purpose Synonyms by Type of Question

ASSESSMENT	DESCRIPTION	RISK	PREVENTION	INTERVENTION
Assess	Characteristics	Dangerousness	Deterrence	Counseling
Diagnosis	Comorbid	Prediction	Prevention	Intervention
Eligibility	Description	Prognosis		Psychotherapy
Evaluate	Needs assessment	Risk assessment		Treatment
Measure		Threat assessment		

Weaknesses

There is only one glaring weakness in PsycINFO: It does not allow the searcher to use the Boolean operator NOT. Most of the time, this weakness can be surmounted but it would be a vast improvement if PsycINFO added this possibility.

Social Work Abstracts

SWAB is the smaller of the two major proprietary databases. It contains over 45,000 records. It does not indicate how many journals are abstracted but an educated guess would place this number at about 100.

Features

SWAB opens on the Basic Search page. New users should scroll down to the bottom of the page to learn how SWAB handles functions like phrases and truncation. It uses the * sign for truncation and double parenthesis for phrases like "social work." The right side of the Basic Search page allows users to Limit Search; click on the More button for options. The most useful is Publication Year since SWAB goes back 30 years and most users will want studies done in the last 10 years. After pressing the OK button, the database returns to the Basic Search page. Choose the Advanced Search tab to begin since this page allows users to employ all of the Boolean operators.

Sample Search

Let us assume we are interested in improving prevention programs for Hispanic students since they are the most rapidly growing demographic group of students in schools in the United States. We might frame the question as "What are the best prevention programs for children of Hispanic descent?" Once again, we will be searching for evidence that is scientifically based, child and adolescent oriented, school related, and question focused.

Scientifically Based Research. To obtain the best secondary research, use the word roots of the same terms as before: "systematic* review*" and "meta-analy*". Note that because SWAB is the smallest of the private databases; we will have to use truncation to get the broadest possible results. Be sure to use double quotation marks for the phrases and to change the default operator from AND to OR. This should net over 125 results.

To obtain the best primary research, use the word roots of the terms found in Box 4.4 to employ the Scientifically Based Indicators found under Prevention. Begin by going to the Advanced Search page and enter the following terms: "clinical trial*," compar*, "control group*," evaluat*, and random*. Because there are more than three SBIs, we must accomplish this task in three steps. After entering the first three terms, enter the last two terms; note that the default remains at OR. Then go to the Search History tab, select the two searches, and combine them using OR. Accomplished correctly, this should give nearly 12,000 results.

Child- and Adolescent-Oriented Research. As before, use the Boolean operator OR to locate all the articles on adolescen*, child*, teen*, or youth* in the default "Terms Anywhere." Since there are four terms, users must use the same three-step process described earlier. Be sure to combine all terms using the OR operator. Done correctly, you should receive over 19,000 results.

School-Related Research. Now use the school-related terms: educat*, student*, and teacher* but not the term school*. This is because of a flaw in the SWAB program that will be discussed under Weaknesses later. To find school*, change the default in "Terms anywhere" to Abstract (AB), then search for school* again in Descriptors (DE), and then search for school* again in Source (SO). Maintain the Boolean operator OR for this operation. This should result in about 5,000 records.

Question-Focused Research. Again we have changed both the purpose and problem. We will subdivide this quest as before.

To find *purpose*-related terms, peruse the list in Box 4.6 and use truncation as follows: deter* and prevent*. This should net about 7,500 results.

To find *problem*-related terms, we must brainstorm as many terms as possible for the demographic descriptor, Hispanic. Since Latinos are a diverse group, we'll use three major terms to look for studies about them, including Hispanic*, Latin*, and Mexic*, combining all three with the operator OR. (Practitioners in New York and Puerto Rico will probably want to substitute "Puerto Ric*" and those in Florida will probably want to substitute Cuba* for Mexic*.) These three terms will lead to nearly 1,400 results.

Putting It All Together. Now return to the Search History page. There are two potential "forests" to view—the secondary research on Hispanics or the secondary research on prevention. Let's tackle the former first. Select the combined Hispanic terms and the combined result for systematic reviews. Combine both of these with AND. You should receive fewer than five results. Now let's address the latter forest. Select the combined prevention terms and the combined result for systematic reviews. Combine both with AND and you should obtain about 25 results. To browse either set, click on the Display icon on the far right of this number. The citations will appear on a new page. To see the complete citation and abstract or the complete record, click on the "Change Display" button, choose the "Fields to Display" menu and select Citation and Abstract, and press OK.

Now let's examine the "trees." Return to the Search History page and select the following search results: combined Hispanic terms, combined prevention terms, combined school-related terms, combined child and adolescent terms, and the combined scientifically based indicators. Now combine all five of these with AND. You should receive about 20 results. To browse them, click on the Display icon on the far right of this number. You will not have to change the display again.

Weaknesses

The biggest problem with SWAB is that it is difficult to locate information on schools. This is due to the fact that it is one of the only databases to include the lead author's address as one of the standard citation fields. Since many of these address begin with "School of Social Work," it results in nearly 12,000 false positives in a search using the term: school* in either Terms Anywhere or in Citation (CITN). Unfortunately, using the narrower term "schools" will create too many false negatives. The only way around this problem is to change the default from "Terms Anywhere" and look for school* in three fields: Abstract, Descriptors, or Source. I would have liked to contact the owner of SWAB to report this problem, but there was no external link to the owner's Web site. Eliminating the lead author's address from the citation would be the best solution to this problem. Another major problem with SWAB was that there was no way to save searches to a personal account. One can download results into another program, but one cannot save the searches to run an update or create new combinations in the future.

Screening Abstracts

The goal of using Boolean operators to narrow our results was to provide us with a reasonable number of abstracts to browse. Ideally, this number is less than 100, but more than 10. Assuming it takes about 30 seconds to read an abstract, this means that the screening process will take anywhere from 5 to 50 minutes. We will want to determine whether the studies found meet our four basic search criteria: Are they scientifically based? Are they child or adolescent oriented? Are they school focused? Did they answer the question we asked? To help practitioners stay focused on these four criteria, I've developed the abstract screening tool in Box 4.7.

---

1. What was the level of scientific support?
   ☐ Meta-analysis or systematic review
   ☐ Randomized controlled trial (control group vs. treatment group)
   ☐ Quasi-experimental design (treatment A vs. treatment B)
   ☐ Pretest-posttest design (one group studied before and after intervention)

2. Who was the sample of the study?
   ☐ Children (ages 0–4)
   ☐ Children (ages 5–10)
   ☐ Early adolescents (ages 11–13)
   ☐ Adolescents (ages 14–18)

3. What was the setting of the study?
   ☐ Preschool
   ☐ Elementary school
   ☐ Middle/junior high school
   ☐ High school

4. What clinical question did the study address?
   ☐ Assessment
   ☐ Description
   ☐ Risk
   ☐ Prevention
   ☐ Intervention

Note: The abstract must be able to answer questions 1, 2, and 4 or be rejected from consideration. This assumes that practitioners can adapt other interventions to fit a school setting.

Practical Guidelines

The Individuals with Disabilities Education Improvement Act gives practitioners an easy way out when it mandates that school-based personnel provide services that are "based on peer-reviewed research *to the extent practicable*" (section 614 (d)(1)(a)(i)(IV), emphasis added). It begs the question, what is reasonable and doable for the average practitioner when it comes to investigating the evidence? I would prefer that the three major clearinghouses included more information on small group and individual interventions and I believe that this will come with time. In the meantime, however, practitioners need some common-sense guidelines. One of the basic principles of building a scientific base is to triangulate one's evidentiary support. I like to compare it to building a stool—anything with less than three legs creates problems for the person putting weight on it. Triangulation can be accomplished in at least three ways. First, one can search three places—clearinghouses, electronic databases, and books (see Appendix B). Second, one can search for at least three sources within any one location—three scientifically based articles in an electronic database or three chapters in books on empirically supported treatments. Third, one could search three different electronic databases. The advantage of looking for an odd number is that some controversies can be resolved by simply looking at what the majority support. In the next chapter, we will examine more scientific ways to appraise the research that is found.

Summary

This chapter aimed to teach practitioners how to efficiently and effectively search for the best available evidence. There are three major clearinghouses for systematic reviews: the What Works Clearinghouse, the Campbell Collaboration, and SAMHSA's Registry of Evidence-Based Programs and Practices. All of them collect and evaluate the quality of the interventions before publishing them. The invisible Web dwarfs the visible Web by several hundred times, but school-based practitioners must find a way to access this data. The Web is best searched using Boolean logic and the operators AND, OR, and NOT. This requires learning some syntax tips to help investigators specify exactly what interests them. Ideally, using Boolean operators should enable professionals to complete a search in no more than 1 hour for any database. The public databases can be accessed once professionals know where to look, but much of the full-text information remains proprietary—available only for a fee. There are two major public databases. ERIC presents a wealth of information, some of which is peer reviewed. PubMed is the oldest and largest of the public databases and contains information on health-related conditions, including pediatrics and psychiatry. The private Web must be accessed through a university library and has the best databases by which to find evidence. There are two major private databases for mental health clinicians. PsycINFO is the oldest and most relevant database that school-based practitioners can access. SWAB is the smallest of the databases and will be of most use to school social workers. Finally, practitioners need to screen the evidence they find and triangulate their search to justify their clinical decision making.

Suggested Reading

1. Devine, J., & Egger-Sider, F. (2004). Beyond Google: The invisible Web in the academic library. *Journal of Academic Librarianship, 30* (4), 265–269.

2. Price, G., & Sherman, C. (2001). Exploring the invisible Web: 7 essential strategies. *Online, 25* (4), 32–34.

3. Wouters, P., Reddy, C., & Aguillo, I. (2006). On the visibility of information on the Web: An exploratory experimental approach. *Research Evaluation, 15* (2), 107–115.

Internet Resources

American Institutes for Research
http://www.air.org/

Campbell Collaboration (Social, Behavioral, and Educational Issues)
http://www.campbellcollaboration.org/

Carl Sagan's Baloney Detection Kit
http://users.tpg.com.au/users/tps-seti/baloney.html

Center for the Study and Prevention of Violence's Blueprints for Violence Prevention
http://www.colorado.edu/cspv/blueprints/

Centers for Disease Control's School Health Education Resources
http://apps.nccd.cdc.gov/sher/

Critical Thinking Community
http://www.criticalthinking.org

Cochrane Collaboration (Health Care)
http://www.cochrane.org/index.htm

Education Resource Information Center
http://www.eric.ed.gov/

National Academies Press—Over 3,700 books online (free)
http://books.nap.edu/

National Center for Biotechnology Information
http://www.ncbi.nlm.nih.gov/sites/entrez?db=pubmed

National Guideline Clearinghouse—Agency for Healthcare Research and Quality
http://www.guidelines.gov/

National Library of Medicine's Medical Subject Headings (MeSH)
http://www.nlm.nih.gov/mesh/MBrowser.html

Office of Juvenile Justice and Delinquency Prevention's Model Programs
http://www.dsgonline.com/mpg2.5/mpg_index.htm

SAMHSA's National Registry of Evidence-Based Programs and Practices
http://www.nrepp.samhsa.gov/index.htm

What Works Clearinghouse
http://ies.ed.gov/ncee/wwc/

5

Appraising the Evidence

Preview

Chapter 4 addressed how to efficiently and effectively investigate the evidence. The purpose of this chapter is to help practitioners learn how to appraise the evidence that was found using the previous chapter's search techniques. The five types of answerable questions lead to five types of research studies, but do not correspond in a one-to-one manner (see Figure 5.1). This chapter will address the best way to appraise each of the five types of research studies.

Both prevention and intervention questions lead to effectiveness studies, which require the same approach to appraisal (Guyatt, Sackett, & Cook, 1993). First, I will begin with effectiveness studies of both preventions and interventions since this is the type of research that most practitioners will want to put to use. This will be done in two stages. I will begin by describing the process of secondary research and the potential problems that may result. Then I will discuss the two types of primary research that meet the U.S. Department of Education's definition of scientifically based research. Both will be appraised using the Department of Education's three broad criteria: relevance, strength, and consistency. Second, I will then move to assessment studies that involve measurement of a problem and discuss how to appraise instrument studies, employing 10 critical questions. Third, I will discuss why risk questions lead to cohort studies and describe six essential questions used to evaluate these. Fourth, I will address the two types of studies that result from description questions: quantitative surveys and qualitative case studies. Finally, I will describe how to choose the best intervention to employ with one's clients.

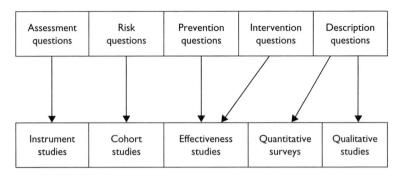

Assessment questions	Risk questions	Prevention questions	Intervention questions	Description questions
Instrument studies	Cohort studies	Effectiveness studies	Quantitative surveys	Qualitative studies

FIGURE 5.1. Types of questions into types of studies.

Appraising Effectiveness Studies

Chapter 4 introduced the difference between secondary research and primary research. Secondary research is helpful for gaining a broad view of a problem or the effectiveness of a technique across multiple studies over many years. Primary research is helpful for gaining the most recent research with a specific group at a specific time. The two approaches complement each other to give clinicians a glimpse of both the forest and trees. These two types of research, however, must be appraised differently. Since Chapter 4 recommended that practitioners read the secondary research first, I will address how to appraise these studies first. Then I will discuss how to appraise the primary research.

Meta-Analyses and Systematic Reviews

Few studies are more attractive to a busy professional than a review that purports to systematically collect, cull, and compare all of the primary research on a topic of interest. Ideally, such reviews are rigorous, transparent, and auditable. By *rigorous*, we mean that they utilize the highest standards to decide which studies to include in the review. By *transparent*, we mean that they explicitly state how the studies are collected, the criteria by which they are judged, and how they reach their conclusions. This transparency should allow another researcher to audit the results. By *auditable*, we mean that there is sufficient specificity so that another researcher can attempt to replicate the findings. This has actually occurred several times in the professional literature and the published debates make for interesting reading. For an example, read a recent debate about a meta-analysis of prevention programs for families with young children at risk for child abuse and neglect

Evidence-Based Practice in School Mental Health

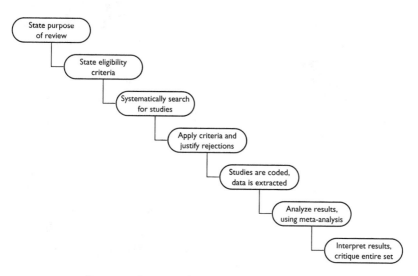

FIGURE 5.2. Seven steps in meta-analyses.

(original article: Geeraert, Van den Noortgate, Grietens, & Onghena, 2004; critique: Miller, 2006; and rebuttal: Van den Noortgate, Geeraert, Grietens, & Onghena, 2006).

The Review Process

Before we address the issue of how to appraise a systematic review or meta-analysis, however, it is necessary to understand how such a review is accomplished. Torgerson (2003) states that the process of a systematic review should have seven basic steps (see Figure 5.2). First, the reviewers state the purpose of the review and a protocol for answering the research question. Second, the eligibility or inclusionary criteria are determined. Common criteria for randomized controlled trials (RCTs) and quasi-experimental designs (QEDs) will be described later. Third, the reviewers must systematically search for studies that seem to fit these criteria. This means that they include the search terms used, the databases searched, the range of dates used, and the subject-specific journals that were hand searched. Ideally, two researchers working independently of each other do simultaneous searches. Fourth, the studies are retrieved and read thoroughly to determine whether they fit the criteria for inclusion. The studies are appraised for their internal (and external) validity. Eligibility criteria are strictly applied and the weaker studies are rejected. The separate reviewers must come to some consensus about any differences of opinion. Fifth, the remaining studies are coded

---

(e.g., RCT or QED), and then the following data is consistently extracted: sample characteristics, duration and intensity of the intervention, and the outcome measures employed. Means and standard deviations at the beginning, middle, end, and follow-up periods are recorded. Sixth, quantitative studies with complete statistics can be analyzed using meta-analysis where feasible. Feasibility requires that the studies have used similar outcome measures so that their results can be reasonably combined. Let's use the Drug Abuse Resistance Education (DARE) program as an example. Most evaluations of this program focused on its explicit goal: to teach youth drug abuse resistance skills; so most researchers looked for self-reported denial of illicit drug use as the outcome measure. Birkeland, Murphy-Graham, and Weiss (2005) have argued, however, that DARE has an implicit goal: to improve the relationship between youth and police. Obviously, these two disparate goals cannot be added together to determine effectiveness. In short, you may be able to add apples and oranges to obtain a total number of fruit, but cabbages won't fit the category. This issue of comparability is the most hotly contested controversy in meta-analysis (Greenhalgh, 2006). Seventh, all of the data should be synthesized and interpreted. Ideally, this includes a critical review of both the strengths and weaknesses of the entire set. (This helps set the direction for future research in the field.) This synthesis will then be subject to blind peer-reviews before it is published.

If the process is done correctly, then research consumers can easily see why so many scholars put this kind of secondary research at the pinnacle of the pyramid (see Figure 4.1). We must, however, take the hierarchy of evidence with a grain of salt. Unfortunately, not all meta-analyses are created equal and consumers should be able to distinguish the good ones from the merely mediocre ones. As Greenhalgh (2006) states, "not even the most hard-line protagonist of evidence-based medicine would place a sloppy meta-analysis or randomized controlled trial that was seriously methodologically flawed above a large, well-designed cohort study" (p. 53). This requires that school-based practitioners understand how systematic reviews should look and know how to critique a systematic review or meta-analysis.

Critique of Meta-Analyses

What can go wrong with a systematic review? For each step in the process, there are potential missteps that must be avoided (Oxman, 1995). The first possible misstep is to have an unclear purpose or research question at the start of the review. Reviews should be clear about the specific population of

Evidence-Based Practice in School Mental Health

interest, the range of interventions (e.g., dosage and duration), and the range of outcomes that will be studied. For example, we could expect a meta-analysis of interventions meant to reduce the dropout rate to first define the term "dropout." This is not as easy as it appears because there are many conflicting definitions that lead to vastly different estimates of the size of the problem (Samuels, 2007; Viadero, 2001). Should those students who cease attending school in order to obtain their GEDs be considered dropouts? In Chicago, for example, the estimates of dropouts range from 30% to 66% depending on who is doing the measuring (Tonn, 2005). The second misstep can occur in the development of inclusionary criteria. Criteria that are too rigid may exclude too much of relevant literature and criteria that are too loose may include sloppy research. A third misstep can occur in the systematic search for studies. Sometimes, the systematic search will inadvertently (but systematically) miss certain types of literature. For example, many meta-analyses exclude multiple-baseline single-subject designs even though some of those designs may be as rigorous as RCTs (Erion, 2006; Maughan, Christiansen, Jenson, Olympia, & Clark, 2005). A widely suspected form of bias in the professional literature is publication bias—the tendency for journals to publish studies that confirm the beliefs of editors and/or offer statistically significant results (Lane & Dunlap, 1978). Sometimes this is referred to as the "file drawer problem"—the tendency for studies with nonsignificant findings to be confined to the primary author's filing cabinet (Rosenthal, 1979). The most commonly proposed solution is a search for "grey literature"— unpublished studies, such as theses or other works by authors in the field who have previously published (Conn, Valentine, Cooper, & Rantz, 2003; Martin, Perez, Sacristen, & Alvarez, 2005). This task has been rendered easier with the introduction of the System for Information on Grey Literature in Europe (Bradshaw, Lovell, & Harris, 2005; Sampson, Ritchie, Lai, Raven, & Blanchard, 2005). The fourth possible misstep may occur when there is only one researcher conducting the research. The omission of a collaborator has three potential problems. The researcher is less likely to develop a standardized protocol for assessing the literature and resort to "scientific gerrymandering" (O'Sullivan, 2006). The lack of a research partner means that there is no one to provide an alternative viewpoint on an ambiguous study. The solitary researcher may inadvertently be more critical of research that conflicts with previously held beliefs. This is known as confirmation bias—the tendency to both perceive and recall evidence that confirms a previously held point of view (Beier & Ackerman, 2005;

Wood & Nezworski, 2005). For example, there have been conflicting results on the study of how confirmation bias affects eligibility decisions by school-based practitioners (Huebner, 1990 vs. O'Reilly, Northcraft, & Sabers, 1989). The fifth misstep has to do with the consistent extraction of the data. Owing to space limitations by journals, research results written by one team rarely meet all the requirements for meta-analysis by another group. The best way around this predicament is for the meta-analysis team to contact the original researchers to determine if they have the statistics that were left out of their published work. When systematic reviewers do not go this extra mile, it reduces their ability to compare studies effectively. The sixth misstep is the misuse of statistics, in this case, meta-analysis. Computer analysts have a saying, "Garbage in, garbage out," by which they mean that the quality of the result is dependent on the quality of the input. Sophisticated statistical analysis cannot make a silk purse out of a sow's ear. If the studies are too dissimilar, combining their results will only confuse matters more. Readers who want to learn more about the statistical results for meta-analyses should look at Valentine and Cooper's (2003) article on effect sizes at the What Works Clearinghouse (http://ies.ed.gov/ncee/wwc/pdf/essig.pdf). The final misstep can occur during the interpretation of results. Oxman (1995) warns readers of the medical literature about two common misinterpretations. First, "no evidence of effect" should not be confused with "evidence of no effect." For example, just because the Institute of Medicine (2004) found no evidence that thimerosal, the mercury-based preservative once common in childhood vaccines, ever caused autism (McCormick, 2003) does not mean that there was evidence that thimerosal never caused autism (Parker, Schwartz, Todd, & Pickering, 2004). Second, meta-analysis of an intervention's effect on subgroups (e.g., a particular ethnic group or age group) can be misleading. Specifically, it is more likely that a subgroup will have a quantitative difference (i.e., a difference in how often a treatment worked) than a qualitative difference (i.e., whether a treatment worked). Thus, when a meta-analysis concludes that an intervention works with the large group but does not work with a specific subgroup, this interpretation should be viewed with caution (Brookes et al., 2001).

For a summary meta-analysis evaluation form, see Box 5.1. Readers who would like a more definitive list of criteria for systematic reviews should see the QUORUM guidelines at the end of the chapter (see Internet Resources).

BOX 5.1 Meta-Analysis Summary Evaluation Form

	NO	YES
1. Is the research question clear? (Are major search terms defined?)	☐	☐
2. Are the inclusionary criteria rigorous? (e.g., RCTs, QEDs, and multiple baseline designs)	☐	☐
3. Was the search for studies comprehensive? (Was the grey literature searched?)	☐	☐
4. Was the meta-analysis performed by more than one researcher? (In order to avoid confirmation bias)	☐	☐
5. Did the researchers collect pretest and posttest means and standard deviations for each study?	☐	☐
6. Did the researchers use a standard statistical for measuring effect size? (e.g., standardized mean difference, absolute risk reduction or number needed to treat)	☐	☐
7. Did the researchers interpret the results with caution? (Did they avoid confusing "no evidence of effect" with "evidence of no effect"? Did they avoid overreaching conclusions about subgroup effects?)	☐	☐
Totals		

Primary Research

The U.S. Department of Education evaluates primary effectiveness studies along three major criteria: relevance, strength, and consistency (What Works Clearinghouse, 2006b). Let us discuss each of these in detail.

Relevance

Relevance is determined by the study's topic area, adequacy of the outcome measures, and adequacy of the reported data. Each of these will be addressed in more detail now.

Relevance of the Topic

Relevance of the topic is defined in four ways. First, the study must have been done within a *relevant timeframe*. The What Works Clearinghouse, for example, does hand searches of scholarly journals going back 20 years. Studies done before that period do not meet the relevant timeframe criterion. Second, the study must have a *relevant intervention*. Interventions can include programs (e.g., Check and Connect, a dropout prevention program), products (e.g., Positive Action, a character education curriculum), techniques (e.g., cognitive-behavioral therapy), and school policies (e.g., looping—when teachers and related services personnel advance with the same group of children for 2–3 years). An intervention for attention-deficit/hyperactivity disorder is unlikely to help a student with selective mutism open up to others. On the other hand, an intervention using pair discussion groups might be a relevant intervention (Watson, 1995). Third, the study must be based on a *relevant sample*. School refusal behavior may occur for different reasons for primary age children than it does for high school students (Kearney, 2007). Interventions that work for young pupils are likely to fall flat for older adolescents (Gosschalk, 2004). Fourth, there must be a *relevant outcome*. Student outcomes include the achievement of long-term goals, such as improved grades, raised test scores, or graduation from school. They may also include instrumental goals such as attendance, good behavior, supportive relationships, and study skills. Sexual abstinence, for example, would not be an expected outcome for a drug prevention program, but reduced HIV incidence might be anticipated (Griffin, Botvin, & Nichols, 2006).

Adequate Outcome Measures

Adequate outcome measures must be both reliable and valid. *Reliability* refers to the instrument's consistency. For example, we would expect that a parent who filled out the Child Behavior Checklist for her child would not have wildly different results 1 month apart. (It is common for parents and teachers to have different results because of the fact that they observe the child in two radically different contexts.) Reliability is a prerequisite to validity. *Validity* refers to the instrument's accuracy—does it measure what it intends to measure? Students with externalizing behavior disorders, for example, are notoriously poor judges of their own behavior (Achenbach, McConaughy, & Howell, 1987; Handwerk, Larzelere, Soper, & Friman, 1999). They may give a reliable/consistent self-report, but that does not mean it is *accurate*. A more valid result would be obtained by asking for a teacher rating of the student's conduct (e.g., Achenbach's Teacher Report Form).

Adequate Reporting of Data

Adequate reporting of data means that the study must provide sufficient statistics for other researchers to check the results or combine them in a meta-analysis. At a minimum, this means that the study must report both means and standard deviations for the treatment group and the control/comparison group both before and after the intervention. The study should also report the sample sizes for the two groups (What Works Clearinghouse, 2006b). *Means* describe the average effect of the intervention or the comparison condition. *Standard deviations* describe the amount of dispersion in the scores. Generally, researchers want means to increase and standard deviations to decrease with intervention.

Strength

The strength of a research study is determined by the study's design and whether it meets important quality standards for its respective design. The two strongest designs are RCTs and QEDs.

Randomized Controlled Trials

RCTs are studies that assign participants to an intervention or control group randomly. Because they compare a treatment group to a nontreatment group, they provide evidence for the efficacy of the intervention. In short, this kind of study answers the question, "What works?" RCTs must demonstrate seven quality standards. These include specific random assignment procedures, baseline equivalence, low overall attrition, equivalent attrition, a lack of intervention contamination, lack of teacher-intervention confound, and congruence between the unit of assignment and the unit of analysis.

First, RCTs must have *specific random assignment procedures* that include details about how the randomization procedure was carried out (e.g., a roll of dice), the role of the person making the random assignment (e.g., university researcher vs. building principal), and how the results of the random assignment were concealed from the participants. Second, *baseline equivalence* refers to the need for the intervention group and the control/comparison group to reasonably similar at the start of the study. For example, they should be relatively similar on demographic characteristics, such age, race, or gender and on assessment measures (e.g., the Behavioral Assessment Schedule for Children's Self-Report of Personality). It simply makes no sense to only measure differences in outcome if they do not begin at the same starting point. For example, Eikeseth, Smith, Jahr, and Eldevik (2007) did a comparison of behavioral therapy and eclectic therapy for young children with autism. The behavioral group had a gender mix of 8 boys and 5 girls while the comparison group had 11 boys and 1 girl. When the two groups are not equivalent at the start, it makes it nearly impossible to draw firm conclusions at the end. Third, *low overall attrition* means an acceptable number of participants did not drop out, move, or become otherwise unavailable during the course of the study. There are exceptions to this rule. For example, some urban schools have mobility rates over 50%—meaning that there are at least as many student transfers as half the total student population for the school. Studies conducted in these real life settings might reasonably be expected to mirror the broader transiency rate. The fourth criterion for randomization is *equivalent attrition*—both the intervention group and the control/comparison groups must have similar dropout rates. For example, if the treatment group of adolescent girls who received individual pregnancy prevention counseling dropped out of school at a much lower rate than the group that received a group pregnancy prevention program, one might begin to suspect that something other than the intervention was keeping one group in school while the other group left. Fifth, there should be a *lack of intervention contamination*. Intervention contamination can occur when participants in the intervention group and the control/comparison group discuss the intervention, thereby diffusing the intervention to a broader group of participants than originally intended (Craven, Marsh, Debus, & Jayasinghe, 2001). Sixth, the *lack of teacher-intervention confound* is necessary because of the fact that some studies have one teacher institute one intervention while a colleague uses the alternative. Under such conditions, there is no way to tell whether it was the teacher's (or therapist's) individual style or the actual treatment that made a difference (What Works Clearinghouse, 2006a). Finally, *congruence between the unit of assignment and the unit of analysis* means that if the researcher assigned entire classrooms to either a treatment group or control/comparison group, then the outcomes should be analyzed by classrooms rather than by individual students (Jaycox et al., 2006; St. Pierre & Rossi, 2006). For another example, studies that assign neighboring schools to different conditions should analyze the results by schools, not

Evidence-Based Practice in School Mental Health

classrooms (Skara, Rohrbach, Sun, & Sussman, 2005; Slater & McKeown, 2004). In either case, the units should be the same.

Quasi-Experimental Designs

QEDs are studies in which the participants are not randomly assigned to a control and intervention group, but are assigned to comparison groups based on similarity. Because they typically compare one kind of intervention to another kind of intervention under real world conditions, they provide evidence for the effectiveness of the new intervention. In short, this kind of study answers the question, "What works better?" QEDs are potentially strong if they have one of three designs: baseline equating, regression discontinuity, or single-case designs.

Baseline equating means that, even though participants are not randomly assigned to a treatment or control group, there is an effort to ensure that the two groups used for comparison are equated on important demographic or outcome characteristics before treatment (e.g., number of office disciplinary referrals). For example, students may be purposely matched by gender and race as well as by grade point average if the intervention was meant to improve academic achievement. *Regression discontinuity* refers to designs where the participants are assigned to their respective groups based on a cutoff score on an outcome measure prior to the intervention (e.g., both groups of students may score in the "clinical range" on a standardized behavioral measure). *Single-case designs* involve repeated measurements of a single individual or group over different phases of intervention (e.g., baseline, intervention-A, no intervention, intervention-B, postintervention, and 3-month follow-up). If a quasi-experimental design meets at least one of the above criteria, it must then meet the last six criteria described for a randomized controlled trial.

Consistency

The consistency of an intervention's effects involves comparing findings across several studies to determine its generalizability. An intervention's generalizability is determined by looking at three characteristics: (1) variations in participants, school settings, and measured outcomes; (2) differential effects on subgroups, settings, and outcome measures; and (3) statistical reporting.

Variations

Variations in studies evaluating the same intervention can include participants, settings, or outcome measures (What Works Clearinghouse, 2006b).

Variations in participants can include different races, genders, and age groups. It is not uncommon for an intervention to be designed for one group, be found successful, and then evaluated for its success with other groups. It can be expected that some interventions may be effective for one ethnic group, but not for another (Cardemil, Reivich, Beevers, Seligman, & James, 2007). It can also be expected that the same intervention may have different effects for different genders (O'Donnell et al., 1995). Variations in settings can include rural, suburban, and urban neighborhoods; elementary, middle/junior high schools, and high schools; and general education versus special education milieus. Hennessey (2007), for example, found that students in an urban area progressed more than suburban students in her study of the Open Circle Program. A meta-analysis, for example, found that students with mild disabilities do not attain better academic or social skills in a special education than in regular classes, thus raising the question about greater inclusion for these students (Sindelar et al., 1988). Outcome measures can include cross-informant instruments, such as parent, student, and teacher measures or multimodal measures, such as observations, self-reports, and clinical interviews. Ogden and Hagen (2006), for example, used multi-informant assessments to evaluate the use of Multisystemic Treatment for youth at risk for placement outside of the home because of behavioral problems. Rahill and Teglasi (2003), however, used cross-modality evaluations to determine which of two social competency programs worked better for students with emotional disabilities.

Differential Effects

An intervention might be expected to have somewhat different levels of effectiveness based on three variables. First, the demographic characteristics of the sample may change its effectiveness. As the next chapter will make clear, clinicians will tend to adapt an intervention if it does not seem to meet the needs of their clients. Second, the setting in which the intervention was employed can make a difference. An intervention designed to work in an urban area may fall flat in a rural one. Finally, the outcome measures that were used to evaluate the intervention can change the results. For example, there are multiple standardized scales for measuring self-esteem. Which instrument is chosen can have a significant impact on the findings.

Statistical Reporting

In order to know whether a study can be generalized to other students, we must know the answers to three questions. First, we must know whether the sample was sufficiently large to adequately represent the larger population.

For example, any population of 1,000 or less should be represented by a sample at least half as large. Second, we need to know if there was any evidence of response bias—did at least half of those invited to participate actually agree to take part? Finally, did those who improve the most with the intervention share any attribute or characteristic that was not controlled during the assignment procedure?

For a summary effectiveness evaluation form, see Box 5.2. Readers who would like to see a more definitive list of criteria for effectiveness studies should see the CONSORT statement at the end of this chapter (see Internet Resources).

BOX 5.2 Effectiveness Studies Evaluation Form

	NO	YES
Relevance of the Timeframe		
1. Was the study carried out within the past 20 years?	☐	☐
2. Was the intervention logically related to the problem?	☐	☐
3. Did the study use a relevant sample (group of students)?	☐	☐
4. Was the outcome measured logically related to the problem?	☐	☐
Adequacy of Outcome Measures		
1. Was the instrument's reliability coefficient (α) $\geq$ .80?	☐	☐
2. Was the instrument's validity data provided?	☐	☐
Adequate Reporting of Data		
1. Were means and standard deviations before the intervention reported?	☐	☐
2. Were means and standard deviations after the intervention reported?	☐	☐
For RCTs		
1. Did the study specify how random assignment occurred?	☐	☐
2. Was there baseline equivalence between the control and intervention groups?	☐	☐

(continued)

	NO	YES
3. Was the overall attrition (dropout) rate less than 20%?	☐	☐
4. Were the attrition rates for the control and intervention groups similar?	☐	☐
5. Did the study document any steps to avoid contamination/diffusion effects?	☐	☐
6. Did the study document any steps to avoid teacher-intervention confound?	☐	☐
7. Did the unit of assignment match the unit of analysis?	☐	☐

For QEDs*

	NO	YES
1. Were the two treatment groups similar at the baseline?	☐	☐
2. Were participants assigned to groups based on their pretest score on an outcome measure?	☐	☐
3. For single-case designs, were multiple measurements taken during each phase?	☐	☐

Consistency

	NO	YES
1. Was the effectiveness of the intervention consistent across variations? (e.g., demographic groups, settings, or outcome measures)	☐	☐
2. Were any differential effects of the intervention reported?	☐	☐
3. Did the statistical description of the sample support generalization? (Did most of the sample agree to participate?)	☐	☐

Totals

Note: A "Yes" to any of the three questions qualifies the study as a QED; now answer the last six questions for RCTs.

Appraising Instrument Studies

In an earlier article (Raines, 2003a), I suggested that clinicians should consider adding standardized rating scales to their arsenal of assessment techniques. Three guiding principles stated there deserve repetition. First, rating scales are just part of a complete assessment process. This principle has three corollaries. Scales should be balanced by interviews with the referred student, parents, and/or teacher to gain qualitative information that scales are unlikely to uncover. The information from standardized scales should also be balanced with nonreactive measures, such as a systematic archival record search for attendance, tardiness, disciplinary referrals, extracurricular activities, grades, and test scores (Raines, 2002b). Since most rating scales focus on (or blame) the individual student, they should be balanced with an assessment of the environment as well (Heller, Holtzman, & Messick, 1982). Second, those who administer a standardized scale should be qualified to do so. Reputable test developers require that test administrators submit their qualifications before purchasing a test. Teachers will generally qualify as Level A users, school counselors and school social workers will typically qualify as Level B users, and school psychologists will qualify as Level C users because of having a graduate course in psychometrics. Third, as discussed in Chapter 3, school-related personnel are required to take a strengths-based approach. Scales that only focus on negative symptoms or pathological states have no place in the school environment. Unfortunately, this requirement alone will significantly reduce the number of clinical measures that can be employed.

Greenhalgh (2006) correctly observes that good assessment measures should have five key characteristics. These are sensitivity, specificity, positive predictive value, negative predictive value, and accuracy. Let us address each one in order. *Sensitivity* addresses the question "How good is this instrument at identifying students who have this problem?" In other words, it aims to get the "true positive" rate—all of those who really have the problem are identified by the assessment measure. Sensitivity is usually determined by employing a test of validity, comparing the results of one test with the results of a widely accepted standard. *Specificity* addresses the question, "How good is this instrument at screening out students who do not have this problem?" In other words, it aims to get the "true negative" rate—all of those who really do not have the problem are excluded by the measure. Both sensitivity and specificity tell us about how well the instrument works in large groups. *Positive predictive value* addresses the question, "If a student is identified by the instrument, what is the probability that he/she actually has the problem?" In other words, it aims to obtain the posttest probability that the test identifies the right youth. *Negative predictive value* addresses the question, "If a student is screened out by the instrument, what is the probability that he/she really does not have the problem?" In other words, it aims to obtain the posttest probability that the test screens out the right youth. Both predictive values tell us how well the instrument works for the individual student. Finally, *accuracy* addresses the question, "Does the instrument correctly identify those students with the problem *and* correctly screen out those who do not have the problem?" In other words, it aims to be both sensitive and specific for large groups and balance positive predictive value with negative predictive value for individuals.

With these goals in mind, let us proceed to identifying 10 questions for assessment measure studies (Greenhalgh, 2006; Raines, 2003a). First and foremost, is the instrument relevant to school-related problems? *Relevance* in this context refers to the rating scale's application to problems that create an adverse effect on a child's ability to learn in school. Tests developed solely for adults might be able to be used for some adolescents, but they are probably inappropriate for children. Second, was the instrument tested for reliability? *Reliability* is a precondition of validity and strives for consistent results. It is typically measured one of three ways. Inter-rater reliability is established when independent evaluators rate behavior in similar ways, such as parents rating the same child. Test-retest reliability is established when respondents score similarly over time (e.g., 2 weeks apart). Split-half reliability is established when scores on one half of an instrument are similar to scores on the other half (e.g., even items vs. odd items). Reliability is usually expressed in terms of a correlation coefficient ranging from 0 to 1. Coefficients less than .80 are considered substandard (Wasserman & Bracken, 2002). Third, was the instrument tested for validity? *Validity* depends on reliability and strives to accurately measure the desired construct. It is also typically measured one of three ways. Content validity refers to whether each item relates to the concept being measured. A panel of experts determines whether the items cover both the breadth and depth of the concept. Criterion validity refers to the relationship between the instrument and an external standard. External standards may be either another well-established instrument or subscale (i.e., concurrent validity) or a future performance. For example, a new depression scale might be compared to the Beck Depression Inventory or hope to predict those who would attempt suicide. Construct validity is the highest form of validity and refers to whether the scale measures what it purports to measure. This is accomplished only through repeated studies across multiple populations. Self-esteem, for example, is a multifaceted concept, including academic, behavioral, social, and physical attributes. Fourth, was the instrument piloted on a broad spectrum of participants? *Diversity* concerns include age, gender, race-ethnicity, and disability status. Wasserman & Bracken (2002) argue that questions that disadvantage one group over another should be discarded. The instrument must also be tried out on a range of youth, including some who have the target problem and some who do not. This is crucial for determining the positive or negative prediction value of the rating scale. Fifth, did the developers take measures to avoid bias? *Bias* can occur in three ways. Workup bias occurs when only those who are identified as having the problem are given the concurrent instrument. Expectation bias occurs when a scale administrator thinks they know what the results should be and subtly (and sometimes unconsciously) influence the findings. Bias is therefore avoided when all participants are treated the same and all administrators are blind to the intended results. Language bias occurs when the instructions or sample items are difficult to understand. School-based professionals work with students with low reading ability or parents with limited English proficiency on a regular basis. Language that is too sophisticated will actually bias the results. Sixth, were percent statistics provided for the instrument's sensitivity? Remember that sensitivity is the ability of the scale to determine who has the problem. The more severe or dangerous the problem, the higher we may want sensitivity to be—even if it results in many false positives. For example, we might want an instrument that identifies potential school shooters to be very sensitive, but we would still want to take these findings with a grain of salt and do a complete assessment. Seventh, were percent statistics provided for the instrument's specificity? Remember that specificity is the ability of the scale to screen out those who do not have the problem. The more embarrassing the problem, the higher we may want specificity to be—even if it results in many false negatives. For example, we might want an instrument that identifies children with elimination disorders to be very specific so that we would recommend only a few students to receive urological or gastroenterological examinations. Eighth, does the scale take steps to reduce response bias? *Response bias* is the tendency to answer questions in a predisposed manner (Kamphaus & Frick, 2002). It usually occurs in two different ways. Students filling out a self-report measure are likely to give socially desirable responses, making themselves look as good as possible. On the other hand, third parties who want to ensure that the student qualifies for services may be tempted to give socially undesirable responses to make the child look as problematic as possible. Typical solutions are to either have some irrelevant items thrown in the mix of questions (e.g., "I brush my teeth after every meal.") or to vary the direction of the response category, so that a 5 may denote adaptive behavior on one item, but denote maladaptive behavior on another. These items are then scored on a separate scale to warn clinicians to view the results warily. Ninth, has the study provided a "normal range" for results? *Normal range* refers to the set of scores that are regarded as both ordinary and acceptable. Usually this is expressed in terms of the participant's score being normal or near normal. Finally, has the study identified a clinical cut score? *Clinical cut scores* are usually the upper limit for the normal range, typically set anywhere between one and two standard deviations from the mean or average. In a normal (symmetrical) bell-shaped curve (see Figure 5.3), this means that anywhere from 16% to 2.5% of the population will be considered at risk for having the problem (Feil et al., 2005). In problem-based scales, clinicians look for scores at least a standard deviation above the mean; while in strengths-based scales, clinicians look for scores at least a standard deviation below the mean. The closer the clinical cut scores are to the mean, the more sensitive the results, while further away from the mean, cut scores lead to more specific results (Cowell, Gross, McNaughton, Ailey, & Fogg, 2005; Hussey & Guo, 2003). Ideally, clinical cut scores are subjected to a criterion validity check. The ultimate aim of identifying the instrument's sensitivity, specificity, and clinical cut score is that the clinician can then calculate the likelihood ratios to determine whether to utilize a given rating scale.

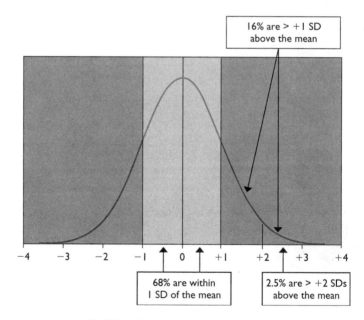

FIGURE 5.3. Normal bell-shaped curve with standard deviations (SD).

Evidence-Based Practice in School Mental Health

For a summary instrument evaluation form, see Box 5.3. Readers who would like a more definitive list of criteria should see the STARD initiative at the end of this chapter (see Internet Resources).

Appraising Cohort Studies

School-based professionals often see children who are facing some kind of harmful situation. Situations beyond their control include exposure to parental alcoholism and drug use, child abuse and neglect, lead-based paint, or parental mental health issues. Experiences within their control include alcohol and drug use, bullying, eating disorders, and sexual activity. All of these have potential long-term consequences and sequelae. Risk questions are usually examined through cohort studies because of the ethical complications of deliberately exposing children to dangerous conditions. In a cohort study, researchers identify a group of children who experienced

---

BOX 5.3 Instrument Study Evaluation Form

	NO	YES
1. Is the instrument relevant to school-related problems?	☐	☐
2. Did the study report a reliability coefficient (α) $\geq$ .80?	☐	☐
3. Did the study test the instrument for validity?	☐	☐
4. Was the instrument piloted on a broad spectrum of participants?	☐	☐
5. Did the developers take steps to avoid bias?	☐	☐
6. Does the study provide a percentage for sensitivity for the test?	☐	☐
7. Does the study provide a percentage for specificity for the test?	☐	☐
8. Does the study take precautions against response bias?	☐	☐
9. Does the study provide a "normal range" for test results?	☐	☐
10. Does the study provide a clinical cut score?	☐	☐

Totals

---

a harmful situation and another similar group of children who were not exposed to the adverse event (Levine et al., 1994).

Cohort studies can be either retrospective or prospective. In prospective cohort studies, both groups are followed in a longitudinal study that takes a variety of outcome measures at regular intervals. These intervals may range from every year to every 5 years (e.g., Guxens, Nebot, & Ariza, 2007; Smith, Ireland, & Thornberry, 2005). In retrospective cohort studies, large samples are surveyed about past adverse experiences and then differences between the groups are determined (e.g., Dube et al., 2006). Regardless of the subtype, it is important to remember that without a control group, causation cannot be determined—only correlations can be noted (Coffey, Carlin, Lynskey, Patton, & Ismail, 2004). Research consumers, therefore, must read results cautiously and consider whether potentially confounding factors such as economic deprivation have been controlled (Ensinger, Hanson, Riley, & Juon, 2003).

Levine et al. (1994) identify five essential questions to ask about cohort studies and imply one more. First and foremost, how similar were the comparison groups other than on the target risk factor? The more the two groups varied in terms of age, race, gender, socioeconomic status, or other potential intervening variables, the greater the threat to internal validity. Second, were the two groups measured in the same way as related to both adverse exposure and subsequent outcomes? Different measurement techniques can lead to incomparable results that may invalidate the study. Third, was the follow-up period long enough for the potential consequences to become evident? Some sequelae to toxic experiences do not show up until years or even decades later. For example, childhood sexual abuse has been shown to later affect attitudes toward and behavior in marriage (Cherlin, Burton, Hurt, & Purvin, 2004; Larson & Lamont, 2005). While longer follow-up periods allow for more intervening variables to occur, shorter follow-up periods risk a lack of sufficient time for the true costs to be apparent. Fourth, did the comparison groups have a similar rate of attrition? It is inevitable that some participants will be lost over a long prospective cohort study, but if the groups lose members at different rates (and death is not a potential outcome of the risk factor), then a confounding influence may be at work. Fifth, is there a dose-response gradient? A *dose-response gradient* is a positive correlation between the amount of exposure and the amount of the effect. For example, many children have lived in houses built prior to 1978, when use of lead-based paint was no longer allowed, so one might expect that the higher their blood lead levels the greater the harm. When scientists examined the evidence, this is exactly what they found. Children with low lead levels had smaller impairments in intelligence, reaction time, visual-motor integration, fine motor skills, attention, and off-task behavior than children with high lead levels (Chiodo, Jacobson, & Jacobson, 2004). In a long-term study, Fergusson, Horwood, and Lynskey (1997) found that children with higher lead levels had poorer reading ability, were more often to dropout of school, and did worse on standardized tests. Studies that can quantify the amount of exposure to the adverse circumstance are more likely to determine the dose-dependent response. Finally, does the study provide the relative risk? *Relative risk* is the ratio of the adverse effect in the exposed group when divided by the risk of the adverse effect in the unexposed group. Values greater than 1 represent an increased risk for the exposed group. For example, Cooper and Speece (1988) examined the relative risk for children with poor work-related skills (i.e., disorganization, distractibility, and noncompliance) to be referred to a teacher assistance team. The relative risk was 23.1, meaning that these children were 23 times more likely than their peers to be referred.

For a summary cohort evaluation form, see Box 5.4. Readers who would like a more definitive list of criteria should examine the STROBE initiative at the end of this chapter (see Internet Resources).

BOX 5.4 Cohort Study Evaluation Form

	NO	YES
1. Were the comparison groups similar regarding traits other than the risk factor?	☐	☐
2. Did the two groups receive the same measurements for both risk exposure and adverse effects?	☐	☐
3. Was the follow-up period long enough to allow the adverse effects to show up?	☐	☐
4. Did the two groups have a similar attrition (dropout) rates?	☐	☐
5. Did the study measure the dose-response relationship?	☐	☐
6. Did the study calculate the relative risk ratio?	☐	☐
Totals		

Quantitative Surveys

Greenhalgh (2006) has identified 10 crucial questions for evaluating quantitative survey research. First, was a survey questionnaire the most appropriate means of answering the question? She uses an example that is relevant to school-based practitioners. If the question is about the prevalence of asthma in school-aged children, then a survey of their parents may not be the best way to answer the question for three reasons. The parent may not know the child has asthma, the parent may think the child has asthma when they really do not, or they may choose to withhold information that they perceive as socially embarrassing. She recommends that a better method would be a systematic content analysis of medical records. Second, was the survey questionnaire reliable and valid? Remember that reliability is about consistency, a prerequisite for validity. Surveys are standardized in an effort to increase reliability; any deviation from the standard form decreases the reliability. Validity addresses accuracy—the questionnaire must measure what it intends to measure. If one were to ask obese children how much they ate in an average day, you would not discover how much they ate, but how much they admitted they ate. This subtle difference may be quite significant! It is important to remember that most surveys are self-report instruments that may reflect a desire for social desirability. Third, what was the form and content of the questionnaire? Form issues include the form's appealing qualities, its length, and its terminology. Forms that are written in 10-point font, or more than two pages long, or with lots of big words can be off-putting for children or adolescents. It is especially important in research related to children that the questions be written in simple language that children can easily understand. Content issues include whether the items were closed (respondents choose from limited option) or open (respondents write whatever they please); whether some items were deliberately reversed so that participants could not simply "strongly agree" that they loved school. Greenhalgh also warns against "weasel words" in questions, such as commonly, many, some, or usually. These words are simply too ambiguous to obtain clear answers. Fourth, were the instructions clear? Unlike interviews where researchers can explain the material and answer questions, surveys get only one chance to communicate with participants. Ideally, they identify the purpose of the research, give an assurance of anonymity or confidentiality (never both), possible ways to contact the researcher, a stamped addressed return envelope, instructions about how to complete the survey, and a small token of appreciation (e.g., a pen or pencil). Fifth, was the questionnaire adequately piloted? Even surveys that have been checked and double-checked for grammar and spelling cannot predict cognitive or emotional reactions of the respondents. Well-constructed questionnaires, then, are piloted on a similar set of respondents; they provide details about how the piloting was done, and what changes were made as a result of the piloting exercise. Sixth, did the survey use a probability sample? Researchers rarely have sufficient funds to do a population study that involves sending a questionnaire to the entire group affected by the issue, so they resort to using samples. There two broad types of samples. *Probability samples* use a randomized strategy that provides an equal chance for every person in the population to be selected. For example, in telephone surveys, researchers often use random digit dialing to select which members of the population are selected to participate. *Nonprobability samples*, however, use a strategy that provides each person with an unknown chance of being selected. Haphazard samples, for example, often select the first set of people who are available at the time. While this may seem fairly random, it allows for an unknown variable to be part of the selection process as when the first students available for a survey on anxiety are constantly worried that they might be late! Seventh, was the response rate at least 50%? Even the most well-designed surveys can fail to obtain valid results because of inadequate response rates. Low response rates are usually an indication that a nonresponse bias exists. A nonresponse bias occurs when nonresponders differ from responders in an unknown but important characteristic. For example, an Internet survey regarding school service providers' use of electronic databases may inadvertently create a nonresponse bias due to the fact that those who are less computer savvy may not respond (Braithwaite, Emery, de Lusignan, & Sutton, 2003). Ways to increase the response rate include personalization, offering incentives for completion and return, keeping the content concise, and addressing interesting topics (Van Kenhove, Wijnen, & DeWulf, 2002). Eighth, are the correct statistical tests used to analyze the data? There are two broad categories of statistical tests (Weinbach & Grinnell, 2007). *Parametric tests* require that at least one variable (usually the outcome) is measured at an interval or ratio level, that the dependent (or outcome) variable is normally distributed in the population, and that the cases are randomly selected. The most common parametric tests include one-way ANOVA, Pearson's *r*, and *t*-tests. *Nonparametric tests* are designed for research in which the above requirements cannot be met. The most common nonparametric tests include chi-square, Kendall's tau, Spearman's rho, and Wilcoxon sign (see Box 5.5). If the tests used in the survey do not sound familiar to readers, they should review the results with caution. Ninth, are both nonsignificant and significant findings reported? Some authors believe that scholarly journals are interested only in significant results and do not report nonsignificant results even when they are highly relevant to the research question. They seem to believe that nonsignificant = insignificant, and this is incorrect. An important caveat to insert at this point is a warning about data dredging (see Box 5.6). Finally, have the findings been placed in the larger context? An important part of the Discussion section is to return to the literature review and place the new findings in the context of previous findings. Generally, the new results will confirm, complement, or contradict the old results. This is also the place for researchers to identify the limitations of their study. Since there is no such entity as perfect research, the absence of a paragraph on limitations should raise readers' suspicions.

For a summary survey evaluation form, see Box 5.7. Readers who would like a more definitive list of criteria should examine the STROBE initiative at the end of this chapter (see Internet Resources).

BOX 5.5 Parametric and Nonparametric Alternatives

COMMON PARAMETRIC TESTS	NONPARAMETRIC ALTERNATIVES
Paired *t*-test	Wilcoxon sign
Independent *t*-test	Kolmogorov-Smirnov or Mann-Whitney *U*
One-sample *t*-test	Chi-square goodness of fit
One-way ANOVA (analysis of variance)	Kruskal-Wallis
Pearson's *r* (Pearson's correlation)	Kendall's tau or Spearman's rho

---

Evidence-Based Practice in School Mental Health

BOX 5.6 Data Dredging: The Desperate Search for Significance

Supervising hundreds of graduate research projects has taught me to beware of the ubiquitous phenomenon of data dredging. Data dredging occurs when researchers (students and professors alike) have collected an enormous amount of data that is then subjected to dozens of statistical tests in order to find some result that is statistically significant. It is usually born of a disappointment in finding any significant result to the primary research question. Having failed in their primary mission, these researchers embark on a crusade to find something of lasting value in their data. There are two problems with this approach. First, they falsely believe that significance = importance. These two terms may be synonymous in other fields, but not in the field of statistics! Finding a nonsignificant relationship may be very important, such as when the Institute of Medicine (2004) found no relationship between thimerosal and autism. Second, mere chance alone will virtually guarantee that if enough tests are run on a sufficiently large data set, then at least one test will demonstrate statistical significance. Since the study was never designed to test this relationship, the supposedly significant result will most likely prove spurious when subjected to research that is designed to test the relationship. The general rule of thumb, then, is that researchers should run only those statistical tests that are designed to answer the research question or hypothesis. Guyatt, Sackett, and Cook (1994) offer the following tests for studies that discover different results for different subgroups. First, is the difference large (e.g., more than 25%)? Second, is it unlikely to occur by chance (e.g., $p < .01$)? Third, was the analysis driven by a hypothesis before the research was conducted? Fourth, were there only a few (e.g., less than five) subgroup analyses conducted? Finally, have the differences been replicated in other studies? If a research study fails any of these criteria, then the results should be viewed with suspicion.

BOX 5.7 Survey Evaluation Form

	NO	YES
1. Was the survey the best way to answer the research question?	☐	☐
2. Was the survey instrument both reliable and valid?	☐	☐
3. Was the survey's length and language appropriate to its purpose?	☐	☐
4. Were the survey instructions clear and appropriate to the participants?	☐	☐
5. Was the survey piloted before the large survey was initiated?	☐	☐
6. Did the survey use a probability (random) sample?	☐	☐
7. Was the response rate at least 50%?	☐	☐
8. Did the survey employ the appropriate statistical tests?	☐	☐
9. Are both nonsignificant and significant findings reported?	☐	☐
10. Did the authors place the new findings in context with previous findings?	☐	☐

Totals

Qualitative Studies

Appraising qualitative research studies requires a different set of criteria than the ones used to judge quantitative research. This is because it is essentially unfair to hold qualitative researchers to standards that they never had any intention of achieving. While a few qualitative studies might hold positivist assumptions (Giacomini & Cook, 2000), most will take a social constructivist or interpretive approach (Raines, 2008). This means that instead of talking about rigor, qualitative researchers prefer the term trustworthiness, meaning the practitioners must be able to trust the results enough to act upon them (Lincoln & Guba, 2000). For each of the major terms regarding

QUANTITATIVE TERMS	QUALITATIVE TERMS
Rigor	Trustworthiness
Objectivity	Confirmability
Reliability	Dependability
Internal validity	Credibility
External validity	Transferability

rigor in quantitative research there is a corresponding term for qualitative research (see Box 5.8). *Confirmability* asks, "Can these findings be confirmed by independent observers?" For example, a qualitative researcher should provide details about how the interpretive codes were created and revised using either experts or the participants themselves. *Dependability* asks, "Can these results be regarded as congruent with the context and characteristics of the participants?" A qualitative researcher, for instance, should provide in-depth descriptions about the participants and places of the study. *Credibility* asks, "Can these findings be regarded as truthful?" For example, credibility is enhanced if the research occasionally repeats a question to see if the same answer is given again in a later interview. *Transferability* asks, "Can these results be generalized outside of the current context?" A qualitative researcher may cautiously apply the findings to other members of the population that share proximal similarity with the study's participants (Shadish, 1995). For an extensive list of criteria for qualitative studies, see Raines's (2008) chapter in *Social Work Research and Evaluation: Foundations for Evidence-Based Practice*, 8th ed. (New York: Oxford University Press).

Choosing the Best Intervention

After practitioners have investigated the evidence (Chapter 4) and appraised the evidence (Chapter 5), it is necessary to choose the intervention that we wish to employ. There are two fundamental tests at this juncture. First, which intervention meets the four requirements for "best evidence" (Figure 4.2)? Second, which intervention enjoys the highest level of scientific support (Figure 4.1)? The best intervention, then, is a combination of client-environment fit and a matter of scientific support. The exact amount of weight to be placed on each one is part of the art of evidence-based practice (Pollio, 2006).

Summary

In this chapter, I addressed five types of studies that result from the five types of questions discussed in Chapter 3. First, effectiveness studies covered both prevention and intervention questions. These studies were identified as the type of study that practitioners will want to use the most. They included both secondary and primary research. I began by describing the process of systematic reviews and the potential problems that could occur. Then I discussed the two types of primary research that meets the U.S. Department of Education's definition of scientifically based research—randomized controlled trials and quasi-experiment designs. Both were appraised using the Department of Education's three broad criteria: relevance, strength, and consistency. Second, assessment studies involve measurement of a problem. There are 10 basic questions to employ in appraising these studies. Third, cohort studies examine risk questions. There were six essential questions used to evaluate these. Fourth, quantitative and qualitative surveys result from description questions. Finally, I described how to choose the best intervention to employ with one's clients, using a combination of factors. Chapter 6 will discuss how to adapt and apply an intervention with one's clients.

Suggested Reading

1. Bossuyt, P. M., Reitsma, J. B., Bruns, D. E., Gatsonis, C. A., Glasziou, P. P., Irwig, L. M., et al. (2003). Towards complete and accurate reporting of studies of diagnostic accuracy: The STARD initiative. *British Medical Journal, 326*, 41–44.

2. Katrak, P., Bialocerkowski, A. E., Massy-Westropp, N., Kumar, V. S. S., & Grimmer, K. A. (2004). A systematic review of the content of critical appraisal tools. *BMC Medical Research Methodology, 4* (22), Retrieved on May 19, 2007 from: http://www.pubmedcentral.nih.gov/picrender.fcgi?artid=521688&blobtype=pdf

3. Moher, D., Cook, J. C., Eastwood, S., Olkin, I., Rennie, D., & Stroup, D. F. (1999). Improving the quality of reports of meta-analyses of randomised controlled trials: The QUORUM statement. *Lancet, 354*, 1896–1900.

4. Vlayen, J., Aertgeerts, B., Hannes, K., Sermeus, W., & Ramaekers, D. (2005). A systematic review of appraisal tools for clinical practice guidelines: Multiple similarities and one common deficit. *International Journal for Quality in Health Care, 17* (3), 235–242.

Internet Resources

Appraisal of Guidelines Research and Evaluation (AGREE)
http://www.agreecollaboration.org/

Centre for Evidence Based Medicine's Levels of Evidence
http://www.cebm.net/index.aspx?o=1025

CONSORT Guidelines
http://www.consort-statement.org/

National Health Service's Public Health Resource Unit's Appraisal Tools
http://www.phru.nhs.uk/pages/PHD/resources.htm

Quack Watch
http://www.quackwatch.com/

QUORUM Statement Checklist for Systematic Reviews
http://www.consort-statement.org/QUOROM.pdf

STARD Initiative
http://www.stard-statement.org/website%20stard/

STROBE Initiative
http://www.strobe-statement.org/

SUNY Medical Library Tutorials on Evaluating Studies
http://servers.medlib.hscbklyn.edu/ebmdos/5toc.htm

6

Adapting and Applying the Evidence

Preview

The purpose of this chapter is to help school-based practitioners adapt and apply empirically supported treatments (ESTs) introduced in Chapter 4 and appraised in Chapter 5. Perhaps the biggest complaint about evidence-based practice is that it supposedly turns therapists into technicians and clients into widgets. Before we move on to address the issue of adapting and applying the evidence, we will confront this misconception directly. We will identify the reasons to adapt an EST, and then examine three critical issues in adapting ESTs. First, we will discuss how to adapt EST to the developmental level of the child. This will incur consideration of therapeutic engagement, affective education, cognitive capacities, homework tasks, and parental involvement. Second, we will address cultural sensitivity for the major racial-ethnic groups in American schools, such as Hispanics, African Americans, and Asians. Finally, we will consider the contextual constraints of delivering services in a host institution where the primary concern is education, not mental health. This entails conceptualizing the delivery of services as a three-part funnel devoted to universal prevention delivered through educational personnel, selected short-term group interventions, and indicated intensive individual treatment.

The Science and Art of Therapy

The argument on art versus science goes something like this, "Clinical practice is an art because the interpersonal relationship evolves like a dance that is more emotional than logical" (Nelson, Steele, & Mize, 2006). One of the consistent criticisms of EBP is that it assumes a medical model that is strictly linear and top-down: patients come for consultation; they are diagnosed, given treatment, outcomes are evaluated, and the patient goes home (Pollio, 2006). Anyone who has done psychotherapy knows that clients often seek consultation for a surface problem and receive help for that one before revealing a deeper problem and then working on the new one. Like peeling an onion, people choose to reveal their problems gradually as trust is developed in a collaborative relationship. As Ackerman et al. (2001) conclude, "Concurrent use of empirically supported relationships and ESTs tailored to the patient's disorder and characteristics is likely to generate the best outcomes" (p. 496). The model of evidence-based practice discussed in this book is not linear, but recursive (see Figure 2.1). As practitioners deal with one problem in an iterative evidence-based process, they actually generate practice-based evidence for the next cycle. Good therapists constantly rechoose and refine their intervention strategies over the life of the change effort. As Pollio (2006) states,

> Clinicians need to be willing to combine the existing evidence from the literature with their own analysis of the dynamics of the situation to guide specific responses and strategies to situations. This is perhaps the clearest example of the art of EBP. (p. 228)

Step 4 in the process (Figure 2.1) is what this chapter is all about and it involves the integration of scientifically based research and interpersonal artful application. As Carolyn Saari (1986), former editor of the *Clinical Social Work Journal*, states, "The practice of clinical social work is neither an art nor a science, since such a division is artificial—it is both" (p. 12).

Furthermore, the process is not top-down; it assumes a collaborative relationship where practitioners are familiar with more than one method to help a client (Kaslow, 2002; Nelson, 2002; Shapiro, Welker, & Jacobson, 1997) and proffer informed choices about how to do so. We will be discussing this in more detail in the chapter on ethics.

Adapting and Applying the Evidence

A repeated question in evidence-based medicine is, "What are the results and will they help me in caring for my patients?" (Guyatt, Sackett, & Cook, 1994; Jaeschke, Guyatt, & Sackett, 1994; Richardson & Detsky, 1995). This is a relevant question for all helping professionals. The literature usually provides two reasons for adapting the evidence, to which we will add a third that is specific to schools.

Evidence-Based Practice in School Mental Health

The most commonly cited reason for adapting the evidence is client complexity (or in medical terms, comorbidity). Since human beings are complex creatures and not manufactured widgets, most clinicians advocate that one size will not fit all (Ruscio & Holohan, 2006). Furthermore, any visitor to a junior high school will readily admit that even children who are roughly the same age develop socially and mature physically at vastly different rates (Manning, 2002). Guyatt et al. (1994) put the problem of applying prevention and intervention effectiveness studies this way.

> The first issue to address is how confident you are that you can apply the results to a particular patient or patients in your practice. If the patient would have been enrolled in the study had she been there—that is, she meets all the inclusion criteria and doesn't violate any of the exclusion criteria—there is little question that the results are applicable. If this is not the case, and she would have been ineligible for the study, *judgment is required.* (p. 61, emphasis added)

It has been estimated that the average randomized controlled trial excludes 30% to 70% of potential participants (Westen, 2006); this means that there is a large chance that clinical judgment is needed to determine whether or not to apply the research to a given client. For example, in a National Institute of Mental Health (NIMH) study on the treatment of adolescent depression (March et al., 2004), researchers excluded all the adolescents who were abusing drugs, absent more than 25% of the time from school over the previous 2 months, or diagnosed with bipolar disorder or severe conduct disorder (Westen, 2006a). While these might seem reasonable precautions to ensure that the study enrolled only adolescents with depression (and no severe comorbid disorders), the study also makes this caveat:

> Patients were excluded for dangerousness to self or others if they had been hospitalized for dangerousness within 3 months of consent or were deemed by a cross-site panel to be "high risk" because of a suicide attempt requiring medical attention within 6 months, clear intent or an active plan to commit suicide, or suicidal ideation with a disorganized family unable to guarantee adequate safety monitoring. (p. 808)

Despite the exclusion of a wide range of confounding factors and the most severe cases, the study did manage to include a large number of total participants (439 adolescents) that was quite diverse—54.4% female, 73.8% White, 12.5% African American, and 8.9% Hispanic. Concurrent diagnoses included 15.3% with generalized anxiety disorder, 13.7% with attention deficit/hyperactivity disorder, 13.2% with oppositional defiant disorder, 10.7% with social phobia, and 10.5% with dysthymia (Treatment for Adolescents with Depression Study Team, 2005). In short, this large NIMH-funded study was able to evaluate four treatment conditions for adolescents with depression: pharmacotherapy with fluoxetine, cognitive behavioral therapy (CBT), the combination, and a placebo drug. Outcome evaluation occurred after 12 weeks, a suitable time period for most interventions within a public school year (March, Silva, & Vitiello, 2006). The results indicated that most adolescents (12–17) were better off with a combination of fluoxetine and CBT than either intervention alone or the placebo therapy. Guyatt et al. (1994) recommend that an even better approach than rigid application of the study's exclusionary or inclusionary criteria is to ask the question, "Is there a compelling reason why the results should *not* be applied to the client?" If one cannot be found, then clinicians should go ahead and apply the intervention.

Westen (2006b) raises the interesting issue of exactly what should be applied—a manualized empirically supported treatment (EST) or the principals upon which the empirically supported treatment is based (e.g., cognitive behavioral theory and techniques). While there are some manuals adapted to meet the needs of minority clients, such as CBT for Latino immigrants with depression (Stirman, Crits-Christoph, & DeRubeis, 2004), manuals seem to have the reputation that they assume that one size fits all. Kendall, Chu, Gifford, Hayes, and Nauta (1998), however, have this to say about their own manual:

> Perhaps it goes without saying that a manual requires implementation with good clinical skills… . The rampant misunderstanding of treatment manuals, along with the overzealous assumptions about the potency of manuals, combined to reaffirm the need to explicitly state that a manual operationalizes the treatment but *practitioners must be able to breathe life into a manual.* (p. 197, emphasis added)

Kendall and his colleagues seem to be admitting that even manualized ESTs require both science and art. Once clinicians understand that Westen's either-or dichotomy is no longer valid, then the real question becomes,

"How do I adapt what I find in the literature to make the intervention a good fit?" The remainder of this chapter will address three pertinent issues: developmental level, cultural sensitivity, and school-based contextual constraints.

Developmental Level

Since most intervention research started with adults, then adolescents, and finally children, the most common concern of school-based practitioners is whether the intervention needs to be adapted for the developmental level of the child (Nock, Goldman, Wang, & Albano, 2004). It is important to remember that age and developmental stage do not always go hand in hand. Some gifted children will be advanced for their age and some low achievers will be behind for their age (Gowan, 2004; Hanline, Milton, & Phelps, 2007; van Baar, Ultee, Gunning, Soepatmi, & de Leeuw, 2006). Ideally, children's developmental level will be assessed prior to the intervention (Schultz, Selman, & LaRusso, 2003).

For example, CBT has common elements that are used across age-groups, including an agenda, goal-setting, a collaborative process, and homework, but given the sometimes radical differences in cognitive ability, CBT must be adapted for children (Barrett, 2000; Holmbeck, O'Mahar, Abad, Colder, & Updegrove, 2006; Piacentini & Bergman, 2001). While some CBT manuals have been explicitly designed for children (e.g., Kendall & Hedtke, 2006) and adults with disabilities (e.g., Taylor & Novaco, 2005), Kingery et al. (2006) warn that simply employing one is not good enough.

> Although chronological age provides a general framework for a child's expected abilities, it is important for clinicians to understand a particular child's level of cognitive, social, and emotional development, as these skills can greatly impact his or her ability to effectively participate in, and ultimately benefit from treatment. When implementing manualized CBT for anxious youth, clinicians must be knowledgeable, creative, and flexible—from implementing creative strategies for engaging youth in treatment and modifying various components of CBT to fit a child's developmental level, to involving family members and school personnel in the treatment process. (p. 264)

Kingery and colleagues then discuss four common issues in adapting CBT to the child's level of development: engagement, affective education, cognitive restructuring, and family involvement. Two more common developmental issues will be added: self-determination and homework. For specific examples of adaptation for individual clients, see Box 6.1.

Engagement

Unlike adults and some adolescents, children almost never seek help for themselves. They are referred by parents, teachers, or other well-meaning adults. Engagement is improved when clinicians focus on engagement prior to intervention (McKay, Nudelman, McCadem, & Gonzalez, 1996). Three techniques are especially useful. First, since children often feel like they don't have a choice about attending therapy, it is important to give them some control of the parameters. Individual students can determine (within limits) when they meet (i.e., which classes they'll miss) and student groups can select the name and norms of the group (Kingery et al., 2006). Second, since children often look for cues from parents about how to respond to therapeutic intervention, specifically focusing on the parents' support for sessions can be useful (Miller & Feeny, 2003; Waldron, Kern-Jones, Turner, Peterson, & Ozechowski, 2007). For children, this may mean that a parent attends the first session with the child, while for adolescents it might be preferable for parents to have their own orientation to the work ahead and their role in facilitating therapeutic compliance. Third, clinicians can normalize the discussion of sensitive subjects, such as substance abuse, sexual behavior, violence, and peer relationships, by generalizing, "Many of the kids that come here talk about such topics as..." Another possibility is the use of an instrument that serves as a broad screen of sensitive student concerns (Elliott et al., 2004). Thereafter, clinicians can let students determine the order in which each of these topics would be addressed (Mithaug & Mithaug, 2003). When a topic is deemed too taboo for discussion, a conversation can deal with what makes some subjects more taboo than others and what it might be like to break the taboo without actually doing so. In general, children need to feel like they have some control over the process and that their rights to some degree of self-determination will not be abrogated.

Affective Education

CBT requires participants to both identify a wide range of emotional states and move toward emotional regulation. The identification of *emotional states* involves providing children help in learning the names of feelings prior to being expected to discuss them. This actually involves two skills that many adults take for granted. The first is the ability to name categorical affects, such as happy, sad, angry, surprised, disgusted, and afraid (Ribordy, Camras,

Evidence-Based Practice in School Mental Health

BOX 6.1 Adapting Treatment Manuals

Weisz (2004), a strong proponent of ESTs, applied four different treatment manuals to real cases. He then carefully tracked the adaptations necessary in each case. They provide clues to the kinds of adaptations that are routinely necessary.

CASE	MANUAL	ADAPTATIONS
Sean, 9 years old, anxiety disorder	The Coping Cat Manual (Kendall et al., 1990). See Web resource: www.childanxiety.org	1. Therapist must avoid role of comforter/protector and allow the child to face challenging exposures. 2. For resistant children, break exposure tasks into components (talking in front of two people rather than a group) or making it fun (imitating Jim Carey or Adam Sandler). 3. For children who cannot identify nonanxious thoughts, have them identify their favorite hero and how they might think. 4. Avoid using the manual woodenly and pay attention to the therapeutic relationship (Kendall et al., 1998).

(continued)

CASE	MANUAL	ADAPTATIONS
Megan, 13 years old, depression	The Coping with Depression Course for Adolescents (CDW-A) (Clarke, Lewisohn, & Hops, 1990). See web resources: http://www. kpchr.org or http://www.feelbetter.org	1. Follow up with no-shows and do problem solving to address transportation, schedule conflicts, or social anxiety. Aim for a four-session commitment before an informed decision. 2. For adolescents with co-occurring problems, either use another EST in combination or apply the same CDW-A principles to the other problem. 3. Skill building occurs quickly, so therapist must use initial session for relationship building only. 4. Adolescents may be too pessimistic to try, so therapists must become cheerleaders and encourage students to look at the exercises as experiments. Use praise and rewards liberally. 5. Adolescent may not do the homework, so try to catch them doing some pleasant activity or thinking and reward those accidental efforts.
Kevin, 8 years old, attention deficit/hyperactivity disorder	Pelham's Summer Treatment Program for ADHD (Pelham, Greiner, & Gnagy, 1998). See Web resource: http://ccf. buffalo.edu/STP.php	1. For children with co-occurring problems, individualize treatment through functional behavioral assessment and adding items to the daily report card given to parents. Add other ESTs as necessary. 2. For parents or teachers who fail to follow up with maintenance activities, conduct a functional behavioral assessment of the parent or teacher and increase contingency rewards for them. 3. For locales who do not have access to such a program, work with community-based providers to obtain funding for a summer program.

		4. The gains made in the summer program will not last without continued intervention, especially social skills training for those low in peer acceptance and study skills training for those low in academic performance.
Sal, 13 years old, conduct disorder	Behavioral Parent Training for Youth Conduct Problems (Patterson, 1976; Patterson, Reid, & Dishion, 1992).	1. For parents who say "I can't," do NOT try to convince them that they can, but empathize that then it is difficult. Offer to compartmentalize tasks or offer more support (e.g., phone calls). 2. For parents who say "I won't," do NOT try to propose different solutions, but ask parents to identify another strategy and support their efforts. 3. For parents who say "I didn't," do NOT ask if the assignment was done, but ask what they did ask their child to do during the week and how the request worked.
	Anger Control Training with Stress Inoculation (Feindler & Guttman, 1994), Anger Coping Program (Lochman, Fitzgerald, & Whidby, 1999).	1. For youths with low motivation to change because of externalizing the problem, focus on a cost-benefit analysis of a fight that lead to school suspension or grounding at home. 2. For youths who get overly aroused in role-plays, act as coach close at hand or use a peer buddy to help out. 3. For youths who disengage from problem-solving, use real-life situations (not theoretical ones) to reengage them in brainstorming alternative solutions.

Stefani, & Spaccarelli, 1988). There are many feeling charts available that enable viewers to match facial expressions to feelings. These are great for helping children recognize the feelings of others, but few children are facing a mirror when asked how they are feeling in the moment. They need to be taught about somatic clues to their affective experience (e.g., dry mouth, racing pulse, shallow breathing, and pounding chest for anxiety). The second is the ability to name affects by their level of intensity (e.g., annoyed, angry, or furious). This can be done by creating feeling thermometers for each emotion and identifying low, middle, and high intensity terms for each category affect. *Emotional regulation* involves helping children realize that they can control their emotional reactions. Children are notoriously labile when it comes to emotional control. They often externalize their own affects by blaming someone else for them (e.g., "He made me cry/laugh/mad."). These children may be helped by identifying the exaggerated facial expressions of a cartoon character or acting out feelings in an imaginary game of charades where they can demonstrate emotional control. Developing emotional regulation skills may require taking more time to practice controlled breathing and relaxation techniques.

Cognitive Restructuring

Cognitive therapy requires the meta-cognitive skill of thinking about one's own thinking. For children who are concrete and egocentric, this requires some modification. One useful technique is the use of situational cartoons with empty thought bubbles above the characters so that children can surmise for themselves what the character is thinking. For artistically inclined therapists, cartoons can be drawn on a dry-erase board. For artistically challenged therapists, cartoons can be clipped from the local paper and words inside the bubbles can be blanked out. Another useful method is to translate cognitive distortions to "thinking traps" such as "I always fail" and translate cognitive restructuring to "coping clues" such as "I can do it" (Kingery et al., 2006). Listing these on a poster board that is kept for future reference serves as a visual reminder for children apt to forget the lessons. Another possibility is to create a deck of "game cards" with various tasks and corresponding rewards based on difficulty or complexity (Miller & Feeny, 2003).

Parent Involvement

Not only do children rarely seek treatment for themselves, but legally also, they cannot consent for treatment; so involvement of parents is both an ethical and legal necessity. There are two answerable questions that the research can help practitioners to decide. First, which types of problems are best addressed by having parents collaborate in treatment? Second, what type of parent involvement works best? Let's deal with each question in order. First, the problems that are best addressed through parental involvement are the externalizing disorders, such as oppositional defiant disorder (Behan & Carr, 2000), attention deficit/hyperactivity disorder (Nolan & Carr, 2000), conduct disorders (Maughan et al., 2005), and substance abuse (Petrie, Bunn, & Byrne, 2006). This is not surprising because the child's symptoms are primarily alloplastic, affecting others more than the self. For these problems, parents are often receiving training in child management skills and positive behavioral support. Children may also receive some form of social skills training or problem-solving therapy, but parental involvement is absolutely essential for effective treatment. For example, McCart, Priester, Davies, and Azen (2006) found in their meta-analysis that behavioral parent training had a stronger effect for antisocial youth than CBT for the youth themselves. This was most pronounced, however, when the children were younger (ages 6–12). They provided two possible explanations. One possibility is that parent training worked best because younger children were more dependent on their parents than adolescents would be. The other possibility is that younger children with externalizing problems lack the meta-cognitive skills to benefit from CBT (Durlak, Fuhrman, & Lampman, 1991).

Children with internalizing disorders may also need parents to be involved on a collateral basis if they are inadvertently supporting the child's symptomatology, such as when anxious parents encourage anxious behavior on the part of their children (Kingery et al., 2006; Miller & Feeny, 2003; Nock et al., 2004) or depressed parents facilitate depression among their children (Reissland, Shepherd, & Herrera, 2003). This is also not surprising given that children often look to parents for cues about how to respond to new situations. On other occasions, there are times when parents need support because of their internalizing response to their children's externalizing disorders (Chronis, Gamble, Roberts, & Pelham, 2006). McCart et al. (2006), for example, found that parents often received side-benefits from parent training in terms of their own mental health or marital relationship.

The question of which type of parental involvement works best is also complicated. O'Halloran and Carr (2000) found that for children whose parents were undergoing separation or divorce, it was best if parental intervention was kept separate from the child's therapy. Since children may need to discuss their anger at parents or pressure due to parental triangulation in a safe venue, this type of parallel therapy makes sense. Parent-child interaction therapy seems to work best in preschool children or elementary-age children with developmental disabilities (McDiarmid & Bagner, 2005; Nixon, Sweeney, Erickson, & Touyz, 2003, 2004). Given that the primary bond at this age or developmental level is still between parent and child, this also seems sensible. As peer relationships become more important, one might reasonably expect group therapy to take precedence over family therapy. Research, however, fails to substantiate this intuitive stance. Both elementary and middle-school children have repeatedly done better with a parent-involvement component than without one (Bernstein, Layne, Egan, & Tennison, 2005; Lowry-Webster, Barrett, & Dadds, 2001; Storr, Ialongo, Kellam, & Anthony, 2002). Perhaps counterintuitive to some is the research that demonstrates that multidimensional family therapy also works best for adolescents with substance abuse disorders (Liddle et al., 2001; Rowe, Parker-Sloat, Schwartz, & Liddle, 2003; Schurink, Schippers, & de Wildt, 2004). One explanation for this may be that drug addiction can be so powerful that teenagers are unable to solve the problem on their own and need to once again depend upon the support of family members just as some forms of therapy for addicted adults recommend dependence on a higher power.

Tasks/Homework

It is common practice for CBT therapists to give homework assignments to be completed before the next session. Children, however, often regard "homework" as a loaded term. To understand why homework carries so much baggage, clinicians need to understand the current research on academic homework. The research on academic homework consistently demonstrates four facts.

First, the benefit of homework is a mixed bag. A recent meta-analysis has shown that academic homework does not necessarily lead to either better grades or improved test scores, leading many to wonder if homework is worth the hassle. Cooper, Robinson, and Patall (2006) found a positive and strong relationship between the amount of homework and student achievement, but only for adolescents, not elementary students and only for intermediate outcomes (e.g., unit tests), not for long-term outcomes (e.g., grades or standardized test scores). Second, homework is complicated by more factors than any other academic strategy (Cooper, 2001). It involves multiple actors, multiple purposes, tasks of varying quality, and impacts subsequent teaching routines (Trautwein & Köller, 2003). Third, academic homework has often been noted as a source of friction between children and parents (Cooper, 2001; Solomon, Warin, & Lewis, 2002). There are few school-related issues that lead to more triangulation of vested parties than homework (Margolis, McCabe, & Alber, 2004). Fourth, children who are referred for help with academic and behavioral issues have more difficulties doing homework than their nonreferred peers (Habbousche et al., 2001; Power, Werba, Watkins, Angelucci, & Eiraldi, 2006; Swanson & Deshler, 2003). What is the key to helping these children? Swanson and Deshler recommend moving along a continuum from teacher-guided practice to student-guided practice in four stages: (1) verbal practice where students talk about the steps involved in the strategy; (2) controlled practice and feedback where students practice using the strategy in front of others (e.g., therapist or small group) and receive constructive criticism; (3) advanced practice where students use the strategy in more difficult situations and receive feedback; and (4) generalization where students apply the strategy to new and unrehearsed situations.

It is not difficult to see the application of these principles to therapy. Children in a cognitive behavioral group for anger control might begin by talking about the steps involved in defusing a situation in which they have previously exploded in anger. Then they could do short and simple two-character role-plays meant to help them apply the steps. Next, they could do longer and more complex role-plays involving more than two characters. Finally, they could experiment with trying these steps in real-life situations, such as the playground, cafeteria, or school bus, which are often undersupervised environments (Guerra, Boxer, & Kim, 2005). The words "experiment" or "project" are preferable to homework because they do not have negative connotations and imply a hands-on activity that most children enjoy.

Self-Determination Skills

As children mature, so do their decision-making skills. Martsch (2005) compared two group applications of cognitive behavioral treatment for adjudicated male adolescents who were randomly assigned to two different treatment conditions. Youths were divided by age group (12–15 years and 15–18 years). Both treatments consisted of ten 2-hour weekly group sessions. One treatment condition was identified as "high process," meaning that there was greater emphasis on cohesion building, more leadership opportunities, and more member decision making on agenda items. The other condition was identified as "low process," meaning that there was less member-to-member dialogue, more of a didactic approach, and a preset agenda. Results indicated that the younger adolescents fared better in the low process groups while older adolescents did better in the high process groups. Martsch concluded that the older adolescents were more able to handle the more interactive and self-determined format whereas the younger adolescents needed the firmer, more structured approach.

Cultural Sensitivity

Minority groups are not well represented in the research literature. There have been relatively few systematic reviews of the effectiveness of therapy with African American (Baytop, 2006; Ward, 2007), Hispanic (Navarro, 1993), or Asian (Lei, Askeroth, Lee, Burshteyn, & Einhorn, 2004) clients. This paucity may be due to the diverse approaches to healing in non-Western cultures, such as dance, traditional healers, and herbal remedies, which Western researchers are inclined to ascribe to anthropological, religious, or placebo effects (Gielen, Fish, & Draguns, 2004). Fortunately, most of the treatments that are effective for majority youths have also been found to effective for minority youths with few differences in effect (Arnold et al., 2003; Kazdin, 2002; Pina, Silverman, Fuentes, Kurtines, & Weems, 2003). The evidence on cultural adaptation is mixed. Kumpfer, Alvarado, Smith, and Bellamy (2002), for example, examined the effect of adapting the Strengthening Families Program for a wide variety of ethnic groups and found that the cultural adaptations that omitted core components increased family engagement, but decreased positive outcomes (Elliott & Mihalic, 2004). In general, the evidence indicates that cultural sensitivity training can benefit service providers, but there remains a lack of evidence that this training benefits service recipients (Anderson, Scrimshaw, Fullilove, Fielding, & Normand, 2003; Beach et al., 2005). This section will examine the critical factors that mental health providers should consider, and how they can adapt psychosocial interventions to the major racial-ethnic minorities in the United States.

Critical Factors

Turner (2000) recommends that practitioners pay attention to seven critical factors when adapting programs for ethnic minorities. First, professionals should attend to the degree of influence that certain protective factors have in the culture. For example, church attendance is far more likely among African American families than other groups. Second, clinicians should observe the degree of cultural assimilation, identity, and lifestyle preferences. Families living within an ethnic enclave, for instance, are often slower to acculturate than families who choose to live in a majority community. Third, practitioners should be aware that different individuals acculturate at different rates. Even siblings may demonstrate different levels of acculturation depending on what age they were when the family migrated. Fourth, professionals should attend to family migration patterns and relocation history. It is easier for families who voluntarily emigrate than for those who are forced to suddenly leave their homeland because of political or military oppression. Fifth, clinicians should be alert to the possibility of trauma, loss, or post-traumatic stress for those who have experienced ethnic "cleansing" or torture. Sixth, practitioners should familiarize themselves with the family's work status and economic stressors. For example, it is common that respected professionals (e.g., doctors, lawyers, and teachers) from the old country not to have their credentials recognized by their new nation. Finally, school staff should assess both the family's preferred language as well as their degree of literacy in that language. Many immigrants leave their homeland with only a rudimentary education, so merely translating notes home does little to facilitate home-school communication. For example, Jensen (2001) notes that nearly 70% of Mexican immigrants have not completed high school while nearly 45% of Filipino immigrants have a college degree.

Hispanic Families

Certain minority groups are growing faster than others. While the U.S. population grew at a rate of 13% between 1990 and 2000, the Hispanic population grew at a rate of 58% (U.S. Census Bureau, 2001). The need for culturally sensitive interventions is essential if immigrant children are going to successfully navigate the American school system (Matthews & Mahoney, 2005). Furthermore, school-based practitioners must be sensitive to the worldview conflicts between immigrant parents and their American-raised children (Roysircar-Sodowsky & Frey, 2003). Martinez and Eddy (2005) adapted a standard eight-session parent management training program for Hispanic families. Working with bicultural practitioners, they adapted the eight standard elements and added four culturally specific sessions: Latino roots, family roles, cross-cultural bridging, and addressing structural barriers to success, such as ethnic discrimination, for a total of 12 sessions. They then piloted the adapted program with focus groups of Hispanic parents. This culturally enhanced version of parent management training showed positive effects for engagement (80% attended all sessions) and for both youth and adult outcome measures. Interestingly, in the control group that did not receive any services, families with U.S.-born children fared much worse than those with immigrant children. This may be explained by the double gap, both generational and cultural, between foreign-born parents and their American-raised offspring (Santisteban, Muir-Malcolm, Mitrani, & Szapocznik, 2002). In general, it is probably more important to offer culturally sensitive treatment to immigrant parents than to their English-speaking children, but clinicians must always be aware of the double risk faced when youth and parents are at different levels of acculturation.

African American Families

Obesity of African Americans in poverty is a major cause of health risks, especially cardiovascular disease. While there is a lack of rigorous research on the adaptation of interventions for African Americans in general, one exception to that rule is a dissertation completed by Willet (1996). Noting that previous research had shown that African American women had the highest overall age-adjusted prevalence of obesity, she adapted a health risk reduction program for African American women and their school-age daughters. Researching several school-based programs, she found that the Know Your Body program (Resnicow et al., 1992) was effective for inner-city school children. The culturally sensitive version was a brief (10-session) program that involved mothers and their adolescent daughters in low-impact aerobics, making healthier choices at fast food restaurants, and creating a rap to remember the program's principles. Results indicated mothers in the intervention group did significantly better on cognitive and behavioral measures than mothers in the control group. Unfortunately, the intervention did not change the adolescents' attitudes or behavior around nutrition. A major problem in the evaluation was missing data because of skipped items in the daughter's response to adult-oriented outcome measures. Willett (1996) surmised that there were three possible explanations. The reading level of the instruments may have been too hard for the adolescents to complete accurately. Alternatively, the intervention may have been too short-term to make a significant difference. Finally, none of the girls were overweight at the beginning of the study and may have been less motivated to maintain a healthy lifestyle. While it is difficult to determine exactly why the results were not significant for the school-age children, the study demonstrates the level of rigor that studies about cultural adaptation must meet.

Asian Families

Yu (1999) observed that Chinese students with high levels of depression also suffered from school conduct problems and low academic achievement. Family conflict also seemed to predict future depression. He adapted the

Penn Prevention Program for 220 school-age children (ages 9–14), who were selected from a larger sample based on two criteria: depressive symptoms and family conflict. The culturally sensitive version reduced the total number of sessions from 12 to 10, retained the cognitive therapy portions to correct pessimistic thinking, but compacted the sessions on problem solving and decision making. The biggest change was made to the assertiveness training component since this skill was incongruent with acceptable Chinese behavior, especially when directed toward adults. Thus, the Chinese children were taught "negotiation" skills to use with family members. Finally, the program was delivered by school teachers rather than a mental health professional because of the limited availability of such professionals with knowledge of Chinese culture. Results indicated that children in the intervention group had significantly lower depression scores than children in the control group, both at program termination and at the 3-month follow-up.

In summary, interventions that work for most families are also likely to work with families across racial-ethnic groups (Kumpfer et al., 2002). This does not mean that everyone is the same, but that differences are likely to be minor, not major (Deffenbacher & Swaim, 1999). In other words, one is more likely to find differences of degree, such as how well a program works, rather than differences of type, such as whether it works. Practitioners should also not be afraid to adapt ESTs for fear of losing effectiveness. Two of the three adapted programs demonstrated effectiveness when compared to control groups that received no intervention. None of these rigorous studies on culturally sensitive adaptations of ESTs, however, compared their effectiveness to unedited versions of the same treatments. It would have proved interesting to find out if the culturally relevant editions outperformed the original ESTs. Furthermore, only one set of the researchers (Martinez & Eddy, 2005) reported doing a pilot test of the modified program before using it on a larger sample. Clearly, there is much more work to be done in the evaluation of culturally adapting ESTs to new populations.

Contextual Constraints

There are two reasons that ESTs must be adapted before being applied to schools. First, there is a great disparity between the mental health needs of children in schools and the availability of help. Approximately 20% of all American school-age children need some form of mental health services (American Academy of Pediatrics Committee on School Health, 2004; U.S. Public Health Service, 2000), but less than a third actually receive the help they need (Paternite, 2005). Of those who do receive help, the vast majority receive it in school (Rones & Hoagwood, 2000). Consequently, most school mental health programs, however, are overwhelmed and understaffed. Second, most of the over 1,500 randomized controlled trials of treatment efficacy have been carried out in or by university laboratories. These laboratory conditions, while ideal for controlling extraneous variables, have little in common with community-based conditions. As Hoagwood and Johnson (2003) correctly observe, "These differences imply that treatments developed through efficacy trials *need adaptation to fit* into clinics, schools, or other service settings" (p. 9, emphasis added).

The contextual constraints of working in a host setting where mental health services are viewed as ancillary and tenuously supported are serious (Masia-Warner, Nangle, & Hansen, 2006; Sedlak, 1997). As the American Academy of Pediatrics Committee on School Health (2004) recommended, school-based practitioners must conceptualize service delivery as a funnel with three sections (see Figure 6.1). Readers familiar with the response-to-intervention model will recognize that the funnel is, in fact, an upside-down pyramid. First, school social workers, psychologists, and counselors must work with and through education personnel to ensure that universal prevention services are rendered for children with mild or temporary problems. Second, they must serve selected children with moderate problems primarily in groups or short-term individual counseling. Finally, they must ensure that students with indicated chronic problems receive appropriately intensive services (Schaeffer et al., 2005). This section will deal with three important issues: teacher consultation for early prevention, group therapy and short-term services for intermediate intervention, and case coordination for community-linked intensive intervention.

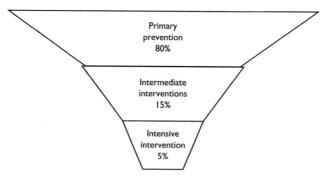

FIGURE 6.1. The funnel approach to mental health services in schools.

Evidence-Based Practice in School Mental Health

Teacher Consultation

In the first tier of the funnel model, universal prevention activities are applied to all students. Teacher consultation is ideal for elementary-age children with mild problems or temporary adjustment issues because the student has a single teacher for most of the school day (Schill, Kratochwill, & Elliott, 1998). After 5th grade, this is increasingly not the case and other avenues must be explored. For the first 6 years of school, however, the teacher-student relationship is critical for both academic and social success (Hughes, Cavell, & Willson, 2000). Need assessments show that teachers may have both more and stronger needs for support when trying to educate children with special needs (Granlund & Roll-Pettersson, 2001). New teachers are especially vulnerable to a lack of knowledge and experience with school-based mental health concerns (Kos, Richdale, & Jackson, 2004; Sciutto, Terjesen, & Bender-Frank, 2000). Fortunately, research demonstrates that classroom consultation works whether it involves the functional assessment of an individual child or general principles for behavioral management of an entire group (DuPaul & Weyandt, 2006; Schill et al., 1998). For example, Viggiani, Reid, and Bailey-Dempsey (2002) conducted an experiment where two classrooms received collaborative services and two classrooms were assigned as controls in an impoverished urban neighborhood in New York. The social workers focused on behavioral and attendance issues while teachers focused on academic concerns. They met weekly and used a collaborative task-centered problem-solving approach (Reid, 1992). In a situation where children were frequently out-of-seat, the teacher and social worker agreed that she would carry an egg-timer during class. When it went off, those children who were in their seats received an animal cracker. Gradually, this simple solution was reduced to just twice per week without losing effectiveness. Results indicated improved attendance, homework completion, self-control, and academic-related behavior (i.e., improved effort in math, science, and language) for those classrooms receiving the intervention. The great advantage of such universal interventions is that they empower teachers to help entire classrooms of children across multiple years, making them a very efficient use of school resources.

Han and Weiss (2005) reviewed four factors that increase the likelihood that teachers will sustain mental health programs in schools. These include the following: support for the program by the building principal, the teacher's sense of self-efficacy in teaching, the level of professional burnout, and beliefs about the acceptability of the program. First, principals, as gatekeepers of any new innovation in their buildings, serve a critical role in the successful implementation of prevention programs (Kam, Greenberg, & Walls, 2003). Second, teachers who are already confident in their teaching ability are more willing to entertain new ideas and experiment with new techniques. Third, professional burnout saps the energy and enthusiasm required to implement new approaches to old problems. Finally, the acceptability of an intervention by teachers is determined by the severity of the problem, the type of intervention, the amount of effort or time required to implement it, compatibility with their previously held beliefs, and its anticipated effectiveness. For example, teachers' beliefs about adolescent sexual behavior can affect how faithfully they implement a teen pregnancy prevention program.

Short-term Groupwork

In the second tier of the funnel model, practitioners identify children who have not responded as hoped to the universal preventions administered by teachers in the general education curriculum. Rather than assume that these children are in need of intensive treatments, wise practitioners will often try short-term group interventions as an efficient use of their (and the students') time. This has the distinct advantage of giving the group leaders an opportunity to see how troubled children interact with their peers when they have to share the attention of a caring adult. Since this situation parallels the classroom experience of the teacher, it allows the related services professional to recreate the child's social milieu and observe his/her behavior in its natural environment.

Most cognitive behavioral groups perform best by having six to eight members (Schaeffer et al., 2005). This number is large enough so that one to two absences will not decrease the group's interpersonal resources, but small enough to ensure that each member has sufficient time to participate and practice their skills. By short-term, we mean interventions that last no more than 10 weeks, a quarter of the standard 40-week school year. Short-term group interventions have been found effective for a wide range of school-age students, including those with aggressive behavior (Lochman, Powell, Boxmeyer, Deming, & Young, 2007), anxiety (Bernstein et al., 2005), post-traumatic stress disorder (Salloum, Avery, & McClain, 2001), pregnant or parenting teens (Harris & Franklin, 2003), self-harming behaviors (Burns, Dudley, Hazell, & Patton, 2005), sexual abuse survivors (DeLuca, Boyes, Grayston, & Romano, 1995), and pupils with self-control problems (see Box 6.2). Harris and Franklin (2003), for example, developed the Taking Charge curriculum based on a previous research review (Seitz & Apfel, 1999) for use with pregnant and/or parenting Hispanic adolescents in a school-based setting. The cognitive behavioral intervention was comprised of eight

BOX 6.2 Cognitive Behavior Therapy for Students With Poor Self-Control

Squires (2001) developed a six-session group therapy intervention for students with low self-control. The goals of the group were to reduce office disciplinary referrals, improve classroom compliance, and improve peer relationships. Pretest and posttest measures included Hudson's (1982) Index of Peer Relations; Humphrey's (1982) Children's Self-Control scales; and Faupel, Herrick, and Sharp (1998) Classroom Observation Checklist. While the group followed a similar preset format for each session and a standard curriculum was used, Squires also thought

> Flexibility was considered important so that issues brought in by the children and young people could be used instead of the materials developed specifically for the course. For example, during Session 4, one of the pupils expressed the view that one of his teachers was always picking on him. He said he thought this was unfair and it made him feel angry. When he felt angry he often shouted out at the teacher, and he had been sent out of the room several times. This was developed with the group and then linked to the theme for the session (experiments and action plans). He was able to test out his belief after deciding that in the next lesson with this teacher he would do a bar count of the times the teacher "picked on him" compared to other children in the class. During the next session, the child was able to report that the teacher only picked on him four times and many other children in the class exceeded this. He now thought the teacher was being fair and he no longer felt angry when the teacher addressed him. (pp. 321–322)

Results of the intervention found no significant differences for peer relations (even though 59% of the group improved), but did find significant improvement for both self-control ($p = .04$) and classroom behavior ($p = .028$). Squires provides three appendices to his article. Appendix A provides details on his entire 6-week CBT program. Appendix B provides an optional set of CBT strategies for flexibility. Appendix C provides a Situations Sheet on which students can record their reactions to a variety of circumstances.

1-hour sessions led by social workers and cofacilitated by young adults with experience in adolescent parenting. They found that participants had made significant gains in coping skills, problem solving, school attendance, and grade point average. A 30-day follow-up showed that the group members had maintained their growth.

Short-term groups have also been found effective for parent management training (Barlow & Stewart-Brown, 2005). Some versions have been found effective in as few as six sessions (Morgan & Hensley, 1998; Zimmerman, Jacobsen, MacIntyre, & Watson, 1996). A number of school-based practitioners find parent training onerous regardless of consistent findings of its effectiveness. Like teachers, they reject certain ESTs because they are not convinced that the extra effort is worth the effect. Parents attend infrequently or dropout prematurely without a concerted effort (Katz et al., 2001; Orrell-Valente, Pinderhughes, Valente, & Laird, 1999). Lim, Stormshak, and Dishion (2005), therefore, developed a single-session 2-hour parenting program that included videotape modeling followed by group discussion. Participants included parents of 6th grade students at four public middle schools. They watched a 30-minute video demonstrating both counterproductive and constructive parenting techniques, Parenting in the Teenage Years (Dishion, Kavanagh, & Christianson, 1995). Then they debriefed the presentation with a professional therapist and were given a handout with a summary of the principles covered. Results indicated that parents improved on both self-reported and observed measures of parent-adolescent interaction 4 weeks after the training. The authors did not pretend that such a brief training is effective with all families: those with deeper problems may require a longer intervention or family counseling at a community agency.

Intensive Treatment

School mental health practitioners are between a rock and a hard place. On one hand, the most *efficient* use of their time is to refer students who need long-term individual psychotherapy to community agencies or private practitioners. The former, however, are also overworked and understaffed and the latter are often expensive and/or require excellent insurance coverage. The sad fact remains that those children who do receive mental health services are most likely to obtain help through a school-based program (Rones & Hoagwood, 2000). For all the reasons outlined by Crisp, Gudmundsen, and Shirk (2006) (see Box 6.3), schools are the most *effective* location to deliver mental health services.

BOX 6.3 Adolescent Mood Project (Denver, CO)

Researchers from the University of Denver (Crisp et al., 2006) worked to translate an empirically supported treatment for depression to four public high schools. They wanted to see if a cognitive behavioral intervention developed as a randomized controlled trial could work in a real community setting. They posited that schools were an ideal setting for four reasons. First, schools are a community agency that is familiar to youths and their parents, and attendance is free from any psychological stigma (unlike community mental health centers). Second, since adolescents are already present, there are no transportation barriers to overcome. Third, schools are a natural environment when youths demonstrate some of functional impairments caused by depression, making it easier to monitor how treatment affects their functioning. Fourth, students can learn the cognitive behavioral skills in an environment where they can be readily tested.

To establish a foundation for the experiment, the researchers took three initial steps. First, they established contacts with local school districts and community mental health agencies to assess their interest and support for the proposed project. Second, after choosing four high schools, they worked with school staff to tailor the implementation to the institutional culture. For example, the schools varied on how students were reminded on coming to sessions (e.g., sending hall passes, therapist going to retrieve the student, or sending an intercom message). Another difference was whether the school would allow sessions to be carried on during core classes, auxiliary classes, lunch, or study periods. Finally, they built close relationships with the school's administrative assistants who could help them with accessing the students' schedules or making photocopies.

In two of the schools, the program worked closely with the high school counseling departments. In the other two schools, the program worked closely with community mental health centers that staffed school-based "health clinics" on a part-time basis. They

(continued)

began by piloting the program with six therapists and six students from three of the schools. Based on this initial experiment, they made five modifications to the treatment manual developed by Rosselló and Bernal (1999). First, they changed the cognitive therapy module to address cognitive coping with truly severe circumstances (e.g., sexual abuse, family violence, and chronically sick parents). Second, they modified the behavior therapy module to focus more on relationship activities that students can use to relieve stress, to have adolescents make their own list of pleasant activities, and to include relaxation training. Third, they altered the relational therapy module to focus on real interpersonal issues (i.e., anger management, social problem solving, social anxiety, and assertiveness) and changed the final sessions from developing a "philosophy of life" to exploring short-term goals. Fourth, they created a Personal Mood Manager to provide students with a workbook that provided a summary of the treatment principles and organized homework activities into their daily routine. Finally, they adapted the sessions to fit the 45-minute class periods and allowed the three main modules to be completed with 1- to 2-week gaps caused by school holidays or vacation schedules.

They expanded the typical inclusionary criteria to include more comorbid disorders, including attention deficit/hyperactivity disorder, anxiety disorders, conduct disorders, and substance abuse. They also reduced the usual exclusionary criteria to include students with a history of suicide attempts, parasuicidal behaviors (e.g., cutting), and suicidal ideation. Thus, their clientele was considerably more diverse than the NIMH TADS project mentioned earlier in this chapter. Project participants were 59% white, 11% African American, and 26% Hispanic. Concurrent diagnoses included 37% with generalized anxiety disorder, 7% with ADHD, 33% with conduct disorder, 26% with social phobia, and 26% with dysthymia. In fact, only 37% of the sample had depression as their only diagnosis!

Preliminary project results were encouraging. Of the 20 students who completed treatment, their scores on the Beck Depression Inventory (1961) showed an average reduction of 22 points, and

(continued)

15 no longer met the diagnostic criteria for depression. They concluded there were three main obstacles to the dissemination of ESTs in schools. First, there were not enough school-employed mental health professionals to identify and refer students for the help they needed. The two high schools that had full-time school-based practitioners did a much better job than the two high schools that outsourced this function to community mental health agencies. Second, those school-employed mental health professionals who do exist spend too much time on administrative tasks rather than having opportunities to learn and implement ESTs. Third, even for those school-based mental health professionals who had the time seldom had the funding available for training and support for evidence-based practice. If schools could employ more mental health practitioners, reserve more of their time for treatment, and provide adequate support for continuing education and supervision, then ESTs could flourish within the school setting.

Guidelines for Adaptation

Ruscio and Holohan (2006) posit that the decision to adapt an empirically supported treatment is a two-step process. First, under what conditions should a clinician adapt an EST? Second, how should a clinician modify an EST?

They identify four conditions under which therapists should always adapt an EST, and I will add a fifth. First, if the treatment is unacceptable to the student or his/her family or both, then the EST should be modified or another one chosen. The rationale for this is simple—clients who do not agree with a treatment decision will undermine its effectiveness through noncompliance. Second, an EST should be changed if the clients' symptoms or environment are so turbulent that client safety is a legitimate threat. For example, exposure therapy for a child with post-traumatic stress disorder may have the short-term adverse effect of causing them overwhelming anxiety. In such cases, therapists would be wise to back off from direct exposure and try a more indirect approach, such as merely imagining the threatening situation. Third, an EST should be changed if other problems are more urgent—this may change weekly for adolescents. A client being seen for self-esteem problems may need to have this treatment set aside if he/she is suddenly referred to the principal's office for peer violence. Fourth, if the client does not have the intrapersonal coping resources to deal with an intensive EST, then it should be changed. This could occur in two ways—sessions could be of shorter duration or the frequency of the sessions could be slowed down. Fifth, it also seems prudent to adapt an EST when the client is involuntary (e.g., students with externalizing disorders). The primary adaptation would be to spend more time working on engaging them in the therapeutic relationship prior to trying to change their behavior (Murphy, 1999).

Ruscio and Holohan (2006) also provide three guidelines for adapting ESTs, to which I will add a fourth. First, an EST may be "augmented" by supplementary interventions designed to address other clinical problems or complex features of the client. This can be accomplished two different ways. A therapist may attempt to apply multiple ESTs sequentially or blend two or more ESTs into a concurrent treatment. Second, if the most empirically supported treatment is not a good fit, the clinician can move down the hierarchy of evidence (see Figure 4.1) to find the next most effective treatment. This tiered approach may have the added benefit of providing more time for the therapeutic relationship to solidify so that more effective treatments can be tried later on. Third, try to identify the core ingredients of the EST and adapt the peripheral aspects to the needs of the client. A child with little ability to self-reflect on his/her own thought might be given CBT with a reduced cognitive component. This type of modification, of course, raises the question as to when an adapted EST is no longer empirically supported. This important issue will be addressed in the next section. Fourth, it is also wise not to reduce the duration of the intervention. None of us would consider giving half the prescribed dosage of medicine to a sick child, yet some practitioners think this is permissible for ESTs. ESTs are designed and evaluated to work within certain parameters—if we curtail these boundaries then we will surely reduce their effectiveness.

Treatment Fidelity

While I have argued for flexibility in the application of ESTs to specific clients, this should not be interpreted to mean that "anything goes." ESTs are validated under carefully controlled conditions for a reason—to specify exactly who they help and how long this help should take. If there is no rational reason for adapting an EST, then a practitioner should implement it as it was designed to work. This has three implications. First, clinicians should remain faithful to the theory behind the EST—one cannot employ a cognitive behavioral intervention from a psychodynamic viewpoint and expect that it will work exactly the same. Second, practitioners should be sure to implement all of the principal elements of the EST. If homework is part of the intervention, then eliminating homework will reduce the EST's effectiveness. Finally, as mentioned, therapists should not shorten the EST. Squires' (2001) group for students with poor self-control (see Box 6.2) was administered in six 1-hour sessions. If one of the contextual constraints of a school is a maximum of 45-minute sessions, then obviously the number of sessions would have to be increased to administer the full dose of Squire's intervention. One way to check the validity of an adaptation is to obtain approval from the developer of the EST (Franklin & Hopson, 2007). Sometimes this approval is contingent upon evaluation of the results and sharing the data with the original developer—this is exactly what will be addressed in Chapters 7 and 8.

Summary

This chapter began with an important discussion about the integration of science and art in therapy. Eschewing the either-or debate, we argued that evidence-based practice requires the integration of both. Combining scientifically based research and the art of the therapeutic relationship requires considerable clinical wisdom and skill. We then addressed three crucial issues in the adaptation and application of ESTs in clinical practice. These included developmental considerations, cultural sensitivity, and contextual constraints. Developmental considerations included thinking about how to engage nonvoluntary minor clients, how to educate children about affective issues, how to work with their cognitive capacities, and how to involve parents in the process. Cultural sensitivity involved a consideration of some general principles for cross-cultural work and specific ideas for adapting interventions for the major racial-ethnic groups that attend American schools, including Hispanics, African Americans, and Asians. A three-level approach to systematically addressing mental health concerns within the contextual constraints of schools was described. The first level was universal prevention activities delivered through educational staff via teacher consultation and collaboration. The second level was selected intervention delivered through mental health practitioners via short-term groupwork. The third level was indicated intervention delivered by mental health practitioners via long-term individual psychotherapy. Finally, I provided some specific guidelines for adaptation and identified three principles for implementation fidelity.

Suggested Reading

1. Crisp, H. L., Gudmundsen, G. R., & Shirk, S. R. (2006). Transporting evidence-based therapy for adolescent depression to the school setting. *Education and Treatment of Children, 29* (2), 287–309.

2. Harris, M. B., & Franklin, C. G. (2003). Effects of a cognitive-behavioral, school-based, group intervention with Mexican American pregnant and parenting adolescents. *Social Work Research, 27* (2), 71–83.

3. Schaeffer, C. M., Bruns, E., Weist, M., Stephan, S. H., Goldstein, J., & Simpson, Y. (2005). Overcoming challenges to using evidence-based interventions in schools. *Journal of Youth and Adolescence, 34* (1), 15–22.

Internet Resources

American Academy of Child and Adolescent Psychiatry Practice Parameters
http://www.aacap.org/page.ww?section=Practice+Parameters&name=Practice+Parameters

American Psychological Association's Guide to Empirically Supported Interventions
http://www.apa.org/divisions/div12/rev_est/

Empirically Supported Interventions in School Mental Health—Center for School Mental Health
http://csmh.umaryland.edu/resources.html/resource_packets/download_files/empirically_supported_2002.pdf

National Guideline Clearinghouse—Agency for Healthcare Research and Quality
http://www.guideline.gov/index.aspx

National Institute on Drug Abuse's Principles of Drug Addiction Treatment
http://www.drugabuse.gov/PODAT/PODATIndex.html

National Institutes of Health Consensus Statement on ADHD
http://consensus.nih.gov/1998/1998AttentionDeficitHyperactivityDisorder110html.htm

Office of Juvenile Justice and Delinquency Prevention's Model Programs
http://www.dsgonline.com/mpg2.5/mpg_index.htm

SAMHSA's National Registry of Evidence-Based Programs and Practices
http://www.nrepp.samhsa.gov/index.htm

U.S. Department of Education's Safe, Disciplined, and Drug-Free Exemplary Programs
http://www.ed.gov/admins/lead/safety/exemplary01/panel_pg2.html

U.S. Department of Health and Human Services—Matrix of Children's Evidence-Based Interventions
http://www.systemsofcare.samhsa.gov/headermenus/docsHM/MatrixFinal1.pdf

7

■ ■ ■

Evaluating Group Outcomes Using Descriptive Designs

Preview
The previous chapter addressed how to adapt and apply an empirically supported treatment (EST) for children and adolescents. The purpose of this chapter is to discuss the process of evaluating group outcomes using descriptive research designs. It will address five important points about outcome evaluation. First, it will remind readers of the difference between dependent and independent variables. Second, it will describe three major types of research designs. Third, it will identify six sources of data. These include archival student records, teacher interviews, daily or weekly logs, standardized instruments, direct observation, and scaled questions. Fourth, it will introduce readers to using Microsoft Excel to record and analyze results. This will include a primer on data entry, descriptive statistics, and inferential statistics. The chapter will conclude with two important distinctions. First, it will discuss the difference between correlation and causation. Second, it will address the difference between clinical significance and statistical significance. In school-based practice, we are far more likely to discover a correlation rather than causation, primarily due to ethical concerns about control groups or even paired comparison groups. Many students and beginning professionals mistakenly equate the statistical and clinical significance or confuse which one should have the highest priority. For practitioners, clinical significance should always take precedence.

Importance of Outcome Evaluation
There is a hidden cost for adapting ESTs before applying them. As an observant seminar attendee once asked, "If I change the

intervention, how do I know that it is still empirically supported?" "You don't," I candidly responded, "at least not yet." Nock, Goldman, Wang, and Albano (2004) make the same point and identify the implications for the flexible practitioner:

> To be sure, making modifications will result in the implementation of a treatment that is different in content and structure than that supported by the research (e.g., in the case of pharmacological treatment, one is now prescribing "off label"). As a means of ensuring that the treatment is effective as delivered, we strongly advocate the use of scientific method in each case. Decisions about the nature of the modifications should be rooted firmly in psychological science, and each case should be treated as a scientific experiment with systematic data collection and analysis performed to test the effectiveness of the modified treatment. The use of this method provides empirical support for the intervention as implemented as well as immediate feedback to the clinician and patient that may be useful in guiding future treatment planning. (p. 778)

In fact, outcome evaluation is important for two reasons. First, as mentioned earlier, if we have modified an EST, then we must evaluate it to see if the evidence continues to support its use. Second, while ESTs have been established using another set of students, we really don't know if they work for our set of students until we evaluate our efforts. Outcome evaluation and dissemination of results, then, is the culmination of an evidence-based process. Having converted our need for information into answerable questions; we have searched effectively and efficiently for the best available evidence; appraised that evidence for relevance, strength, and consistency; adapted and applied the evidence to the developmental level, cultural affiliation, and contextual constraints of a particular client; and now we must hold ourselves accountable for the results.

Dependent Variable

The dependent or outcome variable is the effect that therapists hope to create through their intervention. Traditionally, the dependent variable is demonstrated vertically on a graph (the y-axis). The list of potential dependent variables is broad—they include both internalized symptoms and externalized signs. There are at least six possible ways to measure dependent variables (described later).

Independent Variable

The independent or predictor variable is the presumed cause of the effect or it at least temporally precedes any change in the dependent variable. Traditionally, the independent variable is demonstrated horizontally on a graph (the x-axis). Therapists usually hope that it is their intervention that is the independent variable. The independent variable must have two qualities. First, the independent variable must be subject to manipulation or control. Second, the independent variable must be provided with fidelity. *Treatment fidelity* refers to the consistency with which the intervention is provided across time or across providers. Fidelity in no way implies that the intervention cannot be adapted from client to client; it simply refers to the provision of the principal elements in a similar manner.

Group Research Designs

Most research textbooks identify three major types of group designs. These include exploratory designs, descriptive designs, and explanatory designs.

Exploratory Designs

Exploratory designs consist of two common subtypes used for group or program evaluations (Grinnell, Unrau, & Williams, 2008). First, there is the *single group posttest-only* design. The most common use of this design is the client satisfaction survey given toward the end of treatment. In this example, treatment is the independent variable and satisfaction is the dependent variable. Second, there is the *longitudinal posttest-only* design. The main difference between this one and the first is that multiple measurements are taken after the group receives the intervention (e.g., at termination, 3-month follow-up, and 6-month follow-up).

Descriptive Designs

Descriptive designs are midway between the relatively weak exploratory designs and the rigorous explanatory designs. There are four commonly used subtypes. First, there is the *single group pretest-posttest* design. A measurement of the dependent variable is taken prior to the intervention (the independent variable) and then again after the intervention. We can now determine if there was a statistically significant change between the two administrations of the measurement. Second, there is the *comparison group posttest-only* design. This kind of design allows practitioners to compare two different interventions (or independent variables). For example, the participants in one treatment group might be compared to participants of another

---

kind of treatment group (e.g., cognitive behavioral group therapy vs. interpersonal group therapy). The dependent variable is measured only at the end of the intervention. Third, there is the *comparison group pretest-posttest* design. This combines features of the previous two designs—taking before and after measurements of the dependent variable and comparing two kinds of intervention (or independent variables). The advantage is obvious—we can now compare the growth rates of the two groups of participants and determine which intervention led to the most improvement. Finally, there is the *interrupted time-series* design. Since this is most common in single-subject designs, it will be addressed in the next chapter.

The reason this chapter focuses on descriptive designs is that they are the most rigorous designs normally used in everyday practice. Each design has its own weaknesses or threats to internal validity (see Box 7.1), but there are no research designs that are impervious to such threats. Threats to internal validity can be understood as rival plausible explanations for the change in

---

BOX 7.1 Research Designs and Their Threats to Internal Validity

TYPE OF DESIGN	COMMON THREATS TO INTERNAL VALIDITY*
Single group posttest only	History; maturation, mortality; and selection
Longitudinal posttest only	History; maturation, mortality; and selection
Single group pretest-posttest	History; maturation; reactive effects; testing
Comparison group posttest only	Intervention contamination; mortality; and selection bias
Comparison Group pretest-posttest	Intervention contamination; reactive effects; and selection bias
Randomized controlled trial	Intervention contamination
Quasi-experimental design	Intervention contamination

*See Appendix C for descriptions of each threat.

Evidence-Based Practice in School Mental Health

outcome. For a description of the most common threats to internal validity, see Appendix C.

Explanatory Designs

Explanatory designs are rigorous research projects that are most capable of providing a scientific base for practice. They include randomized controlled trials and quasi-experimental designs with baseline equating. For more on these two types of designs, review federal legislation section in Chapter 1 and the effectiveness studies section in Chapter 5.

Sources of Data

In a now classic article, Achenbach, McConaughy, and Howell (1987) argued that the best way to get a complete view of the child within his or her environment was to use multiple informants and multiple methods. We will begin with a survey of data mining techniques. Several years ago, I posited five ways to obtain data about student functioning, including archival school records, teacher interviews, daily or weekly logs, standardized instruments, or direct observation (Raines, 2002b). In 2006, I gave the keynote address to a summer symposium at Loyola University of Chicago and a newly minted doctoral graduate was invited to respond to my address on evidence-based practice. She kindly informed me ahead of time that she planned to disagree with me about outcome measurement. She intended to tell the audience that if something cannot be seen, it certainly cannot be measured. In short, invisibility equaled immeasurability! I carefully considered her position and concluded that I could not possibly agree. At recent doctor visits, I noticed that nurses now routinely measured five vital signs rather than four. They still took my pulse, measured my respiratory rate, checked my temperature and blood pressure, but an increasing number of clinics had added pain as the fifth vital sign (American Pain Society Quality of Care Committee, 1995; Joint Commission on Accreditation of Healthcare Organizations, 2004). They could not see my pain, but they allowed me to subjectively measure it on a scale from 1 to 10. Let's discuss how each of these can be used in clinical practice.

Archival School Records

Schools routinely track an increasing amount of information on students, many of which can be utilized as broad measures of student functioning, including school attendance, tardiness, disciplinary referrals, and grade retention (Mattison, 2000). Fortunately, many of these records are now kept in the school's relational database system, making retrieval of the information even easier (Patterson, 2006). Archival records are the least reactive of student measures because neither the student nor the therapist has any control over record retention. School attendance is probably the most important of these records for two reasons. First, students who do not attend school cannot learn at school. Many schools have established an operational definition of truancy that establishes any more than 10% of the days absent as being truant from school. Using a standard 180-day school year, this means any student who misses more than 18 days or more than 9 days per semester. Second, many states establish local education agency funding based on its attendance rate (Dibble, 2004). More students require more resources, so fewer students require less. There is a broad range of mental health problems that can interfere with school attendance—conduct disorder, depression, drug abuse, separation anxiety, and social phobia to name a few. It is reasonable to assume that as students with these disorders get better, their attendance should improve as well.

Teacher Interviews

Most teachers who have taught the same grade for several years have an intuitive sense of the normal range for that developmental level. They can be excellent at determining which child problems are age-appropriate phases or deviations and which ones require intervention. Bilenberg, Petersen, Hoerder, and Gillberg (2005), for example, compared results of a screening using the Achenbach's Child Behavior Checklist to teacher interview assessments. They found that the teachers outperformed the standardized scale in correctly classifying which children had a psychiatric diagnosis. The teachers were correct 87% of the time while the Achenbach's Child Behavior Checklist was correct 72% of the time. While this may represent a high degree of sensitivity rather than specificity, school-based practitioners should take this information seriously, given the importance of the student-teacher relationship for both academic and social prognosis (Hughes, Cavell, & Willson, 2000).

Teachers have also yielded useful information for functional behavioral assessments, correctly identifying the antecedents and consequences of misbehavior over 80% of the time and the purpose of a child's misbehavior on nearly two thirds of the occasions (Murdock, O'Neill, & Cunningham, 2005). Kinch, Lewis-Palmer, Hagan-Burke, and Sugai (2001) found that the most useful reports came from teachers accustomed to dealing with high rates of problem behavior rather than those who rarely witnessed problems. For children with behavioral deficits, then, it makes sense to routinely inquire about three issues: (1) the problem behaviors; (2) the classroom contexts, antecedents, and consequences associated with the problem behavior; and

(3) a hypothesis about the purpose of the misbehavior (Hoff, Ervin, & Friman, 2005; Raines, 2002a). For those interested in measuring progress, one might ask whether there are a wider variety of contexts in which the student performs acceptably, fewer antecedents that lead to misbehavior, or whether the quality of consequences has changed over time, such as concrete reinforcement (food) to social reinforcement (approval). Finally, Ervin et al. (2000) have created a brief (six-item) social validity questionnaire for teachers to provide feedback about the functional behavioral assessment process.

At the elementary level, astute teachers can also name the child's strengths and weaknesses. For those of us interested in measurement, however, this simple recital can become a ratio of strengths to weaknesses. It will vary for each student and it will probably vary over time. A teacher may initially name only two strengths and four weaknesses, but what matters for clinicians implementing change is how this ratio changes over the course of treatment. A perfectly reasonable treatment goal is to have the same teacher eventually name more strengths than weaknesses.

Daily/Weekly Logs

Logs have been used to track children's behaviors and critical incidents for decades (Sadler & Blom, 1970). Logs can also be used to track invisible problems, such as children's pain (McGrath & Gillespie, 2001) or emotional states (Kellner & Tutin, 1995; Kerns, Abraham, Schlegelmilch, & Morgan, 2007). Logs are perhaps the most reactive of measures because children are aware that they are monitoring their own emotions or behaviors or others are tracking them. Both subjective moods and objective behaviors can be tracked using daily or weekly logs. Behavior can be tracked by third parties, such as teachers, who rate a student's observable behavior. Moods can be tracked by the client themselves by having them count the number of negative thoughts or uncomfortable feelings they had during the day. Kellner and Tutin (1995), for example, utilized the Hassle Log (Feindler & Ecton, 1986) to help students keep track of (1) the setting associated with their anger; (2) the incident that triggered their angry reactions; (3) how they handled the incident; (4) a self-appraisal of the intensity of their anger; and (5) a self-appraisal of how they handled the situation. The students, interestingly, decided to rename the instrument the Mad Log! From an outcome evaluation point of view, we might inquire whether the number of settings or situations had decreased and whether the number of adaptive coping responses had increased. Kerns et al. (2007), however, utilized the Youth Everyday Social Interaction and Mood scales (Repetti, 1996) to track children's self-perceptions of their moods (positive and negative) three times per day (morning, afternoon, and night). The secret to both behavioral and emotional logs is consistency. Daily measures should be conducted by the same persons each day (see Box 7.2). Weekly measures should also be completed by the same persons for each day of the week (see Box 7.3).

Rating Scales

While school psychologists probably feel more comfortable using standardized scales than school social workers or school counselors, all three groups should be familiar with them. In Chapters 3 and 5, we addressed some of the qualities that good rating scales should have. These include identification of student strengths, brevity, specificity, sensitivity, reliability, and validity. It is important to remember that the Individuals with Disabilities Education Act requires that schools inquire about both academic achievement and functional performance. As the President's New Freedom Commission on Mental Health (2003) reminds us,

> Functional impairment is defined as difficulties that substantially interfere with or limit role functioning in one or more major life activities, including basic daily living skills (e.g., eating, bathing, dressing); instrumental living skills (e.g., maintaining a household, managing money, getting around the community, taking prescribed medication); and *functioning in social, family, and vocational/ educational contexts.*
>
> Section 1912 (c) of the Public Health Services Act, as amended by Public Law 102-321; p. 10, emphasis added

It is therefore essential to measure exactly *how* a child's emotional or behavioral impairment affects daily functioning. Readers who want to learn more about standardized instruments should review the assessment section in Chapter 3 and the appraising instrument studies section in Chapter 5 (see also Box 7.4).

Direct Observation

Direct observation entails the systematic study of behavior within a specific setting. As with rating scales, the precise technique of observation should match the intended purpose (Hintze, 2005; Landau & Swerdlik, 2005). There are two primary environments in which school-based therapists observe children.

First, most clinicians will gain some direct observations of the child during the administration of a rating scale and/or clinical interviews. There are at least three standardized methods for doing so (McConaughy, 2005). For example, both the Guide to Assessment of Test Session Behavior

BOX 7.2 Daily Goals Log

Student: Grade: Date:

Did student achieve goals today? Y = Yes; N = No; U = Unclear/unsure

Goal #s	Language arts	Math	Science	Social studies	Art	Music	P.E.	Technology	Goal totals
1									
2									
3									
4									
5									
Class totals									

Scoring: All cells should be filled in. Count the Ys only. Record goal totals on Excel/graph.

BOX 7.3 Weekly Goals Log

Student: _____   Grade: _____   Date: _____

Did student achieve goals this week? Y = Yes; N = No; U = Unclear/unsure

Class/period	Monday	Tuesday	Wednesday	Thursday	Friday	Class totals
1						
2						
3						
4						
5						
6						
7						
8						
Daily totals						

Scoring: All cells should be filled in. Count the Ys only. Record class totals on Excel/graph.

BOX 7.4 Referral Issues Covered by Common Standardized Instruments

REFERRAL ISSUE	MAJOR SCALE	MINOR SCALE*	INSTRUMENTS
Activities of daily living		x	BASC-2
Adaptive behavior/ skills		x	BASC-2
	x		SIB-R
	x		VABS-2
Aggression		x	ASEBA
Anger control		x	BASC-2
Anxiety		x	ASEBA
		x	BASC-2
Attention problems		x	ASEBA
		x	BASC-2
Atypicality/unusual		x	BASC-2
		x	SIB-R
Behavioral symptoms	x		BASC-2
Bullying		x	BASC-2
Communication	x		SIB-R
	x		VABS-2
Community living skills		x	SIB-R
		x	VABS-2
Coping skills		x	VABS-2
Daily living skills	x		SIB-R
	x		VABS-2
Delinquency/ conduct problems		x	ASEBA
		x	BASC-2

(continued)

REFERRAL ISSUE	MAJOR SCALE	MINOR SCALE*	INSTRUMENTS
Depression		x	ASEBA
		x	BASC-2
Destructive to property		x	SIB-R
Disruptive behavior		x	SIB-R
Domestic living skills		x	SIB-R
		x	VABS-2
Dressing		x	SIB-R
Eating and meal preparation		x	SIB-R
Emotional self-control		x	BASC-2
Executive functioning		x	BASC-2
Externalizing	x		ASEBA
	x	x	BASC-2
			VABS-2
Fine motor skills		x	SIB-R
		x	VABS-2
Functional communication		x	BASC-2
Gross motor skills		x	SIB-R
		x	VABS-2
Hurtful to others		x	SIB-R
Hurtful to self		x	SIB-R
Hyperactivity/ overactive		x	BASC-2
Inattentive		x	VABS-2
Internalizing	x		ASEBA
	x	x	BASC-2
			VABS-2

(continued)

REFERRAL ISSUE	MAJOR SCALE	MINOR SCALE*	INSTRUMENTS
Interpersonal relations		x	VABS-2
Language—Expressive		x	SIB-R
		x	VABS-2
Language—Receptive		x	SIB-R
		x	VABS-2
Language—Written		x	VABS-2
Leadership		x	BASC-2
Locus of control		x	BASC-2
Maladaptive	x		SIB-R
	x		VABS-2
Money and value		x	SIB-R
Motor skills	x		SIB-R
	x		VABS-2
Negative emotionality		x	BASC-2
Obsessive-compulsive		x	ASEBA
Personal living skills		x	SIB-R
		x	VABS-2
Play and leisure skills		x	VABS-2
Positive qualities		x	ASEBA
Post-traumatic stress		x	ASEBA
Repetitive habits		x	SIB-R
Resiliency		x	BASC-2
Sluggish cognitive tempo		x	ASEBA
Social skills/ interaction		x	BASC-2
		x	SIB-R

(continued)

REFERRAL ISSUE	MAJOR SCALE	MINOR SCALE*	INSTRUMENTS
Social problems/		x	ASEBA
stress		x	BASC-2
Socially offensive behavior		x	SIB-R
Socialization	x		VABS-2
Somatization		x	ASEBA
		x	BASC-2
Study skills		x	BASC-2
Time and punctuality		x	SIB-R
Thought problems		x	ASEBA
Toileting		x	SIB-R
Uncooperative		x	SIB-R
Withdrawal		x	ASEBA
		x	BASC-2
		x	SIB-R
Work skills		x	SIB-R

*Minor scales are typically smaller components of the major scales. Users should refer to the respective test manual for more detailed explanations.

ASEBA, Achenbach System for Empirically Based Assessment; BASC-2, Behavior Assessment System for Children (2nd ed.); SIB-R, Scales of Independent Behavior—Revised; VABS-2, Vineland Adaptive Behavior Scales (2nd ed.).

(Glutting & Oakland, 1993) and the Test Observation Form (McConaughy & Achenbach, 2004) help to assess children's performance while completing a standardized instrument, while the Observation Form for the Semistructured Clinical Interview for Children and Adolescents measures their behavior during an individual interview. Both of these situations have the advantage of offering uniform conditions under which to compare children rather than the complex natural environment of the classroom. The Guide to Assessment of Test Session Behavior has 29 items for the clinician to reflect on and results in four scales: avoidance, inattentiveness, uncooperative mood, and a total score (note that this is a negative total). The Test Observation Form has 125 items for reflection and results in eight scales: withdrawn/depressed, language/thought problems, anxious, oppositional, attention problems, internalizing, externalizing, and total problems (note that this is also a negative total). The Observation Form for the Semistructured Clinical Interview for Children and Adolescents has 121 items and results in the same scales as the Test Observation Form. Evaluators using such measures should be cautious not to overgeneralize the results. Behavior is usually situation specific so the child's behavior within a test-administration or clinical interview will reflect that unique situation (Shapiro & Kratochwill, 2000). Thus, children's office behavior may be indicative of being removed from a noisy, competitive environment into a setting where they are the sole recipient of attention from a kind, empathic, and understanding adult.

Second, many school-based practitioners will want to observe children in their natural environments, most often the classroom (Shapiro & Heick, 2004). Volpe, DiPerna, Hintze, and Shapiro (2005) evaluated seven widely available observational coding systems. They compared the Academic Engaged Time Code (Walker & Severson, 1990), ADHD School Observation Code (Gadow, Sprafkin, & Nolan, 1996), Behavioral Observation of Students in Schools (Shapiro, 2004), Classroom Observation Code (Abikoff & Gittelman, 1985), Direct Observation Form (Achenbach, 1986), State-Event Classroom Observation system (Saudargas, 1997), and the Student Observation System of the BASC (Reynolds & Kamphaus, 2004). The observation systems averaged about 6.5 behavioral categories but varied greatly in the number of observed behaviors ranging from just 1 behavior for the Academic Engaged Time Code to 11 behaviors for the Classroom Observation Code. The length of observation time also varied from a low of 10 minutes for the Direct Observation Form to 32 minutes for the Classroom Observation Code. Only two systems could be used with a Palm or personal digital assistant—the Behavioral Observation of Students in Schools and the Student Observation System. Five of the systems recommend that practitioners use index peer(s) as a means of obtaining normative data. It is important for clinicians to remember that this comparison student should be the same gender and age as the observed student. The younger the student the more important age similarity becomes. Volpe et al. (2005) concluded that most observational systems are treatment sensitive and can therefore be used to monitor progress when applied consistently (i.e., in the same classroom).

Scaled Questions

As mentioned previously, nurses now routinely ask patients to rate their pain on a scale from 1 to 10. Solution-focused therapists have been using this same technique for psychosocial issues (Sklare, 1997). It is particularly useful for students with internalizing problems that are not easily observable by others. Pupils suffering from anxiety, depression, and social phobia, for example, can be asked to rate their feelings on a scale from 1 to 10. While this may seem too subjective for hard-nosed evaluation, each child's self-report becomes their own baseline from which to monitor progress and evaluate outcomes.

Frequency of Data Collection

It is important to know when and how often to collect data. There are three important considerations in determining how frequently to monitor progress. First, it depends on the type of research design. Pretest-posttest research designs require the administration of a test at least twice—before treatment and at the end of treatment (before termination). Ideally, they also follow up on discharged students 3 to 6 months later to make sure the improvement has been maintained. Single-subject designs (discussed in the next chapter) require multiple measurements during each phase of the treatment—assessment, intervention, and follow-up. How often one can collect data also depends on the scale chosen. For example, the directions for Children's Global Assessment Scale asks the responder to consider the child's lowest level of functioning over the past 28 days—so obviously one cannot fill out the Children's Global Assessment Scale more frequently than monthly. Clinicians who choose to use scaled questions, however, may adjust their inquiry so that data could be collected weekly. An example would be, "How would you rate your depression on a scale from 1 to 10 this past week?" Practitioners who use a Daily Log for teachers to fill out might ask the question, "Did this student achieve his goal(s) today?" (see Box 7.2). Finally, as intervention intensity increases so should the frequency of data collection. All children are required by law to receive progress reports on a quarterly basis—for most schools, this means every 10 weeks. As students receive indicated services, then progress monitoring should increase too. Thus, students in tier two of the Response to Intervention model should have their progress monitored at least monthly. Students receiving intensive services in tier three of the Response to Intervention model should have their progress monitored at least every couple of weeks (National Association of State Directors of Special Education, 2006).

Crunching Numbers

Most practitioners go into social work, psychology, or counseling not because they love numbers, but because they care about people. Caring about people requires, however, that we care about their progress (or lack of it) and that we care about being able to continue serving them by justifying what we do to those who hold the purse strings. Gibbs (2003) provides four basic reasons for collecting data in practice. First, as mentioned in the Introduction, we must make our own observations. It is simply impossible to know if we have been effective without some hard evidence. Sometimes this can be sobering when we determine that despite all our best efforts, an intervention has not worked. We have a moral obligation to our clients to ensure that we are providing the best services possible. Second, merely extrapolating scientifically based research to our clients can still place them at risk of harm. Some ESTs demonstrate statistically significant improvement *even if* a few participants have regressed in their functioning. This can occur because the vast majority of studies are about group effects, not individual ones. As long as most of the clients have been helped, it can still be an empirically supported intervention. Third, data collection does not have to be complicated. As mentioned earlier, there are many ways to collect data—some as simple as asking a client a scaled question on a regular basis. Some scales, such as the Strengths and Difficulties Questionnaire (SDQ) (Goodman, 2001), are incredibly brief and easy to score. Finally, research supports the idea that clients actually prefer outcome evaluation over clinician opinion (Campbell, 1990). Since the definition of evidence-based practitioners puts the client's benefits first (see Chapter 2), outcome evaluation helps build trust in the relationship.

Before we address how to analyze your own data in Excel, it is important to address a basic fact about statistics and computers. No computer will tell the user that they are using an inappropriate means of statistical analysis. I will provide some box inserts about some essential statistical concepts (e.g., Box 7.5) to serve as reminders to those who need them without interrupting the flow of the chapter for those who need no refresher course. For those who need more help, please see the suggested reading at the end of this chapter or consult your school's math teacher. (There are very few statistical formulas that require any more than knowledge of 5th grade mathematics.)

Excel

For a decade, I taught graduate-level research using the Statistical Package for the Social Sciences. It is an excellent computer program, which has improved

BOX 7.5 Levels of Measurement

Nominal: Categories without any rank order, such as gender, type of therapist (social worker, psychologist, or counselor), or type of treatment (group, individual, or family)

Ordinal: Categories with a rank order but no standard intervals between them, such as educational attainment (elementary, junior high, or high school), level of satisfaction (very dissatisfied, dissatisfied, satisfied, or very satisfied), preference rank (first, second, or third choices), or socioeconomic status (low, middle, and upper classes)

Interval: Categories with a rank order and a standard interval, but no true zero, such as IQ score, points earned or lost, temperature, or year

Ratio: Categories with a rank order, standard interval and true zero point, such as age, height, number of sessions, or weight

Category values must possess two qualities. They must be mutually exclusive and exhaustive. *Mutually exclusive* means that no case should simultaneously belong to both category values. *Exhaustive* means that the category values should cover every possible variation. Many scales, for example, use an "other" value to include low frequency possibilities. Thus, the category "gender" might have three response categories: female, male, or other to include transgendered individuals.

over time and is relatively user friendly. Students would learn how to set up their data entry sheets and how to analyze the data in exactly the right way, but there was a problem—no one actually owned the Statistical Package for the Social Sciences. They would use it in the university's computer lab, save the data onto their floppy disk (this preceded jump drives), and not be able to look at the data between class sessions. Somewhat reluctantly, I switched to using Microsoft Excel and immediately noticed a difference.

Every student and every agency owned it, so some were actually excited about learning this tool that regularly popped up every time they turned on their computer. They could even enter their data and analyze from the comfort of their home or office. Gradually, I have become a convert to Excel and I hope to convert some of you as well.

Fast Facts

Spreadsheets have four common uses in social service settings (Patterson & Basham, 2006). First, they can graph the progress that individual clients make over the course of treatment. Second, they can analyze how groups of clients change over time. Third, they can analyze service-related expenses, such as books, journals, or treatment manuals. Finally, they can generate tables for reporting results to school administrators, school boards, and district officials.

Spreadsheets have existed as long as humans have kept financial records, but they were traditionally called ledgers. Readers born more than 20 years ago may remember their teachers keeping track of attendance and grades in legal-sized, green-papered registers with a pencil and eraser. Electronic spreadsheets are a vast improvement on these old registers because they automatically update the results as new information is entered (no erasers needed). Excel is neither the oldest nor the only electronic spreadsheet program. The first electronic spreadsheet was VisiCalc, designed in 1979 (Bricklin, 2003). It was quickly followed by Lotus 1-2-3, Excel, and QuattroPro over the next 10 years. Since the advent of electronic spreadsheets, there have been three major improvements. First, they have gradually expanded the range of tools and features, especially the number of statistical functions. Second, they are increasingly integrated with other computer applications, such as Word and PowerPoint, making the copying and pasting of charts easy. Finally, they are used by an ever greater number of helping professionals, including school psychologists, social workers, and counselors (Alberts & Ankenmann, 2001; Carr & Burkholder, 1998; Ware & Galassi, 2006). I use Excel simply because it is part of the Window Office Suite and thus the most widely available spreadsheet for both individuals and agencies. I strongly advise readers to peruse the rest of this chapter in front of computer so that you can look at Excel while reading.

Data Entry

The information in spreadsheets is entered into boxes called cells. There are three kinds of information that cells can hold. They can contain field labels, values, and formulas. *Field labels* are simply the names of the major variables belonging to a group of cases (e.g., age, grade, gender, etc.). *Values* are the textual or numerical information describing a specific case (e.g., 7, 2nd, female, etc.). *Formulas* are algebraic equations that analyze the values in other cells to produce a result in the current cell (e.g., average, sum, or standard deviation). Formulas include both simple manually created equations (see Box 7.6) and advanced functions chosen from a list, such as the statistical formulas we will describe later.

Data can be entered in one of three ways (Patterson & Basham, 2006). First, the data entry can be done manually by typing the data directly into the Excel spreadsheet. Second, the data can be entered by creating a data entry

BOX 7.6 Common Operators in Excel

SYMBOL	PURPOSE	EXAMPLE
=	Equals, used at the beginning of every equation	= C2 + 3
+	Plus, used for addition	= C2 + C3
−	Minus, used for subtraction	= C2 − C3
×	Multiply, used for multiplication	= C2 × C3
/	Divide, used for division	= C2/C3
%	Percent, used for percentage	= C2 × 10%
^	Exponent, used for exponentiation	= C2^2 (C2 squared)
:	Range, used to specify a range of cells	= C2:C10 (all cells in between)
,	Separate, used to separate to cell references	= C2,C10 (only two cells)
Σ	Sigma, used to sum a set of cells	= Σ (C2:C10)
( )	Order, used to specify an operation's priority	= Σ (B2 × B10) + (C2 × C10)

Evidence-Based Practice in School Mental Health

form similar to an agency intake form. Finally, the data can be imported from another program, such as a school database or intranet.

The cells are organized into columns and rows. Columns are vertical lines of alphabetized cells that typically pertain to the variable labels under analysis. Rows are horizontal lines of numbered cells that typically pertain to the individual cases that belong to the dataset. Any cell can be specified by its exact vertical and horizontal location. Thus, the cell C4 would be in the third column and fourth row. If you are worried about running out of room, each worksheet contains 256 columns and over 65,000 rows meaning that there are over 16 million cells (Dretzke, 2005).

Let's begin with Schaeffer et al.'s (2005) advice to start small and evaluate just one intervention. Knowing that psycho-educational support groups are an empirically supported strategy for both parents and children struggling with divorce (Gwynn & Brantley, 1987; Wallerstein, 1991; Zimpfer, 1990), suppose we are doing a short-term adjustment group for children whose parents are going through a divorce using a standard curriculum (Kalter & Schreier, 1994). Let's keep track of five variables: the stage of the parents' divorce (separated, divorced, or remarried), the grade level of the child (1st through 5th grade), the number of sessions they've attended, and their score on the Parent version of the SDQ at pretest and posttest. There is an assumption that parents are more likely to see divorce-related problems than teachers. There are eight children in the group, so we enter the information into Excel, as seen in Box 7.7.

Before getting started in Excel, it will be necessary to ensure that the analysis tool pack is loaded into your program. This is a simple process. Open Excel; along the top of the page, there should be three rows of words/icons. The top row is the Menu bar, the middle row is the Standard Toolbar, and the third row is the Formatting Toolbar. If you do not see all three rows, go to View on the Menu bar, select Toolbars, and ensure that both Standard and Formatting are checked. Now go to the word Tools on the Menu bar, select Add-Ins, and check the Analysis Toolpak option and press OK.

Frequency Distributions

As anyone can tell by looking at the table (Box 7.7) that it is difficult to get a bird's eye view of such a diverse group; so before any data can be analyzed, it needs to be summarized. The most common method of summarization of a single variable (or field) is a frequency distribution. A *frequency distribution* is an array or ordering of the values from lowest to highest or vice versa. Thus, an ordering of the field "grade level" for elementary students would

BOX 7.7 Excel Spreadsheet: Data Entry

	A	B	C	D	E
	A	**B**	**C**	**D**	**E**
1	STAGE	GRADE	SESSIONS	SDQ-1	SDQ-2
2	S	1	6	22	23
3	D	3	8	16	8
4	S	2	7	20	13
5	R	4	6	16	17
6	D	3	7	22	15
7	S	2	7	25	14
8	D	3	8	18	10
9	S	2	8	20	11

likely tell us how many clients were in 1st grade, 2nd grade, 3rd grade, and so on. It enables a researcher to quickly "eyeball" the data and notice which values are most common. The easiest way to do this in Excel is with the pivot table option because it works on both qualitative (nominal) and quantitative (ordinal, interval, or ratio) data. Go to Data in the Menu bar and select PivotTable and PivotChart Report. Click Next to maintain the default for PivotTable and Next again to maintain the default for the entire data set (note that PivotTables must include the Field Labels in Row 1). (Warning: There is a flaw in most versions of Excel so that this range can be changed only by using the mouse, not the cursor keys on the keyboard. Hopefully, this defect will be corrected in future versions.) Then click on Finish to open the PivotTable in a new worksheet. You will now see three boxes. On the far left is the blank PivotTable. On the right, there is the PivotTable Field List. Above this is a small tool bar marked PivotTable. To see the Frequency Distribution of any variable, click and drag the Field button from Field List to the Row section of the PivotTable, then repeat this to drag the same Field button to the Data section. If we drag the field Stage to both the Row and Data sections, we get a distribution as seen in Box 7.8.

This maneuver allows us to see a summary array of how many children are in each stage of the divorce process. We note that most are in the earliest stage, separation, and only one is in the last stage, remarriage. We can also click and drag these field labels back to the PivotTable Field List and select other fields to see different frequency distributions. Users can also create charts for each frequency distribution by clicking on the Chart Wizard button on the PivotTable tool bar.

Descriptive Analysis

There are two levels of statistical analysis. The simplest is called *descriptive* because it "describes" the set of cases under scrutiny. There are two types of descriptive statistics: measures of central tendency and measures of variability. *Measures of central tendency* tell us what is typical about a data set and include the mode, median, and mean/average. Their specific use is governed both by the level of measurement (see Box 7.5) and the characteristics of the sample (see Box 7.9). *Measures of variability* tell how a data set is dispersed and include the range, variance, and standard deviation. Their specific use is also governed by the level of measurement and characteristics of the sample.

Let us say we would like to understand the central tendency for the number of sessions attended by members of the divorce support group. Returning to worksheet 1, click on the empty cell, C10. Now click on the word Insert on the Menu bar and select Function. Select the category Statistical, scroll down to AVERAGE and click OK. By default, Excel chooses all of the numbers above C10. Since this is exactly the data set we would like to average, hit OK and the result should be 7.125. In other words, the average group member attended seven of the eight sessions. Now let's learn about the dispersion. Click on the empty cell, C11. Now click on the word Insert on the

BOX 7.9 Levels of Measurement and Descriptive Statistics

LEVEL OF MEASUREMENT	CENTRAL TENDENCY	VARIABILITY
Nominal	Mode	Number of value categories
Ordinal	Mode or median	Range
Interval	Mode, median, or mean*	Range, variance, standard deviation
Ratio	Mode, median, or mean*	Range, variance, standard deviation

*Caution: The mean or average is not always the best measure of central tendency. If there are a few values that are extreme, called outliers, then the median may be a better choice. When this occurs, then interquartile range or semi-interquartile range may be better measures of variability.

Menu bar and select Function again. Select the category Statistical, scroll all the way to STDEV and click OK. Once again, Excel chooses all of the numbers above, but this time we do not want to include the previous result, so we must change the default range from C2:C10 to C2:C9. To do so, simply move your cursor to the end of the range, backspace over the 10 and type 9, press OK, and the result should be .834523. In other words, most members came within one session of attending the average number of times. We can repeat this process for other ratio level variables, such as the pretest and posttest scores on the SDQ. We would learn that the average pretest score is 19.875 and the average posttest score is 13.875.

Inferential Statistics

The second level of statistics is called *inferential* because it allows researchers to "infer" the results from the sample to the broader population. There are two broad types of inferential research hypotheses or questions. The first type is a hypothesis/question of difference. A hypothesis predicts a direction of the findings, resulting in a "one-tailed" hypothesis. Sometimes the hypothesis involves the difference between two or more separate groups; sometimes the hypothesis involves the difference within one group over the course of time.

Evidence-Based Practice in School Mental Health

It is not difficult to tell that our group made progress during the 8-week group. Their average scores went down six points on the SDQ. What we do not know is whether this difference is statistically significant. This is where inferential statistics can help. We may have hypothesized at the beginning of the group that, "Children enrolled in an 8-week psycho-educational support group for elementary pupils whose parents are going through a divorce will demonstrate improved functioning." In research terms, we have made a positive prediction about our intervention and this has direct implications for our choice of inferential tests. Since we are interested in measuring the difference, we will use a t-test. Since we are interested in the measuring the differences of the same group over time, we should use a paired-sample t-test (see Box 7.10). Since we have made a positive prediction, we should choose a one-tailed over a two-tailed test. (Readers interested in publishing their findings, however, are better off using the more rigorous two-tailed test.) Begin by clicking on empty cell E11. Go to Insert, then Function, then Statistical, then scroll down to TTEST, and hit OK. This time Excel does not fill in the array of numbers for you, so you will need to enter the range yourself. In Array 1, type D2:D9 and tab down. In Array 2, type E2:E9 and tab down. Next to Tails, type 1, and tab down. Next to Type, type 1 again. Note, if you click "Help on this function," Excel will provide a pop-up Excel Help box for further explanation—try it! This box gives the important information that Excel does not actually provide a t statistic, but provides the probability (p) statistic. Traditionally, statisticians have chosen $p < .05$ as significant. Close the Help box and click OK. The result should be .003501, which is statistically significant!

Let's try another example of inferential statistics. The second type of inferential research hypotheses is a hypothesis/question of association. A research question does not predict the direction of the findings, resulting in a "two-tailed" question, meaning the findings could go either way—negative or positive. Sometimes this question involves the similarities between two variables; sometimes it involves the similarities between more than two variables. Looking at the raw data, one cannot help but notice that two of our eight group members actually got worse, instead of better. We might also notice that these same two had the two lowest rates of attendance, so we develop a research question that goes like this, "Is there an association between group attendance and change?" Physicians call this type of inquiry a dose-response question since the dose differed slightly for each client. Returning to our worksheet, we will have Excel create a new

BOX 7.10 Level of Measurement and Commonly Used Inferential Tests

INDEPENDENT (PREDICTOR) VARIABLE	DEPENDENT (CRITERION) VARIABLE	TEST OF DIFFERENCE	TEST OF ASSOCIATION	EXCEL FUNCTION
Nominal	Nominal		Yules-Q	N/A
Large groups—30+		Chi-square (χ^2)		CHITEST
Small groups		Fisher's exact		FISHERINV
Related groups		McNemar's		N/A
Nominal	Ordinal			N/A
Two groups		Wilcoxin-pairs		N/A
Three groups		Kruskal-Wallis	• Mann-Whitney U	N/A
Nominal	Interval/ratio			
One group		Paired t-test*		TTEST (var 1)
Two groups		Independent t-test*		TTEST (var 2)
Three groups		ANOVA F-test*		FTEST
Ordinal	Ordinal		Spearman's rho (ρ)	N/A
Two ranks			Kendall's tau (τ)	N/A
Three ranks			Kendall's w	N/A
Interval/ratio	Interval/ratio		Pearson's r*	PEARSON
Two variables			Linear regression*	LINEST
Three variables			Multiple regression*	LINEST

*Parametric tests must meet three criteria: At least one variable (usually the dependent) must be at the interval or ratio level of measurement; the dependent variable must be normally distributed in the population; cases must be randomly selected from the population and randomly assigned to treatment versus control groups. For nonparametric alternatives, see Box 5.5 or move up one cell.

column for us. Click on empty cell F1 and label this field, Change. Then go to F2 and enter this equation: $=D2-E2$ and press the down cursor. Now place your cursor on the lower right hand corner of F2 (on the small black box) and drag your cursor down to F9. Excel will recreate a matching equation for each row without you having to tell it what to do! Use the average function to determine the average amount of change for the group in F10. As we saw earlier, the result should be six. With this information, we are ready to do a Pearson's correlation (see Box 7.10). Click on empty cell, F11, then go to Insert, then Function, then Statistical, then PEARSON. Like TTEST, Excel allows the user to determine the two arrays or ranges of values. This time for Array 1, click in Array 1, then take your cursor and drag it over cells C2:C9; they will blink and appear in Array 1. Now click in Array 2 and drag the cursor over cells F2:F9. Click on OK and the result should be .798156. Unfortunately, Excel does not tell users whether this result is significant or not the way it did for the t-test, so we have provided two links to obtain this information under Internet Resources. At .798, this result is significant at $p < .02$ for an eight-member group with a two-tailed test (remember we did not predict a direction as we did for the t-test).

For those readers who barely remember their research classes, I strongly recommend befriending a math teacher. They are usually quite patient and adept at explaining these concepts to those who would prefer not to learn them. For those who are computer phobic, we strongly recommend befriending the information technology teacher, who is apt to share the same qualities as the aforementioned math teacher. An excellent (and free) software add-on for advanced inferential statistics in Excel is EZAnalyze (see Internet Resources).

Two Caveats

There are two sets of closely related concepts that can confuse practitioners. The first is the difference between correlation and causation. The second is the difference between clinical and statistical significance.

Correlation Versus Causation

Correlation means that two variables are related, but may have nothing to do with causation. For example, we can correlate the sale of ice cream and death by drowning. Both reach their peak during the summer months, but it would be foolish to think that eating ice cream causes drowning. They are simply both the result of a third variable—increased temperature.

Causation, however, means that one variable (the independent or predictor variable) has a direct effect on another variable (the dependent or outcome variable). The lack of wearing seat belts during car crashes leads to more injury and death. Demonstration of causation requires passing three litmus tests. First, did the intervention temporally precede the change in the dependent/outcome variable? Second, did the intervention and the outcome covary (or correlate) with each other? Finally, did we rule out all of the rival plausible explanations for the change?

Most of the practice-based evidence collected as part of outcome evaluation will demonstrate correlation and not causation for two reasons. First, most therapists would argue that it is unethical to deny treatment to members of control group. Even if the control group was a "waiting list" group to receive treatment, concerned therapists might object that the neediest children should be triaged, thereby creating unequal groups. The most common way around this predicament is to use a comparison group. For example, one group may receive individual treatment while the other group receives group therapy. This brings us to another ethical problem—who decides? If we allow the clients to decide, we may get a *response bias*—those who feel most embarrassed or humiliated about their problems may choose individual therapy. If we allow the therapists to decide, we may get a *sampling bias*—those who think group therapy is the best approach may inadvertently assign the most social or articulate clients to the group condition. Either way, if the two groups are unequal at the beginning of treatment, then their results are not comparable at the end of treatment. The only scientific way around this conundrum is randomized assignment of clients to the two treatment conditions.

This brings us to our divorce support group. Because we did not compare this group to any other comparable group, we cannot know for sure if it was the intervention that caused their improvement. We have passed only the first two tests. We know that the group intervention preceded the change in the outcome measure. We also know that during the 8 weeks that we ran the group, the group improved. We could not, however, rule out other plausible explanations—the members may have become more mature (naturally), received more empathy from teachers, settled into their new family routines, or made new friends. Thus, practice-based evidence can rarely make claims about causation because of the use of less rigorous research designs (Howard & Jenson, 1999; Marino, Green, & Young, 1998; Overbay, Grable, & Vasu, 2006).

Clinicians who believe that they have discovered an intervention that works in a school-based context should collaborate with a university researcher to submit the treatment to a scientific test (randomized controlled trial or quasi-experimental design). Hopefully, this will lead to a joint publication for the benefit of the entire field (Raines & Massat, 2004).

Clinical Significance Versus Statistical Significance

We would be remiss if we allowed readers to think that statistical significance has any relation to clinical significance. Statistical significance is the probability that the difference or association found is due to mere chance. Researchers customarily use the 95% confidence level, often signified by probability sign $p < .05$, meaning that there is only a 5% chance that luck accounted for the results. According to Kazdin (1999), *clinical significance*, however, is

> The practical or applied value or importance of the effect of the intervention—that is, whether the intervention makes any real (e.g., genuine, palpable, practical, noticeable) difference in everyday life to the clients or to others with whom the client interacts. (p. 332)

It might also be described as the degree to which the intervention causes clients to no longer meet the criteria for a clinical disorder. This can be determined in two ways. First, from a quantitative perspective, a client may change from scoring above the cut point on a commonly accepted measure of the problem to scoring below the cut point. For example, if truancy is defined as missing more than 10% of the school year, then a clinically significant improvement would be for the student to attend more than 90% of the school year. Second, from a qualitative perspective, a client may meet the diagnostic criteria on a widely accepted set of criteria, such as the *Diagnostic and Statistical Manual of Mental Disorders* of the American Psychiatric Association (2005). A clinically significant result would mean that the client no longer qualifies for that diagnosis. Statistical and clinical significance are quite separate for two reasons. First, students with high problem scores on a clinical measure, such as the SDQ, can make statistically significant progress, but still score above the clinical cut score. For the SDQ, for example, Goodman (2001) informs users that problem scores on the parent version of the SDQ from 17 to 40 are abnormal. Since we got statistically significant results when the group average was reduced by six points, it becomes clear that if the average pretest score was over 23, then most of our participants could have made statistically significant progress, but still have clinically significant problems! Second, we noted that two out of eight participants (25%) actually got worse over the life of the group. The group made statistically significant progress, but some individuals actually regressed.

In response-to-intervention terms, these two students failed to respond to our scientifically based intervention! The end of the group intervention obviously cannot mean an end to services for every member. We may decide to see these students in individual treatment (moving from Tier 2 to Tier 3) or negotiate an extension of the group for members who are still at risk. We may also decide that our 8-week group was too short and retool it as a full 10-week group (e.g., Kalter & Schreier, 1994; Sanders & Kiester, 1996) since a recent meta-analysis suggests that this length is more effective (Stathakos & Roehrle, 2003). We might also decide that our short-term group intervention needs a parent component, especially if we heed Wallerstein's (1991) warning about children in high-conflict families. Perhaps we could adapt Lim, Stormshak, and Dishion's (2005) 2-hour parent seminar for parents who were separating or divorcing during the next semester. The bottom line is that students who receive intervention must become clinically better, not just statistically so. The next chapter will address progress monitoring using single-subject designs.

Summary

Outcome evaluation is always important whether practitioners adapt an intervention or apply it exactly as it was designed. The scientific method and clinical practice should go hand-in-hand. This chapter began with a reminder about the difference between independent and dependent variables. Then it described three types of research designs. Next, it introduced six ways to collect data on students. These included a search of their archival records, usually from a school database; teacher interviews, especially the degree to which the teacher felt the student was outside of the expected norms for their age group; daily or weekly logs, kept by the teacher and/ or student about emotional or behavioral concerns; standardized instruments that are brief, identify strengths, and aid in treatment planning; direct observation of the student either in the office or the classroom; and scaled questions when the problem is not visible to the human eye (it may be quite visible to the human heart). After this, the frequency of data collection was identified as dependent on three primary factors—the type of research design, the instrument used, and the intensity of intervention. Readers were also introduced to using the Excel spreadsheet to record and analyze the data that was collected. This included some instructions on data entry, descriptive statistics, and inferential statistics. Finally, this chapter concluded with two important cautions. First, there is a difference between correlation and causation. Most practice-based evidence will demonstrate the former, but not the latter. Practitioners can, however, collaborate with researchers to establish scientifically based evidence and disseminate this through a joint publication. Second, there is a difference between clinical significance and statistical significance. Students can make statistically significant progress, but still have clinically significant problems. Good therapists do not quit until their clients can demonstrate clinical improvement.

Suggested Reading

1. Dretzke, B. J. (2005). *Statistics with Microsoft Excel* (3rd ed.). Upper Saddle River, NJ: Pearson/Prentice Hall.

2. Grinnell, R. M. Jr., & Unrau, Y. A. (2008). *Social Work Research and Evaluation: Foundations of Evidence-Based Practice*. New York: Oxford University Press.

3. Patterson, D. A., & Basham, R. E. (2006). *Data Analysis with Spreadsheets*. Boston: Pearson/Allyn & Bacon.

4. Rubin, A. (2007). *Statistics for Evidence-Based Practice and Evaluation*. Belmont, CA: Thomson Brooks/Cole.

5. Weinbach, R. W., & Grinnell, R. M. Jr. (2007). *Statistics for Social Workers* (7th ed.). Boston: Pearson/Allyn & Bacon.

Internet Resources

Measurement Tools

Achenbach System of Empirically Based Assessment
http://www.aseba.org/

Behavior Assessment System for Children
http://ags.pearsonassessments.com/Group.asp?nGroupInfoID=a30000

Scales of Independent Behavior—Revised
http://www.riverpub.com/products/sibr/index.html

Vineland Adaptive Behavior Scales-2
http://ags.pearsonassessments.com/Group.asp?nGroupInfoID=aVineland

Statistical Decisions

Advanced Technology Services—UCLA
http://www.ats.ucla.edu/stat/mult_pkg/whatstat/default.htm

Choosing the Correct Statistical Test—Crystal Hoyt—University
of Richmond
http://www.richmond.edu/~choyt/supportingdocs_spring05/
handout_stattests.doc

EZAnalyze—Data Analysis for Educators
http://www.ezanalyze.com/

Exploratory Data Analysis
http://www.itl.nist.gov/div898/handbook/eda/eda.htm

HyperStat Online Textbook
http://davidmlane.com/hyperstat/index.html

Intuitive Biostatistics—Graphpad.com
http://www.graphpad.com/www/Book/Choose.htm

Matching Statistics with the Research Design—University of Texas
Medical Branch
http://sahs.utmb.edu/pellinore/intro_to_research/wad/sel_test.htm

MedCalc Statistics Menu
http://www.medcalc.be/manual/mpage06.php

Mississippi State University Virtual Statistics Laboratory
http://www.abe.msstate.edu/Tools/vsl/index.php

Professor Gerstman's StatPrimer
http://www.sjsu.edu/faculty/gerstman/StatPrimer/

Rice Virtual Lab in Statistics
http://onlinestatbook.com/rvls.html

Statistical Analysis: Statistics, Mathematics, and Measurement—
A Statistical Flow Chart
http://www.napce.org/articles/Research%20Design%20Yount/
05_analysisflow_4th.pdf

Statistics Demonstrations with Excel
http://sunsite.univie.ac.at/Spreadsite/statexamp/

Statistical Interpretation

Level of Significance for Pearson's *r* Correlation—Illinois State University
http://lilt.ilstu.edu/gmklass/pos138/assignments/level__r.html

Testing the Significance of Pearson's *r*—University of New England (Australia)
http://www.une.edu.au/WebStat/unit_materials/c6_common_statistical_tests/test_signif_pearson.html

8

■ ■ ■

Evaluating Individual Outcomes Using Single-Subject Designs

Preview

The last chapter was about how to evaluate group outcomes using descriptive research designs. This chapter is about how to evaluate individual outcomes using single-subject designs. It will begin with a review of the federal requirements for monitoring the progress of students in special education—having a single standard for progress; planning ahead for progress measurement; reporting progress at regular intervals; changing behavior; and encouraging the return to general education—and then align this with single-subject research designs. Second, establishing a baseline for individual functioning will be described in four ways: ensuring that measures are understandable to parents and students; using a variety of measures, including behavioral rubrics and goal attainment scaling; triangulating the measures to make certain that they truly represent the student's performance level; and being sure to state the baseline in positive terms. Third, the requirements for measurable annual goals will be described, including environmental conditions, services needed, the identity of the student, defined actions, and performance criteria. The last section will provide details on how to evaluate student progress using single-case research procedures using Excel. After an introduction to the many varieties of single-subject design, the chapter will address the requirements in dependent and independent variables; experimental management, visual analysis techniques; student self-monitoring; and how to improve the social validity of the measurement method.

Federal Requirements

Several authors have observed that the new reauthorization of the Individuals with Disabilities Education Improvement Act (IDEA) in 2004 put a new emphasis on monitoring progress (Gartin & Murdick, 2005; Hyatt, 2007; Raines, 2006c). It is helpful to review these legal requirements so that Individualized Education Program (IEP) Teams can meet each of the five mandates regarding progress monitoring.

Single Standard for Progress

The first federal requirement is that students with disabilities are expected to achieve the same standards as students without disabilities. Each state must establish goals that meet four criteria. First, state goals for children with disabilities must meet the primary purpose of IDEA: "To ensure that all children with disabilities have available to them a free appropriate public education that emphasizes special education and related services designed to meet their unique needs and prepare them for further education, employment, and independent living" (section 601 (d)(1)). This is due to the President's Commission on Excellence in Special Education (2002) finding that only 34% of adults with disabilities between the ages of 21 and 64 reported that they were employed and even those who had jobs earned substantially less than their nondisabled peers. Second, the goals must enable the progress of children with disabilities to be "the same as the State's definition of adequate yearly progress" under the Elementary and Secondary Education Act (section 612 (a)(15)(A)(ii)). This was meant to align IDEA with the No Child Left Behind's emphasis on accountability for results (Raines, 2006c). Third, the state goals must address graduation and dropout rates. This is because approximately 80,000 students with disabilities drop out of high school each year (U.S. Department of Education, 2004a). Fourth, the goals must be "consistent, to the extent appropriate, with any other goals and standards for children established by the State" (section 612 (a)(15)(A)(iv)). In other words, students in special education should be judged by the same standards as children in general education.

These state requirements form the reason why each IEP team is expected to use a multimethod assessment strategy that will enable the team to determine "the content of the child's individualized education program, including *information related to enabling the child to be involved in and progress in the general education curriculum*" (section 614 (b)(2)(A)(ii), emphasis added). Based on this assessment, the IEP team must also develop measurable annual goals designed to "meet the child's needs that result from the child's disability to enable the child to be involved in and *make progress in the general education curriculum*" (section 614 (d)(1)(A)(i)(II)(aa), emphasis added). For this reason, states routinely insist that all IEP goals be aligned to state standards for regular education. This requirement has meant that some mental health practitioners must think creatively to apply state education standards to mental health goals. In Illinois, for example, some practitioners find one of the state's physical and health standards useful: "Promote and enhance health well-being through the use of effective communication and decision-making skills" (Standard 24). Fortunately, a few states (e.g., Illinois and New York) have also created social and emotional standards for all children to attain (Collaborative for Academic, Social, and Emotional Learning, 2006).

Progress Measurement Plan

The second federal requirement is that each IEP must delineate an ongoing method for determining the progress of the student toward his or her measurable goals. Thus, each IEP team must include "a description of how the child's progress toward meeting the annual goals...will be measured" (section 614 (d)(1)(A)(i)(III)). Etscheidt (2006) has identified this progress measurement plan as a special area of concern among state administrative review officers. She cites three legal cases where schools lost the hearing because of an inadequate data collection plan. One of the primary complaints of the state hearing officers was that IEP teams failed to identify "objective measures" to determine progress. How does IDEA describe these sorts of measures? The law states that the IEP should use "technically sound instruments that may assess the relative contribution of cognitive and behavioral factors, in addition to physical or developmental factors" (section 614 (b)(2)(C)). Since we have already addressed how to evaluate articles that review the psychometric properties of assessment instruments in Chapter 5, readers should be able to determine which ones meet those criteria.

Regular Reporting

The third federal requirement is that the progress must be reported on a regular basis so that parents know exactly "when periodic reports on the progress the child is making toward meeting the annual goals (such as through the use of quarterly or other periodic reports, concurrent with the issuance of report cards) will be provided" (section 614 (d)(1)(A)(i)(III)). Much has been said about the relaxation of the requirement for writing

---

objectives or benchmarks for most students with disabilities (Hyatt, 2007; Raines, 2006c); practically, there is still a requirement for predetermined standards on how the student is progressing in every grading period. Therefore, school districts would be wise to continue to write objectives or benchmarks even when not specifically required to do so. Etscheidt (2006) found that two districts got into legal trouble on this requirement because the IEP team inappropriately delegated this responsibility to a classroom aide or para-professional who was not a member of the IEP team.

Behavioral Change

Per the fourth federal requirement, for children "whose behavior impedes the child's learning or that of others" (section 614 (d)(3)(B)(i)), the IEP team must consider the use of positive behavior supports, interventions, or other strategies to change that behavior (Raines, 2002a). Since this would create a required goal on the IEP, teams must develop a progress measurement plan to determine whether the behavior has improved. Etscheidt (2006), however, found three occasions where school districts failed to monitor behavioral changes and measure the degree to which these were "significant." The court in this case (*West Des Moines Community School District v. Heartland Area Education Agency*, 2002) did not specify whether they meant statistical or clinical significance, but either one would require specificity of measurement. Given the wide number of behavioral outcome measures available (Cobb & Jordan, 2006; Fischer & Corcoran, 2007), there is no excuse for not using one to evaluate progress under these circumstances.

Revolving Door

One of the chief complaints about special education is that it has not been a revolving door to general education, but a second and separate system (President's Commission on Excellence in Special Education, 2002). Per the fifth federal requirement, at each annual review, the IEP team is expected to revise the IEP to address "*any lack of expected progress* toward the annual goals and in the general education curriculum" (section 614 (d)(4)(A)(ii)(I), emphasis added). This requirement actually implies two important points. First, specific progress must be anticipated. If the measurable annual goals are not specific enough to determine whether the child has met them, then they are inadequate to help with a reevaluation. Second, the reevaluation must include some remeasurement to review how the student has done with respect to the anticipated standards. Students who have met both their individualized annual goals and the standards of the general education curriculum deserve to return to the regular education environment.

Common Problems

Yell and Stecker (2003) provide this portrayal of the IEP process in many, if not most, schools. First, a student is assessed through a predetermined set of standardized instruments to determine eligibility, but this assessment fails to address any instructionally relevant needs that might relate to reason for referral or progress in the general education curriculum. Second, one or more IEP team members writes "cookie-cutter" goals that are transferred from a "goal bank" (computerized or typed). The goals are neither meaningfully based on the assessment nor measurable enough to determine whether they will ever be met. When the parents (and perhaps an older student) show up at the meeting, the prepared IEP is presented to them, and they are expected to review and sign it. Finally, when the IEP has been signed by all the witnesses to this participatory event, it is dutifully placed in a filing cabinet until the IEP team meets again a year later. It never informs intervention, it never is used to monitor progress, and it is little more than a compulsory exercise in legal compliance with educational laws.

Establishing the Baseline

The initial assessment is meant to be a multimethod, multisource evaluation of where the student is at the beginning of the eligibility process. As I have stated elsewhere (Raines, 2002b)

> The demand for measurable goals has implications for the present level of performance (PLOP). Specifically, if annual goals are to be meaningful and measurable, there needs to be measured baseline from which to start. Without such as baseline, there is no way to tell whether a goal is achievable—it may even represent a regression in performance. (p. 59)

By *meaningful*, I mean that there is congruency between the stated problem and the proposed solution or goal. By *measurable*, I mean that there is sufficient specificity to determine if the goal has actually been achieved 12 months later. The latest reauthorization of IDEA has changed the ambiguous phrase "present level of performance," to a clearer phase "present levels of academic achievement and functional performance" to indicate that IEPs are meant to address both academic and social, emotional, behavioral, or daily living skills. The baseline should be understandable, use a variety of measures, be triangulated, and be positively stated.

Understandable Measures

I have spoken to many school districts about IEP writing and have often encountered a common confusion. Many IEP teams think that they cannot mention a measurement within the section on present levels of academic achievement and functional performance. There is no mention of a prohibition on using numbers or statistics in the IEP in either the law or its final regulations. This confusion is based on a misinterpretation of the general principle that all materials should be understandable to parents. Advanced statistical terms, such as z-scores or standard deviations, would be beyond the comprehension of most parents. Most parents can, however, appreciate basic fractions or percentages expressed as, for example, "Juan is late to school 3/5 of the week or 60% of time" or "Serena only plays with 3/15 girls in the class or 20% of her possible playmates," and absorb the information. The important point is that this kind of specificity allows the IEP team to establish a baseline from which to measure progress. Without a baseline, there is simply no way to know if the proposed goals are aiming too high or too low. There is also no way to determine whether the student is responsive or unresponsive to our interventions.

Variety of Measures

This baseline measurement can be established using any of the methods mentioned in Chapter 7. The average number of office disciplinary referrals per quarter might be gleaned from archival records for a student with behavioral problems. The regular education teacher may be able to report how many words a student with a suspected learning disability can read correctly within a 5-minute period on at least three occasions. A log might be kept for a month before the IEP to determine how many times a shy student initiates contributing to a class discussion. If the problem seems too amorphous for an exact measure, then clinicians can help the teacher develop a rubric for the desired behavior (see Box 8.1). The Vineland Adaptive Behavior Scale might be used to measure the adaptive living skills of a student with mental retardation. Occasionally, the IEP team will identify a problem that is difficult to measure using a standardized scale; for these exceptions, they can employ a Goal Attainment scale (see Box 8.2). Direct observation might be used to determine by how much more a student with attention deficit/hyperactivity disorder was off-task than an index peer. A student struggling with depression may be asked to rate his/her own level of sadness each week during the evaluation period. There really are no problems encountered in school that cannot be measured and recorded on initial IEP as a baseline by which to measure improvement.

Triangulated Measures

In order to guarantee that our measurement is sound, however, it is wise to triangulate our approach. This can be accomplished in multiple ways. One might use the same measurement multiple times, as when the teacher tests the student's reading ability on three occasions for 5 minutes a week apart. One could use three different means of measuring the same problem. For example, a log could be kept to record how many times a girl with depression looked sad or about to cry or she could be given the Children's Depression Inventory to see if she fell into the clinical range. Finally, one may possibly ask three different sources the same questions or to fill out related rating scales, such as the BASC or ASEBA scales. Practitioners do this simply to be sure that the measurement is not an aberration or an accident. The more accurate the baseline, the more sure we can be about the level of improvement.

Positive Measures

Finally, the student's level of ability should be stated in positive terms. This is done for two reasons. First, as mentioned in Chapter 3, IDEA requires that IEP teams identify students' strengths from the Individualized Family Service Plan for toddlers to transition planning for students preparing for college or career goals. Second, the current terms "academic achievement" and "functional performance" are meant to focus on what the child can do, not what he or she cannot do. This requires some reframing of the original data. Schools often keep track of negative data—absences, disciplinary referrals, and tardiness. School-based practitioners, however, must be experts at rephrasing some of this information. For example, a student who had 20 absences last year actually attended 160 days in a standard 180-day school year or a student who had 15 office disciplinary referrals last year actually had 165 days when his behavior was appropriate (or at least manageable). Put in terms of percentages, the first student attended school 88% of the required days and the second student behaved himself nearly 92% of the time. The differences in viewpoints are startling—focusing on the negatives conveys the perception that the students are troubled, but concentrating on the positives produces the idea that these

BOX 8.1 Rubrics for Emotional, Behavioral, and Social Issues

The word rubric originally referred to "marks in red" (Finson & Ormsbee, 1998). The marks were used by medieval monks to separate the major sections of a hand-copied sacred book (Wenzlaff, Fager, & Coleman, 1999). Today, rubrics are categories of qualitative criteria that clearly define for the student and teacher the range of performance levels, from unacceptable to exemplary (Pate, Homestead, & McGinnis, 1993). They aim to explicate and systematize the implicit criteria that teachers naturally use to judge student performances or projects (Montgomery, 2000). Rubrics have several strengths: they clearly define the "quality" of the expectation, help teachers assess the current level of the student's skills, and monitor student progress (Goodrich, 1997). They have been used in education for many years, including the training of counselors (Hanna & Smith, 1998) and psychologists (Halonen, Bosack, & Clay, 2003). Teachers are trained in their development and application (Ross-Fisher, 2005), but emotional issues are seldom addressed. Unfortunately, many existing school rubrics for behavior primarily focus on misbehavior and the negative consequences that will ensue when a student acts out—typically a new version of the three-strikes-and-you're-out rule.

The three rubrics below deal with common emotional, behavioral, and social issues that affect a student's performance in the classroom. Readers are encouraged to adapt the rubric below for use in their own work with students and teachers. It is designed to be used by either special education or general education teachers since the ultimate goal of special education should be to return most students to the regular education classroom for most of their day. Ideally, students are asked to judge their own performance in an effort to build self-awareness (Jackson & Larkin, 2002).

Emotional-Behavioral-Social Rubric for Classrooms

| STANDARDS | NEEDS IMPROVING | | APPROACHING GOAL | |
	RARELY	SOMETIMES	USUALLY	ALMOST ALWAYS
Emotional expression	Student expresses his/her feelings appropriately <25% of the time	Student expresses his/her feelings appropriately 25% to 50% of the time	Student expresses his/her feelings appropriately 51% to 75% of the time	Student expresses his/her feelings appropriately >75% of the time
On-task behavior	Student appears engaged or focused <25% of the time	Student appears engaged or focused 25% to 50% of the time	Student appears engaged or focused 51% to 75% of the time	Student appears engaged or focused >75% of the time
Social cooperation	Student works/plays well with others <25% of the time	Student works/ plays well with others 25% to 50% of the time	Student works/plays well with others 51% to 75% of the time	Student works/plays well with others >75% of the time

BOX 8.2 Goal Attainment Scaling

Goal attainment scaling (GAS) has been used since 1968 as a generic method of outcome evaluation in mental health (Kiresuk, Smith, & Cardillo, 1994; Newton, 2002). It has been used in education for over 30 years with a wide variety of students (Keelin, 1977; Maher, 1983; Moyer & deRosenroll, 1984). With the advent of increasing accountability for results in education, it is not surprising that GAS has returned as a method for measuring the progress of students with disabilities (Roach & Elliot, 2005).

There are six basic steps to create any GAS. First, the IEP team identifies the current performance level for an academic or functional skill in specific, measured terms. This is the student's baseline or "0" level of performance. Second, in consultation with the student and parent, identify the "best possible" outcome imaginable over the next 5 weeks. This is the student's "+2" level of performance. Third, identify the "worst possible" outcome over the next over the next weeks. This is the student's "−2" level of performance. Now identify midpoints between where the student is now (0-level) and the two extremes (+2 and −2). These midpoints become halfway markers (+1 and −1).

Let's use an example. Jacob Redbear is a Native American youth struggling with obesity. This problem affects his ability to meet state physical education standards and his social position among the boys in his class. Jacob feels that if he could lose weight, he could be both more athletic and more popular. At age 11 and in 5th grade, Jacob stands 5′ 8″ tall and weighs 143 lbs. The school nurse calculates that he is at the 75th percentile for height, but above the 95th percentile for weight. She informs the IEP team that Jacob's body mass index (BMI) is right at 30 and he is at high risk for developing diabetes if he does not bring his weight under control (Story et al., 2003). Given Jacob and his mother's wish that he was thinner and the prognosis if he does not lose weight, the IEP team decides to set up a GAS for Jacob. They currently know that he weighs 143 lbs and this is easier for his family to track than his BMI score, so they assign this weight to level 0. A member of the IEP team explores the scientifically based research for

(continued)

effective programs targeting obesity in American Indians and finds a promising program called Pathways (Steckler et al., 2003). It involves teaching children about healthy food choices and the importance of increased physical activity. Jacob and his mother appreciate the team's cultural sensitivity and believe that he could probably lose up to 2 lbs per week by following the guidelines. This becomes his +2 level. The worst possible outcome would be for Jacob to gain 2 lbs a week. This becomes his −2 level. The midpoints are obviously to lose or gain 1 lb per week, so they become his +1 and −1 levels respectively. If everything works right, Jacob will lose 10 lbs at the end of 5 weeks. They set up the chart below to graph his performance each week. The physical education teacher gives his mother the URL of a web site (http://www.keepkidshealthy.com) to help Jacob develop healthy habits and the school nurse agrees to weigh him after lunch every Wednesday so that the timing will be consistent. The school social worker agrees to help get Jacob engaged in an active team sport, such as lacrosse, a traditional Native American game.

	WEEK 1	WEEK 2	WEEK 3	WEEK 4	WEEK 5
+2 (−2 lbs)					
+1 (−1 lb)					
0 (143 lbs)					
−1 (+1 lb)					
−2 (+2 lbs)					

GAS level

MacKay, Somerville, and Lundie (1996) question the validity of statistical analysis using the GAS because of its usual reliance on ordinal level data. They do, however, commend it as a process for improving the quality of service delivery "so that the personal growth of clients is always a central focus" (p. 171). The specificity of goal setting anticipates the termination of the treatment and ultimately the self-sufficiency of the client. Thus, it represents a valuable means to promote partnership, encourage strengths, increase accountability, and monitor progress.

pupils are salvageable. Once the IEP team has arrived at this conclusion, it is ready to begin the serious work of goal setting.

Measurable Annual Goals

Annual goals are meant to address the changes that are feasible within a 1-year period. This has two implications for IEP teams. First, goals are meant to be intermediate-term, not long-term. Many organizations are used to thinking in terms of 5-year goals, but IEP teams should resist this temptation. Although there are many long-term goals for a student, the focus should be on the most proximal ones. Second, since goals are reevaluated every year, there is no reason to shoot for all the targets the first year. Some of the goals resulting from the initial three-year evaluation should be postponed until the second or third years. No student (or IEP team) should have more goals than it can reasonably remember without coaxing. This means that three to five annual goals should be the maximum for most students.

Good goals have five inherent parts (Lignugaris/Kraft, Marchand-Martella, & Martella, 2001). These include environmental conditions, services needed, the identity of the student, clearly defined actions, and performance criteria. We will address each of these in detail.

Environmental Conditions

Environmental conditions may consist of either the physical setting or the social situation in which the problem occurs. Possible physical settings that may be targeted for intervention include the classroom, cafeteria, hallways, library, playground, school bus, or study hall. Potential social situations include one-to-one tutoring, small group instruction, special education class, general education class, multiclass teams, or school assemblies. It may be helpful for the IEP team to also consider under which environmental conditions the behavior does not occur since generalizing from this condition can lead to improvement under other conditions.

Services Needed

While some school districts treat the services needed portion of a goal as optional (Pemberton, 2003), there are two reasons to include it. First, there is the ethical reason of informed consent. It is unreasonable to presume that a participating student or parent can understand exactly what a school is offering to do without a statement of services included. Second, there is the practical reason of communication. It frequently happens that one service provider (or even whole IEP team) will write the goals, while another service provider (or team) must implement the goals. Without a clear idea of how the original IEP team had envisioned the interventions to be employed, it is virtually impossible for the following team to provide those services.

Services can be divided between accommodations and modifications. Though often used interchangeably by some school staff, they are not the same (Families & Advocates Partnership for Education, 2001). Accommodations allow

> A student to complete the same assignment or test as other students, but with a change in the timing, formatting, setting, scheduling, response and/or presentation. This accommodation does not alter in any significant way what the test or assignment measures. (p. 1)

Accommodations then are specific supports that enable students to maintain the same standards as their general education peers. Mental health supports might include early morning check-ins to organize the day, regular parental guidance on the phone, group therapy, or solution-focused counseling. The students may need consistent support to succeed, but the standards are never lowered because of their disability. Modifications, however, are adjustments "to an assignment or a test that changes the standard or what the test or assignment is supposed to measure" (p. 1). *Modifications* therefore are major changes to the substance of a standard so that it expects less of the student. Mental health examples include a behavior intervention plan, increased tolerance of emotional outbursts, placement into a special education classroom, or rewarding a forgetful student instead penalizing them. In brief, a modification is any intervention that enables a student to meet a standard that is not afforded to most students. These students require the system to "bend the rules" so that they can still obtain a free appropriate public education.

The key to choosing among the alternatives for an IEP team is determining which interventions enjoy the most empirical support (see Figure 4.1) and which ones offer the best "fit" for the situation (see Figure 4.2). This criterion also avoids the ubiquitous catchphrase "with social work/psychological/ counseling intervention" blandly included in so many IEPs. Such amorphous and generic descriptions are to be avoided for two reasons. First, they are too vague to be replicable and only replicable treatments can be empirically supported (Bloom, Fischer, & Orme, 2006). Second, many school districts have moved to functional rather than discipline-specific roles so that professional role hegemonies are obsolete. Specificity allows any mental health practitioner present to provide the services, not just the one stated in an IEP. This provides more protection to students who deserve to have their needs met by whomever is qualified to do so.

Defined Actions

Defined actions can be broadly conceived of as target behaviors, thoughts, or feelings. While behavior is outwardly observable, thoughts and feelings must be inferred through speech or actions. Behavioral verbs include action words such as raise hand, walk quietly, or comply with directions. Cognitive verbs include words such as describe a situation, analyze motives, or evaluate the pros and cons. Affective verbs include words such as empathize with others, respect adult authority figures, or appreciate differences.

While adults may think that it is difficult to infer another person's thoughts or feelings, it must be remembered that our first "language" is nonverbal communication, which has both para-verbal and nonverbal aspects. Para-verbal clues include the rate, pitch, volume, and quality of the sounds rather than the actual words. Thus, feelings may be expressed through racing speech, high pitch, loud volume, or muttering under one's breath. Nonverbal clues include facial expressions, timing, the use of objects, degree of proximity, and behavior (Keyton, 1999). Thus, feelings can be expressed by grimacing, "flying off the handle," throwing a pencil, backing away, or hitting a peer. Children's "normal" communication methods use para-verbal and nonverbal aspects to a much greater degree than that of adults. Smart IEP teams can utilize these clues when describing both the present level of functioning and writing annual goals.

Performance Criteria

Smith (2000) argues, "every effort should be made to ensure that each annual goal and short-term objective is directly related to the statement of the student's present level of performance" (p. 3). This is why establishing the specific and measured baseline of performance is so important; it makes writing the measurable part of the goal so much easier. The IEP team simply has to extrapolate what a student's positively defined behavior could look like in the future (but see Box 8.3). Using a minimum rate of 10% improvement, if a student attended 150 days of the school year the previous year, the team could expect the same student to attend all 165 days of the following year with increased support. This would result in a clinically significant

BOX 8.3 Myths of Measurability

Bateman and Herr (2003) identify three common myths when it comes to writing measurable IEP goals. Each one is discussed below with an example.

MYTHS AND REALITIES	EXAMPLES AND CRITICAL QUESTIONS
Myth 1: If a goal contains a percentage or fraction, it is measurable. Reality: Nonspecific performances are not made more specific by using a percentage or fraction.	Pat will show good behavior 70% of the day. (What exactly counts as "good behavior"?)
Myth 2: If a goal contains technical language, it is measurable. Reality: Technical language is not more specific than everyday language.	Tony will display the use of democratic values during recess. (Which democratic values will be displayed and evaluated?)
Myth 3: If a goal contains an action verb, it is measurable. Reality: Action verbs can be as indistinct as other words.	Chris will demonstrate an understanding of other students' emotions. (What will this demonstration look like?)

change, since he would miss less than 10% of the school year. The goal, then, might be written as follows:

Environmental condition
Given a mandatory school attendance year of 180 days,

Service
with weekly after-school "possible selves" group (Oyserman, Terry, & Bybee, 2002)

Name of student

Jimmy

Defined action

will attend school

Performance criteria

at least 165 days per year.

Benchmarks

The IEP benchmarks could map this out with greater specificity for each marking period or 10-week interval. Each quarter, the team might expect a student's improvement to go up at least 10% from the year before. Given a baseline average of 37.5 days/quarter (150/4) over the previous year,

> *Quarter 1*: By the end of 1st quarter, Jimmy will attend at least 41 days (37.5 × 110%)
>
> *Quarter 2*: By the end of the 1st semester, Jimmy will attend at least 82 days (75 × 110%)
>
> *Quarter 3*: By the end of the 3rd quarter, Jimmy will attend at least 123 days (112.5 × 110%)
>
> *Quarter 4*: By the end of the year, Jimmy will attend at least 165 days (150 × 110%)

Maintaining quarterly performance expectations enables the team to know quickly whether they need to change or modify the existing level of support before the end of the year in order for the student to successfully achieve the annual goal. Greater specificity leaves no room for doubt. Everyone knows each quarter whether the program is working as planned.

Progress Evaluation and Single-Subject Research Designs

While Chapter 7 dealt with group-level designs related to program evaluation, this section will address case-level evaluation. Single-subject design has been used for many years in clinical psychology (Kazdin, 1982), social work (Gambrill & Barth, 1980; Jayaratne, 1977) and special education (Moore, Fifield, Spira, & Scarlato, 1989; Tawney & Gast, 1984). It is a rigorous, scientifically based method for establishing evidence-based practice (Odom & Strain, 2002). Single-subject designs have a number of strengths. First, they focus squarely on the individual client, not some amorphous group. Second, single-case methods allow practitioners to quickly determine responders versus nonresponders and adapt their interventions accordingly. Third, they provide a practical method for testing the effectiveness of school-based interventions that does not require sophisticated statistical knowledge. Fourth, single-subject research allows practitioners to track how slight modifications in the treatment can have a differential effect on the individual client. Finally, single-case designs offer a cost-effective way to identify small-scale interventions that may be ready to test on a large scale. After all, what works with one student is likely to be effective with many (Horner et al., 2005).

Single-subject designs can build practice-based evidence through either within-subject designs or between-subject designs. *Within-subject* designs are evaluation methods where the evaluation occurs at several points during the treatment phases. There are two main subtypes called reversal designs and alternating treatment designs (Odom & Strain, 2002; Williams, Grinnell, & Unrau, 2008). Reversal designs alternate between no-treatment and treatment conditions (A-B-A-B designs). Alternating treatment designs can be of two more subtypes—treatment-variation designs and different-treatment designs. Treatment-variation designs are those where the therapist adapts the intervention during the treatment phase ($A-B_1-A-B_2$), such as seeing the client more often (a frequency variation) or seeing the client for longer sessions (a duration variation). Different-treatment designs (A-B-C) would be when the therapist uses two different modalities to help the client, such as providing cognitive behavioral therapy and then interpersonal therapy. *Between-subject* designs are those where the results between a small number (usually 3 or more) of individuals are compared to determine the effectiveness of the intervention using multiple baselines. For an excellent example of the latter subtype, readers can peruse the study on self-monitoring by Hughes, Copeland, Wehmeyer, Agran, and Rodi (2002). For our purposes here, however, I will focus only on within-subject designs.

Experimental Method

Within-subject designs demonstrate experimental control when they demonstrate the effects of treatment across at least three different phases of the case. Effectiveness is determined when the desired change in the dependent or outcome variable correlates to changes in the application of the independent or predictor variable. For example, clinicians usually hope that as the therapy is applied the problem is lessened. Using a problem-focused measure like a scaled question about an internalizing disorder, we would expect an inverse relationship—more therapy causes less depression. Thus measurements are taken during the assessment or no-treatment phase, during the treatment phase, and then again during either another no-treatment phase

---

BOX 8.4 Single-Subject Reversal Design

On the first row, begin by labeling the columns (starting Column B) in Excel for each of the phases. The no-treatment phase columns may be labeled Base-1 and Base-2, and Base-3 while the alternating treatment phase columns might be marked Tx-1 and Tx-2. For this example, Row 1 will appear as Base-1; Tx-1, Base-2.

Let's assume that during the assessment phase (Base-1), we measured John's depression using a scaled question as 8, 9, and 7 over 3 weeks. During a brief treatment period (Tx-1), we measured it again with scores 6, 5, 4, 3, and 4 for 5 weeks. Over the Christmas break (Base-2), John's mother helped us measure how he was doing with scores 6 and 7 over 2 weeks. To obtain the 10-week period (or the usual reporting period), graph the results by following the instructions below:

1. Put John's Base-1 scores in Column A, rows 2 to 4; put John's Tx-1 scores in Column B, rows 5 to 9; put John's Base-2 scores in Column C, rows 10 to 11. (Note: The column phases do not share any rows of data.)
2. Drag the cursor over the numbers in columns A to C for rows 2 to 11 (do not include the Field labels in Row 1). Don't worry that most of the columns contain only a few numbers.
3. Click on the Chart Wizard icon on the Standard Tool bar.
4. In the Chart Wizard box, select the Chart Type: Line
5. Next to this, select the Chart Sub-type: Line with markers displayed at each data value.
6. Press Next once.
7. Select the Series tab at the top. For Series1, type: Baseline-1; select Series2 and type: Treatment-1; then select Series3 and type: Baseline-2.
8. Press Next once.
9. The Chart Title should be the name of the Client and Outcome measure, so type: John's CDI Score. Name the Category (X) axis: Weeks (or other regular period, such as months or quarters); name the Value (Y) axis: Level of Depression (or other outcome measure).

(continued)

10. Select the Data Labels tab and choose the Label Contains: TValue
11. Press Next once.
12. Keep the default and place chart as an object in Sheet 1.
13. Press Finish.
14. Now go to Insert on the Main Menu bar, go to Picture, and select AutoShapes.
15. On the AutoShapes tool bar, choose the first option: Lines
16. Draw a straight line between the various phases of treatment.

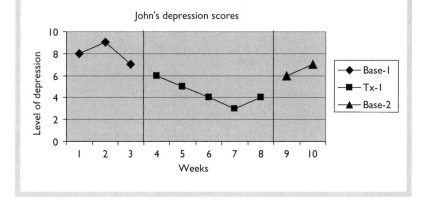

John's depression scores

or alternative-treatment phase. While this can be graphed using Microsoft Access (Jonson-Reid, 2006), it is just as easily performed using Excel (Carr & Burkholder, 1998). For a simplified example of how to do this, see Box 8.4.

Visual Analysis

Single-subject designs can be interpreted using statistical analysis (Edgington, 1987; Jayaratne, 1978; Todman & Dugard, 2001). Unfortunately, these tests usually result in numbers that are difficult to explain to parents, teachers, and students. Horner et al. (2005) recommend a systematic approach to visual analysis of the resulting graph. This is a more user-friendly approach, which has intuitive appeal to other constituents as well.

There are three primary qualities that we should study in the graph: the level, trend, and variability. First, we can analyze the *level* of each phase and determine the mean performance during that period. Looking at the example in Box 8.4, we could easily determine that the level for Base-1 was 8, the level of Tx-1 was 4.4, and the level for Base-2 was 6.5. Clearly then, the level of John's depression (see graph in Box 8.4) went down over the treatment phase and was at least two points higher during the two no-treatment phases. Second, we can study the *trend* of each phase by determining the "best-fit straight line" (Horner et al., 2005, p. 171). In the Base-1 phase, we would probably say that the straight line would probably be horizontal because of the fact that it goes up in Week-2, but down again in Week-3. In the Tx-1 condition, we can clearly see that the straight line would be downward over time. In the Base-3 phase, we can probably conclude that the straight line would be ascending over time. Third, we can analyze the *variability* of each phase and study the fluctuations during the phase. In the Base-1 phase, for example, we see a common pattern of small improvement just before treatment. This is commonly interpreted as improvement because of the expectation that help will be received—it is reflective of the client's hope (Raines, 2004a). In the Tx-1 phase, we notice a steady decline in John's depression with a slight increase just before his impending vacation. This shows that the treatment is working as planned with perhaps a slight concern heading into a period where help will be unavailable. In the Base-2 phase, we notice a steady increase in John's depression as his vacation wears on without help.

Student Self-Monitoring

A number of authors have conducted experiments testing the effects of student self-monitoring. Fuchs and Fuchs (1986) did a meta-analysis and found that the systematic use of formative assessment procedures increased the academic achievement of students with disabilities. Interestingly, their results showed that "when data were graphed, effect sizes were higher than when data were simply recorded (p. 205). DiGangi, Maag, and Rutherford (1991) experimented with having the students do self-graphing and concluded that it enhanced reactivity for both improved behavior and academic achievement. Bloom, Hursh, Wienke, and Wold (1992) also found greater behavioral improvement when progress was regularly monitored. Whether it was done with paper and pencil or with a computer made no difference to the students, but teachers greatly preferred the computer and were more likely to change their interventions when they used the computer.

Gunter, Miller, Venn, Thomas, and House (2002) describe how this can be accomplished by creating a folder for each student on the desktop of the classroom computer. First, each folder is set up containing separate Excel files for each subject or each of the IEP goals, depending on the teacher's or team's preference. Second, a celeration line is superimposed on the graph. A *celeration line* is the gradient of expected progress over the same number of weeks. (This can be done simply by following the same procedure for line drawing described in Steps 14–16 in Box 8.4). The celeration line then allows students to assess their own performance compared to their expected level of achievement. Third, students are trained how to enter data onto the Excel spreadsheet and watch the graphs change as they do so. The graphs can easily be copied and pasted onto weekly progress notes or parent notes so that everyone is aware of how the student is progressing well before the usual reporting period.

Social Validity

Social validity is the acceptability of a treatment or evaluation method across a wide range of constituents, including parents and teachers (Daunic, Smith, Brank, & Penfield, 2006; Frey, Faith, Elliott, & Royer, 2006; Lyst, Gabriel, O'Shaughnessy, Meyers, & Meyers, 2005). The acceptability of a method may be further defined as the degree to which the method is perceived as appropriate, effective, efficient, and fair (Finn & Sladeczek, 2001). Horner et al. (2005) posit that the social validity of single-subject research can be enhanced in four ways. First, the dependent or outcome variables must have high social importance—they should be perceived as highly appropriate or relevant across constituents, including the student. There are many occasions when school personnel fail to understand the link between mental health problems and school achievement. While some authors have chosen to explain the former as a "barrier to learning" (Center for Mental Health in Schools at UCLA, 2007), the research has seldom bothered to demonstrate that improving mental health has led to greater academic achievement (Hoagwood et al., 2007). Second, the independent or predictive variables should possess high fidelity across providers and across service-delivery contexts. This requires that IEP teams identify the intervention with sufficient specificity that it can be replicated by multiple service providers. Vague descriptions of therapy or counseling are insufficient. Third, those who actually implement the interventions should find them to be acceptable, feasible, effective, and easy to use. The more the single-subject design can be woven into the fabric of a provider's daily routine, the greater its social validity. Finally, the outcome must meet a well-defined clinical need. The more clearly the problem can be defined, either qualitatively or quantitatively, the better its chance of being corrected. Problems that are too vague to be described are generally too abstract to be solved.

Summary

The purpose of this chapter was to explain how to evaluate individual outcomes. It began with a review of the IDEA requirements for monitoring the progress of students in special education and aligning this with single-case research designs. First, five federal requirements, including having a single standard for progress; planning ahead for progress measurement; reporting progress at regular intervals; changing behavior; and encouraging the return to general education, were reviewed. Second, establishing a baseline for individual functioning was described in four ways: ensuring that measures are understandable to parents and students; using a variety of measures, including behavioral rubrics and goal attainment scaling; triangulating the measures to make certain that they truly represent the student's performance level, and being sure to state the baseline in positive terms. Third, the requirements for measurable annual goals were described, including environmental conditions, specific services needed, the identity of the student, defined actions, and performance criteria. The last section provided details on how to evaluate student progress using single-case research procedures using Excel. It introduced the many varieties of single-subject design and focused on within-subject designs. It then focused on the requirements in dependent and independent variables; experimental management, visual analysis techniques; student self-monitoring, and how to improve the social validity of the single-subject research.

Suggested Reading

1. Carr, J. E., & Burkholder, E. O. (1998). Creating single-subject design graphs with Microsoft Excel(™). *Journal of Applied Behavior Analysis, 31* (2), 245–251.

2. Etscheidt, S. K. (2006). Progress monitoring: Legal issues and recommendations for IEP teams. *Teaching Exceptional Children, 38* (6), 56–60.

3. Horner, R. H., Carr, E. G., Halle, J., McGee, G., Odom, S., & Wolery, M. (2005). The use of single-subject research to identify evidence-based practice in special education. *Exceptional Children, 71* (2), 165–179.

4. Roach, A. T., & Elliot, S. N. (2005). Goal attainment scaling: An efficient and effective approach to monitoring student progress. *Teaching Exceptional Children, 37* (4), 8–17.

Internet Resources

Behavioral Rubrics

DiscoverySchool.com—Kathy Schrock's Guide to Rubrics
http://school.discovery.com/schrockguide/assess.html#rubrics

Intervention Central (Behavior Report Cards)
http://www.interventioncentral.com/

Princeton Online's Positive Behavior Rubric
http://www.princetonol.com/groups/iad/lessons/middle/Behavior.htm

Professor John Howe's Behavior Rubric
http://www.professorhowe.com/rubricshowc.cfm?code=H6W77&sp=yes&xsite=johnhowe

RubiStar 4 Teachers
http://rubistar.4teachers.org/index.php

Teachnology—Online Teacher Resource
http://www.bestteachersites.com/web_tools/rubrics/

Goal Attainment Scaling

Flinders University (Austrailia) Self-Esteem Goal Attainment Scaling Tool
http://www.socsci.flinders.edu.au/fippm/consult/gasuse.html

Kiresuk, Smith, and Cardillo's Book on Goal Attainment Scaling
http://www.questia.com/PM.qst?a=o&d=28533958&oplinknum=3

Marson and Dran's Goal Attainment Scaling
http://www.marson-and-associates.com/GAS/GAS_index.html

Progress Monitoring

AIMS Web
http://aimsweb.com/

National Center on Student Progress Monitoring
http://www.studentprogress.org/

National Research Center on Learning Disabilities
http://www.nrcld.org

Research Institute on Progress Monitoring
http://www.progressmonitoring.org/

9

▓ ▓ ▓

Ethics for Evidence-Based Practice

Preview
The purpose of this chapter is to address ethical issues related to treatment and research of children in school-based mental health. It is important to remember that evidence-based practice is a process of integrating the "best research evidence with clinical expertise and patient values" (Sackett, Strauss, Richardson, Rosenberg, & Haynes, 2000, p. 1). Since school-based practitioners' primary client is the underage student, the issues that will be covered include informed consent, client self-determination, and parental access and control. Informed consent will begin with the difference between passive and active consent. It will outline the three necessary conditions for informed consent: capacity, information, and voluntariness. Client self-determination begins with the assumption that all adults, even ones with disabilities, have the right to face risks. Educators will need to prepare young people for this eventuality by gradually preparing them to make their own decisions, establish their own goals, and work independently toward them. The primary client in school-based practice is the student. Other constituents may receive professional support and advice, but the ultimate aim of these collateral interventions should be to help students. There are times when clinicians must take paternalistic action, but these should be the exception and not the rule. Parental access and control will introduce the provisions of the Family Educational Rights and Privacy Act (FERPA). It will identify which records are and are not subject to parental inspection and review and how conflicts about the records may be resolved. Finally, this section will distinguish two situations in which information may be

shared without parental or student consent. Each major section concludes with implications for evidence-based practice.

Host Setting Issues

There are three major ethical issues involved in providing school-based mental health services. Some of these are particularly pertinent for mental health professionals working with minors in a host setting. First, mental health professionals are obligated to follow a professional code of ethics whereas there is no universally accepted code of ethics for education personnel. Second, minors have increasing legal rights—society confers these rights gradually as children mature. Gradually, they have a right to drive a car, consent to drug and alcohol treatment, consent to family planning procedures, vote, join the military, and eventually consume alcohol (Advocates for Youth, 1998; Anderson & DuBois, 2007). The ages at which these rights take effect vary widely from state to state (Tillett, 2005). For example, most states confer the right to consent for contraceptive or prenatal care as early as 12 years of age (Guttmacher Institute, 2007). Finally, host settings have some circumstances not usually encountered by community-based mental health professionals, such as delivering services indirectly through teachers (Wesley & Buysse, 2006).

Informed Consent

The idea that children, especially children with disabilities, should have the right to give informed consent or assent is a recent development (see Box 9.1). Schools have a long history of taking informed consent for granted. A common practice is for schools to assume that parents automatically consent unless they specifically object. This practice is known as *passive consent*. For example, a school note may read that all children in the 6th grade will discuss puberty in science class unless parents write a note stating that they do not want their child to participate. It would be dangerous, however, to assume that passive consent would be sufficient for the delivery of mental health services for child and adolescent research purposes (Fisher, 2004).

Basic Concepts

The Center for Mental Health in Schools at UCLA (2004) accurately states that informed consent must possess three qualities. These include capacity, information, and voluntariness. Any breach of informed consent involves some degree of paternalism.

Evidence-Based Practice in School Mental Health

BOX 9.1 The Hepatitis Study at Willowbrook State School

The first case of clinical research using children to bring a call for reform was the hepatitis study conducted at Willowbrook State School in New York from 1956 to 1971. The study was an epidemiological study about how hepatitis was transmitted and its natural course. The subjects of the study were children with mental retardation living in a state facility. When the study was first considered, 73% of the children were estimated to have had IQs of less than 20% and 57% were not toilet trained. Infectious hepatitis was spread easily in this unsanitary environment and was considered a "mild" disease with gastrointestinal and/or upper respiratory symptoms. After getting hepatitis, however, most sufferers were thought to become immune to the disease, much like chicken pox. The medical researchers (Krugman, 1972) believed that giving newly admitted students "controlled exposure" to the ailment would provide "valuable information about the natural history of the disease which could not be learned any other way" and "could lead to the development of a vaccine" (p. 6). They received approval from the Executive Faculty of the New York University School of Medicine, the New York State Department of Health and the Department of Mental Hygiene.

Parental consent was part of the standard operating procedure. The children of parents who did not consent were admitted to different buildings than those who did consent. When enrollment led to overcrowding at the institution, however, admission was apparently closed except to those parents who did consent. Several parents reported that they consented only because they desperately believed it was the only way for their children to obtain admission, according to Willowbrook's Social Work Department (Isaacs, 1972). The researchers then changed their consent procedures to a group method, so that concerned parents could benefit from hearing the response to questions raised by other parents. In 1967, the physicians discovered that some children were not immune, but were contracting hepatitis twice. In 1969, this led to

(continued)

the discovery that there were actually two strains of the hepatitis virus at Willowbrook the entire time and only 40% were immune.

By the end of the study, about 800 children with mental retardation had been deliberately exposed to hepatitis. The results of the study led to the development of an inactivated hepatitis-B vaccine for other children and the use of gamma globulin to reduce the incidence of hepatitis with jaundice for employees and members of the Peace Corps traveling to foreign countries. The situation at Willowbrook came to the public's attention through a week-long televised exposé by Geraldo Rivera in January 1972 (Fordham Urban Law Journal, 1974). The institution was so understaffed that "the loss of an eye, the breaking of teeth, the loss of part of an ear bitten off by another resident, and frequent bruises and scalp wounds" were common occurrences (Barshefsky & Liebenberg, 1974, p. 791). Subsequently, a federal court found the deplorable conditions "inhumane" and ordered that the state meet the institutional standards set by the American Association of the Mentally Deficient (*Association for Retarded Children v. Rockefeller*, 1973).

Discussion Questions

1. Does the likelihood of children naturally contracting the disease provide a rationale for giving them controlled exposure?
2. Should the researchers have studied how to improve hygiene at the institution instead of using its poor hygiene as a reason for experimentation?
3. Should children with high IQs be treated differently than those with very low IQs?
4. If parents have the rights to give legal consent, does the study still have unresolved ethical issues?
5. Do the rewards of this study outweigh the risks? Do the ends justify the means?
6. Would you have given consent for your child to be part of this study? Why or why not?

Capacity is the ability to comprehend the information and appreciate the consequences of the decision. Participants must be able to understand the information given, process the implications for their situations, and justify their choices. It is also important to remember that capacity is decision specific; in other words, it applies only to a specific treatment offered at a specific time (Schacter, Kleinman, & Harvey, 2005). No client can be assessed once and be considered competent to make every decision thereafter. Developmental research suggests that adolescents, 14 and older, are as capable as adults at understanding medical information and weighing the risks and benefits of therapy (Bastiaens, 1995; Kaser-Boyed, Adelman, & Taylor, 1985; Weithorn & Campbell, 1982). Millar (2003), however, found that courts were more likely to find youth with disabilities who reached majority status "incompetent" to make decisions based solely upon their disability label rather than any clear evidence of incapacity.

Information refers to the adequacy of one's knowledge. What must the client know? The Joint Commission on Accreditation of Healthcare Organizations (2007a) provides the following list of six essential points:

A complete informed consent process includes a discussion of the following elements:*
- The nature of the proposed services, medications, interventions, or procedures;
- Potential benefits, risks, or side effects, including potential problems that might occur during recuperation;
- The likelihood of achieving goals;
- Reasonable alternatives;
- The relevant risks, benefits, and side effects related to alternatives, including the possible results of not receiving services;
- When indicated, any limitations on the confidentiality of information learned from or about the patient.

* *Documentation of the items listed may be in a form, progress notes, or elsewhere in the record.* (p. 7)

The Joint Commission on Accreditation of Healthcare Organizations (2007b) also expects clinical caregivers to answer any questions that the patient has before such consent is signed. For a list of points to cover in clinical research, see Box 9.2. It is especially important that this information be in a format that is easy to read. Forty-three percent of Americans have only basic or below-basic literacy skills. Numerical literacy is even worse—fully 55% of

BOX 9.2 Informed Consent and Clinical Research

The Joint Commission on Accreditation of Healthcare Organizations (2007c) recommends that the following points need to be covered with clients before they agree to participate in clinical research:

- It is not known if the experimental treatment will help more than the standard treatment.
- You may not receive the new treatment, but your participation may result in information that will help others in the future.
- You should ask for a copy of the research protocol and a description of the potential side effects.
- Some treatments can have side effects that may be mild, severe, or even life threatening.
- The cost may not be covered by health insurance. Ask if there will be an extra expense to you.
- Clinical research involves several phases, from testing for initial safety and dosage to evaluating long-term safety and effectiveness. Be sure you understand what phase is being evaluated and how it will affect the treatment you receive.
- When asked to sign an informed consent, take the document home, read it thoroughly, and discuss it with your family.
- If you need help understanding the informed consent, seek out a trusted expert or specialist.
- Most clinical studies are reviewed by an Institutional Review Board or IRB, be sure you know how to contact the IRB representative with any concerns.

Questions to ask the researcher or clinicians conducting the research:

- Why is the study being conducted?
- Who is sponsoring the study?
- Will I be able to continue to see my own clinician?
- Is there any cost to me to participate?
- Does anyone receive money for my enrollment?

(continued)

- How long will the study last?
- What tests or treatments will be used?
- What are my options if I don't choose to participate?
- Could I receive a placebo or nontreatment?
- What could happen, good or bad, if I participate?
- Could my problem get worse during the study?
- Can I change my mind about participating after I start?
- Could there be a danger if I stop participating?
- Who would pay if I was injured during the study?
- Will I get a copy of the results at the end of the study?
- Who can I contact outside of the institution about my concerns?
- Who stands to benefit financially from the results of this study?
- Is the research program or overseeing IRB accredited?

Americans have only basic or below-basic mathematic skills. This provides support for the recommendation that most health (and by extension, mental health) information should be at the 5th grade level and discussed rather than just given to patients (Green, Duncan, Barnes, & Oberklaid, 2003; Schacter et al., 2005). The Individuals with Disabilities Education Improvement Act (IDEA) (2004) makes a similar requirement:

> The procedural safeguards notice shall include a full explanation of the procedural safeguards, written in the native language of the parents (unless it clearly is not feasible to do so) and written in an easily understandable manner.
>
> Section 615 (d)(2)

The official regulations clarify the extent to which school districts should go to guarantee that parent's rights are not abrogated because of a language barrier:

> If the native language or other mode of communication of the parent is not a written language, the public agency must take steps to ensure that the notice is translated orally or by other means to the parent in his or her native language or other mode of communication and that the parent understands the content of the notice.
>
> U.S. Department of Education, 2006, p. 46689

It is especially important that children not be inducted into the role of family interpreter since this undermines the authority of the parents and creates a dual-role dilemma for the student who may be tempted to mislead the parents (Fisher, 2004).

Voluntariness is the freedom from constraint, compulsion, or coercion. A person must be able to choose either not to participate or to participate without negative repercussions. This is more difficult than it first appears. When there is a power differential in the relationship, it is more difficult for the more vulnerable party to disagree. Medical research has found, for example, that a substantial minority of parents of preschool children believed that informed consent procedures were unnecessary because they would always do as the physician advised (Harth & Thong, 1995). In American society, it is assumed that adults have the capacity to consent unless proven otherwise. For children, however, the opposite seems to be true—it is assumed that they do not have the capacity to consent except when they approach adulthood. This state of affairs is known as paternalism.

Paternalism occurs whenever adults assume they know what is in the "best interests" of the child without ever consulting that child. While this may be completely justified for preverbal infants and children with severe mental retardation, developmental delay, or psychosis, it may not be justifiable for normal children who can reason and communicate without difficulty (Schacter et al., 2005). As the Center for Mental Health in Schools at UCLA (2004) states:

> It is a paternalistic act whenever a child is made to undergo unwanted assessment, even though the activity is viewed as in the child's "best interests." Whether stated or not, when such actions are taken, the child's autonomy is made less important than the possible harm to the child or others if the child is not assessed or the possible benefits to be gained if the child is assessed. (p. 6)

In short, decisions made by adults to abrogate a child's autonomy sometimes send the message—your rights are less important than my interests.

Constitutional Protections
English (1995) found that the U.S. Supreme Court ruled that the 5th and 14th Amendments to the Constitution applied not only to adults but to children as well. In the famous education case, *In re Gault* (1967), the

high court applied this logic to minors' due process rights when accused of juvenile delinquency. It subsequently affirmed the rights of minors in a wide variety of cases, including those related to first amendment guarantees of free speech (*Tinker v. Des Moines Independent School District*, 1969) and the right to privacy (*Planned Parenthood of Missouri v. Danforth*, 1976).

Parental Consent and Student Assent

Since social institutions exist, in part, to support the family in its responsibilities to and protections of children, it makes sense that the ideal is to obtain consent from both the parent and the student. In cases where the child is clearly underage (younger than 12), it still behooves practitioners to obtain informed assent (Harcourt & Conroy, 2005; Hurley & Underwood, 2002). This entails creating information sheets that are tailored to their developmental level and address their developmental concerns that may be quite different from those of their parents. They must be given relevant information in terms that they can understand (Ford, Sankey, & Crisp, 2007). For research, they need to know how the research will help them, not just unnamed others. They need to know if they will miss valuable classroom learning time and if this academic loss can be made up without penalty. They need to know that unpleasant feelings might be evoked by the probing nature of the questions and how the researcher will protect certain confidences (see Box 9.3). One way to ensure that children truly understand the purpose of the research, its risks and benefits, and their continued right to withdraw is to have children "teach back" these rights in their own words (Joint Commission on Accreditation of Healthcare Organizations, 2007b). Even small children can check off key assurances and spell their own name to assent (see Box 9.4).

Student assent is also supported in IDEA when child involvement is encouraged within the Individualized Education Program (IEP) team. The composition of this team includes parent(s) and "whenever appropriate, the child with a disability" (section 614 (d)(1)(B)(vii)). The Federal regulations expand on this portion of the law as follows:

> Section 614(d)(1)(B)(vii) of the Act clearly states that the IEP Team includes the child with a disability, whenever appropriate. *Generally, a child with a disability should attend the IEP Team meeting if the parent decides that it is appropriate for the child to do so.* If possible, the agency and parent should discuss the appropriateness of the child's participation before a decision is made, in order to help the parent determine whether or not the child's

BOX 9.3 Student Information Letter for a Research Interview

Dear Student,

My name is _____. I work for _____
_____. I want to find out what students like you think about _____.
Your answers will help me answer my questions, but they might also help you understand yourself better too.

To do this, I would like to ask you some questions, such as:

-
-
-

I will record your answers by

_____

Since I just want to find out what you think, there is no right or wrong answer to the questions that I will be asking. You won't be graded on your answers. If some questions make you feel upset, it's okay to tell me that you don't want to answer those questions. You can also change your mind about answering any questions. If you have some questions for me, that's okay too. You can tell others, such as your parents, what we talk about, but I will keep your answers a secret unless you tell me someone might get hurt.

I will try not to pull you out of any important classes. I will also make sure that your teacher knows that you can make up any missed work. I will also try to make sure that you don't miss lunch time with your friends.

When I'm all done, you will get a chance to listen or read your answers to make sure I heard you right. I won't put your name in my paper and I'll make sure no one can guess who you are or what you said. If you don't want your answers in my paper, it's okay to tell me after I write the paper and I'll take your answers out. You won't get in trouble for changing your mind.

Please talk to one of your parents before you decide. They got a letter like this one. You will get a copy of this letter and a copy of the permission note to keep. Your parent will get their own copies too. Thank you for thinking about helping me. Whatever you decide is okay.

BOX 9.4 Student Permission Note for a Research Interview

Put a **T** next to each true sentence below, but put an **F** next to any false ones.

_____I have read the information letter.

_____I talked to my parent or guardian about it.

_____There are no wrong or right answers. I won't be graded on my answers.

_____I can answer the questions without getting upset.

_____I have had all my questions answered.

_____I don't have to do this.

_____I can change my mind and stop answering any questions.

_____I can talk to my parent about the questions asked.

_____My answers will be a secret unless someone might get hurt.

_____I get to keep a copy of the Information letter and this Permission note.

My name: _____

My signature: _____

Today's date: _____

My parent's name: _____

Parent's signature: _____

attendance would be helpful in developing the IEP or directly beneficial to the child, or both. Until the child reaches the age of majority under State law, unless the rights of the parent to act for the child are extinguished or otherwise limited, only the parent has the authority to make educational decisions for the child under Part B of the Act, including whether the child should attend an IEP Team meeting.

> U.S. Department of Education, Office of Special Education and
> Rehabilitative Services, 2006, p. 46671, emphasis added

It makes sense that the more developmentally mature the child, the more their involvement and assent should be encouraged at the IEP team meeting. Generally speaking, early involvement of the student in formulating IEP goals facilitates progress towards achieving IEP goals.

Parental Consent Without Student Assent

Schools frequently allow parents to consent to both assessment and services without student assent. The assessment requirement in IDEA (2004) reads as follows:

> CONSENT FOR INITIAL EVALUATION—The agency proposing to conduct an initial evaluation to determine if the child qualifies as a child with a disability as defined in section 602 shall obtain informed consent from the parent of such child before conducting the evaluation. Parental consent for evaluation shall not be construed as consent for placement for receipt of special education and related services.
>
> Section 614 (a)(1)(D)(i)(I)

This section states the school ideal—parental consent is always obtained before an initial evaluation is begun. It also clarifies that consent to evaluation does not equal consent to services. This consent occurs in the very next paragraph of the law:

> CONSENT FOR SERVICES—An agency that is responsible for making a free appropriate public education available to a child with a disability under this part shall seek to obtain informed consent from the parent of such child before providing special education and related services to the child.
>
> Section 614 (a)(1)(D)(i)(II)

Thus, schools must have separate consents on file for assessment and services. School-based practitioners who also serve children in general education would be wise to do the same—always seek separate parental informed consent for assessment and treatment. This ensures that parents feel included for both the assessment and treatment portion of the therapy.

There are few situations in which therapy should be provided to students over their objection. The first example is students with oppositional defiant disorders who reject therapy precisely because an adult authority figure recommended it (Schacter et al., 2005). The best way to engage such a student may be to join with the student and say something such as, "I know that it is not your choice to be here and generally I don't like to force counseling on anyone, but since we both have to be here, perhaps we can agree to work on some issues that you choose." McKay, Harrison, Gonzales, Kim, and Quintana (2002) also found that multiple-family group counseling improved attendance better than either family therapy or individual therapy alone, but even the families in group counseling attended fewer than half

Evidence-Based Practice in School Mental Health

of the sessions over a 16-week period. The second example would be students with addictions because their compulsion to gamble, use drugs or alcohol, or smoke tobacco is stronger than their volitional control. The best way to engage these students would be to use Prochaska and DiClemente's (2005) stages of change model, preferably using a group treatment approach (Velasquez, Maurer, Crouch, & DiClemente, 2001).

Adolescent Consent Without Parental Consent

Interestingly, there is a general rule that the school can choose to overrule the parents when it comes to the initial evaluation and subsequent reevaluations, but the school cannot overrule the parents when it comes to providing services (see section 614 (a)(1)(D)(ii), IDEA, 2004). The three exceptions to parental consent for an initial evaluation are when the school cannot locate the parents; the parental rights have been terminated in a court of law; and the rights of the parents to make educational decisions have been subrogated by a court of law and bestowed upon an educational surrogate. The ability of a school to overrule parents becomes more lenient at the reevaluation:

> PARENTAL CONSENT—Each local educational agency shall obtain informed parental consent, in accordance with subsection (a)(1)(D), prior to conducting any reevaluation of a child with a disability, except that such informed parental consent need not be obtained if the local educational agency can demonstrate that it had taken reasonable measures to obtain such consent and the child's parent has failed to respond.
>
> Section 614 (c)(3)

Clinically, however, there may be times when services are ethically required even if not legally sanctioned (see ethical-legal typology below). Tillet (2005) states that there are four circumstances in which minors can give

ETHICAL-LEGAL TYPOLOGY		
Legal spectrum	Legal but not ethical issue	Legal and ethical issue
	Neither ethical nor legal issue	Ethical but not legal issue
	Ethical spectrum	

informed consent without parental consent. These include mature minors, emancipated minors, emergency care, and state-mandated situations.

Mature Minors

State courts have also upheld the rights of minors to make decisions for themselves, especially when it involves their health. This right has become known as the "mature minor" doctrine. South Carolina, for example, allows mature minors access to contraceptive services, treatment for sexually transmitted diseases, and prenatal care (Guttmacher Institute, 2007). The Center for Mental Health in Schools at UCLA (2004) provides this explanation:

> The mature minor doctrine emerged from court decisions, primarily state court decisions, addressing the circumstances in which a physician could be held liable in damages for providing care to a minor without parental consent. Pursuant to the doctrine, there is little likelihood that a practitioner will incur liability for failure to obtain parental consent in situations in which the minor is an older adolescent (typically at least age 15) who is capable of giving an informed consent and in which the care is not high risk, is for the minor's benefit, and is within the mainstream of established medical opinion. (p. 21)

Translating this principle to adolescent mental health, an argument can be made that mature minors have a right to consent for mental health treatment that poses a minimal risk to their well-being, protects them from a potentially greater harm, and is established on widely accepted research. Unless state law expressly forbids mental health treatment without parental consent, clinicians can probably use adolescents' access to healthcare treatment (e.g., contraceptive services) as a reliable analogue. The same would hold true for adolescents' consent to participate in research (Fisher, 2004). Another possible analogue would be the federal mandate under IDEA that adolescents' preferences and goals must be considered when formulating transition goals at age 16 (Lohrmann-O'Rourke & Gomez, 2001; Sitlington & Clark, 2007; Wehmeyer, Palmer, Soukup, Garner, & Lawrence, 2007). Practitioners would only need to demonstrate that they have met the criteria of capacity, information, and voluntariness.

Emancipated Minors

Emancipated minors must be of a state-required age (usually 16, but sometimes as young as 14), live independently from their parents, and be economically self-sufficient (Tillett, 2005). Typical examples include those who are married, pregnant, parenting, serving in the military, or found to be emancipated by a court of law. A court will probably side with the adolescent on occasions when the teenager has greater capacity than a parent, such as when parental judgment is impaired by alcohol or other drugs (Fraser & McAbee, 2004).

Emergency Care

There are times when adolescents need care immediately and professionals cannot wait to contact or convince parents of its necessity. For example, while many states require some type of parental consent for a minor to have an abortion, most of these also permit a minor to obtain one in case of a medical emergency, sexual abuse, rape, incest, or neglect (Tillett, 2005). Since psychological emergencies, such as threats of homicide or suicide, pose an equal or greater danger, it makes sense that such laws provide justification for the provision of emergency mental health services unless there is an explicit state-sanctioned prohibition against these. School-based practitioners may also be able to invoke Good Samaritan immunity when the student is not a regular client (Rubin, 2007). Therapists should be warned, however, that such immunity does not cover gross negligence or willful misconduct (Slovenko, 2005).

State-Mandated Situations

There are 25 states plus the District of Columbia that expressly allow all minors (12 and older) to consent to contraceptive services. There are 21 states that restrict contraceptive services to some minors, but not others. Only four states have no policy or case law. All of the states and the District of Columbia permit minors to consent for services related to sexually transmitted diseases (with the exception of HIV). Over a third of the states, however, allow the physician to inform the parents. Most states (28) plus the District of Columbia permit minors to place their newborns up for adoption. Five require legal counsel and five others require parental involvement. Sixty percent of the states allow parenting teens to consent for medical care of their own children. The remaining states have no policies or case law. Finally, only two states and the District of Columbia permit all minors (12 and older) to consent to an abortion. Twenty-nine have parental consent laws, but seven of these are temporarily or permanently blocked by a court order. Eleven states expect parental notification without requiring parental consent (Guttmacher Institute, 2005). Clearly, in situations where both the adolescent and others are at risk (sexually transmitted diseases), there is greater leniency in favor of adolescent rights. The psychological analogue may be students with conduct disorders who threaten the safety of others or themselves through reckless disregard of the consequences of their actions.

No Consent Needed

Perhaps it will come as a surprise that schools still retain legal rights to assess children with neither parent nor student consent. The IDEA (2004) supports this paternalism when it allows for screening without parental or student consent. The relevant section of the law reads as follows:

> RULE OF CONSTRUCTION—The screening of a student by a teacher or specialist to determine appropriate instructional strategies for curriculum implementation shall not be considered to be an evaluation for eligibility for special education and related services.
>
> Section 614 (a)(1)(E)

Furthermore, this type of educational screening has traditionally been exempted from Institutional Review Boards (Thompson, 1990). Thus, these assessments occur frequently, as the Center for Mental Health in Schools at UCLA (2004) notes:

> Many commonplace activities, such as routine achievement, intelligence, and interest testing in schools, can have life-shaping impact and are likely to have an effect on a large segment of the population. In instances in which consent is ignored, coercion is involved and needs to be justified. (p. 7)

Even though screening by a mental health specialist may be permissible under this section of the law, practitioners would be wise to seek active parental consent for all mental health screening activities (Jackson, 2006). This is why the Columbia University TeenScreen Program (2006) now emphasizes the importance of parental informed consent and teen assent prior to any screening for depression or other problems.

Implications for Evidence-Based Practice

School-based practitioners should keep five points in mind when it comes to informed consent. First, they should never rely on passive consent, where the failure to object is assumed to equal approval. Students (and their parents) should at least be consulted in the choice of which empirically supported treatment (EST) should be employed to ameliorate the pupil's problems. Ideally, they are empowered to become full collaborators throughout the process of evidence-based practice (Walker, Briggs, Koroloff, & Friesen, 2007). Second, they should consider the capacity of the participant before engaging them in assessment, treatment, or evaluation procedures. All consent forms, treatment plans, and evaluation activities should be understandable to both parents and children. Third, they should consider what information needs to be provided so that both parents and children can make a thoughtful decision. This should include the level of evidence (see Figure 4.1) and degree of fit (see Figure 4.2) for each proposed treatment. It may also mean exposing hard truths about ESTs—especially that they are empirically supported for groups of people, not individuals. There are no guarantees that what works for most will work for all. Fourth, they should carefully protect parents' and children's voluntariness during the intervention process. Agreement to a mental health assessment does not confer consent to treatment. Consent to treatment can occur only after the parent and student know all the details of intervention plan. Consent to treatment does not necessarily imply consent to participate in research. Both children and their parents should be fully aware that their right to be helped does not depend upon their submission to be studied. Finally, the ideal is always to obtain both parental consent and student assent in every situation. We should generally aim for partnership rather than paternalism (Calder, 1995; DeChillo, Koren, & Schultze, 1994). This should also mean that we regularly update the student and their parents on their progress and be willing to adapt or change interventions that do not seem to be working.

Client Self-Determination

Back in the early 1970s, Perske (1972) wrote that people with disabilities deserve the opportunity to experience "dignity of risk":

> The world in which we live is not always safe, secure, and pre-dictable .... Everyday that we wake up and live in the hours of that day, there is the possibility of being thrown up against a situation where we may have to risk everything, even our lives. This is the way the real world is. We must work to develop every human resource within us in order to prepare for these days. To deny any person their fair share of risk experiences is to further cripple them for health living. (p. 199)

Since the purpose of school is to develop human resources, it makes sense that we must gradually allow students to face a developmentally appropriate share of experiences meant to prepare them for adult life. Interestingly, the President's Commission on Excellence in Special Education (2002) makes a similar argument. It notes, as we did, that IDEA recommends that children with disabilities attend their own IEP team meeting, *if appropriate*, but they object to the italicized phrase: "However, the Commission finds that [it] is *always* appropriate for students with disabilities to be invited and present at IEP meetings" (p. 46, emphasis in the original).

Education for Risk Taking

According to Ward (2005), this right has three implications. First, self-determination is learned through participatory experiences. Youth who learn to set goals, engage in independent performance toward those goals, evaluate their own performance, and learn from their mistakes do better than those who have others make the decisions for them. Second, if we expect youth to become independently functioning adults, we must give them multiple opportunities in school to practice and hone these skills. Ideally, these opportunities begin in elementary school with simple goal setting and self-regulated problem solving (Palmer & Wehmeyer, 2003). Finally, denial of self-determination rights based solely on a student's disability classification is a mistake. Even those with severe disabilities can learn to advocate for themselves and others. Singh et al. (2003), for example, enabled a nonverbal child with profound mental retardation and multiple physical disabilities to select her own meal choices using a simple microswitch.

Thompson (1990) posits that "the principle of respect for persons mandates that researchers guarantee the right of individual self-determination in the research process, and this includes respecting the wishes and decisions of research participants" (p. 3). One of the most vexing questions has been about who is the primary client. Therapists' answer to this issue will decide many other ethical dilemmas.

Defining the Primary Client

One of the more unsettling issues in a host setting is, "Who is the client?" Hus (2001) puts the dilemma this way:

> The very first ethical issue the elementary school counselor faces is determining who is the client. Because the parent is held accountable in many instances for a child or a child's behavior (i.e., property damages and safety), it would be reasonable to assume that technically the parent is the client. This issue is complicated by the uncertainty associated with legal rights of children in the United States. (p. 16)

Many times the answer to this question seems to be avoided by the major professional associations. The National Association of Social Workers (NASW), the National Association of School Psychologists (NASP), and the American School Counselors Association (ASCA) have all struggled with this issue.

NASW

The *NASW Code of Ethics* (National Association of Social Workers, 1999) states only that the term "'clients' is used inclusively to refer to individuals, families, groups, organizations, and communities" (p. 1) There is no doubt that any of these "can" be a client, but it does not answer the question of who "is" the client. Queries for clarification to the Chair of the NASW's Ethics Committee have gone unanswered. Kopels and Lindsey (2006) rightly see this issue as the crux of many ethical dilemmas:

> A social worker's view of who the client is is another factor that complicates decision making about confidentiality. When social workers view students, school administrators, teachers, parents, and the community equally as clients, then it becomes almost impossible to sort out who is entitled to information about a student. When school social workers do not view the student as their *only client*, then the worker is forced to juggle the competing interests of all these other stakeholders. (p. 75, emphasis added)

In short, the primary problem regarding everyone in the school as one's client is the ethical confusion that ensues. To use a child-centered analogy, it is like trying to find Waldo in one of Handford's (1987) numerous picture books!

NASP

NASP's *Principles for Professional Ethics* (National Association of School Psychologists, 2000a) appears to use the terms "student" and "client" interchangeably in the following section:

> The principles in this manual are based on the assumptions that 1) school psychologists will act as advocates for their students/ clients, and 2) at the very least, school psychologists will do no harm. These assumptions necessitate that school psychologists "speak up" for the needs and rights of their students/clients even at times when it may be difficult to do so. (p. 13)

The NASP, however, seems to identify other types of professional relationships when it adds this parenthetical statement later on the very next page:

> The document frequently refers to a school psychologist's relationships with a hypothetical "student/client." Because school psychologists work in a wide variety of settings, there is no single term that neatly identifies the "other" individual in the professional relationship. Therefore, one should apply *Ethical Principles* in all professional situations, realizing that one is not released from responsibility simply because another individual is not strictly a "student" or a "client." (p. 14)

Who are these "other" individuals with whom school psychologists have "professional relationships"? The NASP identifies them as follows: "although a given principle may specifically discuss responsibilities toward 'clients,' the intent is that the standards would also apply to supervisees, trainees, and research participants" (p. 15). Just when a professional thinks it might be clear that they are different stakeholders to whom one might have professional responsibilities, the NASP (National Association of School Psychologists, 2000a) makes this statement:

> Throughout the *Principles for Professional Ethics,* it is assumed that, depending on the role and setting of the school psychologist, the client could include children, parents, teachers and other school personnel, other professionals, trainees, or supervisees. (p. 15)

Like the NASW Code, this leaves school psychologists in a quandary about to whom they owe their primary allegiance.

ASCA

The American School Counselor Association (2004) barely uses the term "client" at all—it is found only once in their *Ethical Standards for School Counselors.* The standards, however, do offer this statement as the very first duty:

> The professional school counselor:
> a. Has a primary obligation to the student, who is to be treated with respect as a unique individual. (p. 1)

Unfortunately, the indefinite article "a" in front of primary does not clarify who is owed "the" primary obligation. Hus (2001) concludes that school counselors must learn to split hairs: Without clear-cut guidelines for determining who is actually the client, it seems appropriate to suggest that *ethically* the student is the client but that *legally* the parent is the client (p. 17, emphasis in the original).

A Solution

There is a middle path between identifying students as the only clients and identifying everyone as a client. This path is to identify students as the primary clients in school-based practice for three reasons. First, they are the most vulnerable group in the school and this vulnerability changes over time (see Box 9.5). Administrators have a great deal of power, teachers have cooperative power, school boards have elected power, and parents have legal authority. The students have virtually no power at all—they cannot vote, they cannot organize (authorities will call it rioting), and they have very few legal rights. Owing to the doctrine of *loco parentis*, no government agency will protect children's rights except under extreme circumstances, such as abuse or neglect. Thus, it is precisely because of their powerlessness that mental health professionals owe them their primary obligation. Second, the essential quality of "clientness" is that the client knows that they have entered into a helper-to-helped relationship. Ideally, this relationship (regardless of whether it is voluntary or involuntary) is formal and contractual (much like an IEP). Professionals try to help and educate many people in the school setting, but many of them would not consider themselves "clients"; some may not even know that they are a target of our change efforts (Loewenberg, Dolgoff, & Harrington, 2000). Some are colleagues/peers who also provide professional services to students. Some are administrators/supervisors who are accountable to ensure that the professional services are delivered appropriately. Some are relatives who have a legal responsibility for the welfare of the student. It is obfuscation, however, to consider all of these our clients (Raines, 2004b). Finally, schools are the only social institution that is supposed to be child centered. Churches, libraries, offices, shopping malls, and government agencies are primarily focused on adults. Schools are the one widely used public institution that focuses solely on children. When school-based mental health practitioners lend their aid to administrators, teachers, colleagues, or parents, it is for instrumental reasons. The ultimate goal of such interactions is to help the children in their care. Helping others within a school context is merely a means to the final end of helping students.

BOX 9.5 Research Vulnerability and Developmental Growth

It is generally assumed that the relationship between research vulnerability and developmental growth is an inverse relationship. This means that children's vulnerability goes down as the developmental growth goes up. We expect better coping skills in older children than younger ones. For example, we would not regard taking a toy away from a 12-year old as a reason to have a tantrum, but this is considered understandable in a child of 2. We assume that as children mature they become less at risk. Thompson (1990), in a classic article, posits two other, often unconsidered, possibilities.

First, some risks increase with developmental growth. Very young children are not easily embarrassed because they have not developed a sense of self-concept or modesty. Cross-dressing, for example, does not pose risks to infants in the same way as it would for older children. Young children are also less anxious than older children. They have not yet developed an appreciation of the temporal dimension to be worried about what procedure will happen next. Young children are also less likely to be stressed by concerns about the researcher's intentions. Their limited perspective-taking ability precludes the possibility of assigning potentially negative motives to adult caretakers. Thus, as their trust remains firm, their potential stress also stays constant.

One might now argue that this trust places them at jeopardy and this is true, but psychological jeopardy is in the eye of the beholder. Consider the classic experiment that uses mother-child separations to determine the quality of the child's attachment to a primary caretaker. Institutional Review Boards have generally concluded that such situations place the child at minimal risk. Given the child's limited temporal understanding, however, would the child concur? Researchers have not always been empathic enough to see that the temporary separation from the eyes of the child could be experienced as abandonment. Instead of interpreting the child's rage or despondency as an indicator of their attachment, perhaps we should consider it a measure of psychological risk. Since young children take their coping cues from trusted adults, when we

(continued)

remove that adult from the situation we remove the major resource for the child's resiliency. In short, we have not always defined risk from a child's perspective.

Second, there are times when the relationship between research vulnerability and child development are curvilinear. For example, shame and guilt are not known in infants and toddlers. Once young children do learn these responses, they are often hypersensitive, blaming themselves and apologizing for things that are not their fault, for example, their parents' divorce. Older children, however, gradually distinguish between bad events for which they are responsible and those for which they are not responsible.

In conclusion, we need to rethink our assumptions about research vulnerability and developmental growth. We must be more sensitive to a child's perspective of the research situation, support their need for trustworthy adults, and weigh the risks and benefits from their point of view. If they are the ones who must bear the risks, then they should have a stronger say in how the research is done.

Discussion Questions

1. What other vulnerabilities are reduced as children grow up?
2. What other vulnerabilities are increased as children mature?
3. What is your view about the level of risk for toddlers in the attachment experiments?
4. How could they be improved to offer more protection to young children?
5. How could young children have a voice in the decision to participate in research?

Research on Self-Determination

The research on the reality of self-determination is quite mixed. Youth generally feel less empowered than their parents or teachers think them to be. We will briefly explore the research on each group below.

Students

According to a recent meta-analysis, Algozzine, Browder, Karvonen, Test, and Wood (2001) found that strategies to promote student self-determination are effective. There are even curricula that schools can employ to build student self-determination skills, such as *Become Your Own Expert* (Carpenter, 1995), *Choicemaker* (Martin & Marshall, 1995), and *The Self-Advocacy Strategy for Education and Transition Planning* (Van Reusen, Box, Schumaker, & Deschler, 1994). Unfortunately, many schools routinely neglect to include any goals for student self-determination on IEPs (Wehmeyer, Agran, & Hughes, 2000). Students also have different experiences and perceptions of their autonomy. Carter, Lane, Pierson, and Glaeser (2006), for example, compared youth with emotional disturbance and youth with learning disabilities, based on the perceptions of teachers, parents, and the youth themselves. They found that youth with emotional disturbance had significantly fewer opportunities to engage in self-determination than youth with learning disabilities. Youth with emotional disturbance were especially more likely to perceive their ability to make informed choices differently than parents or teachers.

Parents

A qualitative study by Karvonen, Test, Browder, and Algozzine (2004) found mixed results of student self-advocacy for parents. Most parents experienced training in self-advocacy in their adolescents as part of the "letting go" process, but a few found it as facilitating adolescent rebellion against their wishes. Parents of different racial backgrounds also have different attitudes toward facilitating their children's autonomy. Zhang (2005), for instance, compared cultural, socioeconomic, and children's special education status factors on how much self-determination was allowed by their parents. White parents were more permissive than their African American or Asian counterparts. Parents with college degrees or higher incomes were more encouraging of autonomy than parents without college degrees or lower incomes. Finally, parents of students with disabilities were less empowering than parents of nondisabled children.

Teachers

Teachers' classroom environments vary in their recognition and empowerment of student rights. Classrooms that support student agency and self-determination experience fewer bullying behaviors than classrooms that are not supportive of student autonomy (Doll, Song, & Siemers, 2004). Assor, Kaplan, and Roth (2002) found that three types of teacher behaviors encouraged student self-determination. First, teachers can help students experience the learning process as relevant to their personal goals and interests. Second, teachers can proffer choices that are consistent with their stated aims. Third, teachers can permit criticism and encourage independent thinking by students. Karvonen et al. (2004) found that some teachers begin teaching self-awareness of strengths and weaknesses as early as middle school and fold student self-advocacy activities into language arts projects. Some IEP teams turn to structured programs to enable successful student self-advocacy, such as the McGill Action Planning System (Vandercook, York, & Forest, 1989) or the Self-Directed IEP (Martin, Marshall, Maxson, & Jerman, 1997).

Effects

All of these self-determination factors influence students' motivation and ability to finish school (Eisenman, 2007). Without direct instruction in foundational skills for making good choices, working toward goals, and self-evaluation of the results, students are less likely to remain engaged in school and follow-through to graduation (Columbus & Mithaug, 2003). Moreover, special education students who actively participate in their own transition planning do better in postsecondary endeavors (Alwell & Cobb, 2006). Involving students in transition planning does not have to be complicated. Benitez, Lattimore, and Wehmeyer (2005) found that the path to postsecondary employment was a simple three-step process: determine individualized career goals; develop and implement the transition plan; and evaluate and adjust progress toward the goals. On the other hand, the failure to include students in participatory decision making tends to lead to greater use of segregated placements, aversive conditioning, and the overuse of restraint and seclusion procedures (Amos, 2004). Since many of these results have been found to be harmful (Arnold & Hughes, 1999; Busch & Shore, 2000; Dishion, McCord, & Poulin, 1999; Dodge, 1999; Masters & Bellonci, 2001), school-based practitioners would be wise to recognize that these iatrogenic interventions are rooted in a philosophy of paternalistic control.

Paternalism

Reamer (2006b) identifies three common types of paternalism. First, sometimes professionals withhold information from a client, such as when a child faces a terminal illness and the family would prefer that she enjoys the little time she has left (Goldie, Schwartz, & Morrison, 2005). Second, sometimes professionals deliberately deceive a client, such as when a nosy adolescent wants to know if the social worker is single and available. Third, sometimes professionals interfere with a client's action, such as when a child attacks a classmate or a teen attempts a self-injurious act.

Reamer (1983) identifies four client attributes that warrant paternalism. First, interference is warranted when clients lack information that would convince them to do otherwise. For example, a student may require urgent intervention if they erroneously believe that a friend or family member has been killed and they wish to join them in the afterlife (e.g., *Romeo and Juliet*). Second, some clients may (temporarily or permanently) be unable to understand the relevant information. A child with moderate mental retardation, for example, may not be able to comprehend a choice between living with aged and ailing parents or going into a community-integrated living arrangement. Third, Reamer argues that when clients have consented to an intervention beforehand, but withdraw their consent afterwards, interference is justified. He uses the example of a client who voluntarily enters a chemical dependency facility only to resent his decision later. The problem with this argument is that the intrusion may have more to do with the attributes of the counselors than the attributes of the patient. Marshall and Marshall (1993), for example, found that religious and minority counselors were significantly more likely to make a paternalistic choice for both adolescents and adults. Furthermore, courts have ruled that psychiatric patients cannot be considered incompetent merely because they are noncompliant (Linzer, 1999). Finally, he posits that if clients are likely to agree with the interference afterwards, then paternalism is warranted. For example, an adolescent suffering from a substance-induced psychotic disorder may appreciate intervention after he has recovered.

Reamer (1983) also posits that there are three clinical situations that warrant paternalism. First, interference is appropriate if the harmful consequences are irreversible, such as when a client plans to maim or murder others. Second, paternalism may be justifiable if the client's range of freedom can be preserved only by temporarily restricting the client's current freedom. Students who have lost the ability to make good choices because of drug or alcohol addictions need responsible adults to make decisions for them. Third, intrusion may be necessary in emergency situations when there is not enough time to persuade a client to think rationally, such as when a student is about to jump off a building.

Overall, paternalism is viewed with skepticism by the major codes of ethics for school-based practitioners. The American School Counselor Association (2004) states that the school counselor "respect the student's values and beliefs and does not impose the counselor's personal values" (p. 1).

The National Association of School Psychologists (2000a) affirms the general principle that

> When a child initiates services, school psychologists understand their obligation to respect the rights of a student or client to initiate, participate in, or discontinue services voluntarily. When another party initiates services, the school psychologist will make every effort to secure voluntary participation of the child/student. (III. B. 3)

The NASW (1999) concurs that "social workers respect and promote the right of clients to self-determination and assist clients in their efforts to identify and clarify their goals" (standard 1.02).

The biggest problem with paternalism is its pervasiveness within the culture of public (and parochial) schools, a situation that has not changed for decades (Goldman, 1972). This is most poignantly demonstrated when we ask the question of who decides the goals of intervention. If it is the school who decides what the goals should be, then the system remains paternalistic and the family remains marginalized. This is one of the criticisms of the positive behavior intervention and support movement (Mulick & Butter, 2005). If the movement is nothing more than Skinnerian behaviorism wrapped in new clothes, then it is tantamount to a new form of educational control. At the risk of being repetitious, both IDEA and the President's Commission on Excellence in Special Education (2002) make it clear—decisions regarding assessment and treatment are meant to be collaborative and fully involve students and their families.

Implications for Evidence-Based Practice

School-based practitioners should remember five key points about client self-determination. First, clinicians have a responsibility to ensure that students become educated to take appropriate risk. One of these risks is the choice of a treatment that does not possess a high degree of empirical support. Second, they should primarily serve the interests and protect the rights of students. Aid provided to other constituents should be instrumental to the goal of ultimately helping students. The bottom line for any outcome evaluation is, "How is the student responding to the intervention?" Third, the evidence suggests that students can learn to be effective decision makers with proper instruction from parents and teachers. Decisions about which EST to use should be made with parents (and teachers) in a coaching role, helping them to ask pertinent questions (see Box 9.6). Fourth, the earlier students are involved as full participants in educational decisions, the harder they will work to achieve their aspirations. Practitioners should be aware about which programs are most likely to help students achieve postsecondary goals, such as college or career objectives. Fifth, paternalism is justified only in exceptional circumstances. School-based clinicians may have to work hard to resist the dominant culture within public schools, but our ethics require that students make most of the decisions on which ESTs to employ.

Parental Access and Control of Records

The primary law guaranteeing parents access and control of student records is the FERPA of 1974. FERPA is a "spending clause" statute because it affects

---

BOX 9.6 Questions for Parents to Ask Before Consenting to Treatment

Mellard (2004) suggests that school service providers be ready to answer a number of parental questions before implementing an intervention. Below is a list of some of the questions that parents might ask.

1. What is the name of the scientifically based intervention that is recommended?
2. What is the level of support for the scientifically based intervention?
3. How long will the intervention last (in weeks)?
4. How often will student progress be monitored?
5. How many minutes of class will my child miss to participate in the intervention?
6. Who will deliver the intervention?
7. Where will the intervention take place?
8. What criteria will be used to judge whether the intervention is working?
9. How will a decision be made to adjust or change the intervention if it's not working?
10. What if my child has an adverse reaction to the intervention?

---

only educational institutions receiving federal funds. These institutions include preschools, elementary and secondary schools, and colleges and universities. The law grants parents and guardians the right to inspect and review all education records directly related to their children.

Education Records

Education records are defined as "those records, files, documents, and other materials which—(i) contain information directly related to a student; and (ii) are maintained by an educational agency or institution or by a person acting for such agency or institution" (FERPA, 1974, section 1234g (a)(4)(B)). There are four common categories of records that parents cannot access.

The first set is "sole possession" files of instructional, supervisory, or administrative personnel that are never revealed to another person except an authorized substitute. The second group is "law enforcement" records maintained by campus police for their use only. In other words, this exemption does not include student disciplinary records. The third set is psychological or psychiatric treatment records of a student who has reached majority. The federal regulations narrow the definition of "treatment" as follows:

> For the purpose of this definition, "treatment" does not include remedial educational activities or activities that are part of the program of instruction at the agency or institution.
>
> U.S. Department of Education, 2004b, 34 CRF 99.3 (a)(4)(iii)

Treatment records would also extend to therapy records kept by school counselors and school social workers.

There is yet a fourth set of records that are subject to only limited access and this is group records:

> If any material or document in the education record of a student includes information on more than one student, the parents of one of such students shall have the right to inspect and review only such part of such material or document as relates to such student or to be informed of the specific information contained in such part of such material.
>
> FERPA, 1974, section (a)(1)(A)

Thus, practitioners who routinely see students in school-based groups that may not qualify as "treatment" groups would be wise to either maintain individual records or convey the personal information contained in a group record through an oral conversation that is then documented. Examples of such groups might include peer mediation groups, peer tutoring groups, service learning groups, student leadership groups, or study skills groups.

Parental Control of Information

FERPA (1974) not only allows for the inspection and review of records, it also allows them to seek the correction of records:

> To challenge the content of such student's education records, in order to insure that the records are not inaccurate, misleading, or otherwise in violation of the privacy rights of students, and to provide an opportunity for the correction or deletion of any such inaccurate, misleading or otherwise inappropriate data contained therein and to insert into such records a written explanation of the parents respecting the content of such records. ((A)(2))

Practitioners, therefore, should be mindful about what statements they make in official school records, such as IEPs. It is best to write official reports with the image of the parent looking over one's shoulder. Practitioners, however, do not have to amend a statement just because a parent disagrees with it. Parents can write rebuttals or explain extenuating circumstances in a separate note that will become part of the official record. In a case where professionals and parents cannot come to agreement, this mechanism allows them to "agree to disagree" without compromise.

Nonconsensual Release of Information

Schools are able to release any records containing "personally identifiable information" without student or parental consent to 10 different groups. Since most these are outside our purview of interest, we will discuss the two most relevant exceptions.

First, FERPA (1974) allows the nonconsensual release of information to a broad range of school personnel:

> Other school officials, including teachers within the educational institution or local educational agency, who have been determined by such agency or institution to have legitimate educational interests, including the educational interests of the child for whom consent would otherwise be required.

> Section (b)(1)(A)

The phrase "legitimate educational interests" has become a point of contention between school-based mental health professionals and other school personnel, especially teachers and principals. Unfortunately, it has not been further defined in the *Code of Federal Regulations* or by case law. It is probably best to

---

limit these interests to those situations involving school and student safety, specific teaching strategies, and special education placement considerations. Even when these situations occur, practitioners would be wise to limit disclosures as narrowly as possible and only provide sufficient information to achieve their purpose. Since FERPA leaves this discretion up to the local education agency or school district (not the building principal), it may also behoove clinicians to volunteer to head a task force made up of representatives from multiple constituent groups to establish district policy on this issue.

Second, FERPA (1974) allows the nonconsensual release of information for research purposes, including

> Organizations conducting studies for, or on behalf of, educational agencies or institutions for the purpose of developing, validating, or administering predictive tests, administering student aid programs, and improving instruction, if such studies are conducted in such a manner as will not permit the personal identification of students and their parents by persons other than representatives of such organizations and such information will be destroyed when no longer needed for the purpose for which it is conducted.

Section (b)(1)(F)

The federal regulations expand the definition of an organization qualifying under this exemption: "the term *organization* includes, but is not limited to, Federal, State, and local agencies, and independent organizations" (34 CFR 99.31(b)(6)(iv)). This allowance is generally meant to engage in research that will improve services to students. This exemption may well include case or group evaluation activities undertaken to improve interventions to students. In short, prior parent and/or student consent to receive treatment could be interpreted as consent to evaluate whether the treatment worked. This exemption, however, does not appear to include large-scale surveys that seek to determine the mental health of students, so researchers would be wise to seek active consent for this kind of research. It is also vitally important that if consent is granted, that the research is careful not permit the identification of any student. The federal regulations recognize that some disaggregated samples are so small that identification of individual students is a risk when they include "a list of personal characteristics that would make the student's identity easily traceable" (34 CFR 99.3). Thus, researchers should be cautious about the cell size in subgroup disaggregation studies. One rule of thumb could be the state-level decision about how many individuals to include in a subgroup for No Child Left Behind (U.S. Department of Education, 2007).

Implications for Evidence-Based Practice

There are three important points for school-based practitioners to remember about parental access and control of records. First, FERPA is clear that the general principle is to allow for parents to inspect and review most school records. While informal "progress notes" will fall under the category of "sole possession" files, formal progress reports should be shared regularly to promote shared decision making. Second, for official school records, parents retain the right to access and seek the correction of those records. Progress reports should identify the baseline measurement and the most current measurement so that parents can clearly determine for themselves how well an intervention is working. Finally, there are two occasions under which information can be shared without student or parental consent. One is the sharing of information with educational personnel who have a legitimate educational interest. Since most mental health interventions require a child to miss class time, teachers and principals have a right to know whether the benefit (i.e., social-emotional growth) is worth the cost (i.e., loss of academic time). This information, however, should be narrowly construed and predetermined at the district level. The other is the sharing of information for research purposes with a view to improving services to students. Mental health practitioners should feel comfortable routinely evaluating their own practice as a result of this statute, but large-scale studies should always seek the permission of both parents and students.

Summary

This chapter has examined three interrelated ethical issues. First, it examined the issue of informed consent. Passive consent was acknowledged to be a common practice in schools, but considered inadequate for protecting student rights. Truly informed consent requires capacity, information, and voluntariness. Each of these needs to be assessed for each situation in which consent is sought. There are exceptions to obtaining the informed consent of parents and the assent of students, but these need to be weighed carefully in each case. Knowledge of state laws allowing mature minors to make their own decisions is critical for providing health and mental health care. Second, we explored the issue of self-determination. This should always involve some developmentally appropriate direct instruction in making good choices, setting realistic goals, and working toward them even if students must learn from their mistakes. A key issue is the determination of one's primary client. This is best assumed to be the student within school-based practice owing to concerns about powerlessness, the definition of client-ness, and institutional priorities. There are a few times when paternalism is appropriate, but these occasions should be few and far between. Third, we investigated the issue of parental access and control of records in schools. FERPA grants parents the right to inspect and review the vast majority of school records. There is one important exception and this is the sole pos-session files belonging to a school employee. FERPA also empowers parents to seek the correction of files they find false or misleading. Practitioners who write official reports are wise to consider this right while drafting their reports. Finally, clinicians should be aware that there are only two relevant circumstances when school-based personnel can share information about a student on a nonconsensual basis—one involves sharing with those who have a legitimate educational interest and the other involves service-related research to improve intervention.

Suggested Reading

1. Eisenman, L. Y. (2007). Self-determination interventions: Building a foundation for school completion. *Remedial and Special Education, 28* (1), 2–8.

2. Fisher, C. B. (2004). Informed consent and clinical research involving children and adolescents: Implications of the revised APA Code of Ethics and HIPAA. *Journal of Clinical Child & Adolescent Psychology, 33* (4), 832–839.

3. Thompson, R. A. (1990). Vulnerability in research: A developmental perspective on research risk. *Child Development, 61* (1), 1–16.

Internet Resources

Advocates for Youth—Legal Issues and School-Based and School-Linked Health Centers
http://www.advocatesforyouth.org/PUBLICATIONS/iag/sbhcslhc.htm
Code of Federal Regulations
http://www.gpoaccess.gov/cfr/index.html

FindLaw Education Laws
http://www.findlaw.com/01topics/37education/index.html

Guttmacher Institute's Adolescent page
http://www.guttmacher.org/sections/adolescents.php

Human Subject Regulations Decision Charts
http://www.hhs.gov/ohrp/humansubjects/guidance/decisioncharts.htm

Legal Information Institute of Cornell University
http://www.law.cornell.edu/

10

■ ■ ■

Systemic Change

Preview

This chapter identifies the complex systemic issues of implementing evidence-based practice (EBP) in the schools. It begins with an overview of organizational change. This overview will provide readers with the cornerstones of change, the different types of implementation, and the different stages of implementation. Along the way, I will provide inserts to assess organizational readiness and explain how to conduct a force field analysis. Then I will address the most common barriers to implementation. These barriers include lack of time, lack of relevant information, lack of technology skills, and institutional issues. I will end on a note of hope—that the gap between researchers and practitioners is surmountable if we learn to work together.

Systemic Issues in Implementation

In the middle of the 18th century, a British naval surgeon discovered a cure for scurvy, a disease that ravaged sailors on long voyages for centuries. Despite the overwhelming need for a cure, the simple dietary solution (increasing vitamin C) was not implemented in the British navy for another century (Walker, 2003). While new discoveries no longer take 100 years to be implemented, recent research indicates that it is still taking up to 20 years before clinical research becomes translated to clinical practice (Brekke, Ell, & Palinkas, 2007). Even with intentional dissemination efforts, it takes 5 years to implement EBP within large organizations (Fixsen, Naoom, Blase, Friedman, & Wallace, 2005).

In the change management literature, there are both early and late adopters of any new technology (Baskin, 2004; Panzano & Roth, 2006). Some will resist EBP because it is based on a medical model that includes differential diagnosis, empirically supported treatments (ESTs), and evaluation of results (Forness & Kavale, 2001; Oswald, 2002). Some will look at EBP as just yet another educational fad that may not last (Dewey, 1902/2001). However, everyone has begun to figure out that, regardless of their field of practice in education (Adams & McCarthy, 2005; Apel, 2001; Bailey, Bornstein, & Ryan, 2007), it is going to affect them and that there is professional literature out there to support their efforts. They have also begun to realize that EBP requires some extra effort that is best shared by a team of committed professionals (Gambrill, 2005; Hunt, Haidet, Coverdale, & Richards, 2003).

The Center for Mental Health in Schools at UCLA (2007) notes that a number of new initiatives have been suggested for schools. Many of these have been good ideas, such as positive behavior intervention and supports, social-emotional learning, and so forth. It can seem as if EBP is just one more add-on. The key, however, is to integrate EBP into the life of an institution that already has its own culture and norms of operation. To do that correctly, practitioners must understand the basic concepts of organizational change.

Organizational Change
Organizational change requires a solid foundation, knowing the different types of implementation, and understanding the stages of change. We will address all of these now.

Cornerstones
Fixsen et al. (2005) identify four cornerstones for successful implementation. First, successful implementation requires coordinated training, coaching, and formative assessment of carefully chosen practitioners. State education agencies or state professional associations, for example, could sponsor key leaders to learn and integrate EBP into their daily practice. Second, it necessitates an organizational infrastructure that provides timely instruction, skillful supervision, and attention to process and outcome evaluation. Again, state education agencies or state professional associations could sponsor training conferences and tools for outcome evaluation. Third, it entails the full involvement of interested and invested constituent groups from beginning to end. As noted in the last chapter, students and their parents are often

the last to be included in school change efforts, and yet both the law and professional ethics require their involvement. Finally, it requires state and federal funding policies that empower the change process by providing the money to make it happen. State education agencies, for example, could purchase access to the proprietary databases mentioned in Chapter 4 to foster ongoing evidence based learning. They could also help offset the expense of adopting expensive proprietary ESTs (Franklin & Hopson, 2007).

Types of Implementation

Fixsen et al. (2005) also identify three types of implementation, including paper implementation, process implementation, and performance implementation. *Paper implementation* refers to the development of policy or procedural manuals that describe in detail how something should be done. The U.S. Department of Education does this every time a new education law is passed. School-based practitioners realize that this step alone takes about 18 to 22 months for the federal government. Administrators recognize that this stage is often a kind of perfunctory compliance with mandates from faraway overseers who are unlikely to actually observe and inspect internal operations. Such distance allows the appearance of compliance with no real transformation of building-level tasks. *Process implementation* refers to the effecting of new procedures for staff training, supervision, or information collection processes that are meant to change organizational practices. School districts often do this yearly with in-service training or the development of school improvement plans that organize building-level data into tables according to district goals. Mere labels and procedural compliance, however, may represent only "lip service" to the new policies. *Performance implementation* refers to the actual use of new interventions in daily practice among frontline staff that benefit the consumer. This requires that the change be integrated with the systems in which it is embedded. It is this last level of change that must occur if ESTs are going to make a difference to the lives of students.

Stages of Change

The change process is often slow and frustrating for those who are advocates of change. It would be wise for change agents to consider the organization's readiness to change before they start (see Box 10.1).

It helps to think of change occurring through six stages, each one with its own challenges and tasks. The first stage is *exploration* of the potential change.

BOX 10.1 Assessing Organizational Readiness to Change

Edwards, Jumper-Thurman, Plested, Oetting, and Swanson (2000) have described seven stages about community readiness to change that can easily be applied to educational communities since both have a shared culture. Fixsen et al. (2005) have suggested corresponding steps that change agents can take to move the community forward.

STAGE OF READINESS	RECOMMENDED STEPS
1. *No awareness*: No consciousness about the need for change.	Raise consciousness by seeking out key leaders and potential change agents. Help them see how the change might contribute to their own vision.
2. *Denial*: Recognition is present, but it is confined to a small group with insufficient power to effect change.	Help small groups to think "outside the box" of their sphere of influence. Encourage them to use social marketing strategies to build bridges to other groups.
3. *Vague awareness*: Recognition is present, but no clarity exists when it comes to details.	Provide explicit examples of what others have done. Focus on feasibility and cost-effective plans.
4. *Preplanning*: Clarity about how things could be exists, but leaders are just beginning to emerge, and no plan has developed.	Assist emergent leaders in developing a plan and identifying potential beneficiaries of the change effort.
5. *Preparation*: Active leaders are focusing on detailed arrangements to effect the change.	Help leaders assess what resources are needed and how to expand the process.
6. *Initiation*: Paper implementation and some process implementation has been accomplished.	Help leaders to see the process through to performance implementation. Help them anticipate potential barriers or challenges.

(*continued*)

STAGE OF READINESS	RECOMMENDED STEPS
7. *Stabilization*: Process implementation is finished and performance implementation has begun. Barriers have been identified.	Help leaders to continue to resolve problems and integrate change with existing policies and programs for a seamless system of service delivery.

During this time, the organization investigates the potential fit between the proposed innovation and the existing needs and resources. Smart change agents demonstrate how the new approach can correspond to such needs with a good return on the investment of resources. Key stakeholders must be recruited and must consent to further work on the change process (Fuchs & Fuchs, 2001). Within a local education agency, these include the director of special education, district superintendent, building principals, the board of education, the union representative, and the parent-teacher organization or association.

The second stage is *installation* of the innovation. During this time, the agency must put in place the structural supports necessary to sustain the change, including funding for training or a realignment of resources to support needed technologies (e.g., computers or database access). Local educational agencies, for example, may choose to use some of the IDEA early intervention or Title 1 funding to support this effort. Contacts with local universities might be made for external program evaluation, technical assistance, or grant writing support. It would be prudent for change agents to consider how to bring about change that will still support institutional stability (see Box 10.2).

The third stage is *initial implementation* of the change. This stage is marked by a sense of awkwardness and trepidation as initiators contend with systemic barriers, including fixed traditions, anxious administrators, mixed messages, interdisciplinary tensions, and plain old inertia. It is best to start small and develop a data-based track record before extending the innovation to other programs (Schaeffer et al., 2005). This is what Miller, George, and Fogt (2005) call starting small, but thinking big. Change leaders need

BOX 10.2 Force Field Analysis

Lewin (1951) developed field theory as a way to explain how a societal unit maintains stability while adapting to the environment and moving forward at the same time, much as a motorcycle learns to negotiate turns on a road. Forces can be either internal or external, since the organization always exists in a social environment. The forces influencing an agency can be driving forces or restraining forces. Driving forces press for change while restraining forces inhibit change. Both are needed to maintain stability or the social unit will crash. Stability is an important concept for change agents to keep in mind—too often, zealots want to bring change at any price and forget that the operation is not a success if the patient dies.

Force field analysis has many applications to counseling, education, psychology, and social work. In social work, it has been used to assess the likelihood of organizational change efforts (Brager & Holloway, 1992) and help implement risk assessment systems for the identification of child abuse (DePanfilis, 1996). Psychologists have used force field analysis to design and implement school consultation services (Fuqua & Kurpius, 1993; Kurpius, 1978). Educators have used it in conflict resolution programs (Ragan, 2000). Counselors have used it to analyze the cultural accommodations necessary to implement effective career counseling programs (Leong, 2002).

Let's apply the use of force field analysis to the implementation of EBP in the schools. Critical actors include the current Secretary of Education, State Education Agency directors, district superintendents, school board members, building principals, union leaders, and parent-teacher organization presidents. The key to dynamic change is to gradually increase the strength of the driving forces while moderating the strength of the restraining forces, resulting in a delicate balance between stability and change. We will list driving and restraining forces on the chart below. As one can see, most of the driving forces are external to schools, while most of the restraining forces are located internally. This implies that evidence-based change agents should consider ways to help schools see how the new approach can help solve their existing problems or felt needs.

(continued)

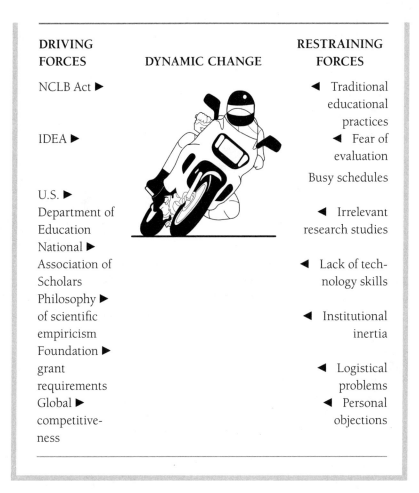

DRIVING FORCES	DYNAMIC CHANGE	RESTRAINING FORCES
NCLB Act ▶		◀ Traditional educational practices
IDEA ▶		◀ Fear of evaluation
		Busy schedules
U.S. ▶ Department of Education		◀ Irrelevant research studies
National ▶ Association of Scholars		◀ Lack of technology skills
Philosophy ▶ of scientific empiricism		◀ Institutional inertia
Foundation ▶ grant requirements		◀ Logistical problems
Global ▶ competitive-ness		◀ Personal objections

to remain flexible and optimistic at this crucial step (Hernandez & Hodges, 2003). Interpersonal support may be extremely important in order to maintain one's courage in the face of mounting obstacles (Elias, Zins, Graczyk, & Weissberg, 2003). Initial pitfalls should be honestly admitted, but be considered part of the "learning curve" in moving forward.

The fourth stage is *full operation* of the innovation. It is at this stage that integration with other parts of the system occurs. For EBP, this means that every level of intervention is involved, including prevention programs, targeted group interventions, and indicated individual interventions, such as response-to-intervention or IEPs. Change agents need to assess process-related fidelity before evaluating outcomes. There is no sense in measuring outcomes if the program has been subject to so much compromise that it is no longer recognizable as an empirically supported intervention (Mowbray, Holter, Teague, & Bybee, 2003). Core elements must remain in place even if slight adaptations have been made to fit the organizational culture.

The fifth stage is *adaptation* of the innovation. As new implementers adopt the proposed change, they will invariably tailor it to suit their own style or local needs (Kratochwill & Shernoff, 2004). Most of these changes will qualify as fortuitous adaptations, but some will be unintentional corruptions or deliberate distortions (Rubin & Parrish, 2007; Sanders & Turner, 2005). Unintentional corruptions of EBP include watering down the complete process to mere adoption of ESTs with no ongoing outcome evaluations or mere outcome evaluations of ongoing programs that have no empirical support (see Chapter 2). Deliberate distortions include journalistic reviews of the research literature to support preferred practices (see Box 4.5), reliance on authority figures who label their pet projects as evidence based with no objective support, or rigid adherence to cookbook practice (see Chapter 2). All of these are caricatures of EBP and represent attempts to adulterate legitimate science with self-indulgent strategies (Gambrill, 2003; Shlonsky & Gibbs, 2006). As mentioned in Chapter 6, practitioners need to maintain a balance between adaptation and treatment fidelity.

The final stage is *sustainability* of the change effort. School systems are dynamic, ever-changing environments—actors move, political agendas sway, and funding streams dry up as new ones emerge (Elias et al., 2003; Hatch, 2000). Commitment to EBP requires that as needs change, the new questions are put into answerable forms, the research literature is searched anew, new studies are appraised for their relevance, strength, and consistency, new adaptations and applications are discovered, and outcomes are reevaluated. The beauty of EBP is its flexibility and accommodation of new problems and new populations. It constantly evolves to fit the needs of a changing world.

Implementation Barriers

Many fields of clinical practice have examined the reasons why ordinary practitioners do not use EBP in their daily work. These reasons can be organized into themes, including lack of time, lack of information, lack of technology skills, and institutional issues. Each of these problems will be addressed along with potential solutions.

Evidence-Based Practice in School Mental Health

Lack of Time

A number of studies have indicated that lack of time is the primary reason that clinicians do not use EBP in their work with clients. Edmond, Megivern, Williams, Rochman, and Howard (2006) surveyed social work field instructors and found that 84% pointed to lack of time as the primary reason. Meline and Paradiso (2003) found that 93% of speech and language professionals working in schools also reported unhappiness with the amount of time they had to stay up-to-date with the recent research. Fully 89% felt that it was difficult to see clients and keep up with the latest findings. Kratochwill and Shernoff (2004) concur that "even when psychologists are aware of the empirical evidence supporting a technique or procedure, they may not infuse this evidence into practice because doing so would require more work than time permits" (p. 36). Part of the time problem has been the limited time for ongoing professional development training. Schools tend to use "institute days" or other in-service venues to provide practitioners with compressed information that is lost if attendees do not immediately integrate it into their daily routine (Addis, 2002). The end result has been a lack of change in professional practice (Cook, Landrum, Tankersley, & Kauffman, 2003; Gersten & Dimino, 2001).

Solutions

There are three possible solutions to the lack of time. First, buy-in by both district-level and building-level supervisors is important from the start. Only they can provide the release time necessary to obtain mentoring or coaching on effective interventions (Boudah, Logan, & Greenwood, 2001). Simply adding EBP as one more professional responsibility onto an already full load will not produce the expected benefits. Administrator support can have its own dangers, however, since any perception of "top-down" imposition can lead to increased staff resistance (Sanders & Turner, 2005). Second, another possibility is the use of university interns to help with the data collection and analysis process. This produces a win-win situation for both the local education agency and the university students. The agency obtains third-party, objectively collected data and the interns gain valuable experience about collecting and analyzing data under real world conditions (Viggiani, Reid, & Bailey-Dempsey, 2002). Third, implementation does not (and should not) occur overnight—it takes up to 5 years for complete integration. Focusing on empirically based prevention first has the benefit of saving time spent on targeted and indicated interventions later on (Gladwell, 2000). Sanders and

Turner (2005), for example, completed their training of professionals over a 3-year period with eight quality control features: skills-based training using small group exercises, follow-up after the initial training, use of a data-based feedback loop, affordable fees, interdisciplinary eligibility, course reading requirements and testing, accreditation of the trainers, and the use of standardized materials to maintain training fidelity.

Lack of Relevant Information

Meline and Paradiso (2003) found that 44% of speech and language therapists felt that the majority of research was not of interest to them and 58% did not find it easy to transfer the findings to their daily practice. Edmond et al. (2006) found that 36% of the social work field instructors claimed there was a lack of relevant information in the professional literature. Feeny, Hembree, and Zoellner (2003) explored the reasons behind psychologists' failure to employ a well-established EST with clients. They discovered four myths about ESTs: beliefs that ESTs should not be altered to fit client needs, beliefs that ESTs are insufficient as a cure and must be augmented by other therapies, beliefs that ESTs work only under laboratory conditions and not in the real world, and beliefs that ESTs will lead to iatrogenic effects, such as a worsening of the symptoms or higher client dropout rates.

Solutions

There are two major problems that must be addressed under relevance. The first major problem is the weakness of the available research. Kazdin (2000) proposed a plan for child and adolescent research that emphasizes four goals. First, researchers must do a better job of connecting treatment with what we know from basic science (especially developmental psychopathology and neurophysiology). Second, researchers need to study the mechanisms or processes by which therapeutic change occurs and situational factors that influence the change. Third, researchers need to broaden the range of issues under study beyond specific treatment techniques, such as cognitive behavioral therapy. For example, future research might compare different psychosocial therapies or study different combinations of therapies. Finally, he suggests that researchers need to expand the range of outcome criteria by which they evaluate effectiveness. Researchers need to go beyond pre- and posttests to real world outcomes such as academic achievement and school functioning (Walker, 2003). This could also include client-generated outcomes determined by children and adolescents as well as long-term outcomes, such high school graduation and gainful employment.

The National Advisory Mental Health Council's (2001) report suggested that researchers can focus their efforts on two major implementation-related issues. First, the National Advisory Mental Health Council posits that psychosocial intervention outcome studies can inform implementation research by providing clues about

> The facets of treatments that are critical to ensure beneficial outcomes, delineating the conditions and parameters under which interventions are most likely to succeed, and identifying the processes and principles by which treatments may be augmented to enhance their success across diverse populations and settings. (p. 55)

This elaborate sentence actually makes three subpoints. First, most of our research efforts have been about "what works" rather than "why it works." When we can tease out the most crucial elements of an effective intervention, it will be more useful to everyday practitioners who can build their own treatments around the essential core (Spielmans, Pasek, & McFall, 2006). Next, when we can delineate the specific conditions under which a given treatment works best, we can differentially apply treatments based on comorbidity or client complexity (Jensen et al., 2001). Finally, when we know how to adapt interventions to fit the diversity needs of our students, we can employ them more effectively (Ruscio & Holohan, 2006). Second, the National Advisory Mental Health Council (2001) suggests that "dissemination research offers crucial information on the factors critical to successful transportation of interventions—information that can be integrated into treatment development, right from the start, to ensure that interventions can be used and sustained" (p. 55). As efficacy research begins to be translated to effectiveness research, we need to pay attention to the process variables (facilitating or obstructive) that affect how a laboratory-generated treatment works under natural conditions (Addis, 2002; Hernandez & Hodges, 2003). This would enable clinicians to anticipate potential roadblocks and take advantage of situational supports to improve client outcomes.

The second major problem is the availability of the good research that does exist. While we mentioned four ways that individual practitioners can get access to the proprietary databases that contain most of this information in Chapter 4, there are two more systemic solutions. First, when universities contact alumni about garnering support, alumni can make their future support contingent on the university's willingness to give alumni access to university databases from the convenience of one's home or office. After all, if university staff and students have this kind of access, why not the alumni? Second, professional associations might negotiate access for their members. This would probably entail an increase in the annual fee, but it would be well worth the cost if it was shared by several thousand professionals in the discipline.

Lack of Technology Skills

Edmond et al. (2006) found that 22% of the social work field instructors admitted that lack of technology skills was an obstacle. Three sets of technology skills are imperative for EBP: electronic search strategy skills (see Chapter 3); research appraisal skills (see Chapter 4); and outcome evaluation skills (see Chapters 7 and 8). Gale, Hawley, and Sivakumaran (2003) tested 150 mental health professionals on 10 basic questions about probability and compared their answers to an equally educated group of nonhealthcare providers (excluding scientists and academics). Overall, the mental health professionals scored no better than their nonhealthcare counterparts. The problem with this result, of course, is that mental health professionals are routinely expected to assess risks in their clients. Kratochwill and Shernoff (2004) found that there were 10 different groups engaged in the systematic appraisal of research studies about prevention or intervention effectiveness, often with their own particular methods. A lack of research appraisal skills can hamper consumers' ability to distinguish strong criteria from weak criteria, leading to a tendency to adopt anything that comes with the label "evidence based" (Rubin & Parrish, 2007).

Solutions

There have been two broad approaches to the lack of technology skills on the part of practitioners. The older model is the *scientist-practitioner model* (Chavkin, 1993; Elliott, Sheridan, & Gresham, 1989; Haring-Hidore & Vacc, 1988). In this model, preservice practitioners are trained in the process of EBP with the hope that they will maintain and hone these skills throughout their careers (Howard, McMillen, & Pollio, 2003; Kratochwill & Shernoff, 2004). There are four problems with this model. First, most practitioners do not work in settings that reward or even reinforce scholarship (Wakefield & Kirk, 1996). Second, as mentioned earlier, universities still routinely cut their students off from research databases the moment they graduate. Third, one of the problems within the helping professions has been that professors within these professions are not required to have any practice experience. For example, while the Council of Social Work Education requires that social work instructors have at least 2 years of practice experience, this requirement is waived if the instructor does not teach practice. This lack of direct practice experience makes it more difficult for such instructors to make research relevant to daily practice. Students are sometimes required to do a research project within their practicum, but the quality of this project often depends heavily on the research skills of the field instructor (Dietz, Westerfelt, & Barton, 2004). Finally, some schools have allowed masters-level adjunct instructors to teach many of the practice courses. While these adjuncts tend to have excellent clinical skills, they often lack the research skills necessary to combine EBP with the usual problem-solving model (Walker, Briggs, Koroloff, & Friesen, 2007).

The newer model is the *researcher-practitioner partnership model* (Barlow, Morrow-Bradley, Elliot, & Phillips, 1993; Franklin & McNeil, 1992; Hess & Mullen, 1995). In this model, practitioners are teamed with researchers who have similar interests. Practitioners bring real world relevance and complex clients to the project and the researchers bring scientific rigor and technological expertise. The primary problem with this model is the imbalance of time and resources between the partners. University researchers are frequently given time and money to work on such projects while their community-based colleagues must scramble to squeeze the required time into an already tight schedule with multiple commitments. Nonetheless, recent research shows that ongoing collaboration is effective in sustaining EBP in community settings (Franklin & Hopson, 2007).

It is important to note that neither of these approaches is necessarily exclusive of the other. Preservice practitioners can be trained in EBP (Howard, McMillen, & Pollio, 2003; Koller & Bertel, 2006) and still team with university-based researchers after graduation (Berninger, Dunn, Lin, Shimada, 2004; Kettlewell, 2004; Regehr, Stern, & Shlonsky, 2007). This two-pronged collaborative approach is, in fact, probably the optimal solution.

Institutional Issues

Hoagwood and Johnson (2003) provide two reasons why ESTs have not been easily transported into schools. First, the very nature of efficacy research that is designed and carried out under laboratory conditions may not mesh well with school-based conditions (Morrison, 2001). School-based conditions are messy at best—students have multiple and complex problems not easily squeezed into diagnostic pigeon holes, the environment does not allow for neat 50-minute periods where clients can be seen individually for weeks without interruption, and school providers are overworked and underappreciated (Crisp, Gudmundsen, & Shirk, 2006; Southam-Gerow, Weisz, & Kendall, 2003).

Second, diffusion studies are few and far between. According to Herschell, McNeil, and McNeil (2004), fewer than 1% of the psychology publications on ESTs dealt with dissemination of child treatment studies. Such studies identify which interventions have been applied to a community context, how they are adapted, and what factors affect their sustainability. Overbay, Grable, and Vasu (2006), for example, found numerous challenges in doing an effectiveness study under school-based conditions, including, the impossibility of random assignment, difficulty in getting cooperation from comparison schools, eliminating interaction effects between schools, legal hurdles, locating developmentally appropriate outcome measures, teachers who refused to cooperate with observations out of concerns that it would be reflected in their performance reviews, difficulties with maintaining neutrality, and logistical difficulties (conflicting schedules and weather catastrophes). Currently, diffusion research on school implementation represents a large gap in the research literature. There have been many studies on school climate and its effect on student outcomes, but there are few studies of the effects that school climate have on service delivery (Hernandez & Hodges, 2003).

Kratochwill and Shernoff (2004) provide a third problem—many prevention programs are delivered through teachers, not mental health professionals. Given the universal aims of these programs, this is not a surprise, but it does raise the issue of teachers' willingness to implement empirically supported interventions. Unfortunately, research on teacher's adoption of empirically supported techniques is no better than the research on mental health practitioners. Carnine (1995) found that there are three aspects to teachers' failure to utilize relevant research. First, many teachers find the existing research untrustworthy. This may be due to the fact that the research designs "do not adequately reflect the realities of classroom teaching" (Vaughn, Klingner, & Hughes, 2000, p. 165), but the result is the same—teachers do not place their confidence in the findings. Second, research has not always been presented in a way that makes application easy. Method sections often lack detailed descriptions of the intervention and contextual conditions, and Discussion sections generally do a poor job of identifying their real world implications (McDonald, Keesler, Kauffman, & Schneider, 2006). Third, the research database has seldom been accessible to teachers after they graduate from school. Part of this may be the fault of teachers who prefer to seek out informal rather formal sources of knowledge (Landrum, Cook, Tankersley, & Fitzgerald, 2002), but the larger fault lies with universities who cut off students from the scholarly databases as soon as they graduate as if access was no longer a professional necessity.

Foorman and Moats (2004) found that the primary obstacle to transporting and sustaining research-based interventions was the lack of informed instructional leaders, such as principals or lead teachers, who can propel an agenda forward over several years (Miller et al., 2005). Indigenous school-based practitioners who have personal experience implementing a technique and who understand the environmental system are key figures for helping to motivate others to adapt and apply empirically supported procedures. Unfortunately, the burnout rate for principals is very high: most superintendents stay for 2 years and only 50% of new teachers stay for more than 3 years (Elias et al., 2003).

Solutions

The contextual challenges of any large complex system are the most difficult to overcome. There are some published research projects that have undertaken the task of implementing ESTs in highly chaotic real world situations (Crisp et al., 2006). Future researchers should study these attempts, particularly the way they handle procedural barriers.

Currently, we can identify four possible solutions. First and foremost, any changes must be intimately linked to the overall vision and goals for the academic community (Miller et al., 2005). If the innovation does not help meet one of the identified objectives of a school, it is both unlikely to be adopted and unlikely to be sustained. Change agents should study the school improvement plan carefully to ferret out how to pitch the new intervention. Second, dissemination researchers must take good process notes or create what qualitative researchers would call an audit trail. Indeed, the best deployment research is likely to include both qualitative and quantitative elements. Such mixed method approaches are most appropriate for complex situations in which either approach would be inadequate to the task (Raines, 2008). Third, the resulting research should also take into account a person-in-environment or student-in-class/school climate perspective. Roach and Kratochwill (2004) identify three measures for school culture (see Box 10.3). There are also an increasing number of scales to measure classroom climate (see Box 10.4). There are very few scales, however, that attempt to assess students' level of functioning within their educational environment (Bowen, Richman, & Bowen, 1997; Hunsucker, Nelson, & Clark, 1986). Fourth, committed implementation should lead to recognition for faculty

BOX 10.3 School Climate Scales

SCALE	CITATION	AVAILABILITY
California School Climate and Safety Survey	Furlong et al., 2005	Michael Furlong, University of California Santa Barbara, Center for School-Based Youth Development, Santa Barbara, CA 93106-9490.
Comprehensive Assessment of School Environment (CASE) Survey	Howard and Keefe, 1991; Kelly et al., 1986; Van Horn, 2003	Out of print—May 1, 2006, National Association of Secondary School Principals, Reston, VA 20191-1537. 1-866-647-7253 www.nassp.org
Organizational Climate Description Questionnaire; Organizational Climate Index; Organizational Health Inventory	Hoy, Smith, and Sweetland, 2002; Hoy, Tarter, and Kottkamp, 1997;	Wayne K. Hoy, Education Administration, 116 Ramseyer Hall, 29 W. Woodruff, Ohio State University, Columbus, OH 43210. http://www.coe.ohio-state.edu/whoy/instruments_6.htm

and staff who lead such efforts. Rewards can be low in cost (e.g., a preferred parking space), but they should be publicly presented so that others will emulate their example (Fuchs & Fuchs, 2001). The flip side of this coin is that outcome evaluation of an intervention should not be used as a summative evaluation of a practitioner's skills—this is a misuse of research and one that is sure to dampen anyone's enthusiasm for EBP.

Schaeffer et al. (2005), for example, examined how to implement evidence-based mental health programs within the Baltimore public schools.

BOX 10.4 Classroom Environment Scales

SCALE	CITATION	AVAILABILITY
Assessment of Practices in Early Elementary Classrooms	Hemmeter, Maxwell, Ault, and Schuster, 2001; Maxwell, McWilliam, Hemmeter, Ault, and Schuster, 2001	Teachers College Press, P.O. Box 20, Williston, VT 05495-0020. 1-800-575-6566 http://www.teacherscollegepress.com/
Classroom Environment Scale	Trickett, Leone, Fink, and Braaten, 1993; Trickett and Moos, 1995	Mind Garden, Inc., 855 Oak Grove Road, Suite 215, Menlo Park, CA 94025. (650) 322-6300 http://www.mindgarden.com
Classroom Literacy Environmental Profile (CLEP)	Wolfersberger, Reutzel, Sudweeks, and Fawson, 2004	Mary E. Wolfersberger, School of Education, California State University, Bakersfield, CA 93311.
Learning Environment Inventory (Secondary grades); My Class Inventory (Primary grades)	Fraser, 1998; Fraser, Anderson, and Walberg, 1982; Sink and Spencer, 2005	Koffman, E. C., McNeely, S. L., & Willerman, M. (1991). *Teachers Helping Teachers: Peer Observation and Assistance.* New York: Praeger. www.questia.com
Student Perceptions of Classroom Support Scale (SPCS)	O'Rourke and Houghton, 2006	John O'Rourke, Edith Cowan University, Bradford St., Mount Lawley, Perth, WA 6050, Australia.

They began by identifying three main principles. First, all stakeholders should be involved in the process, including school-based clinicians, school administrators, teachers, parents, and even youth. Second, the involvement of these various stakeholders should occur simultaneously and address all stages of the change process from identifying which problems should take priority, selecting intervention approaches, and evaluating relevant outcomes. Third, the intensity of the process needs to remain consistently high to ensure that those enlisted to participate will remain involved.

The team then implemented the integration of ESTs in four stages. First, clinicians were trained in the adaptation and application of ESTs in real world settings (e.g., core cognitive behavioral skills). Second, several treatment manuals were purchased and made available at a central location so that practitioners could peruse them at their leisure and select the ones most relevant for their work. Copies were then made to facilitate their use. Third, clinicians were asked to choose just one intervention that would be utilized by all of the clinicians during the coming school year. This would enable them to have concurrent and continuing discussions about the adaptations they felt were necessary. Finally, the practitioners were to implement the interventions using their regular meetings as a forum for ongoing supervision, troubleshooting, or support. Throughout the stages, clinicians were encouraged to adapt the interventions in a way that fit their personal style as therapists.

Personal Objections

Some professionals hold misconceptions about the rigidity or linearity of EBP and thus reject it outright rather than investigate it further. They are simply unwilling to make the "paradigmatic break" with authority-based or idiosyncratic practice (Howard, McMillen, & Pollio, 2003). Many psychologists endorse the "equivalence of therapies" idea that anything is better than nothing and there is no real reason to prefer one method over another (Kratochwill & Shernoff, 2004). In other words, the Dodo bird decree that "all have won and all must have prizes" is alive and well (Luborsky, Singer, & Luborsky, 1975; Smith, Glass, & Miller, 1980; Winter, 2006). Despite their membership in scientifically based professions, sometimes even educated practitioners take radical departures from the laws of logic and reason (Rosen, 2003). Lilienfeld (2002), for example, states that scientific practice requires that "people must be able to cast aside their intuitions and convictions regarding the relations among variables when the data compel them to do so" (p. 186).

Evidence-Based Practice in School Mental Health

Without a certain degree of comfort with sustained uncertainty, clinicians cannot approach empirical knowledge with the required spirit of dispassionate inquiry (Johnston & Fineout-Overholt, 2005).

Drake, Hovmand, Jonson-Reid, and Zayas (2007) identify five essential skills for evidence-based practitioners. First, they "acquire the habit of practicing EBP reflexively" (p. 437). This ability needs to be taught in graduate schools and spread across multiple courses, both practice and research classes. Second, they must learn how to phrase answerable questions. I have attempted to demonstrate this in Chapter 3. Third, they must learn how to search the research literature. This was the subject of Chapter 4. Fourth, they must learn how to evaluate the research found in their search. This was the primary focus of Chapter 5. Fifth, they must learn how to apply the evidence while taking into account client characteristics and professional judgment. This was the main emphasis in Chapter 6. To their list, I would add a sixth skill. They must learn how to evaluate outcomes using both group-level and individual-level research designs. This is what I hoped to teach in Chapters 7 and 8.

There are those scholars who base their objections firmly within a constructivist view of social reality (Gergen, 1985; Tyson, 1992; Witkin, 1991). Most of these seem to place clinical intuition on epistemological par with empirical science (Sundarararjan, 2002; Tyson, 1994). Since philosophical systems are built on a priori assumptions, they can possess high internal consistency and be difficult to criticize from the outside. Nonetheless, the scientific relativism that they engender has important and perilous implications for clinical practice, education, and society at large (Kavale & Forness, 2000; McNeill, 2006; Raines, 2008).

Six Degrees of Separation

In 1967, Stanley Milgram created an experiment regarding the small world phenomenon. He gave the name, address, and some personal data of a resident in Cambridge, Massachusetts, to 150 study participants living in Nebraska. The research participants were told only to pass information along to someone they knew until it got to the target recipient. Milgram found that the average number of contacts it took to reach the intended person was only five persons, providing the basis for the notion of six degrees of separation (Milgram, 1967).

Many authors have discussed the research-practice gap (Cohen, 2001; Herie & Martin, 2002; Walker, 2003), but Milgram's study suggests that the gap may not be as wide as typically assumed. Researchers can locate practitioners who can provide real world relevancy and complex participants. Practitioners can find researchers who can help them locate empirically supported interventions and provide objective outcome evaluation of their efforts (Raines, 2004a). EBP can work if we work together.

Summary

This chapter examined the complex systemic issues of implementing EBP in the schools. It started with a review of the organizational change process. This review provided insights into the cornerstones of change, the different types of implementation, and the different stages of implementation. I also provided inserts to help readers assess organizational readiness and conduct a force field analysis. The largest part of the chapter addressed the most common impediments to implementation. The first impediment was a lack of time and I suggested three strategies to combat the problem, including release time, use of interns, and focusing on prevention first. The second barrier was a lack of relevant information and I advised two broad approaches—increasing the relevancy of research for real world settings and improving practitioners' access to research through their alma maters or professional associations. The third obstacle was the lack of technology skills and I recommended combining the scientist-practitioner model with the researcher-practitioner partnership model. The final roadblock was institutional issues and I advocated for four solutions, including aligning the change to the school's vision, a qualitative focus on process issues encountered during dissemination, more attention to contextual influences in outcome evaluation, and more recognition of school staff that employ an evidence-based process in their practice. I ended with a reflection on the small world phenomenon—that the gap between researchers and practitioners is surmountable if we learn to work together.

Suggested Reading

1. Hernandez, M., & Hodges, S. (2003). Building upon the theory of change for systems of care. *Journal of Emotional & Behavioral Disorders, 11* (1), 19–26.

2. Mowbray, C. T., Holter, M. C., Teague, G. B., & Bybee, D. (2003). Fidelity criteria: Development, measurement, and validation. *American Journal of Evaluation, 24* (3), 315–340.

3. Schaeffer, C. M., Bruns, E., Weist, M., Stephan, S. H., Goldstein, J., & Simpson, Y. (2005). Overcoming challenges to using evidence-based interventions in schools. *Journal of Youth and Adolescence, 34* (1), 15–22.

Internet Resources

National Implementation Research Network
http://nirn.fmhi.usf.edu/

National Institute of Mental Health's Blueprint for Change
http://www.eric.ed.gov/ERICDocs/data/ericdocs2sql/
content_storage_01/0000019b/80/19/e0/57.

Implementation Science (online medical journal)
http://www.implementationscience.com/

Glossary

Accommodations. Specific supports that enable special education students to maintain the same standards as their general education peers (see Modifications).

Answerable questions. Inquiries that can be informed by scientifically based research. They do not include ethical/moral questions or questions about individual clients.

Assessment questions. Questions that ask about the best methods to assess, screen, or diagnose a client's problem, especially with a focus on reliable and valid measurement.

Attrition rate. The percentage of initial research participants who dropped out, moved, or otherwise became unavailable for follow-up.

Authority-based practice. A propensity for following the advice of experts who speak confidently of their knowledge, based on years of experience, advanced degrees, multiple publications, or some combination.

Baseline equivalence. The establishment of similarity between the control group and the treatment group in randomized controlled studies or between the comparison groups in quasi-experimental designs.

Boolean logic. Rational logarithms that employ the operators AND, OR, and NOT to specify the parameters for a computerized search.

Capacity. An element of informed consent: the ability to comprehend the information provided and appreciate all of the consequences of one's decision.

Clinical significance. The practical or applied value or importance of the effect of the intervention—that is, whether the intervention makes any real (e.g., genuine, palpable, practical, noticeable) difference in everyday life (Kazdin, 1999, p. 332).

Cookbook practice. A tendency to rigidly follow the treatment manuals of empirically supported treatments without consideration of the unique needs and characteristics of one's clients.

Critical realism. The belief in an objective reality that is only partially perceived through empirical knowledge. Knowledge only approximates reality at best; it never corresponds to reality and thus must be subjected to critical rationality.

Dependent variable. The outcome or effect caused by the independent variable (qv).

Description questions. Inquiries that ask about the cluster of symptoms that clients with a specific problem are likely to exhibit. They can focus on taxonomy or clinical characteristics.

Descriptive statistics. Numerical expressions that describe the sample in terms of its central tendency or variability. Examples include the mean and standard deviation (see Inferential statistics).

Effectiveness. The potency of a particular intervention when assessed under routine conditions, especially in a community-based agency, such as schools (see Efficacy).

Efficacy. The potency of a particular intervention when assessed under highly controlled conditions, especially under laboratory controls (see Effectiveness).

Empirically supported treatments (ESTs). Discrete interventions that have been subjected to more than one randomized controlled trial, preferably by different evaluators with different samples, and found to be helpful in treating a specific condition.

Evidence-based practice (EBP). A *process* of lifelong learning that involves continually posing specific questions of direct *practical* importance to clients, searching objectively and efficiently for the current best evidence relative to each question, and taking appropriate action guided by evidence (Gibbs, 2003, p. 6, italics added).

External validity. The degree to which the results pertaining to a sample can be generalized to the larger population from which it was drawn.

File drawer problem. The tendency for studies with statistically insignificant results to remain unpublished (see Grey literature). The situation is an obstacle to determining the true effects of intervention or prevention studies.

Functional impairment. Difficulties that substantially interfere with or limit role functioning in one or more major life activities, including basic daily living skills (e.g., eating, bathing, dressing); instrumental living skills (e.g., maintaining a household, managing money, getting around the community, taking prescribed medication); and functioning in social, family, and vocational/educational contexts (Section 1912 (c) of the Public Health Services Act, as amended by Public Law 102-321; p. 10).

Grey literature. Unpublished studies that typically do not have statistically significant results.

Hierarchy of evidence. The ladder of evidentiary support for a specific intervention or prevention technique. The highest level is a meta-analysis, followed by randomized controlled trials, then quasi-experimental designs, etc (See Figure 4.1).

Independent variable. The presumed cause or intervention intended to effect change in the dependent variable (qv).

Inferential statistics. Numerical expressions that allow the research to draw inferences from the results from the study sample to the larger population from which it was drawn. Examples include Pearson's r and the t-test.

Information. An element of informed consent: adequate knowledge of the proposed interventions, potential risks and benefits, likelihood of success, reasonable alternatives, risks and benefits of the alternatives, and limitations on confidentiality.

Informed consent. The active agreement to participate based on capacity, information, and voluntariness.

Internal validity. The degree to which change in the dependent variable is caused only by the presence of the independent variable (see External validity).

Intervention contamination. One of the threats to internal validity in which some external event contributes an unknown amount to the observed change.

Intervention questions. Inquiries about the optimal treatment for a specific problem or disorder.

Journalistic review. A review of the literature that sets out to prove that a hypothesis is true by searching only for confirmatory evidence (see Systematic review).

Meta-analysis. A subtype of systematic review that seeks to quantify the complete set of research on a topic and produce a statistical summary of the findings.

Modifications. Major changes to the substance of a standard so that it expects less of the student than students in general education (see Accommodations).

Nonparametric tests. Statistical procedures used for hypothesis testing when the research design cannot meet all the criteria required for Parametric tests (qv).

Nonprobability sampling. The selection of research participants in such a way that they have an unknown chance of being included with the sample. Examples include convenience samples, quota samples, purposive samples, and snowball samples (see Probability sampling).

Outcome evaluation. The process of evaluating the progress of clients by, minimally, using a pretest and posttest design.

Paper implementation. The development of policy or procedural manuals that describe in detail how something should be done (see Performance implementation or Process implementation).

Parametric tests. Statistical procedures that are employed for hypothesis testing when the research design meets three criteria: At least one variable (usually the dependent) must be at the interval or ratio level of measurement; the dependent variable must be normally distributed in the population; and cases must be randomly selected from the population and randomly assigned to treatment versus control groups (see Nonparametric tests).

Passive consent. The assumption that parents (or students) automatically consent unless they specifically object (see Informed consent).

Paternalism. The assumption that an adult knows what is in a child's "best interests" without needing to consult the child (see Self-determination).

Peer Reviewed. An attribute of manuscripts that are critically evaluated by at least colleagues who are blind to the author's identity or position. These peers then recommend to the editor that the manuscript be published without revision, published with minor revisions, rejected for major revisions, or rejected entirely.

Performance implementation. The actual use of new interventions in daily practice among frontline staff that benefits the consumer (see Paper implementation or Process implementation).

Prevention questions. Inquires about the optimal method to avert a negative condition or problem.

Probability (*p* value). The mathematical likelihood that the result is due to chance, such as a sampling error. Traditionally researchers use $p < .05$ as a minimal standard (see Statistical significance).

Probability sampling. The selection of research participants in such a way that each one has a known chance of being included within the sample.

Examples include random samples, stratified random samples, and cluster random samples (see Nonprobability sampling).

Process implementation. The effecting of new procedures for staff training, supervision, or information collection processes (see Paper implementation or Performance implementation).

Quasi-experimental designs (QEDs). Experimental designs in which participants are assigned to two or more different treatment groups in order to compare their progress. Typically the two groups are designed to have baseline equivalence prior to the intervention.

Randomized controlled trials (RCTs). Experimental designs in which participants are randomly selected and assigned to either a no-treatment control group or a treatment group.

Relevant evidence. Means evidence having any tendency to make the existence of any fact that is of consequence to the determination of the action more probable or less probable than it would be without the evidence (Federal Rule of Evidence 401).

Reliability. The ability of an instrument to obtain consistent measurements of the same variable. It is a prerequisite for validity.

Reliable evidence. Based on "sound science" and meets one of four criteria: (1)whether the theory or technique can be (or has been) tested; (2) whether the theory or technique has been subject to peer review and publication; (3) whether or not the theory or technique has a known error rate and standards controlling its operation; or (4) whether the underlying science has attracted widespread acceptance by the scientific community (Federal Rule of Evidence 702).

Risk questions. Inquiries about the prognosis of clients with a specific problem or diagnosis.

Scientifically based research

a) Means research that involves the application of rigorous, systematic, and objective procedures to obtain reliable and valid knowledge relevant to education activities and programs; and
b) Includes research that
1. Employs systematic, empirical methods that draw on observation or experiment;
2. Involves rigorous data analyses that are adequate to test the stated hypotheses and justify the general conclusions drawn;

3. Relies on measurements or observational methods that provide reliable and valid data across evaluators and observers, across multiple measurements and observations, and across studies by the same or different investigators;
4. Is evaluated using experimental or quasi-experimental designs in which individuals, entities, programs, or activities are assigned to different conditions and with appropriate controls to evaluate the effects of the condition of interest, with a preference for random assignment experiments, or other designs to the extent that those designs contain within-condition or across-condition controls;
5. Ensures that experimental studies are presented in sufficient detail and clarity to allow for replication or, at a minimum, offer the opportunity to build systematically on their findings; and
6. Has been accepted by a peer-reviewed journal or approved by a panel of independent experts through a comparably rigorous, objective, and scientific review.

U.S. Department of Education, 2006, §300.35

Self-determination. The ability, knowledge, and right to engage in goal-directed, self-regulated, autonomous behavior (Karvonen et al., 2004, p. 23).

Sensitivity. The ability of an instrument to accurately include all of the potential persons who have a specific problem (see Specificity).

Single-subject designs. An experimental design with a sample of one, such as one client, one group, or one family. Typically measurements are taken before, during, and after the intervention to determine its effect (see Within-subject designs).

Social validity. The degree to which the method of intervention or evaluation is perceived as appropriate, effective, efficient, and fair by a wide range of constituents.

Specificity. The ability of an instrument to accurately exclude all of the potential persons who do not have a specific problem (see Sensitivity).

Statistical significance. A research result that is considered highly unlikely to have occurred by chance, such as sampling error (see Clinical significance or Probability).

Systematic review. A review of the literature that sets out to answer a research question by examining the highest quality research and deliberately seeking for evidence that contradicts the researcher's preferred point of view (see Journalistic review).

Teacher-intervention confound. One of the threats to internal validity in which researchers are unable to decipher how much of the change in the dependent variable was due to the personal qualities of one doing the intervention as opposed to the intervention itself.

Treatment fidelity. The consistency with which the intervention is provided across time or across providers.

Treatment manual. A standardized guide for therapists that operationalizes the procedures used to treat a specific problem and the recommended order for employing them.

Validity. The ability of an instrument to obtain accurate measurements of the variable. It is dependent upon the establishment of reliability.

Voluntariness. An element of informed consent: freedom from constraint, compulsion, or coercion.

Within-subject designs. The most common type of single-subject design, wherein the evaluation occurs at several points during the treatment phases, including baseline, intervention, and follow-up.

Appendix A: Internet Resources for Evidence-Based Practice

Advocacy Groups

Advocates for Children in Therapy
http://www.childrenintherapy.org

Alliance for Human Research Protection
http://www.ahrp.org

Coalition Against Institutionalized Child Abuse
http://caica.org

Appraisal Tools

Appraisal of Guidelines Research and Evaluation (AGREE)
http://www.agreecollaboration.org/

Centre for Evidence Based Medicine's Levels of Evidence
http://www.cebm.net/index.aspx?o=1025

CONSORT Guidelines
http://www.consort-statement.org/

National Health Service's Public Health Resource Unit's Appraisal Tools
http://www.phru.nhs.uk/Pages/PHD/resources.htm

QUORUM Statement Checklist for Systematic Reviews
http://www.consort-statement.org/QUOROM.pdf

STARD Initiative
http://www.stard-statement.org/website%20stard/

STROBE Initiative
http://www.strobe-statement.org/

SUNY Medical Library Tutorials on Evaluating Studies
http://servers.medlib.hscbklyn.edu/ebmdos/5toc.htm

Assessment Tools

Achenbach System of Empirically Based Assessment
http://www.aseba.org/

Behavior Assessment System for Children
http://ags.pearsonassessments.com/Group.asp?nGroupInfoID=a30000

Children's Global Assessment Scale
http://www.southalabama.edu/nursing/psynp/cgas.pdf

Columbia University TeenScreen Program
http://www.teenscreen.org/

Mood and Feeling Questionnaire
http://devepi.mc.duke.edu/MFQ.html

Scales of Independent Behavior—Revised
http://www.riverpub.com/products/sibr/index.html

School Success Profile
http://www.schoolsuccessprofile.org/

Strengths and Difficulties Questionnaire
http://www.sdqinfo.com/
Vineland Adaptive Behavior Scales-2
http://ags.pearsonassessments.com/Group.asp?nGroupInfoID=aVineland

Behavioral Rubrics

DiscoverySchool.com—Kathy Schrock's Guide to Rubrics
http://school.discovery.com/schrockguide/assess.html#rubrics

Intervention Central (Behavior Report Cards)
http://www.interventioncentral.com/

Princeton Online's Positive Behavior Rubric
http://www.princetonol.com/groups/iad/lessons/middle/Behavior.htm

Professor John Howe's Behavior Rubric
http://www.professorhowe.com/rubricshowc.cfm?code=H6W77&sp=
yes&xsite=johnhowe

RubiStar 4 Teachers
http://rubistar.4teachers.org/index.php

Teachnology—Online Teacher Resource
http://www.bestteachersites.com/web_tools/rubrics/

Critical Thinking

Carl Sagan's Baloney Detection Kit
http://users.tpg.com.au/users/tps-seti/baloney.html

Critical Thinking Community
http://www.criticalthinking.org

Quack Watch
http://www.quackwatch.com/

Database Resources

American Institutes for Research
http://www.air.org/

Campbell Collaboration (Social, Behavioral, and Educational Issues)
http://www.campbellcollaboration.org/

Cochrane Collaboration (Health Care)
http://www.cochrane.org/index.htm

Education Resource Information Center
http://www.eric.ed.gov/

National Academies Press—Over 3700 Books Online (Free)
http://books.nap.edu/

National Center for Biotechnology Information (aka PubMed)
http://www.ncbi.nlm.nih.gov/sites/entrez?db=pubmed

National Library of Medicine's Medical Subject Headings (MeSH)
http://www.nlm.nih.gov/mesh/MBrowser.html

What Works Clearinghouse
http://ies.ed.gov/ncee/wwc/

Empirically Supported Interventions for Children and Adolescents

American Academy of Child and Adolescent Psychiatry Practice Parameters
http://www.aacap.org/page.ww?section=Practice+Parameters&name=
Practice+Parameters

American Psychological Association's Guide to Empirically Supported
Interventions
http://www.apa.org/divisions/div12/rev_est/

Centers for Disease Control's School Health Education Resources
http://apps.nccd.cdc.gov/sher/

Center for the Study and Prevention of Violence's Blueprints for Violence
Prevention
http://www.colorado.edu/cspv/blueprints/

Empirically Supported Interventions in School Mental Health—Center for
School Mental Health
http://csmh.umaryland.edu/resources.html/resource_packets/download_
files/empirically_supported_2002.pdf

National Guideline Clearinghouse—Agency for Healthcare Research and
Quality
http://www.guideline.gov/index.aspx

National Institute on Drug Abuse's Principles of Drug Addiction Treatment
http://www.drugabuse.gov/PODAT/PODATIndex.html

National Institutes of Health Consensus Statement on ADHD
http://consensus.nih.gov/1998/1998AttentionDeficitHyperactivityDisorder1
10html.htm

Office of Juvenile Justice and Delinquency Prevention's Model
Programs
http://www.dsgonline.com/mpg2.5/mpg_index.htm

SAMHSA's National Registry of Evidence-Based Programs and Practices
http://www.nrepp.samhsa.gov/index.htm

U.S. Department of Education's Safe, Disciplined, and Drug-Free
Exemplary Programs
http://www.ed.gov/admins/lead/safety/exemplary01/panel_pg2.html

U.S. Department of Health and Human Services—Matrix of Children's
Evidence-Based Interventions
http://www.systemsofcare.samhsa.gov/headermenus/docsHM/MatrixFinal1.pdf

Ethical and Legal Guidelines

Advocates for Youth—Legal Issues and School-Based and School-Linked
Health Centers
http://www.advocatesforyouth.org/PUBLICATIONS/iag/sbhcslhc.htm

American Counseling Association
http://www.counseling.org

American Psychological Association—Division of School Psychology
http://www.indiana.edu/~div16/index.html

ASCA's Ethical Standards for School Counselors
http://www.schoolcounselor.org/files/ethical%20standards.pdf

Code of Federal Regulations
http://www.gpoaccess.gov/cfr/index.html

FindLaw Education Laws
http://www.findlaw.com/01topics/37education/index.html

Guttmacher Institute's Adolescent Page
http://www.guttmacher.org/sections/adolescents.php

Human Subject Regulations Decision Charts
http://www.hhs.gov/ohrp/humansubjects/guidance/decisioncharts.htm

Legal Information Institute of Cornell University
http://www.law.cornell.edu/

NASP Professional Conduct Manual and Principles for Professional Ethics
http://www.nasponline.org/standards/ProfessionalCond.pdf

NASW Code of Ethics
http://www.socialworkers.org/pubs/code/code.asp

School Social Work Association of America
http://www.sswaa.org

Goal Attainment Scaling

Flinders University (Austrailia) Self-Esteem Goal Attainment Scaling Tool
http://www.socsci.flinders.edu.au/fippm/consult/gasuse.html

Kiresuk, Smith, and Cardillo's Book on Goal Attainment Scaling
http://www.questia.com/PM.qst?a=o&d=28533958&oplinknum=3

Marson and Dran's Goal Attainment Scaling
http://www.marson-and-associates.com/GAS/GAS_index.html

Library Critiques of Web-Based Information

Association of College and Research Libraries
http://www.ala.org/ala/acrl/acrlpubs/crlnews/backissues1998/julyaugust6/
teachingundergrads.htm

Library of Congress
http://www.loc.gov/rr/business/beonline/selectbib.html

Hope Tillman—Librarian, Babson College
http://www.hopetillman.com/findqual.html

University of California–Los Angeles (UCLA's Librarian, Esther
Grassian)
http://www.library.ucla.edu/libraries/college/help/critical/index.htm

Professional Associations

American Counseling Association
http://www.counseling.org

American Psychological Association—Division of School Psychology
http://www.indiana.edu/~div16/index.html

American School Counselor Association
http://www.schoolcounselor.org/index.asp

National Association of School Psychologists
http://www.nasponline.org

National Association of Social Workers
http://www.socialworkers.org

School Social Work Association of America
http://www.sswaa.org

Progress Monitoring

AIMSweb
http://aimsweb.com/

National Center on Student Progress Monitoring
http://www.studentprogress.org/

National Research Center on Learning Disabilities
http://www.nrcld.org

Research Institute on Progress Monitoring
http://www.progressmonitoring.org/

Statistical Decisions

Advanced Technology Services—UCLA
http://www.ats.ucla.edu/stat/mult_pkg/whatstat/default.htm

Choosing the Correct Statistical Test—Crystal Hoyt—University of
Richmond
http://www.richmond.edu/~choyt/supportingdocs_spring05/handout_
stattests.doc

Exploratory Data Analysis
http://www.itl.nist.gov/div898/handbook/eda/eda.htm

EZAnalyze—Data Analysis for Educators
http://www.ezanalyze.com/

HyperStat Online Textbook
http://davidmlane.com/hyperstat/index.html

Intuitive Biostatistics—Graphpad.com
http://www.graphpad.com/www/Book/Choose.htm

Matching Statistics with the Research Design—University of Texas Medical
Branch
http://sahs.utmb.edu/pellinore/intro_to_research/wad/sel_test.htm

MedCalc Statistics Menu
http://www.medcalc.be/manual/mpage06.php

Mississippi State University Virtual Statistics Laboratory
http://www.abe.msstate.edu/Tools/vsl/index.php

Professor Gerstman's StatPrimer
http://www.sjsu.edu/faculty/gerstman/StatPrimer/

Rice Virtual Lab in Statistics
http://onlinestatbook.com/rvls.html

Statistical Analysis: Statistics, Mathematics, and Measurement—A Statistical Flow Chart.
http://www.napce.org/articles/Research%20Design%20Yount/05_analysisflow_4th.pdf

Statistics Demonstrations with Excel
http://sunsite.univie.ac.at/Spreadsite/statexamp/

Statistical Interpretation

Level of Significance for Pearson's r Correlation—Illinois State University
http://lilt.ilstu.edu/gmklass/pos138/assignments/level__r.html

Testing the Significance of Pearson's r—University of New England (Australia)
http://www.une.edu.au/WebStat/unit_materials/c6_common_statistical_tests/test_signif_pearson.html

Systemic Implementation

National Implementation Research Network
http://nirn.fmhi.usf.edu/

National Institute of Mental Health's Blueprint for Change
http://www.eric.ed.gov/ERICDocs/data/ericdocs2sql/content_storage_01/0000019b/80/19/e0/57.pdf

Implementation Science (Online Medical Journal)
http://www.implementationscience.com/

Surgeon General's Conference on Children's Mental Health: A National Action Agenda
http://www.hhs.gov/surgeongeneral/topics/cmh/cmhreport.pdf

University Research Centers

Center for Mental Health in Schools—UCLA
http://smhp.psych.ucla.edu/

Center for School Mental Health Analysis and Action—University of Maryland
http://csmh.umaryland.edu/

Center of Excellence in Children's Mental Health
http://cmh.umn.edu/

Children's Mental Health Research Center
http://www.csw.utk.edu/about/cmhsrc.html

National Center for School Counseling Outcome Research
http://www.umass.edu/schoolcounseling/

National Technical Assistance Center for Children's Mental
Health—Georgetown University
http://gucchd.georgetown.edu/programs/ta_center/index.html

Research and Training Center for Children's Mental Health—University of
South Florida
http://rtckids.fmhi.usf.edu/

Appendix B: Annotated Bibliography on Empirically Supported Interventions

Barrett, P. M., & Ollendick, T. H. (2004). *Handbook of interventions that work with children and adolescents: Prevention and treatment.* Hoboken, NJ: John Wiley.

Treatments for anxiety, ADHD, conduct disorder, depression, obsessive-compulsive disorder, oppositional defiant disorder, panic disorder, phobias, PTSD, school refusal, SAD, social phobia, substance abuse.

Carr, A. (Ed.) (2000). *What works for children and adolescents: A critical review of psychological interventions with children, adolescents, and their families.* Hoboken, NJ: John Wiley.

Treatments for anorexia, anxiety, ADHD, bulimia, child abuse, conduct problems, depression, divorce, drug abuse, enuresis, encopresis, grief, oppositional defiant disorder, pain problems.

Christopherson, E. R., & Mortweet, S. L. (2001). *Treatments that work with children: Empirically supported strategies for managing childhood problems.* Washington, DC: American Psychological Association.

Treatments for adherence to medical treatment, anxiety, conduct disorders, encopresis and enuresis, habit disorders, pain management, sleep problems.

Fonagy, P., Target, M., Cottrell, D., Philips, J., & Kurtz, Z. (2002). *What works for whom: A critical review of treatments for children and adolescents.* New York: Guilford.

Treatments for anxiety, ADHD, eating disorders, conduct disturbances, depression, pervasive developmental disorders (autism, Asperger's, Rett's), physical symptoms, psychotic disorders (schizophrenia and bipolar), self-harming disorders (eating, suicide, and substance abuse), specific developmental disorders, Tourette's disorder.

Franklin, C., Harris, M. B., & Allen-Meares, P. (2006). *The school services sourcebook: A guide for school-based professionals.* New York: Oxford University Press.

One hundred and fourteen chapters divided into 16 sections covering virtually every aspect of school-based services.

Gordon, B., & Schroeder, C. (2002). *Assessment and treatment of childhood problems: A clinician's guide* (2nd ed.). New York: Guilford.

Treatments for anxiety, death, divorce, enuresis, encopresis, habits and tics, sexual abuse, sibling rivalry, sleep problems.

Hibbs, E. D., & Jensen, P. S. (2005). *Psychosocial treatments for child and adolescent disorders: Empirically based strategies for clinical practice* (2nd ed.). Washington, DC: American Psychological Association.

Treatments for aggression, anorexia, anxiety, attention deficits, autism, conduct disorder, depression, foster care, obsessive-compulsive disorder, sexual abuse, social phobia.

Kazdin, A. E., & Weisz, J. R. (Eds.) (2003). *Evidence-based psychotherapies for children and adolescents.* New York: Guilford.

Treatments for anxiety, ADHD, anorexia nervosa, autism, conduct disorder, depression, enuresis, obesity, obsessive-compulsive disorder, oppositional defiant disorder, pervasive developmental disorders.

Reitman, D. (Ed.) (2008). *Handbook of psychological assessment, case conceptualization, and treatment, Vol. 2: Children and adolescents.*

Treatments for AD/HD, anxiety, communication disorders, conduct disorder, depression, encopresis, enuresis, habit disorders, juvenile firesetting, learning disorders, motor disorders, neurological impairment, neglect, oppositional defiant disorder, physical abuse, psychosis, PTSD, sexual abuse, sleep disorders, substance abuse.

Shinn, M. A., Walker, H. M., & Stoner, G. (Eds.) (2002). *Interventions for academic and behavior problems. II. Preventive and remedial approaches.* Bethesda, MD: NASP.

Chapters on addictive behaviors, basic skill deficits, behavior problems, bullying prevention, classroom interventions, classwide peer tutoring, mathematics achievement, reading improvement, school safety, screening for behavior problems, self-monitoring, social skills, study skills, writing interventions.

Spirito, A., & Kazak, A. E. (2006). *Effective and emerging treatments in pediatric psychology.* New York: Oxford University Press.

Treatments for cystic fibrosis, encopresis and enuresis, pain management, sleep disturbances, suicidal attempts.

Weisz, J. R. (2004). *Psychotherapy for children and adolescents: Evidence-based treatments and case examples.* Cambridge: Cambridge University Press.

Treatments for anxiety, ADHD, conduct disorder, depression.

Appendix C: Ten Threats to Internal Validity

THREAT	DESCRIPTION	SCHOOL EXAMPLE
Ambiguity of causal influence	Uncertainty about the temporal ordering of the independent and dependent variables	A school counselor works on a pupil's self-esteem problems and notices that the child's reading grade has improved. Did higher self-esteem improve his reading or did improved reading increase his self-esteem?
History	An external event that might influence the dependent or outcome variable and was not subject to experimental control	During an intervention to reduce teens driving under the influence, a teen icon is arrested for the same offense and sentenced to 45 days in jail. The publicity could have affected the outcome, but since it occurred during the experiment, there is no way to control for it.
Instrumentation	A flaw in the measurement process due to problems with the tool, the administration, or the administrator	An initial measurement of mathematical ability occurs after lunch, when most children are sleepy, but the second occurs mid-morning when most children are more alert. The children appear to have improved in their arithmetic.
Intervention contamination	The possibility that the intervention has been diffused to members of the control group or comparison group	Some participants in the treatment group share what they have learned with members of the control group. The control group members do nearly as well as the treatment group.

(continued)

THREAT	DESCRIPTION	SCHOOL EXAMPLE
Maturation	Psychosocial or physical changes that occur in the participants over time as they get older	A child in individual long-term therapy improves gradually over time, but since no single-subject design was used, it is unknown how much of the improvement is due to the treatment.
Mortality/ attrition	The loss of research participants over time due to dropping out, moving, or death	People who complete a program are asked to fill out a satisfaction survey, but they may have had higher motivation to finish than those who quit before the end.
Reactive effects	The tendency for participants to react to the knowledge that their progress is being monitored	A psychologist asks a student to carry a daily log to monitor his behavior in class during treatment. The student works harder on self-control because he knows that he has to show the daily log to an adult authority figure.
Regression to the mean	A tendency for those with extreme scores to moderate their answers the second time they take the measure	A child gets the lowest score in the class on a reading test and then scores in the middle range on the second administration. It looks like he has progressed in his reading ability.
Selection bias	The possibility that participants were selected for comparison groups using different criteria for inclusion	Social workers decide to see the most dysfunctional students first and assign less needy students to a wait-list group, thus creating baseline inequality prior to any intervention.
Testing	The learning that occurs from taking a pretest that effects change in the posttest	Students who take college entrance exams usually do better the second time around whether or not they have received tutoring between the two exams.

References

Abikoff, H., & Gittelman, R. (1985). Classroom Observation Code: A modification of the Stony Brook Code. *Psychopharmacology Bulletin, 21,* 901–909.

Achenbach, T. M. (1986). *The Direct Observation Form of the Child Behavior Checklist* (rev. ed.). Burlington, VT: Department of Psychiatry, University of Vermont.

Achenbach, T. M. (2007). *ASEBA: Achenbach system for empirically based assessment.* Retrieved June 4, 2007, from http://www.aseba.org/products/manuals.html

Achenbach, T. M., McConaughy, S. H., & Howell, C. T. (1987). Child/adolescent behavioral and emotional problems: Implications of cross-informant correlations for situational specificity. *Psychological Bulletin, 101* (2), 213–232.

Achenbach, T. M., & Rescorla, L. A. (2001). *Manual for ASEBA school-age forms and profiles.* Burlington, VT: Research Center for Children, Youth, and Families, University of Vermont.

Achenbach, T. M., & Rescorla, L. A. (2007). *Multicultural understanding of child and adolescent psychopathology: Implications for mental health assessment.* New York: Guilford.

Ackerman, S. J., Benjamin, L. S., Beutler, L. E., Gelso, C. J., Goldfried, M. R., Hill, C., et al. (2001). Empirically supported therapy relationships: Conclusions and recommendations of the Division 29 task force. *Psychotherapy: Theory, Research, Practice, Training, 38* (4), 495–497.

Adams, T. (2000). The status of school discipline and violence. *Annals of the American Academy of Political and Social Science, 567,* 140–156.

Adams, S., & McCarthy, A. M. (2005). Evidence-based practice and school nursing. *Journal of School Nursing, 21* (5), 258–265.

Addis, M. E. (2002). Methods for disseminating research products and increasing evidence-based practice: Promises, obstacles, and future directions. *Clinical Psychology, 9* (4), 367–378.

Addis, M. E., Wade, W. A., & Hatgis, C. (1999). Barriers to dissemination of evidence-based practices: Addressing practitioners' concerns about manual-based psychotherapies. *Clinical Psychology: Science and Practice, 6* (4), 430–441.

Advocates for Children in Therapy (2006). *Candace Elizabeth Newmaker.* Retrieved August 7, 2006, from http://www.childrenintherapy.org/victims/newmaker.html

Advocates for Youth (1998). *Legal issues and school-based and school-linked health centers.* Retrieved July 23, 2007, from http://www.advocatesforyouth.org/PUBLICATIONS/iag/sbhcslhc.htm

Alberts, K. S., & Ankenmann, B. (2001). Simulating Pearson's and Spearman's correlations in Q-sorts using Excel. *Social Science Computer Review, 19* (2), 221–226.

Alexander, J., & Tate, M. A. (2005). *What web search engines won't find.* Retrieved May 19, 2007, from http://www3.widener.edu/Academics/Libraries/Wolfgram_Memorial_Library/Need_Help_/How_to_Do_Research_/What_Web_Search_Engines_Won_t_Find_/498/

Algozzine, B., Browder, D., Karvonen, M., Test, D. W., & Wood, W. M. (2001). Effects of interventions to promote self-determination for individuals with disabilities. *Review of Educational Research, 71* (3), 219–277.

Alliance for Human Research Protection (2007). *Psychiatrist "diagnosed" child aged 2 as bipolar, Rx fatal drug combination.* Retrieved May 5, 2007, from http://www.ahrp.org

Alwell, M., & Cobb, B. (2006). A map of the intervention literature in secondary special education. *Career Development for Exceptional Individuals, 29* (1), 3–27.

American Academy of Pediatrics Committee on School Health (2004). School-based mental health services. *Pediatrics, 113,* 1839–1845. Retrieved July 14, 2007, from http://pediatrics.aappublications.org/cgi/reprint/113/6/1839

American Counseling Association (2005). *Code of ethics.* Alexandria, VA: American Counseling Association.

American Pain Society Quality of Care Committee (1995). Quality improvement for the treatment of acute pain and cancer pain. *JAMA 274,* 1874–1880.

American Psychiatric Association (2005). *Diagnostic and statistical manual of mental disorders* (4th ed., text revision). Washington, DC: American Psychiatric Association.

American School Counselor Association (2001). *National model for comprehensive school counseling programs.* Herndon, VA: American School Counselor Association.

American School Counselor Association (2004). *Ethical standards for school counselors.* Herndon, VA: American School Counselor Association.

Amos, P. A. (2004). New considerations in the prevention of aversives, restraint, and seclusion: Incorporating the role of relationships into an ecological perspective. *Research and Practice for Persons with Severe Disabilities, 29* (4), 263–272.

Anderson, E. E., & DuBois, J. M. (2007). The need for evidence-based research ethics: A review of the substance abuse literature. *Drug and Alcohol Dependence, 86* (2–3), 95–105.

Anderson, L. M., Scrimshaw, S. C., Fullilove, M. T., Fielding, J. E., & Normand, J. (2003). Culturally competent healthcare systems: A systematic review. *American Journal of Preventive Medicine, 24* (Suppl. 3), 68–79.

Apel, K. (2001). Developing evidence-based practices and research collaborations in school settings. *Language, Speech, and Hearing Services in Schools, 32* (3), 149–152.

Arnold, L. E., Elliott, M., Sachs, L., Bird, H., Kraemer, H. C., Wells, K. C., et al. (2003). Effects of ethnicity on treatment attendance, stimulant response/dose, and 14-month outcome in ADHD. *Journal of Consulting and Clinical Psychology, 71* (4), 713–727.

Arnold, M. E., & Hughes, J. N. (1999). First do no harm: Adverse effects of grouping deviant youth for skills training. *Journal of School Psychology, 37* (1), 99–115.

Association for Retarded Children v. Rockefeller, 357 F. Supp. 752 (E.D.N.Y. 1973).

Assor, A., Kaplan, H., & Roth, G. (2002). Choice is good, but relevance is excellent: Autonomy-enhancing and suppressing teacher behaviors predicting students' engagement in schoolwork. *British Journal of Educational Psychology, 72* (2), 261–278.

August, G. A., Braswell, L., & Thuras, P. (1998). Diagnostic stability of ADHD in a community sample of school-age children screened for disruptive disorder. *Journal of Abnormal Child Psychology, 26* (5), 345–356.

Bailey, D. M., Bornstein, J., & Ryan, S. (2007). A case report of evidence-based practice: From academia to clinic. *American Journal of Occupational Therapy, 61* (1), 85–91.

Banaschewski, T., Coghill, D., Santosh, P., Zuddas, A., Asherson, P., Buitelaar, J., et al. (2006). Long-acting medications for the hyperkinetic disorders: A systematic review and European treatment guideline. *European Child and Adolescent Psychiatry, 15* (8), 476–495.

Barkham, M., & Mellor-Clark, J. (2003). Bridging evidence-based practice and practice-based evidence: Developing rigorous and relevant knowledge for the psychological therapies. *Clinical Psychology and Psychotherapy, 10* (6), 319–327.

Barlow, D. H., Morrow-Bradley, C., Elliot, R., & Phillips, B. N. (1993). Relationship between the scientist and the practitioner. In J. A. Mindell (Ed.),

Issues in clinical psychology (pp. 11–35). Madison, WI: Brown & Benchmark.

Barlow, J., & Stewart-Brown, S. (2005). Behavior problems and group-based parent education programs. *Journal of Developmental and Behavioral Pediatrics, 21* (5), 356–370.

Barnett, J. E. (2006). Evaluating "baby-think-it-over" infant simulators: A comparison group study. *Adolescence, 41* (161), 103–110.

Barrett, P. M. (2000). Treatment of childhood anxiety: Developmental aspects. *Clinical Psychology Review, 20* (4), 479–494.

Barshefsky, C., & Liebenberg, R. (1974). Voluntarily confined mental retardates: The right to treatment vs. the right to protection from harm. *Catholic University Law Review, 23* (4), 787–805.

Baskin, E. F. (2004). Change management concepts and models: Sponsorship, early adopters, and the development of urban teachers. In R. B. Cooter, Jr. (Ed.), *Perspectives on rescuing urban literacy education: Spies, saboteurs, and saints* (pp. 25–40). Mahwah, NJ: Lawrence Erlbaum.

Bastiaens, L. (1995). Compliance with pharmacotherapy in adolescents: Effects of patients' and parents' knowledge and attitudes toward treatment. *Journal of Child and Adolescent Psychopharmacology, 5* (1), 39–48.

Bateman, B. D., & Herr, C. M. (2003). *Writing measurable IEP goals and objectives.* Verona, WI: Attainment Company.

Baxter, S. (2007, April 22). Cold childhood of Cho, the killer who rejected hugs. *The Sunday Times* [UK]. Electronic version, accession number: 7EH1358906945. Retrieved May 19, 2007, from http://www.timesonline.co.uk/tol/news/

Baytop, C. M. (2006). Evaluating the effectiveness of programs to improve educational attainment of unwed African American teen mothers: A meta-analysis. *Journal of Negro Education, 75* (3), 458–477.

Beach, M. C., Price, E. G., Gary, T. L., Robinson, K. A., Gozu, A., Palacio, A., et al. (2005). Cultural competence: A systematic review of health care provider educational interventions. *Medical Care, 43* (4), 356–373.

Behan, J., & Carr, A. (2000). Oppositional defiant disorder. In A. Carr (Ed.), *What works with children and adolescents? A critical review of psychological interventions with children, adolescents and their families* (pp. 102–130). London: Brunner-Routledge.

Beier, M. E., & Ackerman, P. L. (2005). Working memory and intelligence: Different constructs. *Psychological Bulletin, 131* (1), 72–75.

Bender, W. N., Ulmer, L., Baskette, M. R., & Shores, C. (2007). Will RTI work? In W. N. Bender & C. Shores (Eds.), *Response to intervention: A practical guide for every teacher.* Thousand Oaks, CA: Corwin/Sage.

Benitez, D. T., Lattimore, J., & Wehmeyer, M. L. (2005). Promoting the involvement of students with emotional and behavioral disorders in career and vocational planning and decision-making: The self-determined career development model. *Behavioral Disorders, 30* (4), 431–447.

Berliner, D. C. (2002). Educational research: The hardest science of all. *Educational Researcher, 31* (8), 18–20.

Berninger, V. W., Dunn, A., Lin, S.-J. C., & Shimada, S. (2004). School evolution: Scientist-practitioner educators creating optimal learning environments for all students. *Journal of Learning Disabilities, 37* (6), 500–508.

Bernstein, G. A., Layne, A. E., Egan, E. A., & Tennison, D. M. (2005). School-based interventions for anxious children. *Journal of the American Academy of Child and Adolescent Psychiatry, 44* (11), 1118–1127.

Beutler, L. E. (2000). Empirically-based decision making in clinical practice. *Prevention and Treatment, 3* (Article 27). Retrieved May 19, 2002, from http://journals.apa.org/prevention/volume3/pre0030027a.html

Bhaskar, R. (1989). *Reclaiming reality: A critical introduction of contemporary philosophy.* London: Verso.

Bilenberg, N., Petersen, D. J., Hoerder, K., & Gillberg, C. (2005). The prevalence of child-psychiatric disorders among 8-9-year-old children in Danish mainstream schools. *Acta Psychiatrica Scandinavica, 111* (1), 59–67.

Bird, H. R., Andrews, H., Schwab-Stone, M., Goodman, S., Dulcan, M., Richters, J., et al. (1996). Global measures of impairment for epidemiological and clinical use with children and adolescents. *International Journal of Methods in Psychiatric Research, 6* (4), 295–307.

Birkeland, S., Murphy-Graham, E., & Weiss, C. (2005). Good reasons for ignoring good evaluation: The case of the drug abuse resistance education (D.A.R.E.) program. *Evaluation and Program Planning, 28* (3), 247–256.

Bloom, M., Fischer, J., & Orme, J. G. (2006). *Evaluating practice: Guidelines for the accountable professional* (5th ed.). Boston: Pearson.

Bloom, L. A., Hursh, D., Wienke, W. D., & Wold, R. K. (1992). The effects of computer assisted data collection on students' behaviors. *Behavioral Assessment, 14* (2), 173–190.

Boudah, D. J., Logan, K. R., & Greenwood, C. R. (2001). The research to practice projects: Lessons learned about changing teacher practice. *Teacher Education and Special Education, 24* (4), 290–303.

Bowen, G. L., Richman, J. M., & Bowen, N. K. (1997). The School Success Profile: A results management approach to assessment and intervention planning. In A. R. Roberts & G. J. Greene (Eds.), *Social workers' desk reference* (pp. 787–793). New York: Oxford University Press.

Bowen, G. L., Ware, W. B., Rose, R. A., & Powers, J. D. (2007). Assessing the functioning of schools as learning organizations. *Children and Schools, 29* (4), 199–208.

Bower, P. (2003). Efficacy in evidence-based practice. *Clinical Psychology and Psychotherapy, 10* (6), 328–336.

Bradshaw, T., Lovell, K., & Harris, N. (2005). Healthy living interventions and schizophrenia: A systematic review. *Journal of Advanced Nursing, 49* (6), 634–654.

Brager, G., & Holloway, S. (1992). Assessing prospects for organizational change: The uses of force field analysis. *Administration in Social Work, 16* (3/4), 15–28.

Breggin, P. R. (2003). Suicidality, violence, and mania caused by selective serotonin reuptake inhibitors (SSRIs): A review and analysis. *International Journal of Risk and Safety in Medicine, 16* (1), 31–49.

Brekke, J. S., Ell, K., & Palinkas, L. A. (2007). Translational science at the National Institute of Mental Health: Can social work takes its rightful place? *Research on Social Work Practice, 17* (1), 123–133.

Bricklin, D. (2003). Was VisiCalc the "first" spreadsheet? Retrieved May 19, 2006, from http://www.bricklin.com/firstspreadsheetquestion.htm

Brookes, S. T., Whitley, E., Peters, T. J., Mulheran, P. A., Egger, M., & Davey-Smith, G. (2001). Subgroup analyses in randomised controlled trials: Quantifying the risks of false-positives and false negatives. *Health Technology Assessment, 5* (33), 1–56.

Brown, R. T., Amler, R. W., Freeman, W. S., Perrin, J. M., Stein, M. T., Feldman, H. M., et al. (2005). Treatment of attention-deficit/hyperactivity disorder: Overview of the evidence. *Pediatrics, 115* (6), e749–e757.

Brown, S., & Eisenberg, L. (Eds.) (1995). *The best intentions: Unintended pregnancy and the well-being of children and families.* Washington, DC: Committee on Unintended Pregnancy.

Burns, B. J., Costello, E. J., Angold, A., Tweed, D., Stangl, D., Farmer, E., et al. (1995). Children's mental health service use across service sectors. *Health Affairs, 14* (3), 147–159.

Burns, J., Dudley, M., Hazell, P., & Patton, G. (2005). Clinical management of deliberate self-harm in young people: The need for evidence-based approaches to reduce repetition. *Australian and New Zealand Journal of Psychiatry, 39* (3), 121–128.

Busch, A. B., & Shore, M. F. (2000). Seclusion and restraint: A review of the recent literature. *Harvard Review of Psychiatry, 8* (5), 261–270.

Calder, M. C. (1995). Child protection: Balancing paternalism and partnership. *British Journal of Social Work, 25* (6), 749–766.

Campbell, D. (1986). Relabeling internal and external validity for applied social scientists. In W. Trochim (Ed.), *Advances in quasi-experimental design and analysis* (pp. 67–77). San Francisco: Jossey-Bass.

Campbell, J. A. (1990). Ability of practitioners to estimate client acceptance of single-subject evaluation procedures. *Social Work, 35* (1), 9–14.

Capuzzi, D. (2002). Legal and ethical challenges in counseling suicidal students. *Professional School Counseling, 6* (1), 36–45.

Cardemil, E., Reivich, K. J., Beevers, C. G., Seligman, M. E., & James, J. (2007). The prevention of depressive symptoms in low-income, minority children: Two-year follow-up. *Behaviour Research and Therapy, 45* (2), 313–327.

Carnine, D. (1995). Trustworthiness, useability, and accessibility of educational research. *Journal of Behavioral Education, 5* (3), 251–258.

Carpenter, W. D. (1995). *Become your own expert! Self-advocacy curriculum for individuals with learning disabilities.* Minneapolis, MN: Minnesota Educational Services.

Carr, A. (2000). *What works for children and adolescents: A critical review of psychological interventions with children, adolescents, and their families.* London: Routledge.

Carr, J. E., & Burkholder, E. O. (1998). Creating single-subject design graphs with Microsoft Excel(™). *Journal of Applied Behavior Analysis, 31* (2), 245–251.

Carter, E. W., Lane, K. L., Pierson, M. R., & Glaeser, B. (2006). Self-determination skills and opportunities of transition-age youth with emotional disturbance and learning disabilities. *Exceptional Children, 72* (3), 333–346.

CBS/AP (2007, April 19). Va. Tech killer picked on, classmates say. *CBS News.* Retrieved May 25, 2007, from http://www.cbsnews.com/stories/2007/04/19/virginiatechshooting.shtml

Center for Mental Health in Schools at UCLA (2004). *An introductory packet on confidentiality and informed consent.* Los Angeles, CA: Center for Mental Health in Schools at UCLA. Retrieved August 7, 2005, from http://smhp.psych.ucla.edu/pdfdocs/confid/confid.pdf

Center for Mental Health in Schools at UCLA (2007). *Systemic change and empirically supported practices.* Los Angeles, CA: Center for Mental Health in Schools at UCLA. Retrieved July 4, 2007, from http://smhp.psych.ucla.edu/pdfdocs/systemic/implementation%20problem.pdf

Centers for Disease Control and Prevention, U.S. Department of Health and Human Services (2007, February 8). CDC releases new data on autism spectrum disorders (ASDs) from multiple communities in the United

States. Retrieved June 5, 2007, from http://www.cdc.gov/od/oc/media/pressrel/2007/r070208.htm

Chavkin, N. F. (1993). *The use of research in social work practice: A case example from school social work.* Westport, CT: Praeger.

Cherlin, A. J., Burton, L. M., Hurt, T. R., & Purvin, D. M. (2004). The influence of physical and sexual abuse on marriage and cohabitation. *American Sociological Review, 69* (6), 768–789.

Christopherson, E. R., & Mortweet, S. L. (2001). *Treatments that work with children: Empirically supported strategies for managing childhood problems.* Washington, DC: American Psychological Association.

Chronis, A. M., Gamble, S. A., Roberts, J. E., & Pelham, W. E. (2006). Cognitive-behavioral depression treatment for mothers of children with attention-deficit/hyperactivity disorder. *Behavior Therapy, 37* (2), 143–158.

Churcher, S. (2007, April 22). Campus killer punched sister in violent rows from the age of eight. *Mail on Sunday* [UK]. Electronic version, accession number: 24874354. Retrieved May 19, 2007, from http://www.dailymail.co.uk

Clarke, G., Lewisohn, P., & Hops, H. (1990). *Leader's manual for adolescent groups: Adolescent coping with depression course.* Eugene, OR: Castalia.

Coalition Against Institutionalized Child Abuse (2007). *The short life of Angellika "Angie" Arndt: "Bubbles in my milk."* Retrieved May 5, 2007, from http://caica.org

Cobb, N. H., & Jordan, C. (2006). Identifying and using effective outcome measures. In C. Franklin, M. B. Harris, & P. Allen-Meares (Eds.), *School social work and mental health worker's training and resource manual* (pp. 1043–1052). New York: Oxford University Press.

Coffey, C., Carlin, J. B., Lynskey, M., Patton, G. C., & Ismail, K. (2004). Evidence in cannabis research: Authors' reply. *British Journal of Psychiatry, 184* (6), 543–544.

Cohen, J. (1988). *Statistical power for the behavioral sciences* (2nd ed.). Hillsdale, NJ: Lawrence Erlbaum.

Cohen, M. R. (2001). Closing the gaps. *Nursing, 31* (9), 26.

Collaborative for Academic, Social, and Emotional Learning (CASEL). (2006). *Standards and policies: SEL policy.* Retrieved August 5, 2007, from http://www.casel.org/standards/policy.php

Columbia University TeenScreen Program. (2006, November 16). How the program works: Setting the record straight. Retrieved January 11, 2007, from http://www.teenscreen.org/cms/content/view/107/139/#1

Columbus, M. A., & Mithaug, D. E. (2003). The effects of self-regulated problem-solving instruction on the self-determination of secondary students with disabilities. In D. E. Mithaug, D. K. Mithaug, J. E. Martin,

& M. L. Wehmeyer (Eds.), *Self-determined learning theory: Construction, verification, and evaluation* (pp. 172–189). Mahwah, NJ: Lawrence Erlbaum.

Conn, V. S., Valentine, J. C., Cooper, H. M., & Rantz, M. J. (2003). Grey literature in meta-analysis. *Nursing Research, 52* (4), 256–261.

Constable, R., & Massat, C. R. (in press). Evidence-based practice: Implications for school social work. In C. R. Massat & R. Constable (Eds.), *School social work: Practice, policy, and research* (7th ed.). Chicago: Lyceum Books.

Conyne, R. K., & Cook, E. P. (Eds.) (2004). *Ecological counseling: An innovative approach to conceptualizing person-environment interaction.* Alexandria, VA: American Counseling Association.

Cook, B. G., Landrum, T. J., Tankersley, M., & Kauffman, J. M. (2003). Bringing research to bear on practice: Effecting evidence-based instruction for students with emotional or behavioral disorders. *Education & Treatment of Children, 26* (4), 345–361.

Cooper, H. (2001). *The battle over homework: Common ground for administrators, teachers, and parents.* Thousand Oaks, CA: Corwin.

Cooper, H., Robinson, J. C., & Patall, E. A. (2006). Does homework improve academic achievement? A synthesis of research 1987–2003. *Review of Educational Research, 76* (1), 1–62.

Cooper, D. H., & Speece, D. L. (1988). A novel methodology for the study of children at risk for school failure. *Journal of Special Education, 22* (2), 186–198.

Corcoran, K., & Vandiver, V. L. (2004). Implementing best practice and expert consensus procedures. In A. R. Roberts & K. Yeager (Eds.), *Evidence-based practice manual: Research and outcome measures in health and human services* (pp. 15–19). New York: Oxford University Press.

Cowell, J. M., Gross, D., McNaughton, D., Ailey, S., & Fogg, L. (2005). Depression and suicidal ideation among Mexican American school-aged children. *Research and Theory for Nursing Practice, 19* (1), 77–94.

Craven, R. G., Marsh, H. W., Debus, R. L., & Jayasinghe, U. (2001). Diffusion effects: Control group contamination threats to the validity of teacher-administered interventions. *Journal of Educational Psychology, 93* (3), 639–645.

Crisp, H. L., Gudmundsen, G. R., & Shirk, S. R. (2006). Transporting evidence-based therapy for adolescent depression to the school setting. *Education and Treatment of Children, 29* (2), 287–309.

Daubert v. Merrell Dow Pharmaceuticals, Inc. 509 U.S. 113 S. Ct. 2786 (1993).

Daunic, A. P., Smith, S. W., Brank, E. M., & Penfield, R. D. (2006). Classroom-based cognitive-behavioral intervention to prevent aggression: Efficacy and social validity. *Journal of School Psychology, 44* (2), 123–139.

DeChillo, N., Koren, P. E., & Schultze, K. H. (1994). From paternalism to partnership: Family and professional collaboration in children's mental health. *American Journal of Orthopsychiatry, 64* (4), 564–576.

Deffenbacher, J. L., & Swaim, R. C. (1999). Anger expression in Mexican American and White non-Hispanic adolescents. *Journal of Counseling Psychology, 46* (1), 61–69.

DeLuca, R. V., Boyes, D. A., Grayston, A. D., & Romano, E. (1995). Sexual abuse: Effects of group therapy on preadolescent girls. *Child Abuse Review, 4* (4), 263–277.

DePanfilis, D. (1996). Implementing child mistreatment risk assessment systems: Lessons from theory. *Administration in Social Work, 20* (2), 41–59

Descry, D. E. (2004). Searching the web: From the visible to the invisible. *Tech Trends, 48* (1), 5–6.

Devine, J., & Egger-Sider, F. (2004). Beyond Google: The invisible web in the academic library. *Journal of Academic Librarianship, 30* (4), 265–269.

Dewey, J. (1902/2001). *The educational situation.* Chicago: University of Chicago. Reprinted: L. Iura (Ed.), *The Jossey-Bass reader on school reform* (pp. 3–4). San Francisco: Jossey-Bass.

Dibble, N. (2004, Spring). Revenues generated for school districts by school social work services. *School Social Work Connection, 1,* 11–12.

Dickey, W. C., & Blumberg, S. J. (2004). Revisiting the factor structure of the Strengths and Difficulties Questionnaire: United States, 2001. *Journal of the American Academy of Child and Adolescent Psychiatry, 43* (9), 1159–1167.

Dietz, T. J., Westerfelt, A., & Barton, T. R. (2004). Incorporating practice evaluation with the field practicum. *Journal of Baccalaureate Social Work, 9* (2), 78–90.

DiGangi, S. A., Maag, J. W., & Rutherford, R. B. (1991). Self-graphing of on-task behavior: Enhancing the reactive effects of self-monitoring on on-task behavior and academic performance. *Learning Disabilities Quarterly, 14* (2), 221–230.

Dishion, T. J., Kavanagh, K., & Christianson, S. (1995). *Parenting in the teenage years* [Video]. Available from InterVision, 261 East 12th Avenue, Eugene, OR 97403.

Dishion, T., McCord, J., & Poulin, F. (1999). When interventions harm: Peer groups and problem behavior. *American Psychologist, 54* (9), 755–764.

Dishion, T. J., & Stormshak, E. A. (2007). *Intervening in children's lives: An ecological, family-centered approach to mental health care* (pp. 219–239). Washington, DC: American Psychological Association.

Dodge, K. A. (1999). Cost-effectiveness of psychotherapy for child aggression: First, is there effectiveness? Comment on Schectman and Ben-David (1999). *Group Dynamics, 3* (4), 275–278.

Doll, B., & Haack, M. K. (2005). Population-based strategies for identifying school-wide problems. In R. Brown-Chidsey (Ed.), *Assessment for intervention: A problem-solving approach* (pp. 82–102). New York: Guilford.

Doll, B., Song, S., & Siemers, E. (2004). Classroom ecologies that support or discourage bullying. In D. L. Espelage & S. M. Swearer (Eds.), *Bullying in American schools: A social-ecological perspective on prevention and intervention* (pp. 161–183). Mahwah, NJ: Lawrence Erlbaum.

Donnermeyer, J. F. (2000). Parents' perceptions of a school-based prevention education program. *Journal of Drug Education, 30* (3), 325–342.

Doss, A. J. (2005). Evidence-based diagnosis: Incorporating diagnostic instruments into clinical practice. *Journal of the American Academy of Child and Adolescent Psychiatry, 44* (9), 947–952.

Drake, B., Hovmand, P., Jonson-Reid, M., & Zayas, L. H. (2007). Adopting and teaching evidence-based practice in Master's-level social work programs. *Journal of Social Work Education, 43* (3), 431–446.

Dretzke, B. J. (2005). *Statistics with Microsoft Excel* (3rd ed.). Upper Saddle River, NJ: Pearson/Prentice Hall.

Dube, S. R., Miller, J. W., Brown, D. W, Giles, W. H., Felitti, V. J., Dong, M., et al. (2006). Adverse childhood experiences and the association with ever using alcohol and initiating alcohol use during adolescence. *Journal of Adolescent Health, 38* (4), e1–e10.

DuPaul, G. J., & Weyandt, L. L. (2006). School-based intervention for children with attention deficit hyperactivity disorder: Effects on academic, social, and behavioural functioning. *International Journal of Disability, Development, and Education, 53* (2), 161–176.

Durlak, J. A., Fuhrman, T., & Lampman, C. (1991). Effectiveness of cognitive-behavior therapy for maladapting children: A meta-analysis. *Psychological Bulletin, 110,* 204–214.

Durlak, J. A., Wells, A. M., Cotton, J. K., & Johnson, S. (1995). Analysis of selected methodological issues in child psychotherapy research. *Journal of Clinical Child Psychology, 24* (2), 141–148.

Edgington, E. S. (1987). Randomized single-subject experiments and statistical tests. *Journal of Counseling Psychology, 34* (4), 437–442.

Edmond, T., Megivern, D., Williams, C., Rochman, E., & Howard, M. (2006). Integrating evidence-based practice and social work field education. *Journal of Social Work Education, 42* (2), 377–396.

Edwards, R. W., Jumper-Thurman, P., Plested, B. A., Oetting, E. R., & Swanson, L. (2000). Community readiness: Research to practice. *Journal of Community Psychology, 28* (3), 291–307.

Eikeseth, S., Smith, T., Jahr, E., & Eldevik, S. (2007). Outcome for children with autism who began intensive behavioral treatment between ages 4 and 7: A comparison controlled study. *Behavior Modification, 31* (3), 264–278.

Eisenman, L. Y. (2007). Self-determination interventions: Building a foundation for school completion. *Remedial and Special Education, 28* (1), 2–8.

Elias, M. J., Zins, J. E., Graczyk, P. A., & Weissberg, R. P. (2003). Implementation, sustainability, and scaling up of social-emotional and academic innovations in public schools. *School Psychology Review, 32* (3), 303–319.

Elkin, I. (1999). A major dilemma in psychotherapy outcome research: Disentangling therapists from therapies. *Clinical Psychology: Science and Practice, 6* (1), 10–32.

Elliott, D. S., & Mihalic, S. (2004). Issues in disseminating and replicating effective prevention programs. *Prevention Science, 5* (1), 47–54.

Elliott, J., Nembhard, M., Giannone, V., Surko, M., Medeiros, D., & Peake, K. (2004). Clinical uses of an adolescent intake questionnaire: Adquest as a bridge to engagement. *Social Work in Mental Health, 3* (1-2), 83–102.

Elliott, S. N., Sheridan, S. M., & Gresham, F. M. (1989). Assessing and treating social skills deficits: A case study for the scientist-practitioner. *Journal of School Psychology, 27* (2), 197–222.

English, A. (1995). The legal framework for minor consent. Introduction. In A. English, M. Matthews, K. Estavour, C. Palamountain, & J. Yang (Eds.), *State minor consent statutes: A summary* (pp. 3–7). San Francisco: National Center for Youth Law.

Ennett, S. T., Tobler, N. S., Ringwalt, C. L., & Flewelling, R. L. (1994). Resistance education? A meta-analysis of Project D.A.R.E. outcome evaluations. *American Journal of Public Health, 84* (9), 1394–1401.

Ensinger, M. E., Hanson, S. G., Riley, A. W., & Juon, H.-S. (2003). Maternal psychological distress: Adult sons' and daughters' mental health and educational attainment. *Journal of the American Academy of Child and Adolescent Psychiatry, 42* (9), 1108–1115.

ERIC (1980). School counseling. Education Resources Information Center, retrieved May 19, 2006, from http:www.eric.ed.gov

Erion, J. (2006). Parenting tutoring: A meta-analysis. *Education and Treatment of Children, 29* (1), 79–106.

Ervin, R. A., Kern, L., Clarke, S., DuPaul, G. J., Dunlap, G., & Friman, P. C. (2000). Evaluating assessment-based intervention strategies for students with ADHD and comorbid disorders within the natural classroom context. *Behavioral Disorders, 25* (4), 344–358.

Etscheidt, S. K. (2006). Progress monitoring: Legal issues and recommendations for IEP teams. *Teaching Exceptional Children, 38* (6), 56–60.

Evidence-Based Medicine Working Group. (1992). A new approach to teaching the practice of medicine. *Journal of the American Medical Association, 268,* 2420–2425.

Expert Consensus Guideline Series. (2006). Retrieved October 6, 2006, from http://www.psychguides.com/methodology.php

Ezpeleta, L., Granero, R., & de la Osa, N. (1999). Evaluacion del deterioro en ninos y adolescents a traves de la Children's Global Assessment Scale (CGAS). *Revista de Psiquiatria Infanto-Juvenil, 1,* 18–26.

Families and Advocates Partnership for Education. (2001). *School accommodations and modifications.* Minneapolis, MN: Families and Advocates Partnership for Education. Retrieved May 19, 2002, from http://www.fape.org/pubs/FAPE-27.pdf

Family Educational Rights and Privacy Act (FERPA) of 1974, PL 93-380, 20 U.S.C. §1232g (1974).

Faupel., A., Herrick, E., & Sharp, P. (1998). *Anger management: A practical guide.* London: David Fulton.

Federal Rules of Evidence. (1975). Retrieved on August 7, 2006, from http://www.law.cornell.edu/rules/fre/rules.htm

Feeny, N. C., Hembree, E. A., & Zoellner, L. A. (2003). Myths regarding exposure therapy for PTSD. *Cognitive and Behavioral Practice, 10* (1), 85–90.

Feil, E. G., Small, J. W., Forness, S. R., Serna, L. A., Kaiser, A. P., Hancock, T. B., et al. (2005). Using different measures, informants, and clinical cut-off points to estimate prevalence of emotional or behavioral disorders in preschoolers: Effects on age, gender, and ethnicity. *Behavioral Disorders, 30* (4), 375–391.

Feindler, E. L., & Ecton, R. B. (1986). *Adolescent anger control: Cognitive-behavioral techniques.* New York: Pergamon.

Feindler, E. L., & Guttman, J. (1994). Cognitive-behavioral anger control training for groups of adolescents: A treatment manual. In C. W. LeCroy (Ed.), *Handbook of child and adolescent treatment manuals* (pp. 170–199). New York: Lexington Books.

Fineout-Overholt, E., & Johnston, L. (2005). Teaching EBP: Asking searchable, answerable questions. *Worldviews on Evidence-Based Nursing, 2* (3), 157–160

Finn, C. A., & Sladeczek, I. E. (2001). Assessing the social validity of behavioral interventions: A review of treatment acceptability measures. *School Psychology Quarterly, 16* (2), 176–206.

Finson, K. D., & Ormsbee, C. K. (1998). Rubrics and their use in inclusive science. *Intervention in School and Clinic, 34* (2), 79–88.

Fischer, J., & Corcoran, K. (2007). *Measures for clinical practice and research: A sourcebook, Vol. 1: Couples, families, and children* (4th ed.). New York: Oxford University Press.

Fisher, C. B. (2004). Informed consent and clinical research involving children and adolescents: Implications of the revised APA Code of Ethics and HIPAA. *Journal of Clinical Child and Adolescent Psychology, 33* (4), 832–839.

Fixsen, D. L., Naoom, S. F., Blase, K. A. Friedman, R. M., & Wallace, F. (2005). *Implementation research: A synthesis of the literature.* Retrieved July 10, 2007, from http://nirn.fmhi.usf.edu/resources/publications/Monograph/pdf/Monograph_full.pdf

Fletcher, J. M., Lyon, G. R., Barnes, M., Stuebing, K. K., Francis, D. J., Olson, R. K., et al. (2001, August). *Classification of learning disabilities: An evidence-based evaluation.* Paper presented at the Learning Disabilities Summit: Building a foundation for the future, Washington, DC (ED 458-762).

Flinn, S. K., & Hauser, D. (1998). *Teenage pregnancy: The case for prevention: An analysis of recent trends and federal expenditures associated with teenage pregnancy.* Washington, DC: Advocates for Youth.

Fonagy, P., Target, M., Cottrell, D., Phillips, J., & Kurtz, Z. (2002). *What works for whom? A critical review of treatments for children and adolescents.* New York: Guilford.

Foorman, B. R., & Moats, L. C. (2004). Conditions for sustaining research-based practices in early reading instruction. *Remedial and Special Education, 25* (1), 51–60.

Ford, K., Sankey, J., & Crisp, J. (2007). Development of children's assent documents using a child-centered approach. *Journal of Child Health Care, 11* (1), 19–28.

Fordham Urban Law Journal (1974). Civil rights—Right to treatment—Neither due process nor equal protection clause of the 14th Amendment guarantees the "right to treatment" for mentally retarded children confined in a state institution through noncriminal procedures. *Fordham Urban Law Journal, 2* (2), 363–375.

Forness, S. R., & Kavale, K. A. (2001). Ignoring the odds: Hazards of not adding the new medical model to special education decisions. *Behavior Disorders, 26* (4), 269–281.

Franklin, C. (2001). Onward to evidence-based practices for schools. *Children and Schools, 23* (3), 131–134. Editorial.

Franklin, C., Grant, D., Corcoran, J., O'Dell, P., & Bultman, L. (1997). Effectiveness of prevention programs for adolescent pregnancy: A meta-analysis. *Journal of Marriage and the Family, 59* (3), 551–567.

Franklin, C., & Hopson, L. M. (2007). Facilitating the use of evidence-based practice in community organizations. *Journal of Social Work Education, 43* (3), 377–404.

Franklin, C., & McNeil, J. S. (1992). The Cassata project: A school-agency partnership for practice research integration. *Arete, 17* (1), 47–52.

Fraser, B. J. (1998). Classroom environment instruments: Development, validity, and applications. *Learning Environments Research, 1* (1), 7–34.

Fraser, B. J., Anderson, G. J., & Walberg, H. J. (1982). *Assessment of learning environments: Manual for Learning Environment Inventory (LEI) and My Class Inventory (MCI)* (3rd ed.). Perth, Australia: Western Australia Institute of Technology.

Fraser, J. J., & McAbee, G. N. (2004). Dealing with the parent whose judgment is impaired by alcohol or drugs: Legal and ethical considerations. *Pediatrics, 114* (3), 869–873.

Frey, A., Faith, T., Elliott, A., & Royer, B. (2006). A pilot study examining the social validity and effectiveness of a positive support model in Head Start. *School Social Work Journal, 30* (2), 22–44.

Frye v. United States, 293 F. 1013, 1014 (D.C. Cir. 1923).

Fuchs, L. S., & Fuchs, D. (1986). Effects of systematic formative evaluation: A meta-analysis. *Exceptional Children, 53* (2), 199–208.

Fuchs, L. S., & Fuchs, D. (2001). Principles for sustaining research-based practice in the schools: A case study. *Focus on Exceptional Children, 33* (1), 1–14.

Fuqua, D. R., & Kurpius, D. J. (1993). Conceptual models in organizational consultation. *Journal of Counseling and Development, 71* (6), 607–618.

Furlong, M. J., Greif, J. L., Bates, M. P., Whipple, A. D., Jimenez, T. C., & Morrison, R. (2005). Development of the California School Climate and Safety Survey—Short form. *Psychology in the Schools, 42* (2), 137–149.

Gadow, K. D., Sprafkin, J., & Nolan, E. E. (1996). *ADHD School Observation Code.* Stony Brook. NY: Checkmate Plus.

Gale, T. M., Hawley, C. J., & Sivakumaran, T. (2003). Do mental health professionals really understand probability? Implications for risk assessment and evidence-based practice. *Journal of Mental Health, 12* (4), 417–430.

Gambrill, E. (2003). Evidence-based practice: Sea change or the emperor's new clothes? *Journal of Social Work Education, 39* (1), 3–23.

Gambrill, E. (2005). *Critical thinking in clinical practice: Improving the quality of judgments and decisions* (2nd ed.). Hoboken, NJ: John Wiley.

Gambrill, E. (2006a). *Social work practice: A critical thinker's guide* (2nd ed.). New York: Oxford University Press.

Gambrill, E. (2006b). Evidence-based practice and policy: Choices ahead. *Research on Social Work Practice, 16* (3), 338–357.

Gambrill, E. (2007). Views of evidence-based practice: Social workers' code of ethics and accreditation standards as guides for choice. *Journal of Social Work Education, 43* (3), 447–462.

Gambrill, E. D., & Barth, R. P. (1980). Single-case study designs revisited. *Social Work Research and Abstracts, 16* (3), 15–20.

Gambrill, E., & Gibbs, L. (2002). Making practice decisions: Is what's good for the goose good for the gander? *Ethical Human Sciences and Services, 4* (1), 31–46.

Garbarino, J. (2001). An ecological perspective on the effects of violence on children. *Journal of Community Psychology, 29* (3), 361–378.

Gartin, B. C., & Murdick, N. L. (2005). IDEA 2004: The IEP. *Remedial and Special Education, 26* (6), 327–331.

Gaub, M., & Carlson, C. L. (1997). Gender differences in ADHD: A meta-analysis and critical review. *Journal of the American Academy of Child and Adolescent Psychiatry, 36* (8), 1036–1045.

Geeraert, L., Van den Noortgate, W., Grietens, H., & Onghena, P. (2004). The effects of early prevention programs for families with young children at risk for physical child abuse and neglect: A meta-analysis. *Child Maltreatment, 9* (3), 277–291. See comment by Miller.

General Electric Co. v. Joiner, 118 S. Ct. 512 (1997).

Gerber, M. M. (2003, December). *Teachers are still the test: Limitations of response to instruction strategies for identifying children with learning disabilities.* Paper presented at the Learning Disabilities Responsiveness-to-Intervention Symposium, National Research Center, Kansas City, MO.

Gergen, K. J. (1985). The social constructivist movement in modern psychology. *American Psychologist, 40* (3), 260–275.

Gersten, R., & Dimino, J. (2001). Realities of translating research into classroom practice. *Learning Disabilities Research and Practice, 16* (2), 120–130.

Germain, C. B. (1979). *Social work practice: People and environments, an ecological perspective.* New York: Columbia University Press.

Gettinger, M., & Kohler, K. M. (2006). Process-outcome approaches to classroom management and effective teaching. In C. M. Evertson, & C. S. Weinstein (Eds.), *Handbook of classroom management: Research, practice, and contemporary issues* (pp. 73–95). Mahwah, NJ: Lawrence Erlbaum.

Gibbs, L. (2003). *Evidence-based practice for the helping professions: A practical guide with integrated multimedia.* Pacific Grove, CA: Thomson-Brooks/Cole.

Gielen, U. P., Fish, J. M., & Draguns, J. G. (Eds.) (2004). *Handbook of culture, therapy, and healing.* Mahwah, NJ: Lawrence Erlbaum.

Gladwell, M. (2000). *The tipping point: How little things can make a big difference.* Boston: Little, Brown.

Glutting, J. J., & Oakland, T. (1993). *Manual for the guide to the assessment of test behavior.* San Antonio, TX: Psychological Corporation.

Goldie, J., Schwartz, L., & Morrison, J. (2005). Whose information is it anyway? Informing a 12-year-old patient of her terminal prognosis. *Journal of Medical Ethics, 31* (7), 427–434.

Goldman, L. (1972). Psychological secrecy and openness in the public schools. *Professional Psychology, 3* (4), 370–374.

Goldstein, B. (2007, April 24). Cho Seung-Hui's commitment papers. Retrieved May 25, 2007, from http://www.slate.com/id/2164842

Goodman, R. (2001). Psychometric properties of the Strengths and Difficulties Questionnaire. *Journal of the American Academy of Child and Adolescent Psychiatry, 40* (11), 1337–1345. Available from http://www.sdqinfo.com

Goodrich, H. (1997). Understanding rubrics. *Educational Leadership, 54* (4), 14–17.

Gosschalk, P. O. (2004). Behavioral treatment of acute onset school refusal in a 5-year-old girl with separation anxiety disorder. *Education and Treatment of Children, 27* (2), 150–160.

Gowan, J. C. (2004). The use of developmental stage theory in helping gifted children become creative. In D. J. Treffinger (Ed.), *Creativity and giftedness* (pp. 21–33). Thousand Oaks, CA: Corwin.

Granlund, M., & Roll-Pettersson, L. (2001). The perceived needs of support of parents and classroom teachers—A comparison of needs in two micro-systems. *European Journal of Special Needs Education, 16* (3), 225–244.

Green, W. H. (2001). *Child and adolescent clinical psychopharmacology* (3rd ed.). Philadelphia: Lippincott.

Green, J., Duncan, R. E., Barnes, G. L., & Oberklaid, F. (2003). Putting the "informed" into "consent": A matter of plain language. *Journal of Pediatrics and Child Health, 39* (9), 700–703.

Greenhalgh, T. (2006). *How to read a paper: The basics of evidence-based medicine* (3rd ed.). Oxford, UK: Blackwell.

Greenhill, L. L., Halperin, J. M., & Abikoff, H. (1999). Stimulant medications. *Journal of the American Academy of Child and Adolescent Psychiatry, 38* (5), 503–512.

Griffin, K. W., Botvin, G. J., & Nichols, T. R. (2006). Effects of a school-based drug abuse prevention program for adolescents on HIV risk behavior in young adulthood. *Prevention Science, 7* (1), 103–112.

Grinnell, R. M., Jr., Unrau, Y. A., & Williams, M. (2008). Group-level designs. In R. M. Grinnell, Jr., & Y. A. Unrau (Eds.), *Social work research and evaluation: Foundations of evidence-based practice* (8th ed., pp. 177–204). New York: Oxford University Press.

Grove, W. M., & Barden, R. C. (1999). Protecting the integrity of the legal system: The admissibility of testimony from mental health experts under *Daubert/Kumho* analyses. *Psychology, Public Policy, and Law, 5* (1), 224–242.

Guerra, N. G., Boxer, P., & Kim, T. E. (2005). A cognitive-ecological approach to serving students with emotional and behavioral disorders: Application to aggressive behavior. *Behavioral Disorders, 30* (3), 277–278.

Gunter, P. L., Miller, K. A., Venn, M. L., Thomas, K., & House, S. (2002). Self-graphing to success: Computerized data management. *Teaching Exceptional Children, 35* (2), 30–34.

Guttmacher Institute (2007). *State policies in brief: An overview of minor consent laws.* New York: Guttmacher Institute. Retrieved July 24, 2007, from http://www.guttmacher.org/statecenter/spibs/spib_OMCL.pdf

Guxens, M., Nebot, M., & Ariza, C. (2007). Age and sex differences in factors associated with the onset of cannabis use: A cohort study. *Drug and Alcohol Dependence, 88* (2–3), 234–243.

Guyatt, G. H., Sackett, D. L., & Cook, D. J. (1993). Users' guide to the medical literature. II. How to use an article about therapy or prevention A. Are the results of the study valid? *JAMA, 270* (21), 2598–2601.

Guyatt, G. H., Sackett, D. L., & Cook, D. J. (1994). Users' guide to the medical literature II: How to use an article about therapy or prevention B. What were the results and will they help me in caring for my patients? *JAMA, 271* (1), 59–63.

Gwynn, C. A., Brantley, H. T. (1987). Effect of a divorce group intervention for elementary school children. *Psychology in the Schools, 24* (2), 161–164.

Habbousche, D. F., Daniel-Crotty, S., Karustis, J. L., Leff, S. S., Costigan, T. E., Goldstein, S. G., et al. (2001). A family-school homework intervention program for children with attention-deficit/hyperactivity disorders. *Cognitive and Behavioral Practice, 8* (2), 123–136.

Halonen, J. S., Bosack, T., & Clay, S. (2003). A rubric for learning, teaching, and assessing scientific inquiry in psychology. *Teaching of Psychology, 30* (3), 196–208.

Han, S. S., & Weiss, B. (2005). Sustainability of teacher implementation of school-based mental health programs. *Journal of Abnormal Child Psychology, 33* (6), 665–679.

Handford, M. (1987). *Where's Waldo?* Boston, MA: Little, Brown.

Handler, M. W., & DuPaul, G. J. (1999). Pharmacological issues and iatrogenic effects on learning. In R. T. Brown (Ed.), *Cognitive aspects of chronic illness in children* (pp. 355–385). New York: Guilford.

Handwerk, M. L., Larzelere, R. E., Soper, S. H., & Friman, P. C. (1999). Parent and child discrepancies in reporting severity of problem behaviors in three out-of-home settings. *Psychological Assessment, 11* (1), 14–23.

Hanline, M. F., Milton, S., & Phelps, P. C. (2007). Influence of disability, gender, and time engaged on the developmental level of children's art work: Findings from three years of observation. *Journal of Early Intervention, 29* (2), 141–153.

Hanna, M. A., & Smith, J. (1998). Using rubrics for documentation of clinical work supervision. *Counselor Education and Supervision, 37* (4), 269–278.

Harcourt, D., & Conroy, H. (2005). Informed assent: Ethics and processes when researching with young children. *Early Child Development and Care, 175* (6), 567–577.

Haring-Hidore, M., & Vacc, N. A. (1988). The scientist-practitioner model in training entry-level counselors. *Journal of Counseling and Development, 66* (6), 286–288.

Harris, M. B., & Franklin, C. G. (2003). Effects of a cognitive-behavioral, school-based, group intervention with Mexican American pregnant and parenting adolescents. *Social Work Research, 27* (2), 71–83.

Harter, K. (2007). *Wisconsin clinic fined $100,000 in girl's death; employee gets 60 days jail.* Retrieved May 5, 2007, from http://www.twincities.com

Harth, S. C., & Thong, Y. H. (1995). Parental perceptions and attitudes about informed consent in clinical research involving children. *Social Science and Medicine, 41* (12), 1647–1651.

Hatch, T. (2000). What does it take to break the mold? Rhetoric and reality in New American Schools. *Teachers College Record, 102* (3), 561–589.

Hauser, D. (2004). *Five years of abstinence-only-until-marriage education: Assessing the impact.* Washington, DC: Advocates for Youth.

Heller, K., Holtzman, W., & Messick, S. (1982). *Placing children in special education: A strategy for equity.* Washington, DC: National Academies Press.

Hemmeter, M. L., Maxwell, K. L., Ault, M. J., & Schuster, J. W. (2001). *Assessment of practices in early elementary classrooms.* New York: Teachers College Press.

Hennessey, B. (2007). Promoting social competence in school-aged children: The effects of the Open Circle Program. *Journal of School Psychology, 45* (3), 349–360.

Herie, M., & Martin, G. W. (2002). Knowledge diffusion in social work: A new approach to bridging the gap. *Social Work, 47* (1), 85–95.

Hernandez, M., & Hodges, S. (2003). Building upon the theory of change for systems of care. *Journal of Emotional and Behavioral Disorders, 11* (1), 19–26.

Herschell, A. D., McNeil, C. B., & McNeil, D. W. (2004). Clinical child psychology's progress in disseminating empirically supported treatments. *Clinical Psychology: Science and Practice, 11* (3), 267–288.

Hess, P. M., & Mullen, E. J. (Eds.) (1995). *Practitioner-researcher partnerships: Building knowledge from, in, and for practice.* Washington, DC: NASW Press.

Hintze, J. M. (2005). Psychometrics of direct observation. *School Psychology Review, 34* (4), 507–519.

Hoag, M. J., & Burlingame, G. M. (1997). Evaluating the effectiveness of child and adolescent group treatment: A meta-analytic review. *Journal of Clinical Child Psychology, 26* (3), 234–246.

Hoagwood, K., & Johnson, J. (2003). School psychology: A public health framework I. From evidence-based practices to evidence-based policies. *Journal of School Psychology, 41* (1), 3–21.

Hoagwood, K. E., Olin, S. S., Kerker, B. D., Kratochwill, T. R., Crowe, M., & Saka, N. (2007). Empirically based school interventions targeted at academic and mental health functioning. *Journal of Emotional and Behavioral Disorders, 15* (2), 66–92.

Hoff, K. E., Ervin, R. A., & Friman, P. C. (2005). Refining functional behavioral assessment: Analyzing the separate and combined effects of hypothesized controlling variables during ongoing classroom routines. *School Psychology Review, 34* (1), 45–57.

Holmbeck, G. N., O'Mahar, K., Abad, M., Colder, C., & Updegrove, A. (2006). Cognitive-behavioral therapy with adolescents: Guides from developmental psychology. In P. C. Kendall (Ed.), *Child and adolescent therapy: Cognitive-behavioral procedures* (3rd ed., pp. 419–464). New York: Guilford.

Horner, R. H., Carr, E. G., Halle, J., McGee, G., Odom, S., & Wolery, M. (2005). The use of single-subject research to identify evidence-based practice in special education. *Exceptional Children, 71* (2), 165–179.

Howard, M. O., & Jenson, J. M. (1999). Clinical practice guidelines: Should social work develop them? *Research on Social Work Practice, 9* (3), 283–301.

Howard, E. R., & Keefe, J. W. (1991). *The CASE-IMS school improvement process.* Reston, VA: National Association of Secondary School Principals.

Howard, M. O., McMillen, C. J., & Pollio, D. E. (2003). Teaching evidence-based practice: Toward a new paradigm for social work education. *Research on Social Work Practice, 13* (2), 234–259.

Hoy, W. K., Smith, P. A., & Sweetland, S. R. (2002). The development of the Organizational Climate Index for high schools: Its measure and relationship to faculty trust. *High School Journal, 86* (2), 38–49.

Hoy, W. K., Tarter, C. J., & Kottkamp, R. B. (1991). *Open and healthy schools: Measuring organizational climate.* Thousand Oaks, CA: Sage.

Hudson, W. W. (1982). *The clinical measurement package: A field manual.* Chicago, IL: Dorsey.

Huebner, E. S. (1990). The generalizability of the confirmation bias among school psychologists. *School Psychology International, 11* (4), 281–286.

Hughes, J. N., Cavell, T. A., & Willson, V. (2000). Further support for the developmental significance of the quality of the teacher-student relationship. *Journal of School Psychology, 39* (4), 289–301.

Hughes, C., Copeland, S. R., Wehmeyer, M. L., Agran, M., & Rodi, M. S. (2002). Using self-monitoring to improve performance in general education high school classes. *Education and Training in Mental Retardation and Developmental Disabilities, 37* (3), 262–272.

Humphrey, L. L. (1982). Children's and teachers' perspectives on children's self-control: The development of two rating scales. *Journal of Consulting and Clinical Psychology, 50* (5), 624–633.

Hunsucker, P. F., Nelson, R. O., & Clark, R. P. (1986). Standardization and evaluation of the Classroom Adaptive Behavior Checklist for school use. *Exceptional Children, 53* (1), 69–71.

Hunt, D. P., Haidet, P., Coverdale, J. H., & Richards, B. (2003). The effect of using team learning in an evidence-based medicine course for medical students. *Teaching and Learning in Medicine, 15* (2), 131–139.

Hurley, J. C., & Underwood, M. K. (2002). Children's understanding of their research rights before and after debriefing: Informed assent, confidentiality, and stopping participation. *Child Development, 73* (1), 132–143.

Hus, S. N. (2001). Navigating the quagmire of inherent ethical dilemmas present in elementary school counseling programs. In D. S. Sandhu (Ed.), *Elementary school counseling in the new millennium* (pp. 15–25). Alexandria, VA: American Counseling Association.

Hussey, D. L., & Guo, S. (2003). Measuring behavioral change in young children receiving intensive school-based mental health services. *Journal of Community Psychology, 31* (6), 629–639.

Hyatt, K. J. (2007). The new IDEA: Changes, concerns, and questions. *Intervention in School and Clinic, 42* (3), 131–136.

Individuals with Disabilities Education Improvement Act of 2004, PL 108-446, 118 Stat. 2647 (2004).

Institute of Medicine (2004). *Immunization safety review: Vaccines and autism.* Washington, DC: National Academies Press. Retrieved May 19, 2007, from http://www.nap.edu/execsumm_pdf/10997.pdf

Isaacs, E. (1972, May 4). Response. In *Proceedings of the symposium on ethical issues in human experimentation: The case of Willowbrook State Hospital research* (pp. 19–25). New York: Urban Health Affairs Program and New York University Medical Center.

Jackson, G. E. (2006). Mental health screening in schools: Essentials of informed consent. *Ethical Human Psychology and Psychiatry, 8* (3), 217–224.

Jackson, C. W., & Larkin, M. J. (2002). RUBRIC: Teaching students to use grading rubrics. *Teaching Exceptional Children, 35* (1), 40–45.

Jaeschke, R., Guyatt, G., & Sackett, D. L. (1994). Users' guides to the medical literature. II. How to use an article about a diagnostic test. B. What are the results and will they help me in caring for my patients? *JAMA, 271* (9), 703–707.

Jayaratne, S. (1977). Single-subject and group design in treatment evaluation. *Social Work Research and Abstracts, 13* (3), 35–42.

Jayaratne, S. (1978). Analytic procedures for single-subject designs. *Social Work Research and Abstracts, 14* (3), 30–40.

Jayaratne, S., & Levy, R. L. (1979). *Empirical clinical practice.* New York: Columbia University Press.

Jaycox, L. H., McCaffrey, D., Eiseman, B., Aronoff, J., Shelley, G. A., Collins, R. L., et al. (2006). Impact of a school-based dating violence prevention program among Latino teens: Randomized Controlled Effectiveness Trial. *Journal of Adolescent Health, 39* (5), 694–704.

Jennings, J., Pearson, G., & Harris, M. (2000). Implementing and maintaining school-based mental health services in a large, urban school district. *Journal of School Health, 70* (5), 201–205.

Jensen, L. (2001). The demographic diversity of immigrants and their children. In R. G. Rumbaut & A. Portes (Eds.), *Ethnicities: Children of immigrants in America* (pp. 21–56). Berkeley, CA: University of California Press.

Jensen, P. S., Hinshaw, S. P., Kraemer, H. C., Lenora, N., Newcorn, J. H., Abikoff, H. B., et al. (2001). ADHD comorbidity findings from the MTA study: Comparing comorbid subgroups. *Journal of the American Academy of Child and Adolescent Psychiatry, 40* (2), 147–158.

Jensen, A. L., & Weisz, J. R. (2002). Assessing match and mismatch between practitioner generated and standardized interview-generated diagnoses for clinic-referred children and adolescents. *Journal of Consulting and Clinical Psychology, 70* (1), 158–168.

Johnston, L., & Fineout-Overholt, E. (2005). Teaching EBP: "Getting from zero to one." Moving from recognizing and admitting uncertainties to asking searchable, answerable questions. *Worldviews on Evidence-Based Nursing, 2* (2), 98–102.

Joint Commission on Accreditation of Healthcare Organizations (2004, February 17). *Assessment: Nutritional, functional, and pain assessment and screens.* Oakbrook Terrace, IL: Joint Commission on Accreditation of

Healthcare Organizations. Retrieved April 7, 2005, from http://www.jointcommission.org/AccreditationPrograms/Hospitals/Standards/FAQs/Provision+of+Care/Assessment/nfp_assessments.htm

Joint Commission on Accreditation of Healthcare Organizations (2007a, July 22). *Standards sampler for ambulatory surgery centers.* Oakbrook Terrace, IL: Joint Commission on Accreditation of Healthcare Organizations. Retrieved April 7, 2005, from http://www.jointcommission.org/NR/rdonlyres/A88E7A36-0C20-4C37-B67D-CD8638538E09/0/ASC_stdsampler_07.pdf

Joint Commission on Accreditation of Healthcare Organizations (2007b, July 22). *What did the doctor say? Improving health literacy to protect patient safety.* Oakbrook Terrace, IL: Joint Commission on Accreditation of Healthcare Organizations. Retrieved July 24, 2007, from http://www.jointcommission.org/NR/rdonlyres/F53D5057-5349-4391-9DB9-E7F086873D46/0/health_literacy_exec_summary.pdf

Joint Commission on Accreditation of Healthcare Organizations (2007c, July 15). *What you should know about research studies: A speak-up initiative.* Oakbrook Terrace, IL: Joint Commission on Accreditation of Healthcare Organizations. Retrieved July 24, 2007, from http://www.jointcommission.org/NR/rdonlyres/6DCE201D-78BC-4E36-A673-BC46F42A77F2/0/speakup_research.pdf

Jones, J. (2004). Mood disorders. In F. M. Kline & L. B. Silver (Eds.), *The educator's guide to mental health issues in the classroom* (pp. 193–209). Baltimore, MD: Paul H. Brookes.

Jonson-Reid, M. (2006). Constructing data management systems for tracking accountability. In C. Franklin, M. B. Harris, & P. Allen-Meares (Eds), *School social work and mental health worker's training and resource manual* (pp. 1031–1042). New York: Oxford University Press.

Judge, B., & Billick, S. B. (2004). Suicidality in adolescence: Review and legal considerations. *Behavioral Sciences and the Law, 22* (5), 681–695.

Kalafat, J. (2005). Suicide. In T. P. Gullotta & G. R. Adams (Eds.), *Handbook of adolescent behavioral problems: Evidence-based approaches to prevention and treatment* (pp. 231–254). New York: Springer.

Kalodner, C. R., Alfred, A. F., & Hoyt, W. T. (1997). Group research in applied settings: Examples and recommendations. *Journal for Specialists in Group Work, 22* (4), 253–265.

Kalter, N., & Schreier, S. (1994). Developmental facilitation groups for children of divorce: The elementary school model. In C. W. LeCroy (Ed.), *Handbook of child and adolescent treatment manuals* (pp. 307–342). New York: Lexington Books.

Kam, C., Greenberg, M. T., & Walls, C. T. (2003). Examining the role of implementation quality in school-based prevention using the PATHS curriculum. *Prevention Science, 4* (1), 55–63.

Kamphaus, R. W., & Frick, P. J. (2002). *Clinical assessment of child and adolescent personality and behavior* (2nd ed.). Boston: Allyn & Bacon.

Kamphaus, R. W., VanDeventer, M. C., Brueggemann, A., & Barry, M. (2007). Behavior Assessment System for Children. In S. R. Smith & L. Handler (Eds.), *The clinical assessment of children and adolescents: A practitioner's handbook* (2nd ed., pp. 311–326). Mahwah, NJ: Lawrence Erlbaum.

Kanner, A. M., & Dunn, D. W. (2004). Diagnosis and management of depression and psychosis in children and adolescents with epilepsy. *Journal of Child Neurology, 19* (Suppl. 1), S65–S72.

Karvonen, M., Test, D. W., Browder, D., & Algozzine, B. (2004). Putting self-determination into practice. *Exceptional Children, 71* (1), 23–41.

Kaser-Boyed, N., Adelman, H. S., & Taylor, L. (1985). Minors' ability to identify risks and benefits of therapy. *Professional Psychology: Research and Practice, 16* (3), 411–417.

Kaslow, F. W. (Ed.) (2002). *Comprehensive handbook of psychotherapy: Integrative/eclectic* (Vol. IV). Hoboken, NJ: John Wiley.

Katz, K. S., El-Mohandes, A., Johnson, D. M., Jarrett, M., Rose, A., & Cober, M. (2001). Retention of low income mothers in a parenting intervention study. *Journal of Community Health, 26* (3), 203–218.

Kauffman, J. M. (2005). *Characteristics of emotional and behavioral disorders of children and youth.* Saddle River, NJ: Prentice-Hall.

Kavale, K. A., & Forness, S. R. (2000). History, rhetoric and reality: An analysis of the inclusion debate. *Remedial and Special Education, 21* (5), 279–296.

Kavale, K. A., Holdnack, J. A., & Mostert, M. P. (2006). Responsiveness to intervention and the identification of specific learning disability: A critique and alternative proposal. *Learning Disability Quarterly, 29*(2), 113–127.

Kazdin, A. E. (1982). *Single case research designs.* New York: Oxford University Press.

Kazdin, A. E. (1999). The meanings and measurement of clinical significance. *Journal of Consulting and Clinical Psychology, 67* (3), 332–339.

Kazdin, A. E. (2000). Developing a research agenda for child and adolescent psychotherapy research. *Archives of General Psychiatry, 57* (9), 829–835.

Kazdin, A. E. (2002). Psychosocial treatments for conduct disorder in children and adolescents. In P. E. Nathan & J. M. Gorman (Eds.), *A guide to treatments that work* (2nd ed., pp. 57–85). New York: Oxford University Press.

Kazdin, A. E. (2003). Psychotherapy for children and adolescents. *Annual Review of Psychology, 54,* 253–276.

Kazdin, A. E. (2005). Evidence-based assessment for children and adolescents: Issues in measurement development and clinical application. *Journal of Clinical Child and Adolescent Psychology, 34* (3), 548–558.

Kearney, C. A. (2007). Forms and functions of school refusal behavior: An empirical analysis of absenteeism severity. *Journal of Child Psychology and Psychiatry, 48* (1), 53–61.

Keelin, P. (1977). Goal attainment scaling and the elementary school counselor. *Elementary School Guidance and Counseling, 12* (2), 89–95.

Kelley, M. L. (2003). Assessment of children's behavior in the school setting. In M. L. Kelley, G. H. Noell, & D. Reitman (Eds.), *Practitioner's guide to empirically based measures of school behavior* (pp. 7–22). New York: Kluwer Academic.

Kellner, M. H., & Tutin, J. (1995). A school-based anger management program for developmentally and emotionally disabled high school students. *Adolescence, 30* (12), 813–825.

Kelly, E. A., Glover, J. A., Keefe, J. W., Halderson, C., Sorenson, C., & Speth, C. (1986). *School climate survey.* Reston, VA: National Association of Secondary School Principals.

Kendall, P. C., Chu, B., Gifford, A., Hayes, C., & Nauta, M. (1998). Breathing life into a manual: Flexibility and creativity with manual-based treatments. *Cognitive and Behavioral Practice, 5* (2), 177–198.

Kendall, P. C., & Hedtke, K. (2006). *Cognitive-behavioral therapy for anxious children: Therapist manual* (3rd ed.). Ardmore, PA: Workbook.

Kendall, P. C., Kane, M., Howard, B., & Siqueland, L. (1990). *Cognitive-behavioral treatment of anxious children: Therapist manual.* Ardmore, PA: Workbook.

Kerns, K. A., Abraham, M. M., Schlegelmilch, A., & Morgan, T. A. (2007). Mother-child attachment in later middle childhood: Assessment approaches and associations with mood and emotion regulation. *Attachment and Human Development, 9* (1), 33–53.

Kettlewell, P. W. (2004). Development, dissemination, and implementation of evidence-based treatments: Commentary. *Clinical Psychology: Science and Practice, 11* (2), 190–195.

Keyton, J. (1999). *Group communication: Process and analysis.* Mountain View, CA: Mayfield.

Kinch, C., Lewis-Palmer, T., Hagan-Burke, S., & Sugai, G. (2001). A comparison of teacher and student functional behavior assessment interview information from low-risk and high-risk classrooms. *Education and Treatment of Children, 24* (4), 480–494.

Kingery, J. N., Roblek, T. L., Suveg, C., Grover, R. L., Sherrill, J. T., & Bergman, R. L. (2006). They're not just "little adults": Developmental considerations for implementing cognitive-behavioral therapy with anxious youth. *Journal of Cognitive Psychotherapy, 20* (3), 263–273.

Kirby, D. (2002). Do abstinence-only programs delay the initiation of sex among young people and reduce teen pregnancy? Washington, DC: The National Campaign to Prevent Teen Pregnancy. Retrieved May 19, 2007, from http:www.teenpregnancy.org/resources/data/pdf/abstinence_eval.pdf

Kiresuk, T. J., Smith, A., & Cardillo, J. E. (Eds.) (1994). *Goal attainment scaling: Applications, theory, and measurement.* Hillsdale, NJ: Lawrence Erlbaum.

Klein, J. D. (2005). Adolescent pregnancy: Current trends and issues. *Pediatrics, 116* (1), 281–286. Retrieved May 19, 2007, from http://www.pediatrics.org/cgi/content/full/116/1/281

Kleinfield, N. R. (2007, April 22). Before deadly rage, a lifetime consumed by a troubling silence. *New York Times,* Sec. 1, Col. 1, p. 1. Electronic version. Retrieved May 19, 2007, from http://www.nytimes.com/

Koller, J. R., & Bertel, J. M. (2006). Responding to today's mental health needs of children, families, and schools: Revisiting the preservice training and preparation of school-based personnel. *Education and Treatment of Children, 29* (2), 197–217.

Kopels, S., & Lindsey, B. (2006). The complexity of confidentiality in schools today: The school social worker context. *School Social Work Journal,* (special 100th anniversary issue), 61–78.

Kos, J. M., Richdale, A. L., & Jackson, M. S. (2004). Knowledge about attention deficit/hyperactivity disorder: A comparison of in-service and pre-service teachers. *Psychology in the Schools, 41* (5), 517–526.

Kratochwill, T. R., & Shernoff, E. S. (2004). Evidence-based practice: Promoting evidence-based interventions in school psychology. *School Psychology Review, 33* (1), 34–48.

Krishnamurthy, K. (2007, April 20). "You never noticed him": Classmates recall shooter, graduates of Centreville high school remember a quiet and reclusive Cho. *Richmond Times-Dispatch* [VA]. Electronic version, accession number 2W62W6175224447. Retrieved May 19, 2007, from http://www.timesdispatch.com/cva/ric/times_dispatch.html

Krugman, S. (1972, May 4). Presentation. In *Proceedings of the symposium on ethical issues in human experimentation: The case of Willowbrook State Hospital research* (pp. 4–12). New York: Urban Health Affairs Program and New York University Medical Center.

Kuhn, T. S. (1970). *The structure of scientific revolutions* (2nd ed.). Chicago: University of Chicago Press.

Kumho Tire Co. Ltd. v. Carmichael, 119 S. Ct. 1167 (1999).

Kumpfer, K. L., Alvarado, R., Smith, P., & Bellamy, N. (2002). Cultural sensitivity and adaptation in family-based prevention interventions. *Prevention Science, 3* (3), 241–246.

Kurpius, D. J. (1978). Defining and implementing a consultation program in schools. *School Psychology Review, 1* (3), 4–17.

Landau, S., & Swerdlik, M. E. (2005). Commentary: What you see is what you get: A commentary on school-based direct observation systems. *School Psychology Review, 34* (4), 529–536.

Landrum, T. J., Cook, B. G., Tankersley, M. T., & Fitzgerald, S. (2002). Teachers' perceptions of the trustworthiness, useability, and accessibility of information. *Remedial and Special Education, 23* (1), 42–48.

Lane, D. M., & Dunlap, W. P. (1978). Estimating effect size: Bias resulting from the significance criterion in editorial decisions. *British Journal of Mathematical and Statistical Psychology, 31* (2), 107–112.

Lavoie, D. (2007, March 23). Girl's overdose death raises questions. *Washington Post.* Retrieved May 5, 2007, from http://www.washingtonpost.com

Lee, J. H. (2007, April 22). Virginia Korean community still reeling. Retrieved May 27, 2007, from http://www.washingtonpost.com/wp-dyn/content/article/2007/04/22/AR2007042200936_pf.html

Lei, T., Askeroth, C., Lee, C.-T., Burshteyn, D., & Einhorn, A. (2004). Indigenous Chinese healing: A criteria-based meta-analysis of outcomes research. In U. P. Gielen, J. M. Fish, & J. G. Draguns (Eds.), *Handbook of culture, therapy, and healing* (pp. 213–251). Mahwah, NJ: Lawrence Erlbaum.

Leong, F. T. L. (2002). Challenges for career counseling in Asia: Variation in cultural accommodation. *Career Development Quarterly, 50* (3), 277–284.

Levine, M., Walter, S., Lee, H., Haines, T., Holbrook A., & Moyer, V. (1994). Users' guides to the medical literature. IV. How to use an article about harm. *JAMA, 271* (20), 1615–1619.

Levitt, E. E. (1957). The results of psychotherapy with children: An evaluation. *Journal of Consulting Psychology, 21* (3), 189–196.

Lewczyk, C. M., Garland, A. F., Hurlburt, M. S., Gearity, J., & Hough, R. L. (2003). Comparing DISC-IV and clinician diagnoses among youth receiving public mental health services. *Journal of the American Academy of Child and Adolescent Psychiatry, 42* (3), 349–356.

Lewin, K. (1951). *Field theory in social science.* New York: McGraw-Hill.

Liddle, H. A., Dakof, G. A., Parker, K., Diamond, G. S., Barrett, K., & Tejeda, M. (2001). Multidimensional family therapy for adolescent drug abuse: Results of a randomized clinical trial. *American Journal of Drug and Alcohol Abuse, 27* (4), 651–688.

Lignugaris/Kraft, B., Marchand-Martella, N., & Martella, R. C. (2001). Writing better goals and short-term objectives or benchmarks. *Teaching Exceptional Children, 34* (1), 52–58.

Lilienfeld, S. O. (2002). When worlds collide: Social science, politics, and the Rind et al. (1998) child sexual abuse meta-analysis. *American Psychologist, 57* (2), 176–188.

Lilienfeld, S. O., Lynn, S. J., & Lohr, J. M. (Eds.) (2003). *Science and pseudoscience in clinical psychology.* New York: Guilford.

Lim, M., Stormshak, E. A., & Dishion, T. J. (2005). A one-session intervention for parents of young adolescents. *Journal of Emotional and Behavioral Disorders, 13* (4), 194–199.

Lincoln, Y. S., & Cannella, G. S. (2004). Qualitative research, power, and the radical right. *Qualitative Inquiry, 10* (2), 175–201.

Lincoln, Y. S., & Guba, E. G. (2000). Paradigmatic controversies, contradictions, and emerging confluences. In N. K. Denzin & Y. S. Lincoln (Eds.), *Handbook of qualitative research* (2nd ed., pp. 163–188). Thousand Oaks, CA: Sage.

Lindo, E. J. (2006). The African American presence in reading intervention experiments. *Remedial and Special Education, 27* (3), 148–153.

Linzer, N. (1999). *Resolving ethical dilemmas in social work practice.* Boston: Allyn & Bacon.

Lochman, J. E., Fitzgerald, D. P., & Whidby, J. M. (1999). Anger management with aggressive children. In C. Schaefer (Ed.), *Short-term psychotherapy groups for children* (pp. 301–349). Northvale, NJ: Jason Aronson.

Lochman, J. E., Powell, N., Boxmeyer, C., Deming, A. M., & Young, L. (2007). Cognitive-behavior therapy for angry and aggressive youth. In R. W. Christner, J. L. Stewart, & A. Freeman (Eds.), *Handbook of cognitive-behavior group therapy with children and adolescents: Specific settings and presenting problems* (pp. 333–348). New York: Routledge.

Loewenberg, F., Dolgoff, R., & Harrington, D. (2000). *Ethical decisions for social work practice* (6th ed.). Itasca, IL: F. E. Peacock.

Lohrmann-O'Rourke, S., & Gomez, O. (2001). Integrating preference assessment with the transition process to create meaningful school-to-life outcomes. *Exceptionality, 9* (3), 157–174.

Lomonaco, S., Scheidlinger, S., & Aronson, S. (2000). Five decades of children's group treatment—An overview. *Journal of Child and Adolescent Group Therapy, 10* (2), 77–96.

Lopez, S. A., Torres, A., & Norwood, P. (1998). Building partnerships: A successful collaborative experience between social work and education. *Social Work in Education, 20* (3), 165–176.

Lowry-Webster, H. M., Barrett, P. M., & Dadds, M. R. (2001). A universal prevention trial of anxiety and depressive symptomatology in childhood: Preliminary data from an Australian study. *Behaviour Change, 18* (1), 36–50.

Luborsky, L., Singer, B., & Luborsky, L. (1975). Comparative studies of psychotherapies: Is it true that everyone has won and all must have prizes? *Archives of General Psychiatry, 32* (8), 996–1008.

Lyon, G. R., Fletcher, J. M., Shaywitz, S. E., Shaywitz, B. A., Torgesen, J. K., Wood, F., et al. (2001, May). Rethinking learning disabilities. In C. E. Finn, Jr., A. J. Rotherham, & C. R. Hokanson, Jr. (Eds.), *Rethinking special education for a new century* (pp. 259–287). Washington, DC: Thomas B. Fordham Foundation and the Progressive Policy Institute. Retrieved April 7, 2003, from http://www.excellence.net/library/specialed/index.html

Lyst, A. M., Gabriel, S., O'Shaughnessy, T. E., Meyers, J., & Meyers, B. (2005). Social validity: Perceptions of Check & Connect with early literacy support. *Journal of School Psychology, 43* (3), 197–218.

MacKay, G., Somerville, W., & Lundie, J. (1996). Reflections on goal attainment scaling (GAS): Cautionary notes and proposals for development. *Educational Research, 38* (2), 161–172.

Maher, C. A. (1983). Goal attainment scaling: A method for evaluating special education services. *Exceptional Children, 49* (6), 529–536.

Manicas, P. T., & Secord, P. F. (1983). Implications for psychology of the new philosophy of science. *American Psychologist, 38* (4), 399–413.

Manning, M. L. (2002). *Developmentally appropriate middle level schools* (2nd ed.). Olney, MD: Association for Childhood Education International.

March, J. S., Silva, S., Petrycki, S., Curry, J., Wells, K., Fairbank, J., et al. (2004). Fluoxetine, cognitive-behavioral therapy, and their combination for adolescents with depression: Treatment for adolescents with depression study (TADS) randomized controlled trial. *Journal of the American Medical Association, 292* (7), 807–820.

March, J. S., Silva, S., & Vitiello, B. (2006). The treatment for adolescents with depression study (TADS): Methods and message at 12 weeks. *Journal of the American Academy of Child and Adolescent Psychiatry, 45* (12), 1393–1403.

Marchetti, A., Magar, R., Lau, H., Murphy, E. L., Jensen, P. S., Conners, C. K., et al. (2001). Pharmacotherapies for attention-deficit/hyperactivity disorder: Expected-cost analysis. *Clinical Therapeutics, 23* (11), 1904–1921.

Margolis, H., McCabe, P. P., & Alber, S. R. (2004). Resolving struggling readers' homework difficulties: How elementary school counselors can help. *Journal of Educational and Psychological Consultation, 15* (1), 79–104.

Marino, R., Green, R. G., & Young, E. (1998). Beyond the scientist-practitioner model's failure to thrive: Social workers' participation in agency-based research activities. *Social Work Research, 22* (3), 188–192.

Marks, I. M. (1974). Empirical psychotherapeutic methods. *Psychotherapy and Psychosomatics, 24* (4–6), 222–237.

Marshall, M. J., & Marshall, S. (1993). Treatment paternalism in chemical dependency counselors. *International Journal of the Addictions, 28* (2), 91–106.

Marston, D. (2001, August). *A functional and intervention-based assessment approach to establishing discrepancy for students with learning disabilities.* Paper presented at the Learning Disabilities Summit: Building a foundation for the future, Washington, DC.

Martin, M. W., Levin, S., & Saunders, R. (1999). Secondary school tobacco policy and prevention curricula in South Carolina. *Nicotine and Tobacco Research, 1* (4), 341–346.

Martin, J. E., & Marshall, L. H. (1995). Choicemaker: A comprehensive self-determination transition program. *Intervention in School and Clinic, 30* (2), 147–156.

Martin, J. E., Marshall, L. H., Maxson, L. M., & Jerman, P. L. (1997). *The self-directed IEP.* Longmont, CO: Sopris West.

Martin, J. L. R., Perez, V., Sacristen, M., & Alvarez, E. (2005). Is grey literature essential for a better control of publication bias in psychiatry? An example from three meta-analyses of schizophrenia. *European Psychiatry, 20* (8), 550–553.

Martinez, C. R., Jr., & Eddy, J. M. (2005). Effects of culturally adapted parent management training on Latino youth behavioral health outcomes. *Journal of Consulting and Clinical Psychology, 73* (5), 841–851.

Martinussen, R., Hayden, J., Hogg-Johnson, S., & Tannock, R. (2005). A meta-analysis of working memory impairments in children with attention-deficit/hyperactivity disorder. *Journal of the American Academy of Child and Adolescent Psychiatry, 44* (4), 377–384.

Martsch, M. D. (2005). A comparison of two group interventions for adolescent aggression: High process versus low process. *Research on Social Work Practice, 15* (1), 8–18.

Mash, E. J., & Hunsley, J. (2005). Evidence-based assessment of child and adolescent disorders: Issues and challenges. *Journal of Clinical Child and Adolescent Psychology, 34* (3), 362–379. Special issue on evidence-based assessment.

Masia-Warner, C., Nangle, D. W., & Hansen, D. J. (2006). Bringing evidence-based child mental health services to the schools: General issues and specific populations. *Education and Treatment of Children, 29* (2), 165–172.

Masters, K. J., & Bellonci, C. (2001). The HCFA one-hour rule. *Journal of the American Academy of Child and Adolescent Psychiatry, 40* (11), 1243–1244.

Masui, C., & DeCorte, E. (2005). Learning to reflect and to attribute constructively as basic components of self-regulated learning. *British Journal of Educational Psychology, 75* (3), 351–372.

Matthews, L., & Mahoney, A. (2005). Facilitating a smooth transitional process for immigrant Caribbean children: The role of teachers, social workers, and related professional staff. *Journal of Ethnic and Cultural Diversity in Social Work, 14* (1/2), 69–92.

Mattison, R. E. (2000). School consultation: A review of research on issues unique to the school environment. *Journal of the American Academy of Child and Adolescent Psychiatry, 39* (4), 402–413.

Maughan, D. R., Christiansen, E., Jenson, W. R., Olympia, D., & Clark, E. (2005). Behavioral parent training as a treatment for externalizing behaviors and disruptive behavior disorders: A meta-analysis. *School Psychology Review, 34* (3), 267–286.

Maxwell, K. L., McWilliam, R. A., Hemmeter, M. L., Ault, M. J., & Schuster, J. W. (2001). Predictors of developmentally appropriate classroom practices in kindergarten through third grade. *Early Childhood Research Quarterly, 16* (4), 431–452.

Maynard, R. A. (Ed.) (1996). *Kids having kids: A Robin Hood Foundation special report on the costs of adolescent childbearing.* New York: Robin Hood Foundation.

McCart, M. R., Priester, P. E., Davies, W. H., & Azen, R. (2006). Differential effectiveness of behavioral parent training and cognitive-behavioral therapy for anti-social youth: A meta-analysis. *Journal of Abnormal Child Psychology, 34* (4), 527–543.

McCloskey, D. M., Hess, R. S., & D'Amato, R. C. (2003). Evaluating the utility of the Spanish version of the Behavior Assessment System for Children—Parent report system. *Journal of Psychoeducational Assessment, 21* (4), 325–337.

McConaughy, S. H. (2005). Direct observational assessment during test aessions and child clinical interviews. *School Psychology Review, 34* (4), 490–506.

McConaughy, S. H., & Achenbach, T. M. (2004). *Manual for the Test Observation Form for Ages 2–18.* Burlington, VT: Research Center for Children, Youth, and Families, University of Vermont.

McCormick, M. C. (2003). The autism "epidemic": Impressions from the perspective of immunization safety review. *Ambulatory Pediatrics, 3* (3), 119–120.

McDiarmid, M. D., & Bagner, D. M. (2005). Parent child interaction therapy for children with disruptive behavior and developmental disabilities. *Education and Treatment of Children, 28* (2), 130–141.

McDonald, S.-K., Keesler, V. A., Kauffman, N. J., & Schneider, B. (2006). Scaling-up exemplary interventions. *Educational Researcher, 35* (3), 15–24.

McGrath, P. A., & Gillespie, J. (2001). Pain assessment in children and adolescents. In D. C. Turk & R. Melzack (Eds.), *Handbook of pain assessment* (2nd ed., pp. 97–118). New York: Guilford.

McKay, M. M., Harrison, M. E., Gonzales, J., Kim, L., & Quintana, E. (2002). Multiple-family groups for urban children with conduct difficulties and their families. *Psychiatric Services, 53* (11), 1467–1468.

McKay, M. M., Nudelman, R., McCadem, K., & Gonzalez, J. (1996). Evaluating a social work engagement approach to involving inner-city children and their families in mental health care. *Research on Social Work Practice, 6* (4), 462–472.

McNeill, T. (2006). Evidence-based practice in an age of relativism: Toward a model for practice. *Social Work, 51* (2), 147–156.

Meiland, J. W. (1999). Category mistake. In R. Audi (Ed.), *The Cambridge dictionary of philosophy* (2nd ed., p. 123). Cambridge, UK: Cambridge University Press.

Meline, T., & Paradiso, T. (2003). Evidence-based practice in schools: Evaluating research and reducing barriers. *Language, Speech, and Hearing Services in Schools, 34* (4), 273–283.

Mellard, D. (2004). Responsiveness to intervention: Implementation in schools. Retrieved August 7, 2007, from http://www.schwablearning.org/articles.aspx?r=1057

Mercer, C. D., Jordan, L., Allsopp, D. H., & Mercer, A. R. (1996). Learning disabilities definitions and criteria used by state education departments. *Learning Disability Quarterly, 19* (4), 217–232.

Mercer, J., Sarner, L., & Rosa, L. (2003). *Attachment therapy on trial: The torture and death of Candace Newmaker.* Westport, CT: Praeger.

Meyer, J. R., Reppucci, N. D., & Owen, J. A. (2006). Criminalizing childhood: The shifting boundaries of responsibility in the justice and school systems. In K. Freeark, & W. S. Davidson, II (Eds.), *The crisis in youth mental health: Critical issues and effective programs, Vol. 3: Issues for families, schools, and communities* (pp. 219–247). Westport, CT: Praeger.

Milgram, S. (1967). The small world problem. *Psychology Today, 1* (1), 60–67.

Millar, D. S. (2003). Age of majority, transfer of rights and guardianship: Considerations for families and educators. *Education and Training in Developmental Disabilities, 38* (4), 378–397.

Miller, M. G. (2006). Letter to the editor: Comment. *Child Maltreatment, 11* (1), 95–97. Critique of Geeraert.

Miller, D. N., George, M. P., & Fogt, J. B. (2005). Establishing and sustaining research-based practices at Centennial School: A descriptive case study of systemic change. *Psychology in the Schools, 42* (5), 553–567.

Miller, V. A., & Feeny, N. C. (2003). Modification of cognitive-behavioral techniques in the treatment of a five year-old girl with social phobia. *Journal of Contemporary Psychotherapy, 33* (4), 303–319.

Mithaug, D. K., & Mithaug, D. E. (2003). The effects of choice opportunities and self-regulation training on the self-engagement and learning of young children with disabilities. In D. E. Mithaug, & D. K. Mithaug (Eds.), *Self-determined learning theory: Construction, verification, and evaluation* (pp. 141–157). Mahwah, NJ: Lawrence Erlbaum.

Moncloa, F., Johns, M., Gong, E. J., Russell, S., Lee, F., & West, E. (2003). Best practices in teen pregnancy prevention practitioner handbook. *Journal of Extension, 41* (2).

Monette, D. R., Sullivan, T. J., & DeJong, C. R. (2002). *Applied social research: Tool for the human services* (5th ed.). Belmont, CA: Wadsworth.

Montgomery, K. (2000). Classroom rubrics: Systematizing what teachers do naturally. *The Clearing House, 73* (6), 324–328.

Moore, K. J., Fifield, M. B., Spira, D. A., & Scarlato, M. (1989). Child study team decision making in special education: Improving the process. *Remedial and Special Education, 10* (4), 50–58.

Morgan, B., & Hensley, L. (1998). Supporting working mothers through group work: A multimodal psychoeducational approach. *Journal for Specialists in Group Work, 23* (3), 298–311.

Morris, R. D. (2004). Clinical trials as a model for intervention research studies in education. In P. McCardle & V. Chharbra (Eds.), *The voice of evidence in reading research* (pp. 127–149). Baltimore, MD: Paul H. Brookes.

Morrison, K. (2001). Randomised controlled trials for evidence-based education: Some problems in judging "what works." *Evaluation and Research in Education, 15* (2), 69–83.

Mowbray, C. T., Holter, M. C., Teague, G. B., & Bybee, D. (2003). Fidelity criteria: Development, measurement, and validation. *American Journal of Evaluation, 24* (3), 315–340.

Moyer, L. S., & deRosenroll, D. A. (1984). Goal attainment scaling: Its use with pregnant and single-parent teenagers in an alternative education setting. *Canadian Counsellor, 18* (3), 111–116.

Mulick, J. A., & Butter, E. M. (2005). Positive behavior support: A paternalistic utopian delusion. In J. W. Jacobson, R. M. Foxx, & J. A. Mulick (Eds.), *Controversial therapies for developmental disabilities: Fad, fashion and science in professional practice* (pp. 385–404). Mahwah, NJ: Lawrence Erlbaum.

Mullen, E. J., & Dumpson, J. R. (Eds.) (1972). *Evaluation of social intervention.* San Francisco: Jossey-Bass.

Mulrow, C. D. (1995). Rationale for systematic reviews. In I. Chalmers & D. G. Altman (Eds.), *Systematic reviews* (pp. 1–8). London: BMJ.

Munger, R. L. (2000). Comprehensive needs-based assessment with adolescents. In W. E. Martin, Jr., & J. L. Swartz-Kulstad (Eds.), *Person-environment psychology and mental health: Assessment and intervention* (pp. 11–37). Mahwah, NJ: Lawrence Erlbaum.

Murdock, S. G., O'Neill, R. E., & Cunningham, E. (2005). A comparison of results and acceptability of functional behavioral assessment procedures with a group of middle school students with emotional/behavioral disorders (E/BD). *Journal of Behavioral Education, 14* (1), 5–18.

Murphy, J. J. (1999). Common factors of school-based change. In M. A. Hubble, B. L. Duncan, & S. D. Miller (Eds.), *The heart and soul of change: What works in therapy* (pp. 361–388). Washington, DC: American Psychological Association.

Murphy, J. I. (2005). How to learn, not what to learn: Three strategies that foster lifelong learning in clinical settings. *Annual Review of Nursing Education, 3,* 37–55.

Nathan, P. E., Stuart, S. P., & Dolan, S. L. (2000). Research on psychotherapy efficacy and effectiveness: Between Scylla and Charybdis? *Psychological Bulletin, 126* (6), 964–981.

National Advisory Mental Health Council (2001). *Blueprint for change: Research on child and adolescent mental health.* Washington, DC: National Institute of Mental Health. Retrieved May 19, 2006, from http://www. nimh.nih.gov/publicat/nimhblueprint.pdf

National Association of School Psychologists (2000a). *Principles for professional ethics.* Bethesda, MD: National Association of School Psychologists.

National Association of School Psychologists (2000b). *Guidelines for the provision of school psychological services.* Bethesda, MD: National Association of School Psychologists.

National Association of Social Workers (1999). *NASW code of ethics.* Washington, DC: National Association of Social Workers.

National Association of Social Workers (2002). *NASW standards for school social work services.* Washington, DC: National Association of Social Workers.

National Association of State Directors of Special Education (2006). *Response to Intervention: Policy considerations and implementation.* Alexandria, VA: National Association of State Directors of Special Education.

Navarro, A. M. (1993). The effectiveness of psychotherapy with Latinos in the United States: A metaanalytic review [Spanish]. Efectividad de las psicoterapias con latinos en los Estados Unidos: Una revision meta-analitica. *Revista Interamericana de Psicologia, 27* (2), 131–146.

Nelson, M. L. (2002). An assessment-based model for counseling strategy selection. *Journal of Counseling and Development, 80* (4), 416–421.

Nelson, J. C. (2004). Tricyclic and tetracyclic drugs. In A. F. Schatzberg & C. B. Nemeroff (Eds.), *The American Psychiatric Publishing textbook of psychopharmacology* (3rd ed., pp. 207–230). Washington, DC: American Psychiatric Publishing.

Nelson, T. D., Steele, R. G., & Mize, J. A. (2006). Practitioner attitudes toward evidence-based practice: Themes and challenges. *Adminstration and Policy in Mental Health and Mental Health Services Research, 33* (3), 398–409.

Nixon, R. D. V., Sweeney, L., Erickson, D. B., & Touyz, S. W. (2003). Parent-child interaction therapy: A comparison of standard and abbreviated treatments for oppositional defiant preschoolers. *Journal of Consulting and Clinical Psychology, 71* (2), 251–260.

Nixon, R. D. V., Sweeney, L., Erickson, D. B., & Touyz, S. W. (2004). Parent-child interaction therapy: One- and two-year follow-up of standard and abbreviated treatments for oppositional preschoolers. *Journal of Abnormal Child Psychology, 32* (3), 263–271.

No Child Left Behind Act of 2001. PL 107-110. 115 Stat. 1425 (2002).

Nock, M. K., Goldman, J. L., Wang, Y., & Albano, A. M. (2004). From science to practice: The flexible use of evidence-based treatments in clinical settings. *Journal of the American Academy of Child and Adolescent Psychiatry, 43* (6), 777–780.

Nolan, M., & Carr, A. (2000). Attention deficit hyperactivity disorder. In A. Carr (Ed.), *What works for children and adolescents? A critical review of psychological interventions with children, adolescents, and their families* (pp. 65–101). London: Brunner-Routledge.

Oder, N. (2000). Web estimated at seven million sites. *Library Journal, 125* (9), 16–17.

Odom, S. L., & Strain, P. S. (2002). Evidence-based practice in early intervention/early childhood special education: Single-subject design research. *Journal of Early Intervention, 25* (2), 151–160.

O'Donnell, J., Hawkins, J. D., Catalano, R. F., Abbott, R. D., & Day, L. E. (1995). Preventing school failure, drug use, and delinquency among low-income children: Long-term intervention in elementary schools. *American Journal of Orthopsychiatry, 65* (1), 87–100.

Ogden, T., & Hagen, K. A. (2006). Multisystemic treatment of serious behaviour problems in youth: Sustainability of effectiveness two years after intake. *Child and Adolescent Mental Health, 11* (3), 142–149.

O'Halloran, M., & Carr, A. (2000). Adjustment to parental separation and divorce. In A. Carr (Ed.), *What works with children and adolescents? A critical review of psychological interventions with children, adolescents and their families* (pp. 280–299). London: Brunner-Routledge

O'Leary, M. (2000). Invisible web discovers hidden treasures. *Information Today, 17* (1), 16–18.

O'Leary, K., & Borkovec, T. (1978). Conceptual, methodological, and ethical problems of placebo groups in psychotherapy groups. *American Psychologist, 33* (9), 821–830.

Ollendick, T. H., & Davis, T. E. (2004). Empirically supported treatments for children and adolescents: Where to from here? *Clinical Psychology: Science and Practice, 11* (3), 289–294.

Olson, L., & Viadero, D. (2002, January 30). Law mandates scientific base for research. *Education Week, 21* (20), 1, 14–15.

O'Reilly, C., Northcraft, G. B., & Sabers, D. (1989). The confirmation bias in special education eligibility decisions. *School Psychology Review, 18* (1), 126–135.

O'Rourke, J., & Houghton, S. (2006). Students with mild disabilities in regular classrooms: The development and utility of the Student Perceptions of Classroom Support Scale. *Journal of Intellectual and Developmental Disability, 31* (4), 232–242.

Orrell-Valente, J. K., Pinderhughes, E. E., Valente, E., Jr., & Laird, R. D. (1999). If it's offered, will they come? Influences on parents' participation in a community-based conduct problems prevention program. *American Journal of Community Psychology, 27* (6), 753–783.

O'Sullivan, D. (2006). Meta-analysis. In G. M. Breakwell, S. Hammond, C. Fife-Schaw, & J. A. Smith (Eds.), *Research methods in psychology* (3rd ed., pp. 466–481). London: Sage.

Oswald, D. P. (2002). The new medical model and beyond: A response to Forness and Kavale. *Behavioral Disorders, 27* (2), 155–157.

O'Toole, M. E. (1999, July). *The school shooter: A threat assessment perspective.* Quantico, VA: U.S. Department of Justice/Federal Bureau of Investigation. Retrieved May 19, 2002, from http://www.fbi.gov/publications/school/school2.pdf

Overbay, A. S., Grable, L. L., & Vasu, E. S. (2006). Evidence-based education: Postcards from the edge. *Journal of Technology and Teacher Education, 14* (3), 623–632.

Oxman, A. D. (1995). Checklists for review articles. In I. Chalmers & D. G. Altman (Eds.), *Systematic reviews* (pp. 75–85). London: BMJ.

Oyserman, D., Terry, K., & Bybee, D. (2002). A possible selves intervention to enhance school involvement. *Journal of Adolescence, 25* (2), 313–326.

Palmer, S. B., & Wehmeyer, M. L. (2003). Promoting self-determination in early elementary school: Teaching self-regulated problem-solving and goal-setting skills. *Remedial and Special Education, 24* (2), 115–126.

Panzano, P. C., & Roth, D. (2006). The decision to adopt evidence-based and other innovative mental health practices: Risky business? *Psychiatric Services, 57* (8), 1153–1161.

Pardeck, J. T. (1996). *Social work practice: An ecological approach.* Westport, CT: Auburn House.

Parker, S. K., Schwartz, B., Todd, J., & Pickering, L. K. (2004). Thimerosal-containing vaccines and autism spectrum disorder: A critical review of published original data. *Pediatrics, 114* (3), 793–804.

Parrish, P. (1992). *Amelia Bedelia.* New York: Harper Trophy.

Pate, P. E., Homestead, E., & McGinnis, K. (1993). Designing rubrics for authentic assessment. *Middle School Journal, 25* (2), 25–27.

Paternite, C. E. (2005). School-based mental health programs and services: Overview and introduction to the special issue. *Journal of Abnormal Child Psychology, 33* (6), 657–663.

Patterson, G. R. (1976). *Living with children: New methods for parents and teachers.* Champaign, IL: Research Press.

Patterson, D. A. (2006). Using the school's database system to construct accountability tools. In C. Franklin, M. B. Harris, & P. Allen-Meares (Eds.), *School social work and mental health worker's training and resource manual* (pp. 1053–1060). New York: Oxford University Press.

Patterson, D. A., & Basham, R. E. (2006). *Data analysis with spreadsheets.* Boston: Pearson.

Patterson, G. R., Reid, J. B., & Dishion, T. J. (1992). *Antisocial boys.* Eugene, OR: Castalia.

Paul, H. A. (2004). Issues and controversies that surround recent texts on empirically supported and empirically based treatments. *Child and Family Behavior Therapy, 26* (3), 37–51.

Paul, R., & Elder, L. (2004). *The thinker's guide to fallacies: The art of mental trickery and manipulation.* Dillon Beach, CA: Foundation for Critical Thinking. www.criticalthinking.org

Pearson Education (2007). BASC-2 Behavior Assessment System for Children (2nd ed.). Retrieved June 5, 2007, from http://ags.pearsonassessments.com/Group.asp?nGroupInfoID=a30000

Pelham, W. E., Jr., Fabiano, G. A., & Massetti, G. M. (2005). Evidence-based assessment of attention deficit/hyperactivity disorder in children and adolescents. *Journal of Clinical Child and Adolescent Psychology, 34* (3), 449–476.

Pelham, W. E., Jr., Greiner, A. R., & Gnagy, E. M. (1998). *Children's summer treatment program manual.* Buffalo, NY: State University of New York (SUNY) at Buffalo.

Pemberton, J. B. (2003). Communicating academic progress as an integral part of assessment. *Teaching Exceptional Children, 35* (4), 16–20.

Perelman, L. J. (1992). *School's out: Hyperlearning, the new technology, and the end of education.* New York: William Morrow.

Perske, R. (1972). The dignity of risk. In W. Wolfensberger (Ed.), *Normalization: The principle of normalization in human services* (pp. 176–200). Toronto, ON: National Institute on Mental Retardation.

Petrie, J., Bunn, F., & Byrne, G., (2007). Parenting programmes for preventing tobacco, alcohol or drugs misuse in children: A systematic review. *Health Education Research, 22* (2), 177–191.

Petrosino, A., Turpin-Petrosino, C., & Buehler, J. (2003). Scared Straight and other juvenile awareness programs for preventing juvenile delinquency: A systematic review of the randomized experimental evidence. *Annals of the American Academy of Political and Social Science, 589,* 41–62.

Piacentini, J., & Bergman, R. L. (2001). Developmental issues in cognitive therapy for childhood anxiety disorders. *Journal of Cognitive Psychotherapy, 15* (3), 165–182.

Pina, A. A., Silverman, W. K., Fuentes, R. M., Kurtines, W. M., & Weems, C. F. (2003). Exposure-based cognitive-behavioral treatment for phobic and anxiety disorders: Treatment effects and maintenance for Hispanic/Latino relative to European-American youths. *Journal of the American Academy of Child and Adolescent Psychiatry, 42* (10), 1179–1187.

Pollack, D., & Marsh, J. (2004). Social work misconduct may lead to liability. *Social Work, 49* (4), 609–612.

Pollio, D. E. (2006). The art of evidence-based practice. *Research on Social Work Practice, 16* (2), 224–232.

Potter, W. Z., Padich, R. A., Rudorfer, M. V., & Krishnan, K. R. R. (2006). Tricyclics, tetracyclics, and monomine oxidase inhibitors. In D. J. Stein, D. J. Kupfer, & A. F. Schatzberg (Eds.), *The American Psychiatric Publishing textbook of mood disorders* (pp. 251–261). Washington, DC: American Psychiatric Publishing.

Power, T. J., Werba, B. E., Watkins, M. W., Angelucci, J. G., & Eiraldi, R. B. (2006). Patterns of parent-reported homework problems among ADHD-referred and non-referred children. *School Psychology Quarterly, 21* (1), 13–33.

Powers, J. D. (2005). *Evidence-based practice in schools: Current status, potential barriers, and critical next steps.* Unpublished doctoral dissertation, School of Social Work, The University of North Carolina at Chapel Hill. UMI number: 3200835.

President's Commission on Excellence in Special Education (2002). *A new era: Revitalizing special education for children and their families.* Washington, DC:

Office of Special Education and Rehabilitative Services, U.S. Department of Education. Retrieved May 19, 2004, from http:www.ed.gov/inits/commissionsboards/whspecialeducation/reports/images/Pres_Rep.pdf

President's New Freedom Commission on Mental Health (2003). *Achieving the promise: Transforming mental health care in America. Final report for the President's New Freedom Commission on Mental Health (SMA publication No. 03-3832).* Rockville, MD: President's New Freedom Commission on Mental Health. Retrieved April 7, 2007, from http://www.mentalhealth-commission.gov/reports/FinalReport/downloads/FinalReport.pdf

Price, G., & Sherman, C. (2001). Exploring the invisible web: 7 essential strategies. *Online, 25* (4), 32–34.

Prochaska, J. O., & DiClemente, C. C. (2005). The transtheoretical approach. In J. C. Norcross & M. R. Goldfried (Eds.), *Handbook of psychotherapy integration* (2nd ed., pp. 147–171). New York: Oxford University Press.

Ragan, N. W. (2000). *Strategies for resolving conflicts.* ERIC document no. ED 453–458. Washington, DC: U.S. Department of Education.

Rahill, S. A., & Teglasi, H. (2003). Processes and outcomes of story-based and skill-based social competency programs for children with emotional disabilities. *Journal of School Psychology, 41* (6), 413–429.

Raines, J. C. (2002a). Brainstorming hypotheses for functional behavioral assessment: The link to effective behavioral intervention plans. *School Social Work Journal, 26* (2), 30–45.

Raines, J. C. (2002b). Present levels of performance, goals, and objectives: A best practice guide. *School Social Work Journal, 27* (1), 68–72.

Raines, J. C. (2003a). Rating the rating scales: Ten criteria to use. *School Social Work Journal, 27* (2), 1–17.

Raines, J. C. (2003b). Multiple intelligences and social work practice for students with learning disabilities. *School Social Work Journal, 28* (1), 1–20.

Raines, J. C. (2004a). Evidence-based practice in school social work: A process in perspective. *Children and Schools, 26* (2), 71–85.

Raines, J. C. (2004b). To tell or not to tell: Ethical issues regarding confidentiality. *School Social Work Journal, 28* (2), 61–78.

Raines, J. C. (2006a). Improving educational and behavioral performances of students with learning disabilities. In C. Franklin, M. B. Harris, & P. Allen-Meares (Eds), *School social work and mental health worker's training and resource manual* (pp. 201–212). New York: Oxford University Press.

Raines, J. C. (2006b). SWOT! A strategic plan for school social work in the twenty-first century. *School Social Work Journal* (Special issue), 132–150.

Raines, J. C. (2006c). The new IDEA: Reflections on the reauthorization. *School Social Work Journal, 31* (1), 1–18.

Raines, J. C. (2008). Evaluating qualitative research studies. In R. M. Grinnell, Jr., & Y. A. Unrau (Eds.), *Social work research and evaluation* (8th ed., pp. 445–461). New York: Oxford University Press.

Raines, J. C., & Massat, C. R. (2004). Getting published: A guide for the aspiring practitioner. *School Social Work Journal, 29* (1), 1–17.

Ray, D., & Bratton, S. (1999, October). Update: What the research shows about play therapy. Presented at the Annual Conference of the Association for Play Therapy in Baltimore, MD. Retrieved June 18, 2007, from http://www.a4pt.org/download.cfm?ID=10935

Reamer, F. G. (1983). The concept of paternalism in social work. *Social Service Review, 57* (2), 254–271.

Reamer, F. G. (2006a). Nontraditional and unorthodox interventions in social work: Ethical and legal implications. *Families in Society, 87* (2), 191–197.

Reamer, F. G. (2006b). *Social work values and ethics* (3rd ed.). New York: Columbia University Press.

Regehr, C., Stern, S., & Shlonsky, A. (2007). Operationalizing evidence-based practice: The development of an institute for evidence-based social work. *Research on Social Work Practice, 17* (3), 408–416.

Reid, W. J. (1992). *Task strategies: An empirical approach to clinical social work.* New York: Columbia University Press.

Reissland, N., Shepherd, J., & Herrera, E., (2003). The pitch of maternal voice: A comparison of mothers suffering from depressed mood and non-depressed mothers reading books to their infants. *Journal of Child Psychology and Psychiatry, 44* (2), 255–261.

Repetti, R. (1996). The effects of perceived daily social and academic failure experiences on school-age children's subsequent interactions with parents. *Child Development, 67,* 1467–1482.

Resnicow, K., Cohn, L., Reinhardt, J., Cross, D., Futterman, R., Kirscher, E., et al. (1992). A three-year evaluation of the Know Your Body program in inner-city school children. *Health Education Quarterly, 19,* 463–480.

Reynolds, C. R., & Kamphaus, R. W. (2004). *Behavior assessment system for children* (2nd ed.). Circle Pines, MN: American Guidance System.

Ribordy, S. C., Camras, L. A., Stefani, R., & Spaccarelli, S. (1988). Vignettes for emotion recognition research and affective therapy with children. *Journal of Clinical Child Psychology, 17*(4), 322–325.

Richardson, W. S., & Detsky, A. S. (1995). Users' guides to the medical literature VII. How to use a clinical decision analysis B. What are the results and will they help me in caring for my patients? *JAMA, 273* (20), 1610–1613.

Ringwalt, C., Ennett, S. T., Vincus, A. A., Rohrbach, L. A., & Simons-Rudolf, A. (2004). Who's calling the shots? Decision-makers and the adoption of effective school-based substance use prevention curricula. *Journal of Drug Education, 34* (1), 19–31.

Roach, A. T., & Elliot, S. N. (2005). Goal attainment scaling: An efficient and effective approach to monitoring student progress. *Teaching Exceptional Children, 37* (4), 8–17.

Roach, A. T., & Kratochwill, T. R. (2004). Evaluating school climate and school culture. *Teaching Exceptional Children, 37* (1), 10–17.

Roberts, R. E., Attkinson, C. C., & Rosenblatt, A. (1998). Prevalence of psychopathology among children and adolescents. *American Journal of Psychiatry, 155,* 715–722.

Roberts, A. R., & Yeager, K. (2004). Systematic reviews of evidence-based studies and practice-based research: How to search for, develop, and use them. In A. R. Roberts & K. Yeager (Eds.), *Evidence-based practice manual: Research and outcome measures in health and human services* (pp. 3–14). New York: Oxford University Press.

Rohrbach, L. A., Ringwalt, C. L., Ennett, S. T., & Vincus, A. A. (2005). Factors associated with adoption of evidence-based substance use prevention curricula in US school districts. *Health Education Research, 20* (5), 514–526.

Romanczyk, R. G., Arnstein, L., Soorya, L. V., & Gillis, J. (2003). The myriad of controversial treatments for autism: A critical evaluation of efficacy. In S. O. Lilienfeld, S. J. Lynn, & J. M. Lohr (Eds.), *Science and pseudoscience in clinical psychology* (pp. 363–395). New York: Guilford.

Romeo, R., Byford, S., & Knapp, M. (2005). Annotation: Economic evaluations of child and adolescent mental health interventions: A systematic review. *Journal of Child Psychology and Psychiatry, 46* (9), 919–930.

Rones, M., & Hoagwood, K. (2000). School-based mental health services: A research review. *Clinical Child and Family Psychology Review, 3* (4), 223–241.

Rosen, A. (2003). Evidence-based social work practice: Challenges and promise. *Social Work Research, 27* (4), 197–208.

Rosenthal, R. (1979). The "file drawer" problem and tolerance for null results. *Psychological Bulletin, 86,* 638–641.

Rosselló, J., & Bernal, G. (1999). The efficacy of cognitive-behavioral and interpersonal treatments for depression in Puerto Rican adolescents. *Journal of Consulting and Clinical Psychology, 67* (5), 734–745.

Ross-Fisher, R. L. (2005). Developing effective success rubrics. *Kappa Delta Pi Record, 41* (3), 131–135.

Rothstein, B. J. (2005). Bringing science to law. *American Journal of Public Health, 95* (Suppl. 1), S4. Retrieved August 29, 2006, from http://www. DefendingScience.org. Editorial introduction to a special issue on scientific evidence and public policy.

Rowe, C., Parker-Sloat, E., Schwartz, S., & Liddle, H. (2003). Family therapy for early adolescent substance abuse. In S. J. Stevens & A. R. Morral (Eds.), *Adolescent substance abuse treatment in the United States: Exemplary models from a national evaluation study* (pp. 105–132). New York: Haworth.

Roysircar-Sodowsky, G., & Frey, I. L. (2003). Children of immigrants: Their worldviews value conflicts. In P. B. Pedersen & J. C. Carey (Eds.), *Multicultural counseling in schools: A practical handbook* (2nd ed., pp. 61–83). Needham Heights, MA: Allyn & Bacon.

Rubin, M. H. (2007). Is there a doctor in the house? *Journal of Medical Ethics, 33* (3), 158–159.

Rubin, A., & Parrish, D. (2007). Challenges to the future of evidence-based practice in social work education. *Journal of Social Work Education, 43* (3), 405–428.

Ruscio, A. M., & Holohan, D. R. (2006). Applying empirically supported treatments to complex cases: Ethical, empirical, and practical considerations. *Clinical Psychology: Science and Practice, 13* (2), 146–161.

Saari, C. (1986). *Clinical social work treatment: How does it work?* New York: Gardner.

Sackett, D. L., Rosenberg, W. M. C., Gray, J. A. M., Haynes, R. B., & Richardson, W. S. (1996). Evidence-based medicine: What it is and what it is not. *British Medical Journal, 312,* 71–72. Editorial.

Sackett, D. L., Strauss, S. E., Richardson, W. S., Rosenberg, W., & Haynes, R. B. (2000). *Evidence-based medicine: How to practice and teach EBM* (2nd ed.). Edinburgh: Churchill Livingstone.

Sadler, J. E., & Blom, G. E. (1970). "Standby": A clinical research study of child deviant behavior in a psychoeducational setting. *Journal of Special Education, 4* (1), 89–103.

Saleebey, D. (1996). The strengths perspective in social work practice: Extensions and cautions. *Social Work, 41* (3), 296–305.

Saleebey, D. (2002). The strengths perspective: possibilities and problems. In D. Saleebey (Ed.), *The strengths perspective in social work practice* (3rd ed., pp. 264–286). Boston: Allyn & Bacon.

Salloum, A., Avery, L., & McClain, R. P. (2001). Group psychotherapy for adolescent survivors of homicide victims: A pilot study. *Journal of the American Academy of Child and Adolescent Psychiatry, 40* (11), 1261–1267.

Sampson, E. L., Ritchie, C. W., Lai, R., Raven, P. W., & Blanchard, M. R. (2005). A systematic review of the scientific evidence for the efficacy of a palliative care approach in advanced dementia. *International Psychogeriatrics, 17* (1), 31–40.

Samuels, C. A. (2007, May 9). Lack of research, data hurts dropout efforts, experts say. *Education Week, 26* (36), 8–9.

Sanders, D. G., & Kiester, A. E. (1996). School-based counseling groups for children of divorce: Effects on the self-concepts of 5th grade children. *Journal of Child and Adolescent Group Therapy, 6* (1), 27–42.

Sanders, M. R., & Turner, K. M. T. (2005). Reflections on the challenges of effective dissemination of behavioural family intervention: Our experience with the Triple P—Positive parenting program. *Child and Adolescent Mental Health, 10* (4), 158–169.

Sandieson, R. (2006). Pathfinding in the research forest: The pearl harvesting method for effective information retrieval. *Education and Training in Developmental Disabilities, 41* (4), 401–409.

Santelli, J., Ott, M. A., Lyon, M., Rogers, J., & Summers, D. (2006). Abstinence-only education policies and programs: A position paper of the Society of Adolescent Medicine. *Journal of Adolescent Health, 38,* 83–87. Retrieved May 19, 2007, from http://www.adolescenthealth.org/PositionPaper_Abstinence_only_edu_policies_and_programs.pdf

Santisteban, D. A., Muir-Malcolm, J. A., Mitrani, V. B., & Szapocznik, J. (2002). Integrating the study of ethnic culture and family psychology intervention science. In H. A. Liddle, D. A. Santisteban, R. F. Levant, & J. H. Bray (Eds.), *Family psychology: Science-based interventions* (pp. 331–351). Washington, DC: American Psychological Association.

Santora, M., & Hauser, C. (2007, April 19). Students knew killer's demons by his writings. *New York Times,* Sec. A, Col. 2, p. 1. Electronic version. Retrieved May 19, 2007, from http://www.nytimes.com/

Saudargas, R. A. (1997). *State-event classroom observation system (SECOS) observation manual.* Knoxville, TN: University of Tennessee.

Schab, D. W., & Trinh, N.-H. T. (2004). Do artificial food colors promote hyperactivity in children with hyperactive syndromes? A meta-analysis of double-blind placebo-controlled trials. *Journal of Developmental and Behavioral Pediatrics, 25* (6), 423–434.

Schacter, D., Kleinman, I., & Harvey, W. (2005). Informed consents and adolescents. *Canadian Journal of Psychiatry, 50* (9), 534–540.

Schaeffer, C. M., Bruns, E., Weist, M., Stephan, S. H., Goldstein, J., Simpson, Y. (2005). Overcoming challenges to using evidence-based interventions in schools. *Journal of Youth and Adolescence, 34* (1), 15–22.

Scheflin, A. W. (2000). The evolving standard of care in the practice of trauma and dissociative disorder therapy. *Bulletin of the Menninger Clinic, 64* (2), 197–234.

Schill, M. T., Kratochwill, T. R., & Elliott, S. N. (1998). Functional assessment in behavioral consultation: A treatment utility study. *School Psychology Quarterly, 13* (2), 116–140.

Schorre, B. E. H., & Vandvik, I. H. (2004). Global assessment of psychosocial functioning in child and adolescent psychiatry: A review of three unidimensional scales (CGAS, GAP, GAPD). *European Child and Adolescent Psychiatry, 13* (5), 273–286.

Schulte, B., & Jenkins, C. L. (2007, May 7). Cho didn't get court-ordered treatment. *Washington Post,* Sec. A, p. 1. Electronic version. Retrieved May 24, 2007, from http://www.washingtonpost.com/wp-dyn/content/article/2007/05/06/AR2007050601403

Schultz, L. H., Selman, R. L., & LaRusso, M. D. (2003). The assessment of psychosocial maturity in children and adolescents: Implications for the evaluation of school-based character education programs. *Journal of Research in Character Education, 1* (2), 67–87.

Schurink, I., Schippers, G. M., & de Wildt, W. A. J. M. (2004). Family therapy in treating adolescents with substance abuse problems. A review of the literature [Dutch]. Gezinstherapie bij de behandeling van adolescenten met verslavingsproblemen: Een literatuuroverzicht. *Gedrag & Gezondheid: Tijdschrift voor Psychologie en Gezondheid, 32* (3), 203–214.

Sciutto, M. J., Terjesen, M. D., & Bender-Frank, A. S. (2000). Teachers' knowledge and misperceptions of attention-deficit/hyperactivity disorder. *Psychology in the Schools, 37* (2), 115–122.

Secemsky, V. O., & Ahlman, C. (2003). Proposed guidelines for school social workers seeking clinical supervision: How to choose a supervisor. *School Social Work Journal, 27* (2), 79–88.

Sedlak M. W. (1997). The uneasy alliance of mental health services and the schools: An historical perspective. *American Journal of Orthopsychiatry, 67,* 349–362.

Seethaler, P. M., & Fuchs, L. S. (2005). A drop in the bucket: Randomized controlled trials testing reading and math interventions. *Learning Disabilities Research and Practice, 20* (2), 98–102.

Seitz, V., & Apfel, N. H. (1999). Effective interventions for adolescent mothers. *Clinical Psychology: Science and Practice, 6* (1), 50–66.

Seper, J. (2007, April 20). A signal of deadly violence to come. *Washington Times* [DC]. Electronic version. Accession number: 4KB520070420064542002. Retrieved May 19, 2007, from http://www.washingtontimes.com/

Shadish, W. R. (1995). The logic of generalization: Five principles common to experiments and ethnographies. *American Journal of Community Psychology, 23,* 419–428.

Shaffer, D., Gould, M. S., Brasic, J., Ambrosini, P., Fisher, P., Bird, H., et al. (1983). A children's global assessment scale (CGAS). *Archives of General Psychiatry, 40,* 1228–1231.

Shapiro, E. S. (2004). *Academic skills problems workbook* (rev. ed.). New York: Guilford.

Shapiro, E. S., & Heick, P. (2004). School psychologist assessment practices in the evaluation of students refined for social/behavioral/emotional problems. *Psychology in the Schools, 41,* 551–561.

Shapiro, E. S., & Kratochwill, T. R. (2000). Introduction: Conducting a multidimensional behavioral assessment. In E. S. Shapiro & T. R. Kratochwill (Eds.), *Conducting school-based assessments of child and adolescent behavior* (pp. 1–20). New York: Guilford.

Shapiro, J. P., Welker, C. J., & Jacobson, B. J. (1997). A naturalistic study of psychotherapeutic methods and client-in-therapy functioning in a child community setting. *Journal of Clinical Child Psychology, 26* (4), 385–396.

Shaywitz, S. E., Fletcher, J. M., Holahan, J. M., Schneider, A. E., Marchione, K. E., Stuebing, K. K., et al. (1999). Persistence of dyslexia: The Connecticut Longitudinal Study at adolescence. *Pediatrics, 104,* 1351–1359.

Shlonsky, A., & Gibbs, L. (2006). Will the real evidence-based practice please stand up? Teaching the process of evidence-based practice to the helping professions. In A. R. Roberts & K. R. Yeager (Eds.), *Foundations of evidence-based practice* (pp. 103–121). New York: Oxford University Press.

Sholomskas, D. E., Syracuse-Siewart, G., Rounsaville, B. J., Ball, S. A., Nuro, K. F., & Carroll, K. M. (2005). We don't train in vain: A dissemination trial of three strategies of training clinicians in cognitive-behavioral therapy. *Journal of Consulting and Clinical Psychology, 73* (1), 106–115.

Silver, L. B. (2004). Attention-deficit/hyperactivity disorder. In F. M. Kline & L. B. Silver (Eds.), *The educator's guide to mental health issues in the classroom* (pp. 35–53). Baltimore, MD: Paul H. Brookes.

Sinclair, M. F., Christenson, S. L., Evelo, D. L., & Hurley, C. M. (1998). Dropout prevention for youth with disabilities: Efficacy of a sustained school engagement procedure. *Exceptional Children, 65* (1), 7–21.

Sinclair, M. F., Christenson, S. L., & Thurlow, M. L. (2005). Promoting school completion of urban secondary youth with emotional or behavioral disabilities. *Exceptional Children, 71* (4), 465–482.

Sindelar, P. T., Allman, C., Monda, L., Vail, C. O., Wilson, C. L., & Schloss, P. J. (1988). The power of hypothesis testing in special education efficacy research. *Journal of Special Education, 22* (3), 284–296.

Singh, N. N., Lancioni, G. E., O'Reilly, M. F., Molina, E. J. Adkins, A. D., & Oliva, D. (2003). Self-determination during mealtimes through microswitch choice-making by an individual with complex multiple disabilities and profound mental retardation. *Journal of Positive Behavior Interventions, 5* (4), 209–215.

Sink, C. A., & Igelman, C. N. (2004). Anxiety disorders. In F. M. Kline & L. B. Silver (Eds.), *The educator's guide to mental health issues in the classroom* (pp. 171–191). Baltimore, MD: Paul H. Brookes.

Sink, C. A., & Spencer, L. R. (2005). My Class Inventory-Short Form as an accountability tool for elementary school counselors to measure classroom climate. *Professional School Counseling, 9* (1), 37–48.

Sitlington, P. L., & Clark, G. M. (2007). Transition assessment process and IDEIA 2004. *Assessment for Effective Intervention, 32* (3), 133–142.

Skara, S., Rohrbach, L. A., Sun, P., & Sussman, S. (2005). An evaluation of the fidelity of implementation of a school-based drug abuse prevention program: Project toward no drug abuse (TND). *Journal of Drug Education, 35* (4), 305–329.

Sklare, G. B. (1997). *Brief counseling that works: A solution-focused approach for school counselors.* Thousand Oaks, CA: Corwin.

Slater, P., & McKeown, M. (2004). The role of peer counselling and support in helping to reduce anxieties around transition from primary to secondary school. *Counselling and Psychotherapy Research, 4* (1), 72–79.

Slawson, D. C., & Shaughnessy, A. F. (2005). Teaching evidence-based medicine: Should we be teaching information management instead? *Academic Medicine, 80* (7), 685–689.

Slovenko, R. (2005). Commentary: Malpractice, non-medical negligence, or breach of contract. *Journal of Psychiatry and Law, 33* (3), 445–467.

Small, M. A., Lyons, P. M., & Guy, L. S. (2002). Liability issues in child abuse and neglect reporting statutes. *Professional Psychology: Research and Practice, 33* (1), 13–18.

Smith, S. L. (2000). Creating useful individualized education programs (IEPs). ED449636 2000-12-00. *ERIC Digest,* #E600. Retrieved May 19, 2007, from http://www.eric.ed.gov/ERICDocs/data/ericdocs2sql/content_storage_01/0000019b/80/16/d3/23.pdf

Smith, M. L., Glass, G. V., & Miller, T. L. (1980). *The benefits of psychotherapy.* Baltimore: Johns Hopkins University Press.

Smith, C. A., Ireland, T. O., & Thornberry, T. P. (2005). Adolescent maltreatment and its impact on young adult antisocial behavior. *Child Abuse and Neglect, 29* (10), 1099–1119.

Solomon, Y., Warin, J., & Lewis, C. (2002). Helping with homework? Homework as a site of tension for parents and teenagers. *British Educational Research Journal, 28* (4), 603–622.

Southam-Gerow, M. A., Weisz, J. R., & Kendall, P. C. (2003). Youth with anxiety disorders in research and service clinics: Examining client differences and similarities. *Journal of Clinical Child and Adolescent Psychology, 32* (3), 375–385.

Spielmans, G. I., Pasek, L. F., & McFall, J. P. (2006). What are the active ingredients in cognitive and behavioral psychotherapy for anxious and depressed children? A meta-analytic review. *Clinical Psychology Review, 27* (5), 642–654.

Spirito, A., & Kazak, A. E. (2006). *Effective and emerging treatments in pediatric psychology.* New York: Oxford University Press.

Springer, D. W., Abell, N., & Hudson, W. (2002a). Creating and validating rapid assessment instruments for practice and research, Part 1. *Research on Social Work Practice, 12* (3), 408–439.

Springer, D. W., Abell, N., & Hudson, W. (2002b). Creating and validating rapid assessment instruments for practice and research, Part 2. *Research on Social Work Practice, 12* (6), 768–795.

Sprott, J. B., Jenkins, J. M., & Doob, A. N. (2005). The importance of school: Protecting at-risk youth from early offending. *Youth Violence and Juvenile Justice, 3* (1), 59–79.

Squires, G. (2001). Using cognitive-behavioural psychology with groups of pupils to improve self-control of behaviour. *Educational Psychology in Practice, 17* (4), 317–335.

Stathakos, P., & Roehrle, B. (2003). The effectiveness of intervention programmes for children of divorce—A meta-analysis. *International Journal of Mental Health Promotion, 5* (1), 31–37.

Steckler, A., Ethelbah, B., Martin, C. J., Stewart, D., Pardilla, M., Gittelsohn, J., et al. (2003). Pathways process evaluation results: A school-based prevention trial to promote healthful diet and physical activity in American Indian third, fourth, and fifth grade students. *Preventive Medicine, 37* (6, Pt. 2), S80–S90.

Stirman, S. W., Crits-Christoph, P., & DeRubeis, R. J. (2004). Achieving successful dissemination of empirically supported psychotherapies: A synthesis of dissemination theory. *Clinical Psychology: Science and Practice, 11* (4), 343–359.

Stone, S., & Gambrill, E. (2007). Do school social work textbooks provide a sound guide for education and practice? *Children and Schools, 29* (2), 109–118.

Storr, C. L., Ialongo, N. S., Kellam, S. G., & Anthony, J. C. (2002). A randomized controlled trial of two primary intervention strategies to prevent early onset tobacco smoking. *Drug and Alcohol Dependence, 66* (1), 51–60.

Story, M., Stevens, J., Himes, J., Stone, E., Rock, B. H., Ethelbah, B., et al. (2003). Obesity in American-Indian children: Prevalence, consequences, and prevention. *Preventive Medicine, 37* (6, Pt. 2), S3–S12.

St. Pierre, R. G., & Rossi, P. H. (2006). Randomize groups, not individuals: A strategy for improving early childhood programs. *Evaluation Review, 30* (5), 656–685.

Sundarararjan, L. (2002). Humanistic psychotherapy and the scientist-practitioner debate: An "embodied" perspective. *Journal of Humanistic Psychology, 42* (2), 34–47.

Swanson, H. L., & Deshler, D. (2003). Instructing adolescents with learning disabilities: Converting a meta-analysis to practice. *Journal of Learning Disabilities, 36* (2), 124–135.

Tan, C. S., (2007). Test review: Behavior Assessment System for Children (2nd ed.). *Assessment for Effective Intervention, 32* (2), 121–124.

Tawney, J. W., & Gast, D. L. (1984). *Single-subject research in special education.* Columbus, OH: Merrill.

Taylor, J. L., & Novaco, R. W. (2005). *Anger treatment for people with developmental disabilities: A theory, evidence and manual-based approach.* New York: John Wiley.

Thomas, E. (2007, April 30). Special report: Tragedy at Virginia Tech. Quiet and disturbed, Cho Seung-Hui seethed, then exploded. His odyssey. *MSNBC/Newsweek.* Retrieved May 25, 2007, from http://www.msnbc.msn.com/id/18248298/site/newsweek/page/0/

Thompson, R. A. (1990). Vulnerability in research: A developmental perspective on research risk. *Child Development, 61* (1), 1–16.

Tillett, J. (2005). Adolescents and informed consent. *Journal of Perinatal and Neonatal Nursing, 19* (2), 112–121.

Todman, J., & Dugard, P. (2001). *Single-case and small-n experimental designs: A practical guide to randomization tests.* Mahwah, NJ: Lawrence Erlbaum.

Tonn, J. L. (February 16, 2005). Chicago dropouts. *Education Week, 24* (23), 16.

Torgerson, C. (2003). *Systematic reviews.* New York: Continuum.

Trautwein, U., & Köller, O. (2003). The relationship between homework and achievement—Still much of a mystery. *Educational Psychology Review, 15* (2), 115–145.

Treatment for Adolescents with Depression Study (TADS) Team (2005). The treatment for adolescents with depression study (TADS): Demographic and clinical characteristics. *Journal of the American Academy of Child and Adolescent Psychiatry, 44* (1), 28–40.

Trickett, E. J., Leone, P. E., Fink, C. M., & Braaten, S. L. (1993). The perceived environment of special education classrooms for adolescents: A revision of the Classroom Environment Scale. *Exceptional Children, 59* (5), 411–420.

Trickett, E. J., & Moos, R. H. (1995). *Classroom Environment Scale manual: Development, applications, research* (3rd ed.). Palo Alto, CA: Consulting Psychologist.

Turner, W. (2000). Cultural considerations in family-based primary prevention programs in drug abuse. *Journal of Primary Prevention, 21* (2), 285–303.

Tyson, K. (1992). A new approach to relevant research for practitioners: The heuristic paradigm. *Social Work, 37* (6), 541–556.

Tyson, K. (1994). Author's reply: Response to "Social work researchers' quest for responsibility." *Social Work, 39* (6), 737–741.

Unrau, Y. A., Grinnell, R. M., Jr., & Williams, M. (2008). The quantitative approach. In R. M. Grinnell, Jr., & Y. A. Unrau (Eds.), *Social work research and evaluation: Foundations of evidence-based practice* (pp. 61–82). New York: Oxford University Press.

Urkin, J., & Merrick, J. (2006). Editorial. *International Journal of Adolescent Medicine and Health, 18* (2), 207–208.

U.S. Census Bureau. (2001). *The Hispanic population: Census 2000 brief.* Washington, DC: U.S. Census Bureau.

U.S. Department of Education (2002a). *A new era: Revitalizing special education for children and their families.* Washington, DC: U.S. Department of Education. Retrieved May 19, 2003, from http://www.ed.gov/inits/commissionsboards/whspecialeducation/[cited in chap 1]

U.S. Department of Education (2002b). *Twenty-fourth annual report to Congress on the implementation of the Individuals with Disabilities Education Act.* Washington, DC: U.S. Department of Education.

U.S. Department of Education (2004a). *Digest of education statistics.* Washington, DC: U.S. Department of Education. Retrieved August 1, 2007, from http://nces.ed.gov/programs/digest/d04/tables/dt04_109.asp

U.S. Department of Education (2004b, April 21). Family educational rights and privacy act. Final rule. *Federal Register, 69* (77), 21669–21672.

U.S. Department of Education (2006). *WWC intervention report: Dropout prevention: Check and Connect.* Retrieved June 11, 2007, from http://w-w-c.org/PDF/Intervention/WWC_Check_Connect_092106.pdf

U.S. Department of Education (2007, May 20). *Final regulations on modified academic achievement standards.* Retrieved July 30, 2007, from http://www.ed.gov/policy/speced/guid/modachieve-summary.html

U.S. Department of Education, Office of Special Education and Rehabilitative Services (2006, August 14). Assistance to states for the education of children with disabilities and preschool grants for children with disabilities: Final rule. 34CFR Parts 300 and 301. *Federal Register, 71* (156), 46540–46845.

U.S. National Library of Medicine (2006, December 11). Fact sheet: Medline. Retrieved June 8, 2007, from http://www.nlm.nih.gov/pubs/factsheets/medline.html

U.S. Public Health Service (2000). *Report of the Surgeon General's Conference on Children's Mental Health: A national action agenda.* Washington,

DC: US Department of Health and Human Services. Retrieved August 7, 2003, from www.surgeongeneral.gov/topics/cmh/childreport.htm

Valentine, J. C., & Cooper, H. (2003). *Effect size substantive interpretation guidelines: Issues in the interpretation of effect sizes.* Washington, DC: What Works Clearinghouse. Retrieved September 24, 2007, from http://ies.ed.gov/ncee/wwc/pdf/essig.pdf

Van Baar, A. L., Ultee, K., Gunning, W. B., Soepatmi, S., & de Leeuw, R. (2006). Developmental course of very preterm children in relation to school outcome. *Journal of Developmental and Physical Disabilities, 18* (3), 273–293.

Van den Noortgate, W., Geeraert, L., Grietens, H., & Onghena, P. (2006). The effects of early prevention programs for families with young children at risk for physical child abuse and neglect: A reply on the comments of Miller. *Child Maltreatment, 11* (1), 98–101.

Van Horn, M. L. (2003). Assessing the unit of measurement for school climate through psychometric and outcome analyses of the school climate. *Educational and Psychological Measurement, 63* (6), 1002–1019.

Van Reusen, A. K., Box, C. S., Schumaker, J. B., & Deschler, D. D. (1994). *The self-advocacy strategy for education and transition planning.* Lawrence, KS: Edge Enterprises.

Vandercook, T., York, J., & Forest, M. (1989). The McGill action planning system (MAPS): A strategy for building the vision. *Journal of the Association for Persons with Severe Handicaps, 14* (2), 205–215.

Vaughn, S., Klingner, J., & Hughes, M. (2000). Sustainability of research-based practices. *Exceptional Children, 66* (2), 163–171.

Velasquez, M. M., Maurer, G. G., Crouch, C., & DiClemente, C. C. (2001). *Group treatment for substance abuse: A stages-of-change therapy manual.* New York: Guilford.

Verhulst, F. C. (2002). Editorial. *Journal of Child Psychology and Psychiatry, 43* (6), 693–694.

Viadero, D. (2001, February 7). The dropout dilemma. *Education Week, 20* (21), p. 26–30.

Viggiani, P. A., Reid, W. J., & Bailey-Dempsey, C. (2002). Social worker-teacher collaboration in the classroom: Help for elementary students at risk of failure. *Research on Social Work Practice, 12* (5), 604–620.

Virginia Tech Review Panel (2007). *Mass shootings at Virginia Tech, April 16, 2007: Report of the review panel presented to Timothy M. Kaine, Governor, Commonwealth of Virginia.* Retrieved September 4, 2007, from http://www.governor.virginia.gov/TempContent/techPanelReport.cfm

Volpe, R. J., DiPerna, J. C., Hintze, J. M., & Shapiro, E. S. (2005). Observing students in classroom settings: A review of seven coding schemes. *School Psychology Review, 34* (4), 454–474.

Vostanis, P. (2006). Strengths and Difficulties Questionnaire: Research and clinical applications. *Current Opinion in Psychiatry, 19* (4), 367–372.

Wakefield, J. C., & Kirk, S. A. (1996). Unscientific thinking about scientific practice: Evaluating the scientist-practitioner model. *Social Work Research, 20* (1), 83–95.

Waldron, H. B., Kern-Jones, S., Turner, C. W., Peterson, T. R., & Ozechowski, T. J. (2007). Engaging resistant adolescents in drug abuse treatment. *Journal of Substance Abuse Treatment, 32* (2), 133–142.

Walker, H. M. (2003). Commentary: Addressing the gap between science and practice in children's mental health. *School Psychology Review, 32* (1), 44–47.

Walker, J. S., Briggs, H. E., Koroloff, N., & Friesen, B. J. (2007). Implementing and sustaining evidence-based practice in social work. *Journal of Social Work Education, 43* (3), 361–375. Guest editorial.

Walker, H. M., & Severson, H. H. (1990). *Systematic screening for behavior disorders: Users guide and administration manual.* Longmont, CO: Sopris West.

Wallerstein, J. S. (1991). Tailoring the intervention to the child in the separating and divorced family. *Family and Conciliation Courts Review, 29* (4), 448–459.

Ward, M. J. (2005). An historical perspective of self-determination in special education: Accomplishments and challenges. *Research and Practice for Persons with Severe Disabilities, 30* (3), 108–112.

Ward, E. C. (2007). Examining differential treatment effects for depression in racial and ethnic minority women: A qualitative systematic review. *Journal of the National Medical Association, 99* (3), 265–274.

Ware, W. B., & Galassi, J. P. (2006). Using correlational and prediction data to enhance student achievement in K-12 schools: A practical application for school counselors. *Professional School Counseling, 9* (5, special issue), 344–356.

Waschbusch, D. A., & Hill, G. P. (2003). Empirically supported, promising, and unsupported treatments for children with attention-deficit/hyperactivity disorder. In S. O. Lilienfeld, S. J. Lynn, & J. M. Lohr (Eds.), *Science and pseudoscience in clinical psychology* (pp. 333–362). New York: Guilford.

Wasserman, J. D., & Bracken, B. A. (2002). Selecting appropriate tests: Psychometric and pragmatic considerations. In J. F. Carlson & B. B. Waterman (Eds.), *Social and personality assessment of school-aged children: Developing interventions for educational and clinical use* (pp. 18–43). Boston: Allyn & Bacon.

Watson, S. (1995). Successful treatment of selective mutism: Collaborative work in a secondary school setting. *Child Language Teaching and Therapy, 11* (2), 163–175.

Wehmeyer, M., Agran, M., & Hughes, C. (2000). A national survey of teachers' promotion of self-determination and student-directed learning. *Journal of Special Education, 34* (2), 58–69.

Wehmeyer, M. L., Palmer, S. B., Soukup, J. H., Garner, N. W., & Lawrence, M. (2007). Self-determination and student transition planning knowledge and skills: Predicting involvement. *Exceptionality, 15* (1), 31–44.

Weinbach, R. W., & Grinnell, R. M., Jr. (2007). *Statistics for social workers* (7th ed.). Boston: Pearson.

Weis, R., & Smenner, L. (2007). Construct validity of the Behavior Assessment System for Children (BASC) Self-Report of Personality: Evidence from adolescents referred to residential treatment. *Journal of Psychoeducational Assessment, 25* (2), 111–126.

Weiss, C. H., Murphy-Graham, E., & Birkeland, S. (2005). An alternate route to policy influence: How evaluations affect D.A.R.E. *American Journal of Evaluation, 26* (1), 12–30.

Weisz, J. R. (2004). *Psychotherapy for children and adolescents: Evidence-based treatments and case examples.* Cambridge: Cambridge University Press.

Weisz, J. R., Chu, B. C., & Polo, A. J. (2004). Treatment dissemination and evidence-based practice: Strengthening intervention through clinician-researcher collaboration. *Clinical Psychology: Science and Practice, 11* (3), 300–307.

Weithorn, L. A., & Campbell, S. B. (1982). The competency of children and adolescents to make informed treatment decisions. *Child Development, 53* (6), 1589–1598.

Welsh, W. (2000). The effects of school climate on school disorder. *Annals of the American Academy of Political and Social Science, 567,* 88–107.

Welsh, M., Parke, R. D., Widaman, K., & O'Neill, R. (2001). Linkages between children's social and academic competence: A longitudinal analysis. *Journal of School Psychology, 39* (6), 463–481.

Wenzlaff, T. L., Fager, J. J., & Coleman, M. J. (1999). What is a rubric? Do practitioners and the literature agree? *Contemporary Education, 70* (4), 41–46.

Wesley, P. W., & Buysse, V. (2006). Ethics and evidence in consultation. *Topics in Early Childhood Special Education, 26* (3), 131–141.

West, S. L., & O'Neal, K. K. (2004). Project D.A.R.E. outcome effectiveness revisited. *American Journal of Public Health, 94* (6), 1027–1029.

Westen, D. I. (2006a). Patients and treatments in clinical trials are not adequately representative of clinical practice. In J. C. Norcross, L. E. Beutler, & R. F. Levant (Eds.), *Evidence-based practices in mental health: Debate and dialogue on the fundamental questions* (pp. 161–171). Washington, DC: American Psychological Association.

Westen, D. I. (2006b). Transporting laboratory-validated treatments to the community will not necessarily produce better outcomes. In J. C. Norcross, L. E. Beutler, & R. F. Levant (Eds.), *Evidence-based practices in mental health: Debate and dialogue on the fundamental questions* (pp. 383–393). Washington, DC: American Psychological Association.

Westen, D., Novotny, C. M., & Thompson-Brenner, H. (2005). EBP ≠ EST: Reply to Crits-Christroph et al. (2005) and Weisz et al. (2005). *Psychological Bulletin, 131* (3), 427–433.

What Works Clearinghouse (2006a). *Teacher intervention confound.* Retrieved June 11, 2007, from http://w-w-c.org/reviewprocess/teacher_confound.pdf

What Works Clearinghouse (2006b). *What Works Clearinghouse evidence standards for reviewing studies.* Retrieved June 11, 2007, from http://w-w-c.org/reviewprocess/study_standards_final.pdf

What Works Clearinghouse (2006c). *What Works Clearinghouse tutorial on mismatch between unit of assignment and unit of analysis.* Retrieved June 11, 2007, from http://w-w-c.org/reviewprocess/mismatch.pdf

Wheat, K. (1999). Liability for failure to diagnose dyslexia. *Journal of Forensic Psychiatry, 10* (2), 355–365.

Willet, S. L. (1996). Health risk reduction among African American females: A one-year follow-up. Northwestern University, AAT 9614861. *Dissertation Abstracts International, Section B: The Sciences and Engineering, 57* (1-B), p. 0717. UMI #9614861.

Williams, M., Grinnell, R. G., Jr., & Unrau, Y. (2008). Case level designs. In R. M. Grinnell, Jr., & Y. A. Unrau (Eds.), *Social work research and evaluation: Quantitative and qualitative approaches* (8th ed., 157–178). New York: Oxford University Press.

Winter, D. (2006). Avoiding the fate of the Dodo bird: The challenge of evidence-based practice. In D. Loewenthal & D. Winter (Eds.), *What is psychotherapeutic research?* (pp. 41–46). London: Karnac.

Winters, W. G., & Easton, F. (1983). *The practice of social work in schools: An ecological perspective.* New York: Free Press.

Witkin, S. L. (1991). Empirical clinical practice: A critical analysis. *Social Work, 36* (2), 158–165.

Woerner, W., Fleitlich-Bilyk, B., Martinussen, R., Fletcher, J., Cucchiaro, G., Dalgalarrondo, P., et al. (2004). The Strengths and Difficulties Questionnaire overseas: Evaluations and applications of the SDQ beyond Europe. *European Child and Adolescent Psychiatry, 13* (Suppl. 2), II47–II54.

Wolfersberger, M. E., Reutzel, D. R., Sudweeks, R., & Fawson, P. C. (2004). Developing and validating the Classroom Literacy Environmental Profile

(CLEP): A tool for examining the "print richness" of early childhood and elementary classrooms. *Journal of Literacy Research, 36* (2), 211–272.

Wood, J. R., & Nezworksi, M. T. (2005). Science as a history of corrected mistakes: Comment. *American Psychologist, 60* (6), 657–658.

Wouters, P., Reddy, C., & Aguillo, I. (2006). On the visibility of information on the Web: An exploratory experimental approach. *Research Evaluation, 15* (2), 107–115.

Yell, M. L., & Stecker, P. M. (2003). Developing legally correct and educationally meaningful IEPs using curriculum-based measurement. *Assessment for Effective Intervention, 28* (3–4), 73–88.

Youngstrom, E. A., & Busch, C. P. (2000). Expert testimony in psychology: Ramifications of Supreme Court decision in Kumho Tire Co. Ltd. v. Carmichael. *Ethics and Behavior, 10* (2), 185–193.

Yu, L. (1999). *Preventing depressive symptoms in Chinese children.* University of Pennsylvania. *Dissertation Abstracts International, Section B: The Sciences and Engineering, 60* (12-B), 2000, 6389. UMI #9953624.

Zhang, D. (2005). Parent practices in facilitating self-determination skills: The influence of culture, socioeconomic status, and children's special education status. *Research and Practice for Persons with Severe Disabilities, 30* (3), 154–162.

Zimmerman, T. S., Jacobsen, R. B., MacIntyre, M., & Watson, C. (1996). Solution-focused parenting groups: An empirical study. *Journal of Systemic Therapies, 15* (4), 12–25.

Zimpfer, D. G. (1990). Groups for divorce/separation: A review. *Journal for Specialists in Group Work, 15* (1), 51–60.

Zins, J. E., Bloodworth, M. R., Weissberg, R. P., & Walberg, H. J. (2004). The scientific base for linking social and emotional learning to school success. In J. E. Zins, R. P. Weissberg, M. C. Wang, & H. J. Walberg (Eds.), *Building academic success on social and emotional learning: What does the research say?* (pp. 3–22). New York: Teachers College Press.

Index

Page numbers in *italics* indicate boxes or figures.